Querying
SQL Server

Run T-SQL Operations, Data Extraction,
Data Manipulation, and Custom Queries to
Deliver Simplified Analytics

Adam Aspin

www.bpbonline.com

Group Product Manager: Marianne Conor
Publishing Product Manager: Eva Brawn
Senior Editor: Connell
Content Development Editor: Melissa Monroe
Technical Editor: Anne Stokes
Copy Editor: Joe Austin
Language Support Editor: Justin Baldwin
Project Coordinator: Tyler Horan
Proofreader: Khloe Styles
Indexer: V. Krishnamurthy
Production Designer: Malcolm D'Souza
Marketing Coordinator: Kristen Kramer

First published: July 2022

Published by BPB Online
WeWork, 119 Marylebone Road
London NW1 5PU

UK | UAE | INDIA | SINGAPORE

ISBN 978.93.55512.376

www.bpbonline.com

About the Author

Adam Aspin is an independent Business Intelligence (BI) consultant based in the United Kingdom. He has worked with SQL Server for over 25 years. During this time, he has developed several dozen database and analytical systems based on Microsoft databases. He has applied his skills for a range of clients in industry sectors across finance, utilities, pharmaceuticals , telecoms, insurance, retail, and luxury goods.

A graduate of Oxford University, Adam moved into IT early in his career. Databases soon became a passion, and his experience in this arena ranges from dBase to Oracle, and Access to MySQL, with occasional sorties into the world of DB2, Informix, and PostgreSQL. He is, however, most at home in the Microsoft universe developing applications with SQL Server, SQL Server Analysis Services, SQL Server Reporting Services, SQL Server Integration Services, and Power BI.

Adam is a frequent contributor to SQLServerCentral.com and Simple Talk. He is a regular speaker at SQL Server User Groups, SQL Saturdays, Power BI Meetups and conferences such as SQL Bits. He has written numerous articles for various French IT publications. A fluent French speaker, Adam has worked in France and Switzerland for many years.

He is the author of SQL Server 2012 Data Integration Recipes (Apress, 2012), High Impact Data Visualization in Excel with Power View, 3D Maps, Get & Transform and Power BI, Second Edition (Apress, 2016), Business Intelligence with SQL Server Reporting Services (Apress, 2015), and Pro Power BI Desktop, Third Edition (Apress, 2019) and Pro Pro Power BI Theme Creation (Apress 2021).

About the Reviewer

Sandra Eaton grew up in Birmingham, UK. After an initial career as a civil servant, Sandra took a short break to raise a family, which then turned into a long career break and a wonderful family.

While bringing up two children, Sandra gained a First Class Honors degree from the Open University. She also qualified as an ISEB software tester. She currently applies her skills testing a range of software from PC applications to ERP implementations—and anything in between.

Currently based in Telford, UK, in her spare time Sandra can usually be found walking the Shropshire hills or wild camping in the mountains of North Wales.

Acknowledgement

Writing a technical book is an arduous project at the best of times. Fortunately, I was lucky to have help and support from a great team.

First, I owe a deep debt of gratitude to Sandra Eaton, who kindly accepted my offer to be the technical reviewer of this book. Sandra brought a wealth of experience to this role, and her training as a software tester shone in the way that she helped me ensure that the code worked exactly as it was intended. Sandra went far beyond the call of duty in her efforts to help me deliver a book that would help readers master SQL.

Finally I we have to thank the production staff at BPB for all their help. Their professionalism in guiding me through the publication process was much appreciated.

Last—but not least—I need to thank my wife and son for putting up with my obsession with writing a book on a subject like SQL. Their good humor and encouragement have helped me considerably on this particular journey.

Preface

If you are looking at this book, it is probably because you have some basic SQL ("Structured Query Language") querying knowledge and you want to raise your game and push your skillset to a higher level.

Whatever the motivation, you know that you want to build on your existing knowledge and use it to learn how to deliver the data analysis that you need. This probably means learning how to slice and filter the data in Microsoft SQL Server, as well as ensuring that you can tweak the presentation and present your results clearly and cogently.

This book is the next step on your journey. It aims to teach you in-depth SQL querying using data stored in a SQL Server database. It presumes that you have some previous knowledge of SQL and SQL Server and is designed to take you beyond the core concepts so that you are empowered to write powerful, polished, and efficient SQL queries that deliver real insight.

Why Microsoft SQL Server?

SQL Server is one of the world's bestselling and most widely used databases. It follows that learning the Microsoft flavor of SQL (called T-SQL) and the basics of the Microsoft database has the potential to be a career-enhancing move. As the data store for innumerable corporate, commercial, and web-driven databases, this mature and impressive system is used to power data analysis across the globe.

What Is T-SQL?

Every database has its own flavor of SQL, and these variants are subtly different. Microsoft uses its own dialect of SQL called T-SQL. Although the core elements are the same as those found in other databases, there are many subtle differences between T-SQL and other flavors.

This means that learning just "plain vanilla" SQL will soon leave you struggling with queries that use SQL Server. It can also mean that you will find yourself unable to extract the deeper insights that mastering T-SQL on SQL Server can provide.

Right from the start, this book takes you into the world of SQL Server and T-SQL. This way you learn to use the Microsoft dialect of SQL to its full capacity immediately, without limiting yourself to underperforming queries or missing out on T-SQL features that other flavors of SQL simply do not have.

T-SQL is, fortunately, very close to the SQL used by rival databases. So learning T-SQL sets you on the path to applying SQL query techniques in most of the available SQL databases that are currently deployed.

Why Learn SQL?

Most of the data that fuels businesses throughout the world is stored in relational databases. Nearly all of these databases are queried using a variant of Structured Query Language (SQL). So, simply put, SQL is key to data analysis. A mastery of SQL helps you delve deep into the data that is stored in corporate databases. You can apply SQL to analyze the data and then present it in a clearly understandable form.

SQL can usually serve a vital role in preparing the data for final delivery—no matter what output application you are using to present your analysis. Most end-user tools have an option for entering SQL to help derive meaning from the underlying data sources. Consequently, a good knowledge of SQL can help you analyze data faster and more clearly. The aims of this book are to give you the necessary mastery of SQL to enable you to get the most out of your data and to deliver the insights that will drive your competitive advantage.

Who This Book Is For

This book is designed to help anyone who wants to extend their knowledge of using SQL to deliver in-depth analysis. This means that you could be

- A data analyst
- A student
- A database developer
- A financial professional
- A business analyst
- A job-seeker looking to get ready for a technical interview
- A trainee preparing for a Microsoft SQL exam

or indeed anyone who needs to deliver accurate analytics from the data stored in a SQL Server database.

What This Book Will Bring You

This book was written to help you become proficient in querying databases using T-SQL. It is designed to help you master a language that can seem arcane, or even weird, at first sight. To overcome any initial reticence that you may have, it progresses step by step through all the concepts and techniques that you need to perfect the skill of writing complex SQL queries.

To make SQL comprehensible, I have chosen to introduce each new concept or keyword individually so that you can learn each new element in isolation. As the book progresses, you see how you can combine SQL keywords to extend the power of SQL as you learn to create ever-more-powerful queries.

That said, no one queries databases purely for fun, so each query that you apply in this book also has a practical purpose. As a result, you also see how to develop real-world queries that deliver essential data analysis. You can then adapt these queries to your own requirements using your own data.

How to Read This Book

I did not design this book only to be read from start to finish. By this I mean that you can use it in several different ways depending on your knowledge of SQL and your real-world requirements.

SQL Novices

If you are a complete beginner, then you can begin with Chapter 1 and progress through the book until you feel that you have attained a level of SQL skills that matches your needs. The book is designed to be a complete SQL querying course that allows readers with no previous SQL experience progressively to gain the skills and experience they need.

Refreshing Your Knowledge

If you are coming back to SQL after a while away, consider skimming through the sections in each chapter until you start encountering techniques and approaches that are less obvious. Then slow down and concentrate on the new elements that interest you and consolidate as well as refresh your knowledge. Of course, how you actually do this depends on your level of SQL proficiency before you start reading this book.

In-Depth Querying

If your needs are more advanced, then you might want to begin by skimming through the initial chapters in this book and use them to provide inspiration on how best to solve your specific problems. You can then take a deep dive into the later chapters to make quite sure that your advanced SQL querying knowledge is up to scratch.

Transferring SQL Knowledge from Another Flavor of SQL

Even if you are already used to a different variant of SQL, you may want to read all the chapters to make sure you are clear on the differences between T-SQL and the version of SQL that you have come from. When you are writing more advanced queries, be aware that there are many subtle nuances that differentiate T-SQL from other dialects of SQL, and it is only through writing and testing SQL queries that these differences become apparent.

Solving Specific Issues

If you have been using SQL for a while but need some guidance to help you solve new kinds of query challenges, then you can use this book as a collection of "recipes."

In this case, I suggest that you look at the table of contents and jump straight to the examples that interest you.

Indeed, each chapter explains the various ways that you can use a core SQL querying technique to deliver actionable insight. So, you may choose to learn—or reacquaint yourself with—a key SQL querying concept by studying a specific chapter independently of the rest of the book.

The Structure of This Book

This book assumes a core level of SQL querying knowledge that you can build on to become proficient in writing complex SQL queries. The book follows a linear pattern of knowledge transfer, where previously acquired knowledge underpins new techniques as you progress through the book.

It consists of the following 21 chapters:

Chapter 1, Writing Basic SQL Queries: This chapter introduces the basic concepts of SQL and SQL Server and shows you how to write simple queries.

Chapter 2, Using Multiple Tables When Querying Data: This chapter extends your knowledge by showing you how to join tables to return data from more than one table at a time. It also explains many of the ways that you can join tables.

Chapter 3, Using Advanced Table Joins: This chapter discusses how to use more advanced table joins.

Chapter 4, Filtering Data: This chapter introduces a fundamental concept: filtering the data that you want to use.

Chapter 5, Applying Complex Filters to Queries: This chapter shows you how to combine filters to produce more complex queries.

Chapter 6, Making Simple Calculations: This chapter shows you some of the ways that you can apply basic math to the data in a SQL Server database.

Chapter 7, Aggregating Output: This chapter explains how you can use SQL to group and aggregate data to deliver analysis.

Chapter 8, Working with Dates in SQL Server: This chapter introduces you to some of the essential ways that SQL handles dates and can use dates to deliver analysis over time.

Chapter 9, Formatting Text in Query Output: This chapter shows you some of the key ways that SQL can be applied to format queries.

Chapter 10, Formatting Numbers and Dates: This chapter introduces a series of techniques that you can use to change the way that dates and numbers appear in the final output.

Chapter 11, Using Basic Logic to Enhance Analysis: This chapter concludes the book with an introduction to using SQL to analyze data and deliver added value.

Chapter 12, Subqueries: This chapter shows you how you can use independent SQL queries inside other queries.

Chapter 13, Derived Tables: This chapter teaches you how to compare data at different levels of aggregation or carry out calculations that mix and match different ways of grouping data.

Chapter 14, Common Table Expressions: This chapter explains a powerful way to simplify working with complex datasets.

Chapter 15, Correlated Subqueries: This chapter shows you how you can use certain kinds of subquery to filter the data in the outer query in a specific way.

Chapter 16, Joining and Filtering Datasets: This chapter introduces methods of handling data spread across a series of tables with identical structures.

Chapter 17, Using SQL for More Advanced Calculations: This chapter teaches you how SQL can go much further than simple addition, subtraction, division, and multiplication and how SQL handles numbers.

Chapter 18, Segmenting and Classifying Data: This chapter introduces ways of prioritizing and classifying lists of data in order to analyze the elements that really matter.

Chapter 19, Rolling Analysis: This chapter covers ways of discerning trends, tracking growth, and establishing a solid factual base that you can use for your analysis.

Chapter 20, Analyzing Data Over Time: This chapter goes deeply into techniques that you can apply to track the evolution of sales, profits, or, indeed, any metric over any time period: from years to days to hours and seconds.

Chapter 21, Complex Data Output: This chapter concludes the book with a look at ways of shaping output so that the essence of your analysis is immediately comprehensible. These techniques will also help you to present your analysis in various ways that can make the results easier to read and understand.

The Sample Data and Sample Queries

To help you learn SQL, I have made the sample data as well as all the SQL queries in this book available on the BPB website — **www.bpbonline.com**. This way you can download and install the sample data into a SQL Server database on your PC, and then you can practice SQL querying using the data that I have elaborated on to help you learn SQL.

If typing the queries is a little laborious (though I do recommend doing so as an excellent way of learning), then you can also download each query in the book and simply copy each into the querying application that you are using to see the query result.

Time to Get Started Querying SQL Server

I have said enough about the theory of SQL Server. It is now time to get up close and personal.

But first, make sure you have a working copy of the latest version of SQL Server. This book is written for SQL Server 2019—but will work with previous versions for nearly all of the queries—and I strongly advise you to install one of the free versions of this database as described in Appendix A.

Once you have a functioning database, you need an application that you can use to test your queries. There are many such apps available, but I advise you to use Microsoft's SQL Server Management Studio, especially since this is the application that I have used throughout this book. You can find out how to download and install this tool in Appendix B.

Finally, you need some sample data to work on. For this (and especially if you want to test your SQL using the examples in this book) you need to download and set up the sample PrestigeCars database. This is described in Appendix C.

That is it! You are now ready to start on your journey toward becoming a SQL-querying maestro.

Have fun!

Code Bundle and Coloured Images

Please follow the link to download the
Code Bundle and the *Coloured Images* of the book:

https://rebrand.ly/n5xkm0o

The code bundle for the book is also hosted on GitHub at **https://github.com/bpbpublications/Querying-SQL-Server**. In case there's an update to the code, it will be updated on the existing GitHub repository.

We have code bundles from our rich catalogue of books and videos available at **https://github.com/bpbpublications**. Check them out!

Errata

We take immense pride in our work at BPB Publications and follow best practices to ensure the accuracy of our content to provide with an indulging reading experience to our subscribers. Our readers are our mirrors, and we use their inputs to reflect and improve upon human errors, if any, that may have occurred during the publishing processes involved. To let us maintain the quality and help us reach out to any readers who might be having difficulties due to any unforeseen errors, please write to us at :

errata@bpbonline.com

Your support, suggestions and feedbacks are highly appreciated by the BPB Publications' Family.

Did you know that BPB offers eBook versions of every book published, with PDF and ePub files available? You can upgrade to the eBook version at www.bpbonline.com and as a print book customer, you are entitled to a discount on the eBook copy. Get in touch with us at :

business@bpbonline.com for more details.

At **www.bpbonline.com**, you can also read a collection of free technical articles, sign up for a range of free newsletters, and receive exclusive discounts and offers on BPB books and eBooks.

Piracy

If you come across any illegal copies of our works in any form on the internet, we would be grateful if you would provide us with the location address or website name. Please contact us at **business@bpbonline.com** with a link to the material.

If you are interested in becoming an author

If there is a topic that you have expertise in, and you are interested in either writing or contributing to a book, please visit **www.bpbonline.com**. We have worked with thousands of developers and tech professionals, just like you, to help them share their insights with the global tech community. You can make a general application, apply for a specific hot topic that we are recruiting an author for, or submit your own idea.

Reviews

Please leave a review. Once you have read and used this book, why not leave a review on the site that you purchased it from? Potential readers can then see and use your unbiased opinion to make purchase decisions. We at BPB can understand what you think about our products, and our authors can see your feedback on their book. Thank you!

For more information about BPB, please visit **www.bpbonline.com**.

Table of Contents

CHAPTER 1
Writing Basic SQL Queries

Welcome to SQL Server and the new world of data and analytics that you are about to experience. As you are standing on the threshold of this voyage into the realms of databases and data analysis, you could be feeling a little apprehensive. Well, don't worry, your journey will be as simple and comprehensible as I can make it. This chapter will start you on your adventure first by outlining the software that you need to install and then by explaining what a database is. Then I will show you how to look at the data itself. As you progress, you will learn how to be more selective about the data that you analyze.

Prerequisites

It may seem obvious, but you will need some data in an accessible database before you can start your analysis. So, throughout this book I will be asking you to develop your analytical skills with the aid of a sample database named PrestigeCars. This database contains a small amount of data concerning sales of vehicles by a fictitious British car reseller. If you want to try the examples in this chapter, you will have to download the sample database from the TetrasPublishing website (www.tetraspublishing.com/sqlserver) and install the database into a version of SQL Server. So, it follows that now could be a good time to set up the sample database as described in Appendix C, unless you have already done so. Of course, you can install the sample database only if you have a version of SQL Server already installed and available. So, if you are not in an enterprise environment where SQL Server is already accessible, you will need to install a version of the database software before anything else. This is described in Appendix A.

Once SQL Server is up and running, you will need somewhere to enter and run your queries. I am presuming that you have also installed SQL Server Management Studio (SSMS) as the interface to the sample database. Installing this piece of software is also described in Appendix B. I presume that you will be trying your queries using this particular application.

SSMS is not the only tool that you can use to query databases. There are indeed many excellent applications that you can use to analyze SQL Server data. So, if you prefer to use another application to test the queries in this book, then that is entirely up to you. However, you will have to handle the specifics of installing and working with that application yourself; there are simply too many of them for us to explain every one!

Whatever the tool that you use to write your queries, this chapter will teach you how to

- Query SQL Server databases using SQL Server Management Studio
- List the contents of tables
- Select only certain fields in tables to display
- Display only a few records from a table
- Give columns new names in your query output
- Sort your output

When you have all the prerequisites in place, it is time to move on to the core focus of this chapter and start querying SQL Server data.

> **Note: If you know a little about the standard Microsoft data tools and if you have a basic knowledge of databases, then feel free to skip past the first few sections of this chapter until you find the parts that are new to you. However, I realize that the first steps for a novice are important. Consequently, I prefer to start from the beginning and provide all the information that you are likely to need to get the most out of your SQL learning experience.**

1.1 Relational Databases

As you have decided to learn to analyze data using SQL queries, you need to know a few basic concepts to begin with.

To start, what is a relational database (or a relational database management system, RDBMS)? At its simplest, a relational database is a method of storing data in a clearly defined way. A database consists of tables (sometimes thousands of tables) that each contain rows of data. All the rows in a table consist of the same number of columns. So, a table is really nothing more than a well-structured list—rather like the ones that you have probably encountered in Excel.

In a well-designed database, tables will be organized to avoid duplicating data. The tables in the database can then be linked together to present the data in different ways.

To resume, then, a relational database is a collection of lists (tables) containing columns (fields) of data in a set of rows (records). These elements can then be accessed independently or joined together to deliver the analysis you are looking for.

Conceptually, a database looks something like *Figure 1.1*.

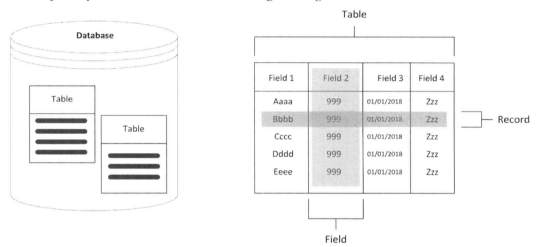

Figure 1.1: *Conceptualizing a relational database*

Note: Please note that all the exercises in this book use a sample database named PrestigeCars. If you need to install this database, then please consult Appendix C.

1.2 Running SQL Server Management Studio

The time has come to start putting the theory into practice. As relational databases can require considerable IT horsepower, they will nearly always reside on powerful servers either on-premises or in the cloud. They are rarely installed on PCs or laptops unless they are being used for learning.

So, what you will nearly always do is connect to the database using a separate piece of software that is, itself, installed on a PC. This is called a client-server model, where you use one application (the client) to connect to the database (the server). While there are many applications that can read data from SQL Server databases, there is one that tends to be used by most analysts and developers. This is SQL Server Management Studio. It is an application written by Microsoft and is (at least at the time that this book went to press) free to install and use. As befits a piece of software that has been evolving for about 20 years, it is both efficient and reliable. Indeed, it is the standard tool that is used by hundreds of thousands of analysts and developers. Consequently, this is the tool that I will be using throughout this book.

I will assume that you have SSMS installed on your PC. If this is not the case, then please consult Appendix B to learn how to find and install this tool.

To connect to a SQL Server database, follow these steps:

1. Double-click the SQL Server Management Studio icon on the desktop, in the taskbar, or in the list of apps.

2. SQL Server Management Studio opens and displays the Connect to Server dialog with the server details, as you can see in *Figure 1.2*.

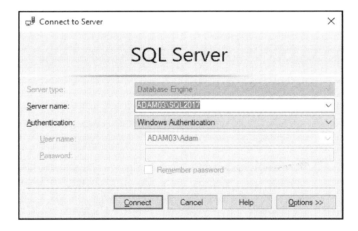

Figure 1.2: The SQL Server Management Studio Connect to Server dialog

3. Select the server name from the pop-up list. If you are in an enterprise environment, you can always ask a system administrator which database to use. If you have just installed a stand-alone version of SQL Server on your laptop or workstation (this is described in Appendix A), then just enter Localhost in the Server Name popup.

4. Click Connect. You will see SQL Server Management Studio, ready for you to begin working, as shown in *Figure 1.3*.

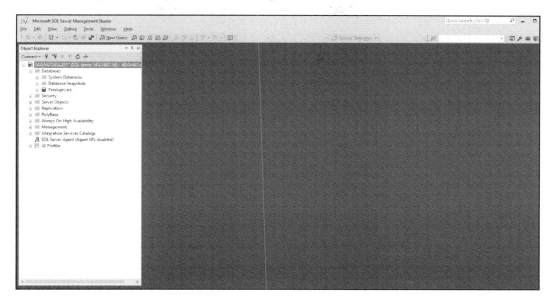

Figure 1.3: SQL Server Management Studio

5. Expand the Databases folder on the left. (You do this by clicking the small plus [+] symbol to the left of the folder.) You will see all the databases that are available for you to work with. If this is a new installation of SQL Server, you will not see any database names except for the PrestigeCars database that you installed following the instructions in Appendix C.

6. Expand the PrestigeCars database in the list by clicking the plus symbol to the left of the database folder. You will then see all the database folders, as shown in *Figure 1.4*.

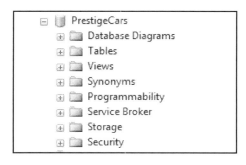

Figure 1.4: The PrestigeCars database

7. Click the PrestigeCars database on the left (this window is known as the Object Explorer).

8. Click the New Query button in the SQL Server Management Studio toolbar at the top of the screen. A new query window opens on the right of the Object Explorer window. You should see something like *Figure 1.5.*

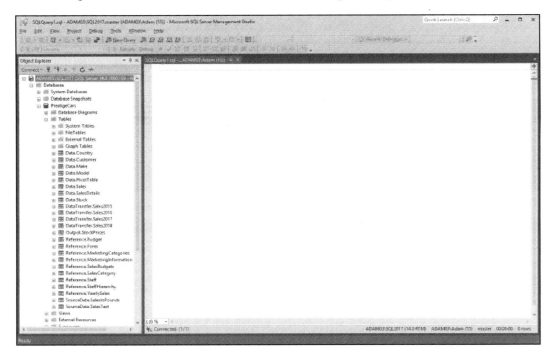

Figure 1.5: *SQL Server Management Studio ready for querying*

Now that you have connected to the database, you are ready to start analyzing the data it contains. I realize that the first time you carry out this sequence of instructions the process may seem a little laborious. However, you will probably launch SQL Server Management Studio only a couple of times a day when you start working with SQL Server. So, it is not really any different than opening Microsoft Word or Excel when you first start creating documents or editing spreadsheets. In any case, this routine will certainly become second nature in a short time.

1.3 Displaying the Tables in a Database

All the data in a SQL Server database is stored in tables. A database can consist of dozens—or even hundreds—of tables of data that have been carefully designed and created by database professionals. The first thing that you will have to do when faced with any database that is new to you is to take a look at the tables it contains. To do this, follow these steps:

1. Expand the Tables folder by clicking the small plus symbol to the left of the Tables folder in the PrestigeCars database. You should see something like the list of tables shown in *Figure 1.6*.

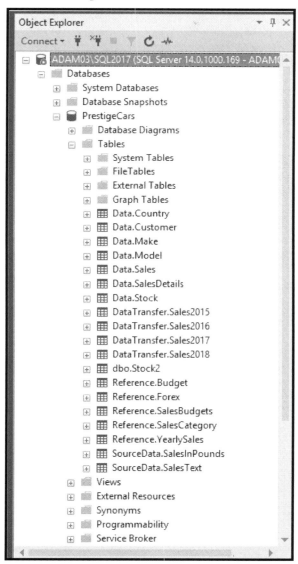

Figure 1.6: *Displaying the tables contained in a database*

As this sample database is small, it contains only a handful of tables. You will learn what they all contain as you progress through this book.

1.4 Finding All the Views in a Database

SQL databases do not just contain tables. Indeed, they can contain hundreds of different items (that are collectively called objects). One of the aims of this book is to introduce you progressively to the essential objects that you will need to learn to manipulate when querying data.

Apart from tables, one kind of object that you need to know about is the view. Quite simply, although all data is stored in tables, you could frequently find yourself querying not only tables but views too. This is because views are a way of looking at data that filter or combine data in some way, essentially making life easier for users by doing some of the work for you.

In SQL queries you can treat views exactly as if they were tables. The first thing to know is how to find the views in a database. Fortunately, this is similar to what you just did when looking at the database tables.

1. Expand the Views folder by clicking the small plus symbol to the left of the Views folder in the PrestigeCars database. You should see something like the list of views in *Figure 1.7*.

***Figure 1.7**: Displaying the views contained in a database*

As you can see, there are even fewer views than tables in the PrestigeCars database. Indeed, there is only a single view named SalesByCountry.

1.5 Schemas

If you take a close look at the tables and views in the PrestigeCars database, you can see that each has a name in two parts. First, there is a shared name (almost like a family name) such as Data or Reference. Then there is there is a period and finally the actual unique name of the table or view. This naming style exists because data can get complicated. Specifically, if you are dealing with thousands of tables and views in a database, you will need to find ways of organizing the elements. One technique is to group tables into schemas. A schema is a kind of virtual "folder" that lets you place together tables and views that you want to consider as sharing common traits. If you prefer, you could consider schemas as a kind of "color-coding" to group items to suit your needs.

Using a schema is not compulsory, but schemas let you apply a common focus to otherwise disparate elements. As you can see in Figure 1.5, all the tables and views that are in the same schemas are grouped together.

As you will see (beginning with the next section), schemas are an essential part of the table or view name. Indeed, when you use a table or view in a piece of SQL code, you should always include the schema name and a period before the table name. If you like, you could consider this to be something similar to referring to a person by their last name and first name to avoid confusing them with someone else.

There will always be at least one schema in SQL Server—the **dbo** schema. However, as this schema is always present, SQL Server calls it the "default" schema, and you do not need to use it when referring to tables in the dbo schema—just use the table name on its own. However, I have made sure that all the tables and views in the PrestigeCars database are in specific schemas to ensure that you learn good SQL habits from the outset.

1.6 Displaying the Data in a Table

Now that you have learned how to look inside a database, it is time to look at some actual data. For your first query, let's suppose you want to see what makes of vehicle are sold by Prestige Cars Ltd.

1. Click the PrestigeCars database in the Object Explorer (the left window) in SQL Server Management Studio.

2. Open a new query window (unless one is already open) by clicking the New Query button in the toolbar at the top of the SSMS window.

3. In the query window, type in the following short piece of SQL:

```
SELECT   *
FROM     Data.Make
```

4. Press the F5 function key to run the code and show the results. The results will appear under the code, as shown in *Figure 1.8.*

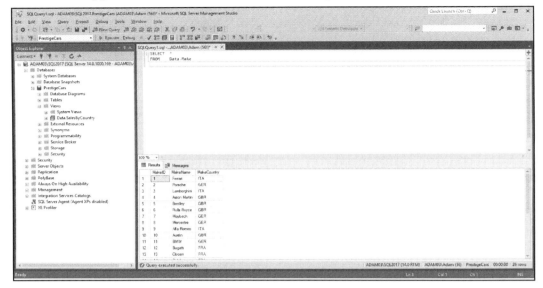

Figure 1.8: *Displaying all the data in a table with SELECT * *

How It Works

In just five words you have said to SQL Server, "Show me the complete contents of the Make table, including all the rows and all the columns of data." All you needed to know is which table you wanted to look at. SQL did the rest.

This code snippet is incredibly simple—five words in all—but that is enough to show you how SQL works in practice. If you issue the right command, then you will get back the data you want to see.

As you can see, this command did more than just list the makes of car. It also showed any other elements that are present in the table, but that is exactly the point of the command. This way you get to see everything that is stored in a table of data.

Of course, you will need to know which table contains the data you want to display when you are dealing with your own data. If you are working in an enterprise environment, this may involve talking to the people in your organization who developed or maintain the databases. Alternatively, there may be documentation that you can read to find the information you require.

If there is no one you can ask and no documentation available, then you can still acquaint yourself with the data by running the SELECT * FROM clause with each data table that you can see in the Tables folder. However, before doing this I advise you to continue a little further in this book and learn how to limit the number of records output by a query.

So, what exactly have you done here? Let's take a closer look at what you have written. *figure 1.9* breaks down the SQL statement into its constituent parts.

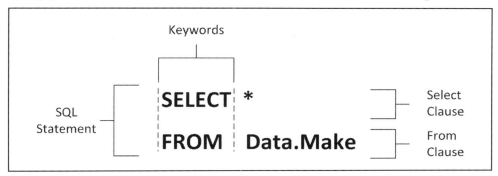

Figure 1.9: *The anatomy of a simple SQL statement*

These constituent parts are:

Keywords	SQL is built using a set of keywords that you combine to produce commands. These commands (or snippets or phrases if you want to call them that) are in English and follow a fairly rigorous syntax. Learning to understand and apply the "grammar" of SQL is what this book is all about.
Clauses	These are a set of short phrases composed of keywords and data elements that make up a SQL statement.

Tricks and Traps

This was a simple SQL command, but the following are nonetheless a few key points that you will need to remember:

- As I mentioned, each SQL Server instance can contain (or host if you prefer) dozens of databases. This means you always have to tell SQL Server which database you want to interrogate. One easy way to do this is to click the appropriate database before opening a new query window, just like you did in this example.

- If you do not indicate the right database to use, SQL Server will either return no data at all or, worse, return the wrong data from another database.

- F5 runs (or executes if you prefer) the SQL code that you have typed or copied into a query window. There are other ways to run a query that you will learn a little later in this chapter.

- It can happen (even when you are an experienced data analyst) that executing a query returns nothing more than an irritating error message like this:

```
Msg 208, Level 16, State 1, Line 1
Invalid object name 'Data.Make'.
```

This probably means you have not clicked a database name in the Object Explorer to specify which database you want to query. In this case, you can set the appropriate database by selecting it from the list of databases that appears when you click the pop-up list at the top left of the SSMS window, as shown in *Figure 1.10.*

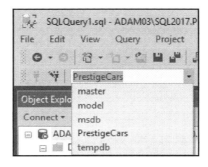

Figure 1.10: *Selecting a database to query*

- In this book I will explain the data tables that you need to use as you meet them. Here you have seen the first of the small set of tables that make up the sample database. As its name suggests, the Make table contains the makes of cars that are stocked and sold by Prestige Cars Ltd.

Note: Make sure you have not selected any of the SQL text before you execute the query. This guarantees that SSMS will run the entire SQL snippet in the query window.

1.7 Limiting the Number of Records Displayed

SQL Server tables can contain millions—or even billions—of records. Each time that you run a query, all the records you see are sent from the server to the querying application. It follows that displaying all the rows in a huge table can place an unnecessary strain on the server that stores the data as well as on the network that connects the server to your workstation. So, in the real world, it is a good idea to display only a small number of records when examining a table. This is particularly true when looking at a table for the first time.

Fortunately, SQL has a way of limiting the number of rows returned by a query. This is nothing more than a simple extension to the command that you used in the previous section. Here you can see how to tweak a piece of SQL code to display only a few makes of vehicle:

1. Delete any SQL that might be in the query window (or open a new query window), and enter the following code snippet:

```
SELECT    TOP 10 *
FROM      Data.Make
```

2. Run the SQL code by pressing F5.

How It Works

Executing this command will display all the columns in the table—but only the first ten records. As this will look like the output shown in Figure 1.3 (limited to the first ten rows), I will not waste space by repeating the results here.

You may well be wondering which records you are seeing when you ask SQL to display the TOP 10 rows (or indeed any other number or records). The answer is that you might not even see the same set of records when you run this command at different times. SQL Server does not necessarily return the first (or last) ten records that were added to a table. Neither does it display the last ten to be updated, viewed, or printed.

This apparently minor question reveals an important fact about SQL databases. They can store records in any order (unless the database programmer instructed them to do otherwise). However, there is no immediate way of telling, when you look at a table, whether the data is stored in any sequence. You need to remember this when querying tables and never trust the data to be returned in any specific order unless you have asked for this to happen. How you do this is explained later in this chapter.

Tricks and Traps

The following are a few points that I think are worth mentioning at this juncture:

*   There are several ways to run the SQL code in a query window. Pressing F5 is only one method. Another is to select Query☐Execute from the SSMS menu. Yet another alternative is to click the Execute button (the red exclamation mark) in the toolbar.

*   In most cases, you can enter the keywords as well as the table and column names in either uppercase or lowercase, or even a mixture of the two. This will depend on how your SQL Server has been configured. In this book, however, I will always enter keywords in uppercase to help them stand out in the code snippet. Ideally, this will make them easier to learn.

- You do not have to write queries in a purely linear fashion, starting with the SELECT clause and continuing to the end of the query. You can start with any part of the query and build it up as you want. In practice, however, you will probably nearly always begin with the FROM clause and then move on to the SELECT clause.

SQL Writing Style

You can format the SQL you write in any way that suits you. You may prefer to write short SQL statements on a single line. Alternatively, you may find it clearer if you place the core keywords like SELECT and FROM on separate lines. The choice is yours.

All you have to remember is that keywords must be separated by a space, a tab character, or a line break. Besides that, the presentation of your SQL is entirely up to you. After all, all that really matters is that it works.

1.8 Displaying Data from a Specific Field

A SQL Server table can contain hundreds of columns. Most of the time you will want to display data from only a few of the available columns in a table. The next piece of SQL shows how you choose a single column to display instead of all the available columns in a table. More specifically, it shows how to list only the customer names.

```
SELECT CustomerName

FROM    Data.Customer
```

Executing this piece of code (using any of the techniques that I pointed out at the end of the previous section) will show you something similar to the output shown in *Figure 1.11*.

Figure 1.11: Choosing a column from a table

How It Works

By replacing the star (or asterisk if you prefer) in your SQL with a specific column name, you have told SQL Server that it is this column—and this column only—that you want to display. This example also makes the point that SQL is an extremely modular and extensible language, and you can easily extend or modify a simple command to make it more specific.

Of course, this approach relies on your knowing the exact name of a column and also typing it exactly as it appears in the table. Fortunately, SSMS has ways of displaying column names and using them in your SQL, as you will discover in the next section.

Tricks and Traps

Even simple SQL commands have their subtleties. When listing data, you need to remember the following:

- You can write short SQL commands like this one on a single line of you prefer. That is, you could write the following instead of placing each clause on a separate line:

```
SELECT CustomerName FROM Data.Customer
```

This is entirely a question of personal choice. As I am presuming that you are new to SQL, we will keep the core SQL statements on separate lines in this book to accentuate the underlying logic of the language. In your queries, you can write the SQL any way you want, as long as it works. All that SQL Server wants is that the "grammar" of the command is technically accurate and that keywords are separated by spaces or returns.

1.9 Finding the Columns in a Table

You may well be wondering how on Earth you can be expected to remember all the columns in each table so that you can type them into your SQL queries. Fortunately, SQL Server Management Studio can help you here by displaying all the columns in a table in a single click.

Displaying the columns in a table is really easy.

1. Click the plus symbol to the left of the table whose columns you want to see (we will use the Country table in this example).

2. Click the plus symbol to the left of the Columns folder. You should see something like *Figure 1.12*.

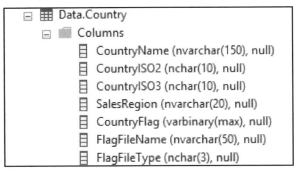

Figure 1.12. Displaying the columns in a table

When you display the list of columns in a table, you can also see some more technical information concerning the type of data that the column contains and possibly the maximum amount of data that each column can hold. While useful, this is not really relevant to the queries that you will be creating in the first few chapters of this book.

Note: SSMS can also list columns (or fields if you prefer) as you enter SQL code. You might see this happening as you enter your SQL. I will explain this more fully in the next chapter.

1.10 Displaying Data from a Specific Set of Fields

SQL does not limit you to displaying all the fields—or only one field—from a table. You can choose not only the fields from a table that you want to display but also the order in which they will appear in the output from the query. The following piece of code shows you how to select two fields (Country Name and Sales Region) from another table in the database—the Country table:

```
SELECT CountryName, SalesRegion
FROM   Data.Country
```

Executing this piece of code will show you something similar to the output in *Figure 1.13*.

Results | Messages

	CountryName	SalesRegion
1	Belgium	EMEA
2	France	EMEA
3	Germany	EMEA
4	Italy	EMEA
5	Spain	EMEA
6	United Kingdom	EMEA
7	United States	North America
8	China	Asia
9	India	Asia
10	Switzerland	EMEA

Figure 1.13. *Displaying multiple fields from the Country table*

Columns or Fields

Whereas spreadsheets prefer the term columns, databases tend to use the word fields. So, despite the fact that we have used the term column up until now in this chapter, I will switch to using the term field from now on.

Both words, however, describe the same thing and can generally be used interchangeably.

How It Works

Here again, you have extended the base SQL that you used at the start of the chapter. Specifically, you have developed the SELECT statement to include the field names containing the data that you want to view. All you had to do was to separate each field name with a comma and place the field names in the order that you want to see their data in the output from left to right.

Tricks and Traps

There is only one major trick to remember when listing a specific set of fields.

- Remember not to add a comma after the final field in a list of fields in the SELECT clause.

1.11 Modifying the Field Name

Many databases have cryptic—or frankly incomprehensible—field names. While as an analyst or data guru you might get used to this, it is not always a good idea to present information to users in a way that makes the data harder to understand than is really necessary. So, SQL allows you to output the data under a different field header to enhance readability. In this example, you will display the country field under another name. Start by taking a look at the code snippet and then at the output it returns in *Figure 1.14:*

```
SELECT CountryName, CountryISO3 AS IsoCode FROM Data.Country
```

Figure 1.14: Changing a field name using an alias

How It Works

In the query output, the original field name is replaced by the name you have chosen—ISOCODE in this example. This technique is called aliasing; you are giving the field another name in the query. Applying an alias has no effect at all on the underlying data and does not change the underlying field name. What it does do is apply a different (and ideally more comprehensible) name in the query output.

Tricks and Traps

Aliases have their own particular set of rules that must be adhered to if they are to work correctly. Essentially you need to remember the following points:

- You may have noticed that all the table and field names that have been used so far contain neither spaces nor special (that is, nonalphanumeric) characters. This is because SQL requires you to specify the names of what it calls objects—that is, fields and tables among other things—in a specific way. However, I do not want to make things appear over-complicated here, so as a starting point, let's just say you are better avoiding all nonalphanumeric characters when creating an alias for a field.

- If you want to add a space to an alias (suppose in the example used in this section you want to see "ISO Code" as the field heading), then you must place the alias inside square brackets or double quotes. That is, you can write either of the following to add a space to the alias ISOCode that you want to use instead of the real field name:

```
SELECT CountryName, CountryISO3 AS [Iso Code] FROM Data.Country
SELECT CountryName, CountryISO3 AS "Iso Code" FROM Data.Country
```

  In practice, many data people advise that you avoid spaces and nonstandard characters if you can, as once you have started down this route, you will have to add the double quotes or square brackets every time you refer to this alias (or table or field) in your code, which can get painful when writing complex queries. So, we will stick to names without spaces or nonalphanumeric characters in this book.

- In some queries you may find that you are faced with field names so cryptic that they are hard to read. In these cases, you could try using the underscore character instead of a space in a field name. This would give an alias that looks like Iso_Code in this example. While this is certainly a little "geeky," this is nonetheless easier to read than a name without any spaces while being much easier to use in more advanced (and complex) queries.

- An alias cannot be more than 128 characters long.

- You can also add an alias using code like this:

```
SELECT CountryName, CountryISO3 = CountryISO3 FROM Data.Country
```

  However, I prefer not to use this technique and so will not be taking this approach when aliasing columns.

Undo and Redo

SSMS is like many other desktop applications in that you can undo changes—and redo them—if you want.

- Ctrl-Z will undo one or more modifications.
- Ctrl-Y will redo modifications that you have undone.

1.12 Sorting Data

Now that you can select the fields that contain the data you want to see in the sequence that you want to see them, you probably also want to sort the data. For example, you might want to sort car sales by increasing sale price. To do this, just run the following snippet and take a look the numbers in the SalePrice field in Figure 1.15. They are now sorted from lowest to highest.

```
SELECT      *
FROM        Data.SalesByCountry
ORDER BY    SalePrice
```

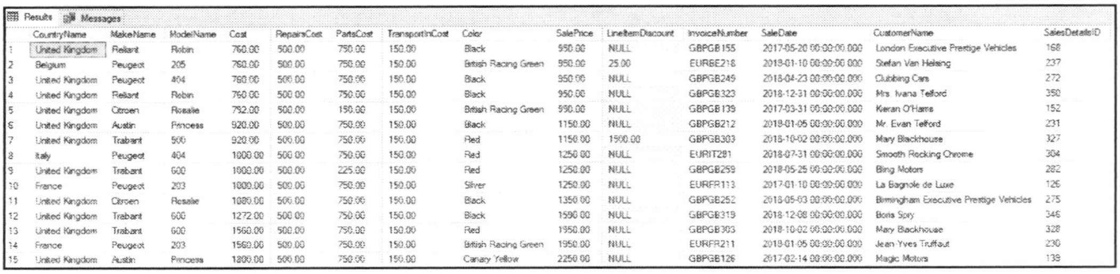

	CountryName	MakeName	ModelName	Cost	RepairsCost	PartsCost	TransportInCost	Color	SalePrice	LineItemDiscount	InvoiceNumber	SaleDate	CustomerName	SalesDetailsID
1	United Kingdom	Reliant	Robin	760.00	500.00	750.00	150.00	Black	950.00	NULL	GBPGB155	2017-05-20 00:00:00.000	London Executive Prestige Vehicles	168
2	Belgium	Peugeot	205	760.00	500.00	750.00	150.00	British Racing Green	950.00	25.00	EURBE218	2018-01-10 00:00:00.000	Stefan Van Helsing	237
3	United Kingdom	Peugeot	404	760.00	500.00	750.00	150.00	Black	950.00	NULL	GBPGB249	2018-04-23 00:00:00.000	Clubbing Cars	272
4	United Kingdom	Reliant	Robin	760.00	500.00	750.00	150.00	Black	950.00	NULL	GBPGB323	2018-12-31 00:00:00.000	Mrs. Ivana Telford	350
5	United Kingdom	Citroen	Rosalie	792.00	500.00	150.00	150.00	British Racing Green	990.00	NULL	GBPGB139	2017-03-31 00:00:00.000	Kieran O'Harris	152
6	United Kingdom	Austin	Princess	920.00	500.00	750.00	150.00	Black	1150.00	NULL	GBPGB212	2018-01-05 00:00:00.000	Mr. Evan Telford	231
7	United Kingdom	Trabant	500	920.00	500.00	750.00	150.00	Red	1150.00	1500.00	GBPGB303	2018-10-02 00:00:00.000	Mary Blackhouse	327
8	Italy	Peugeot	404	1000.00	500.00	750.00	150.00	Red	1250.00	NULL	EURIT281	2018-07-31 00:00:00.000	Smooth Rocking Chrome	304
9	United Kingdom	Trabant	600	1000.00	500.00	225.00	150.00	Red	1250.00	NULL	GBPGB259	2018-05-25 00:00:00.000	Bling Motors	282
10	France	Peugeot	203	1000.00	500.00	750.00	150.00	Silver	1250.00	NULL	EURFR113	2017-01-10 00:00:00.000	La Bagnole de Luxe	126
11	United Kingdom	Citroen	Rosalie	1080.00	500.00	750.00	150.00	Black	1350.00	NULL	GBPGB252	2018-05-03 00:00:00.000	Birmingham Executive Prestige Vehicles	275
12	United Kingdom	Trabant	600	1272.00	500.00	750.00	150.00	Black	1590.00	NULL	GBPGB319	2018-12-08 00:00:00.000	Boris Spry	346
13	United Kingdom	Trabant	600	1560.00	500.00	750.00	150.00	Red	1950.00	NULL	GBPGB303	2018-10-02 00:00:00.000	Mary Blackhouse	328
14	France	Peugeot	203	1560.00	500.00	750.00	150.00	British Racing Green	1950.00	NULL	EURFR211	2018-01-05 00:00:00.000	Jean-Yves Truffaut	230
15	United Kingdom	Austin	Princess	1800.00	500.00	750.00	150.00	Canary Yellow	2250.00	NULL	GBPGB126	2017-02-14 00:00:00.000	Magic Motors	139

Figure 1.15: *Sorting data in descending order*

How It Works

To sort the data returned by a query, just add the ORDER BY keyword (it is considered to be a single keyword even if it is really two words) after the FROM clause of the SQL command. Then you add the field that you are sorting the data on. This creates an ORDER BY clause.

Equally important is the fact that, once again, writing SQL can be all about making simple extensions to the code that you have written so far. So, you do not have to produce instant reams of code that work the first time. You can start with a small snippet of code, test it, and then extend it until it does exactly what you want it to do.

Tricks and Traps

These are several key points to remember here:

- The ORDER BY keyword can also be used on text (in which case it sorts in alphabetical order), on numbers (where it sorts from lowest to highest), or on dates (in which case it places the dates in sequence).

- If you want, you can add the ASC keyword after the sort field name to force an ORDER BY statement to sort the data in ascending order. However, SQL Server sorts data in ascending order out of the box. So, the result would be the same even if you wrote this:

```
SELECT * FROM Data.SalesByCountry ORDER BY SalePrice ASC
```

- If you test this, you will see the same result that you saw when you added the ASC keyword to the ORDER BY clause in the SQL snippet at the start of this section. Techies refer to this as the default sort order.

- If you find that reiterating field names in the ORDER BY clause is somewhat laborious, then you can always apply a shortcut. Instead of using a field name, you can use a number to represent it. So, you could write the SQL query at the start of this section as follows:

```
SELECT    CountryISO3 AS IsoCode, CountryName
FROM      Data.Country
ORDER BY  1
```

The number that you use in the ORDER BY clause stands for the position of the field in the SELECT clause of the SQL statement. So in this example 1 represents IsoCode (aliased as IsoCode). 2 would mean mean CountryName (the second field in the SELECT clause) etc.

1.13 Sorting Data in Reverse Alphabetical Order

As you saw in the previous example, data can be sorted from lowest to highest really quickly and easily. You are can also sort data from highest to lowest (or Z to A). Changing the sort order is as simple as replacing the ASC (short for ascending) keyword that you just met with the DESC (short for descending) keyword. You can see this in the output shown in *Figure 1.16*, which is the result of the following code snippet that sorts the country names in reverse alphabetical order of ISO code:

```
SELECT    CountryISO3 AS IsoCode, CountryName
FROM      Data.Country
ORDER BY  IsoCode DESC
```

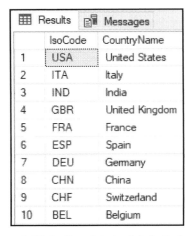

Figure 1.16: Sorting data in alphabetical order

How It Works

Switching the sort order is as easy as adding the ASC keyword to the end of the ORDER BY clause or replacing the DESC keyword with the ASC keyword at the end of the ORDER BY clause of a SQL command. Using DESC forces SQL to sort the results from highest to lowest (if they are numbers), Z to A (if they are text), or latest to earliest (if they are dates).

1.14 Applying Multiple Sort Criteria

Larger data sets can require that you sort data according to multiple criteria. Suppose, for instance, that you want to list all the cars sold first by country, then by make (per country), and finally by model if there are several makes sold for a specific country.

This is easy to do in SQL because it is a simple extension of the techniques that you have seen in the previous two sections. Take a look at the following code snippet:

```
SELECT    CountryName, MakeName, ModelName
FROM      Data.SalesByCountry
ORDER BY  CountryName, MakeName, ModelName
```

Executing this query will return a dataset similar to the one shown in *Figure 1.17*.

	CountryName	MakeName	ModelName
1	Belgium	Alfa Romeo	Giulia
2	Belgium	Alfa Romeo	Spider
3	Belgium	Aston Martin	Rapide
4	Belgium	Aston Martin	Vantage
5	Belgium	Noble	M600
6	Belgium	Peugeot	205
7	Belgium	Peugeot	205
8	Belgium	Triumph	Roadster
9	Belgium	Triumph	TR4
10	Belgium	Triumph	TR6
11	France	Alfa Romeo	1750
12	France	Alfa Romeo	Giulia
13	France	Alfa Romeo	Spider
14	France	Aston Martin	DB4
15	France	Aston Martin	DB5

Figure 1.17: *Sorting sales using multiple fields*

How It Works

Sometimes you will be faced with a table where some fields contain the same data elements repeated several times. A telephone directory is like this. You may have many pages of people named Smith, although nearly all may have different first names. Even if the last name and the first name are the same, they may have different middle initials. In these cases, you need to sort the data on successive fields so that (to continue the telephone directory analogy) you sort first by last name, then by first name, and finally by middle initial.

Entering several fields after the ORDER BY keyword tells SQL to sort the data progressively on the fields that you entered. In this example, it means the following:

- First by the country
- Then by the make (if there is more than one record with the same country)
- Finally by the model (if there is more than one record with the same country and make)

All you have to do is enter the field names separated by a comma in the ORDER BY clause.

Tricks and Traps

Applying a multiple sort order has its own specific set of core requirements. These include the following:

- While there may be technical limits to the number of fields you can sort on, in practice you do not need to worry and can extend the field list that you use in the ORDER BY statement to include many fields.

- In this example, you used the same fields in the SELECT statement that you used in the ORDER BY statement. This is not compulsory in SQL because there is no obligation in a basic SQL query to display the same fields that you use for ordering the data. However, when you are testing your SQL skills (or ensuring that the data looks like you think it should), it can be a good idea to use the same groups of fields in both clauses. This way you can see whether the output is what you expect.

- Sorting query results requires a lot of computing horsepower when you are dealing with large tables or small database servers. I recommend that you sort data only if it is really necessary.

- As was the case for SELECT clauses, you should not add a comma after the final field name in the ORDER BY clause.

1.15 Choosing the Database to Query

Toward the beginning of this chapter you learned to expand a database in the Object Explorer window and click a database before opening a query window. This is not the only way that you can indicate to SQL Server which database you want to query.

Another way to select the database to use (which techies call setting the database context) is as follows:

1. Open a new query window.

2. In the query toolbar, click the pop-up list that contains all the available databases.

3. Select the database to use (PrestigeCars in this example). You can see this in *Figure 1.18*.

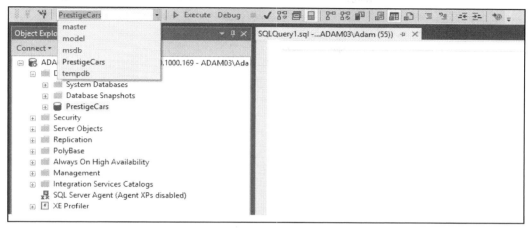

Figure 1.18. *Selecting a database to query*

This is all you have to do to select a database for the query that you are about to write or that you have just written.

Conclusion

This chapter showed you how to perform elementary SQL queries. You saw how to open SQL Server Management Studio and connect to a specific database. Then you saw how to dig into some of the tables that make up a database and take a look at the data they contain.

You then learned how to be a little more selective when outputting data and consequently to choose which fields to display from a query. You also saw how to limit the number of records that a query returned as well as how to sort the data.

All in all, you have already made vast strides toward the basic analysis of SQL Server data. With this knowledge safely acquired, it is time to move on to the next step: using data from multiple tables. This is what you will be looking at in the next chapter.

Core Knowledge Learned in This Chapter

SQL is a language that is built on a collection of core concepts and a set of clearly defined keywords. Using all of these correctly—and understanding exactly what they can and cannot do—is what learning to use SQL is all about. To help you build up your SQL vocabulary, we will always recapitulate any new concepts and keywords that you have met at the end of each chapter. The following are the fundamental keywords that you have learned to use in this chapter:

Concept	Description
Database	A database is a structured way of storing data following a clear set of rules.
Table	A table is a coherent unit of data storage.
Field	A field is a homogenous data definition for a column of data.
Record	A row of data elements made up of fields.
SELECT	This is one of the essential SQL keywords, and you will probably use it in just about every SQL command that you will ever write. It means "isolate and display."
FROM	This is another core keyword. It tells the database which tables you want to look at.
TOP	This keyword restricts the number of rows that a query displays. You can set either a precise number of records to show or a percentage of the total number of records in a table.
AS	This keyword lets you display a field under another name. It is called aliasing a field.
*	The star (or asterisk) keyword means "everything." Yes, this is a keyword too, even if it is only a single character. Using this avoids you having to know what the names of the fields in a table are.
ORDER BY	This keyword combination sorts the output from a query using the selected field or fields as the sort keys.
ASC	Adding this keyword to an ORDER BY clause sorts the data in ascending order.
DESC	Adding this keyword to an ORDER BY clause sorts the data in descending order.

CHAPTER 2

Using Multiple Tables When Querying Data

Now that you are at ease with the basics of querying, it is time to extend your SQL knowledge by looking at how to analyze data that is stored across multiple tables. All SQL databases are based on this simple principle: data is broken down into many separate tables that you then link together to deliver the results you are looking for. Indeed, querying data from several tables at once is so fundamental to SQL that you need to learn to master these techniques early in your SQL apprenticeship.

Storing Data in Multiple Tables

At this stage of your venture into the field of data analysis with SQL, you are probably wondering why data can be placed in several tables at once. It can seem peculiar to break data down into all these separate tables and then spend time joining them together again when you want to query the data.

Well, there are several reasons for taking this approach.

First, one of the main objectives of relational databases is to avoid the duplication of data. Put simply, if an element of data (an address, say) appears in two or more tables, then every time it needed to be updated, it would have to be modified in several places. This is complicated—and a big potential source for errors. One classic consequence is that you end up with multiple different addresses and no way of knowing which is the right one. Relational databases try to prevent this from happening by storing independent but homogenous chunks of data in separate tables once only.

Another advantage of this approach is that avoiding duplication makes the data less voluminous. So, the cost of storing the data is reduced—often considerably in these days of explosive data growth.

Yet another reason to create multiple tables is to centralize reference data—like the table of countries you saw in the previous chapter. This is because certain data elements (such as country names) are likely to be reused frequently in multiple tables. In cases like this, it makes sense to store the country name—as well as any frequently used details—in lookup tables. You can then use a short code in one or more tables to refer to repetitive data in another single table. This way the reference data (such as the country name) will always appear the same way in all your analytical reports because it appears only *once* in the database.

A consequence of this architecture is that database designers often need to add fields that allow tables to be linked, as you will see throughout this chapter. These fields are called *key fields* and may contain numbers or alphanumeric codes. What really matters is that these keys allow data to be mapped across tables so that information can be reconstituted harmoniously and coherently from several tables.

Another (but not the final) reason for storing data in separate tables is that in most cases it allows data to be written to disk (and read from disk) more efficiently. This makes for faster response times. After all, do you want to wait longer than necessary for the answers to their questions?

To get you used to the concept of using multiple tables, this chapter will show you how to

- Join two or more tables.
- Select data from multiple tables.
- Remove duplicates from the output.
- Query **views**, instead of tables. These are, in essence, a way of reusing multiple table joins.

So that is the theory. Now it is time to move on to the practice of the real-world SQL that you will need to master. This chapter teaches you how you can use the links between tables to write more complex and powerful queries. This is an essential step in enabling you to deliver coherent analysis of the source data.

2.1 Joining Tables

As an initial step on your path to analyzing the data for Prestige Cars Ltd., you want to produce a complete list of every vehicle purchased and the amount paid to purchase it. After looking at the PrestigeCars database, you have found the Stock table that contains the price of every car. However, it does not contain the model— only an internal ID number that means nothing to you. However, you have also found a table called Model, and this table contains the list of all the types of model that the company sells, as well as what appears to be the same ID number used in the Stock table. You can see this represented graphically in *Figure 2.1.*

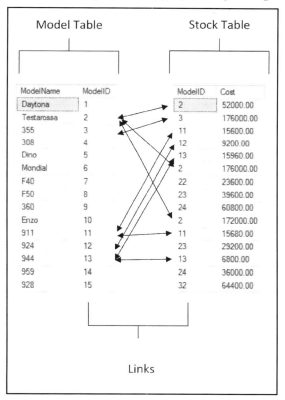

Figure 2.1: *Linking tables*

So, now you need to collate data from both of these tables so that you can see information from both of them in a single query. This will let you see both the model *and* the cost. Here is the SQL that will do exactly this for you:

```
SELECT      ModelName, Cost
FROM        Data.Model

INNER JOIN Data.Stock

            ON Model.ModelID = Stock.ModelID

ORDER BY    ModelName
```

Running this query gives the results shown in *Figure 2.2* (assuming you have scrolled down the list a few rows).

	ModelName	Cost
109	Arnage	61200.00
110	Arnage	68520.00
111	Arnage	45440.00
112	Boxster	18000.00
113	Brooklands	79600.00
114	Brooklands	151600...
115	Cambridge	18000.00
116	Continental	62000.00
117	Continental	45560.00
118	Continental	71600.00
119	Continental	79600.00
120	Corniche	71600.00
121	Countach	2920.00
122	Countach	98800.00

Figure 2.2: Using a join to output data from two tables

How It Works

The code you just wrote to join two tables is a little "dry" to say the least. It is probably easier to understand what you have just done if it is presented in a more visual way. *Figure 2.3* illustrates what joining tables looks like.

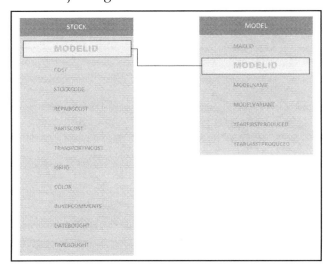

Figure 2.3. Representing table joins visually

Conceptually, joining pairs of tables means knowing which fields can be used to create the "bridge" between the two tables. Once again, this could mean talking to the people who designed the database or delving into any documentation that you may have been given. Sometimes you can easily guess which fields can be used as joins, such as when the two fields have the same name or when the data is clearly the same in both tables. At other times it can be really difficult to guess the join fields just by looking at the tables. For the moment, I will explain how the sample tables are joined each time to avoid you having to guess.

Practically, this code snippet takes three keywords that you already know well (SELECT, FROM, and ORDER BY) and extends the FROM clause with two new keywords: *INNER JOIN* and *ON*. These keywords allow you to create links between tables so that you can display fields from both tables at once. Linking (or joining) two tables in SQL consists of the following steps:

1. Enter the name of the first table to join after the FROM keyword.

2. Add the INNER JOIN keyword after the table name.

3. Enter the name of the second table to join.

4. Add the ON keyword.

5. Enter the names of the two fields that are the link between the two tables, separated by the equal (=) sign.

Each of the fields used to link the tables *must* be preceded by the name of the table that contains the field followed by a period. This enables SQL Server to identify which field can be found in which table when creating the link.

Tricks and Traps

As joining tables is a core concept, you should note these key points from the start:

- The fields that you use to join the two tables may—or may not—have the same name in both tables. If the two field names are different, then you can just enter them "as is," separated by an equal sign without adding the table name. If, however, the two fields have the same name, then you need to precede each field name by the table name and a period. This is because SQL Server gets confused if there is no way of uniquely identifying the field name—almost as if it doesn't know which one to take to finish the join. Adding the table name and a period like this allows SQL to trace the field name back to its source table and consequently identify the correct field to use in the join.

- In practice, it is often best to identify uniquely the fields that are establishing the join by preceding each field with the name of the table it comes from and a period even if the field names are different in the two tables. Once again, this is a little like identifying a person by their last name and first name. In the world of SQL, it avoids confusion by making names uniquely identifiable. In more complex SQL, it allows you to see instantly which field in which table is being linked to which other field in another table. This will help you understand complex queries more easily.

- While taking this "table-field" approach is not strictly necessary, we will apply it as a best practice in the SQL examples in this book.

- The order in which you enter the tables in the FROM clause is unimportant. You could write the FROM clause in this example as follows without altering the result:

```
Data.Stock INNER JOIN Data.Model
```

- Equally, the order of the fields in the ON clause is irrelevant; they do not have to be in the same order as the tables in the query.

- While you **do** have to provide the schema name (Data in this example) for the tables in the FROM clause, you do **not** have to repeat the schema name elsewhere in the SQL. You can precede the table name by the schema in the SELECT and ORDER BY clauses if you want. You can decide whether this makes the SQL easier or harder to read.

- The data in the tables that you are joining is probably not stored in both tables in the same order. However, this is irrelevant to SQL.

Note : I will use keyword to describe core SQL Server terms even when the "keyword" consists of several individual words.

2.2 Removing Duplicates from Query Output

As befits a company that sells its products across the globe, the CEO of Prestige Cars needs to know where its presence is felt the most. It follows that she wants you to produce a list of the countries where the company's customers can be found. A quick look at the database reveals a Customer table that contains a Country field—but it contains only the ISO two-character code for the country of the client. At first sight this is an issue because you want to display the full name for each country. Then you spot the Country table that contains not only the two-character ISO code but also the full name of the country. So, you are hoping that if you can join these two tables, you should be able to obtain the relevant data.

Fortunately, you are right. Here is the SQL that will produce the list you require:

```
SELECT DISTINCT    CountryName

FROM               Data.Customer

INNER JOIN         Data.Country

                   ON Customer.Country = Country.CountryISO2
```

This query returns the results shown in *Figure 2.4.*

Figure 2.4. *Joining tables and returning data from one of the tables*

How It Works

This query joins the Customer table to the Country table. It maps the Country field in the Customer table to the CountryISO2 field in the Country table. As I mentioned earlier, it really helps to know in practice which fields you can use to join tables. Once the two tables are joined, you can select fields from either of the tables. As all you want to display is the country for a customer, the CountryName field is all you need. SQL in effect goes through the Customer table and looks up the country name for each customer. Then it applies the *DISTINCT* keyword to remove any duplicates from the list of countries.

Before looking more deeply into the actual code, I need to make a fairly fundamental point about what this query is doing. A join like this one returns data only when there is a common element in both tables. In other words, the country reference (the Country field in the Customer table and the CountryISO2 field in the Country table) has to exist in both tables for data to be returned from either table. If there is no corresponding element in the two tables, then no data is returned from either table.

If you need to verify this, then look at the contents of the Country table. You will see that it contains two countries (India and China) that have no corresponding cross-reference in the Customer table. Consequently, these countries do *not* appear in the query output.

Another original aspect of this example is the DISTINCT keyword. This keyword is incredibly useful because it removes all duplicates from the query output before you even see the query results. To make this clearer, try running the same query without the DISTINCT keyword using SQL like this:

```
SELECT       CountryName

FROM         Data.Customer

INNER JOIN   Data.Country

             ON Customer.Country = Country.CountryISO2
```

This time you will see the result shown in *Figure 2.5.*

Figure 2.5. Returning data from a joined table without the DISTINCT keyword

As you can see from Figure 2.5, the names of many countries appear several times. Without the DISTINCT keyword, you see several country names repeated as there are a good number of customers in the same country—and SQL would show the country for *each customer*, even if you did *not* ask for the customer to be displayed.

This happens because joining tables will cause SQL to return *all* the records that it can from *both* tables. This will happen whatever the fields that are in the SELECT clause, irrespective of which table they come from.

In the query without the DISTINCT keyword, SQL Server returns all the records from the Customer table (some 87 of them), even if *no* field from the Customer table was requested in the output. This has the effect of duplicating many of the country names because for each customer the query looks up the full country name and displays it in the query result.

Tricks and Traps

With a little practice, joining tables is not difficult. Nonetheless, it can have far-reaching consequences. So, you need to be mindful of the following:

- You may be wondering why you did not just use the Country table directly to produce this list. The reason is that the Country table is essentially a lookup table. It contains a list of country names, but you do not know if it contains all the countries in the world—or only those corresponding to countries where you have customers. So, it is best to use the Customer table as the basis for your query and use the Country table to look up the country name that corresponds to the country code for the actual customers.

- You could, theoretically, not add the table names before the fields in the ON clause. That is, the ON clause could look like this:

  ```
  ON Country = CountryISO2
  ```

- This will work because the field names are unique across the tables used. That is, they are **not identical** in both tables. However, this is far from usual in real-world data analysis, so, as I pointed out in the previous example, I prefer to add the table name to the field in the ON clause as a matter of good practice. This will leave you better prepared to deal with your own data sets.

- In the world of corporate databases, it can sometimes be really hard to find out which fields you need to use to join tables. In practice, nothing will save you quite as much time as acquiring some documentation on the database that you are using for your analysis.

2.3 Joining Multiple Tables

The CEO firmly believes that effective cost control is vital for the company's survival. So, she wants a list of all the cars that have ever been bought since Prestige Cars started trading. In fact, she wants a list of the purchase cost for every make and model ever held in stock.

This query reflects the fact that most databases consist of many tables. In certain queries you will have to join not just two tables—as you did in the previous section—but several tables at once. SQL lets you extend the technique you saw in the previous example to join multiple tables. As an example, suppose you want to list the cost of every make and model of car sold. However, a quick look at the database makes it clear that while the cost is in the Stock table, this contains only the ID for the model and does not contain the make at all. Equally, the Model table contains only an ID for the make and not the full name of the make—which is in the Make table. So, you need to "chain" all three tables (Stock to Model to Make) to return the data that you want to see.

This is probably easier to understand visually. *Figure 2.6* shows you an image of three tables joined together using a different "bridge" field between each pair of tables. This approach allows you to select fields from any or all of the tables.

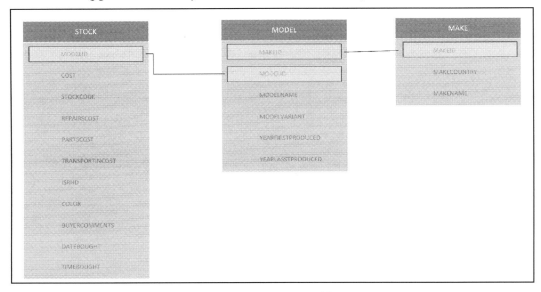

Figure 2.6. *Chaining tables*

The following piece of SQL shows you how this can be done:

```
SELECT     Make.MakeName, Model.ModelName, Stock.Cost
FROM       Data.Stock
INNER JOIN Data.Model
           ON Model.ModelID = Stock.ModelID
INNER JOIN Data.Make
           ON Make.MakeID = Model.MakeID
```

Other Join Syntax

Over time database developers have created several ways of using SQL to join tables.

One traditional technique to join tables uses the WHERE keyword to define table joins. Using this approach, the initial table join that you saw in this chapter would look like this:

```
SELECT     ModelName, Cost
FROM       Data.Model, Data.Stock
WHERE      Model.Modelid = Stock.Modelid
```

This technique lists all the tables to join in the FROM clause (separated by a comma) and then uses a WHERE clause (which is something that you will learn a lot more about about in the next chapter) to define the fields that join the tables.

While there is nothing wrong with this approach, it does detract from the principle use of the WHERE clause, which is to filter data in queries. In practice, this style of coding can lead to extremely complex WHERE clauses.

For these reasons, I prefer using the ON syntax to define table joins. This is because it not only isolates the join criteria more clearly but is also a more modern technique that is used by many development tools (such as SQL Server Management Studio) that generate SQL automatically. Consequently, this is the approach that I will be taking throughout this book.

However, you need to be aware that some legacy SQL Server code uses the WHERE syntax to join tables. So, you need not be surprised if you see this method of joining tables in the real-world databases that you encounter.

Running this query gives the results shown in *Figure 2.7*.

	MakeName	ModelName	Cost
1	Porsche	Testarossa	52000.00
2	Lamborghini	355	176000.00
3	BMW	911	15600.00
4	Bugatti	924	9200.00
5	Citroen	944	15960.00
6	Porsche	Testarossa	176000.00
7	Trabant	DB4	23600.00
8	Peugeot	DB5	39600.00
9	Reliant	DB6	60800.00
10	Porsche	Testarossa	172000.00
11	BMW	911	15680.00
12	Peugeot	DB5	29200.00
13	Citroen	944	6800.00
14	Reliant	DB6	36000.00
15	Lamborghini	355	135600.00

Figure 2.7. Data output from three tables

How It Works

The real work done by this code is in the FROM clause. It works like this:

First:	The Stock table is joined to the Model table (using the shared ModelID field to link the two tables).
Second:	The Make table is then added—with a second INNER JOIN keyword—and linked to the Model table using the ON keyword and the shared MakeID field.
Finally:	Any fields that you want to output are added to the SELECT clause.

The real point of this example is to demonstrate that you can chain together a sequence of virtually any number of tables to analyze data. What is essential is that any two tables share a field (or even several fields) common to both—and that the fields have been designed to be used to join the tables. Each time you want to add another table to the query, you introduce it with the INNER JOIN keyword and then specify which field links it to which field in another table using the ON keyword to "bridge" the tables.

Tricks and Traps

Linking multiple tables in this way will take a little practice before it becomes second nature. To help you when using your SQL skills, here are a few practical considerations that you might want to bear in mind:

- You can begin by adding the fields to the SELECT clause **before** you complete the FROM clause, but it is often easier, conceptually, to concentrate on working out which tables need to be joined (and to join them) before adding the fields that you want to see in the output.

- You do **not** have to say which tables you will be joining **before** you say which fields they will join on. In other words, you can write all the INNER JOIN clauses before you write the ON clauses. However, if you do this, you have to respect a certain structure, which is shown in Figure 2.7:

```
SELECT     Make.MakeName, Model.ModelName, Stock.Cost

FROM       Data.Stock

INNER JOIN Data.Model

INNER JOIN Data.Make
```

```
ON Make.MakeID = Model.ModelID

ON Model.ModelID = Stock.ModelID
```

Join Fields

When you start writing all but the simplest queries, it will rapidly become **absolutely vital** to know which fields you need to use to join tables. Sometimes you will need to join only one field in a table to one other field in another table. Occasionally, you will need to use two or more fields in each table that you are joining. Ideally, the database designers or other users will be able to explain the required fields to you before you start writing queries.

In the PrestigeCars dataset, all table joins are made using a single field. Sometimes these fields contain meaningful data (such as the Countryiso3 field in the Country table). However, other tables use a value such as a number that has no intrinsic meaning to the user; the ModelID field in the Model table is an example. You can even see "meaningless" strings of characters used to join tables. The SalesID field in the Sales table is an example of this.

The point here is that the fields you use to join tables can be letters or numbers. They can be comprehensible to humans or not. This does not matter in the least. All that matters (to data analysts querying databases, anyway) is that you know **which fields to join** and that the dataset has been correctly designed so that the joins will work.

You will probably find that SQL Server databases use numbers as the data type for join fields. While this may seem strange—or even perverse—at first sight, it is a highly efficient way of joining tables and retrieving data.

SQL theorists (yes, they really exist) call the fields that "link" two tables the **join predicate**. This is another way of describing the shared element in the field used to join tables.

You will have to write the ON clauses in *reverse order* of the INNER JOIN clauses if you choose to go down this route. This is because the order of the ON clauses is important if you apply this style of SQL. Indeed, if you place the Make to Model link *after* the Model to Stock link in this kind of clause, the statement will *not* work and will only send back an error message. Because this kind of code can get a little complicated in practice, I will always write each individual join out completely (that is, specifying both the INNER JOIN and ON clauses together) in all the examples in this book.

- You do not **always** have to indicate the table from which a field is drawn before the field name, as I have done here in specifying Make.MakeName, for instance. However, you can only use the field name on its own (without the table name to precede it) if the field name exists **only once** in **all** the selected tables. If there are several fields with the same name in the tables you are joining, SQL Server will not know which field to use and will send back an error message rather than the result that you were expecting. So, once again, preceding each field name with the table name and a period is best practice when writing SQL.

- In this example, I am selecting a single field from each of the three tables that you have joined. In reality, you can select **any** of the fields from any of the joined tables—or even all the fields from **all** of the tables.

- You can simply use the keyword JOIN instead of using INNER JOIN if you prefer. The result will be the same. I will continue to use the "full" INNER JOIN keyword to differentiate basic joins from the other join types that you will encounter throughout the course of this book.

2.4 Using Table Aliases

Analysis is often all about detail. So, it does not come as a surprise when the CEO comes to your desk and requests a list of all vehicles sold along with the selling price and any discounts that have been applied. To keep the CEO happy, you need to know that the PrestigeCars database contains two fairly essential tables called Sales and SalesDetails. These correspond roughly to an invoice header and the individual line items that make up a sale. These two tables contain all the information that you need to look at itemized sales. Let's suppose you need to analyze the discounts that have been applied to make the sales and see how they vary per car sold.

As an example, take a look at the following code snippet:

```
SELECT      S.InvoiceNumber, D.LineItemNumber, D.SalePrice
            ,D.LineItemDiscount
FROM        Data.Sales AS S
INNER JOIN Data.SalesDetails AS D
            ON S.SalesID = D.SalesID
ORDER BY    S.InvoiceNumber, D.LineItemNumber
```

Execute this query, and you should see the output in Figure 2.8. Be aware, however, that Figure 2.8 shows only the first few records and that you will have to scroll down the result set to see all the records returned by this query.

	InvoiceNumber	LineItemNumber	SalePrice	LineItemDiscount
1	EURBE074	1	125000.00	1500.00
2	EURBE125	1	12500.00	750.00
3	EURBE132	1	86500.00	1250.00
4	EURBE171	1	3950.00	750.00
5	EURBE171	2	29500.00	750.00
6	EURBE171	3	12500.00	NULL
7	EURBE193	1	23500.00	NULL
8	EURBE193	2	10500.00	NULL
9	EURBE218	1	950.00	25.00
10	EURBE264	1	6950.00	NULL
11	EURDE004	1	11500.00	NULL
12	EURDE036	1	65890.00	750.00
13	EURDE036	2	6000.00	NULL
14	EURDE043	1	99500.00	500.00
15	EURDE066	1	61500.00	NULL

Figure 2.8. *Using aliases when joining tables*

How It Works

This query joins the Sales and SalesDetails tables on the shared SalesID field. Then it outputs any required fields and sorts them by invoice number, followed by line number (this can be useful in cases where an invoice has more than one line item).

In the previous examples in this chapter, you saw that I added the table name to some field names when we built anything but the simplest query. Now, while this is not difficult, it can soon become extremely laborious because it can mean repeating the schema and table name several times in different parts of the query. Fortunately, there is a way to make your coding easier, even if it has no effect on the final result.

The trick is to use *aliases* for tables—a bit like when you aliased field names in the previous chapter.

First:	Add a space after the table name.
Then:	Add the AS keyword.
Finally:	Enter a short acronym that you will use instead of the table name elsewhere in the query.

Aliases are applied in the FROM clause and then used everywhere else in the query where you would otherwise use the schema and table name.

SQL Writing Style

You have probably noticed that I have a certain way of writing queries in SQL. Our approach is to write all keywords in UPPERCASE and begin each major phrase—such as SELECT, FROM, and ORDER BY—indented in the left margin.

Our approach is not, however, the only one around. Indeed, there are as many ways of writing SQL as there are data analysts and database programmers. So, do not feel that you have to stick to this style. You can write your SQL in lowercase, uppercase, or any case at all. Do what feels right to you.

I advise nonetheless that you try to keep your SQL looking clean and readable. When you have written a query and obtained the results that you were hoping for (or, better still, results that shine a new light on your data), it is easy to forget that the slightly crumpled code that you have crafted could be hard to understand in a few days' time. So, a little effort spent making the code look more elegant can actually help you understand it better—both now and in the future.

Here adding an alias to a table is used not to display the alias but to make the code more comprehensible. This is achieved by rendering the SQL less voluminous and consequently easier to understand.

In this example, the Sales table was given the alias *S*, and the SalesDetails table was given the alias *D*. Once you have aliased the tables, you use the alias instead of the table name everywhere in the code where you would otherwise have used the full table name.

The alias is used in the same way as the table name would be used. So, when you have duplicate field names in separate tables, you can use the alias to distinguish them, rather than having to write out the full name of the table. This is particularly effective in the ON clause, which is consequently much shorter and easier to read.

Tricks and Traps

Aliases, too, have their idiosyncrasies, so you need to be aware of the following:

- Once you have added an alias, you **have to use it instead of the table name**. That is, you **cannot** use the table name elsewhere in the query—in the SELECT or ON clauses, for instance. Once you have created an alias, you are stuck with it—in the current query at least.

- Tools such as SQL Server Management Studio will recognize aliases when they suggest field names to help you write a query. So, this is another reason to begin writing queries with the FROM clause—at least when you are joining tables.

- An alias can be as short as you like. A single character will suffice.

- An alias can be as long as you like (well, 128 characters anyway). However, the main aim of an alias is to make your life easier, so I suggest making aliases as short as possible while trying to balance this with the need for them to be comprehensible as well.

- It can help to try to make aliases memorable. This will help you understand which alias refers to which table when you write SQL queries—and when you revisit them many months later. As you can see in this example, I have tried to use short aliases that remind you of the table name.

- Conversely, while it is easier to alias tables using codes such as T1, T2, and so on, this can make the SQL much harder to understand.

- The AS keyword is optional when aliasing tables. You can simply add the table alias after the table name—and a space to separate the two—if you prefer.

- If you need to visualize the joins between the tables, then you can always jump ahead to Figure 2.10.

2.5 Joining Many Tables

Ideally you are getting to know the PrestigeCars database better. To test your abilities, suppose you want to look at all the important fields from the database in a single query. Specifically, let's imagine you want to produce a list of cars sold that includes all vehicle data as well as all the essential customer data. This means joining virtually all the core tables in a single query. This SQL is quite voluminous compared to the code snippets you have been writing so far, but it is a practical example of the sort of code that you could be producing when analyzing your own data.

```
SELECT      CY.CountryName
            ,MK.MakeName
            ,MD.ModelName
            ,ST.Cost
            ,ST.RepairsCost
            ,ST.PartsCost
            ,ST.TransportInCost
            ,ST.Color
            ,SD.SalePrice
            ,SD.LineItemDiscount
            ,SA.InvoiceNumber
```

```
          ,SA.SaleDate
          ,CS.CustomerName
FROM      Data.Stock ST
INNER JOIN Data.Model MD
          ON ST.ModelID = MD.ModelID
INNER JOIN Data.Make MK
          ON MD.MakeID = MK.MakeID
INNER JOIN Data.SalesDetails SD
          ON ST.StockCode = SD.StockID
INNER JOIN Data.Sales SA
          ON SD.SalesID = SA.SalesID
INNER JOIN Data.Customer CS
          ON SA.CustomerID = CS.CustomerID
INNER JOIN Data.Country CY
          ON CS.Country = CY.CountryISO2
ORDER BY  CY.CountryName
          ,MK.MakeName
          ,MD.ModelName
```

If you run this query, you should see the output in Figure 2.9 (well, you will see all of it in SSMS; in this screenshot, the output has been truncated).

CountryName	MakeName	ModelName	Cost	RepairsCost	PartsCost	TransportInCost	Color	SalePrice	LineItemDiscount	InvoiceNumber	SaleDate	CustomerName
Belgium	Alfa Romeo	Giulia	8400.00	500.00	750.00	150.00	Black	10500.00	NULL	EURBE193	2017-11-06 00:00:00.000	Stefan Van Helsing
Belgium	Alfa Romeo	Spider	10000.00	500.00	750.00	150.00	Black	12500.00	NULL	EURBE171	2017-07-01 00:00:00.000	Stefan Van Helsing
Belgium	Aston Martin	Rapide	69200.00	2000.00	1500.00	750.00	Silver	86500.00	1250.00	EURBE152	2017-03-12 00:00:00.000	Diplomatic Cars
Belgium	Aston Martin	Vantage	100000.00	500.00	2200.00	750.00	Green	125000.00	1500.00	EURBE074	2016-08-23 00:00:00.000	Diplomatic Cars
Belgium	Noble	M600	23600.00	1360.00	750.00	150.00	Black	29500.00	750.00	EURBE171	2017-07-01 00:00:00.000	Stefan Van Helsing
Belgium	Peugeot	205	3160.00	500.00	750.00	150.00	Black	3950.00	750.00	EURBE171	2017-07-01 00:00:00.000	Stefan Van Helsing
Belgium	Peugeot	205	760.00	500.00	750.00	150.00	British Racing Green	950.00	25.00	EURBE218	2018-01-10 00:00:00.000	Stefan Van Helsing
Belgium	Triumph	Roadster	18800.00	1360.00	500.00	150.00	Black	23500.00	NULL	EURBE193	2017-11-06 00:00:00.000	Stefan Van Helsing
Belgium	Triumph	TR4	5560.00	500.00	457.00	150.00	Red	6950.00	NULL	EURBE264	2018-05-03 00:00:00.000	Flash Voitures
Belgium	Triumph	TR6	10000.00	500.00	750.00	150.00	Red	12500.00	750.00	EURBE125	2017-02-12 00:00:00.000	Diplomatic Cars
France	Alfa Romeo	1750	7960.00	500.00	750.00	150.00	Blue	9950.00	NULL	EURFR241	2018-04-15 00:00:00.000	Vive La Vitesse
France	Alfa Romeo	Giulia	2040.00	500.00	750.00	150.00	British Racing Green	2550.00	50.00	EURFR031	2016-01-07 00:00:00.000	M. Pierre Dubois
France	Alfa Romeo	Spider	9200.00	500.00	150.00	150.00	Blue	11500.00	750.00	EURFR194	2017-11-12 00:00:00.000	Mme Anne Duport
France	Aston Martin	DB4	29200.00	500.00	500.00	550.00	Black	36500.00	NULL	EURFR160	2017-05-26 00:00:00.000	Laurent Saint Yves
France	Aston Martin	DB5	55600.00	2000.00	457.00	750.00	Blue	69500.00	NULL	EURFR304	2018-10-02 00:00:00.000	Jacquee Mitterand

Figure 2.9. Outputting all the key data from the database

How It Works

This query joins the Stock, Model, Make, SalesDetails, Sales, Customer, and Country tables. These tables make up the "core" Prestige Cars data set. Then a list of fields from all the tables is added to the SELECT clause to return a list of detailed sales data from all the selected tables. It aliases each table to avoid repeating table names and also sorts the data by country, make, and model (in that order of precedence).

Database Concepts (Continued)

To make it easier for you to communicate with your colleagues when discussing databases, there are a few more essential concepts that you need to know from the start. These include the following (among others):

- **Primary keys**: These are fields that uniquely identify each record (or row) in a table. The key field (or the combination of fields that make up a key) is likely used when creating a join from one table to another. The MakeID field in the Make table is an example of this.

- **One-to-many relationship**: Because one of the main design aims of a well-constructed database is to avoid data duplication, you will frequently encounter tables containing a piece of information that is referred to many times in another table. This is called a one-to-many relationship, where the data that is entered once (such as the make of car in the Make table) is referred to from the multiple models that are available for each make in the Model table.

- **Foreign keys**: When you are joining a table on the "one" side of a one-to-many relationship (such as the Make table to the Model table), then the field that joins on the "many" side (the MakeID field in the Model table) is called a foreign key.

- **Surrogate keys**: When you use an intrinsically meaningless value as a key (primary or foreign) rather than a code or acronym that people can understand, the value is referred to as a surrogate key.

Tricks and Traps

Writing complex table joins comes with its own set of rules and constraints. They include the following:

- The order in which the tables are added to the FROM clause is unimportant. The only thing that matters is that each time a new table is added, you join it to a table that is already present in the list and correctly joined in the ON clause.

- The way we have written the fields in the SELECT clause is purely a formatting choice because I find that this makes the fields easier to handle in voluminous queries. You could just as easily run all the field names together on a single line if you prefer.

- I chose not to output the key fields (those that are used to link tables together) as they are largely meaningless from an analytical perspective because they are largely codes for "internal" use only that have been created by the database designer to allow tables to be joined. You could extend the query to add them if you want.

- You can extend a query up to 4,096 fields in queries like this. Although I suspect that you won't need more than a dozen or so fields in the output, this is another way of saying that there are few practical limits to the number of fields that you can return from a query.

2.6 Visualizing Databases

Even after years of practice it is extremely difficult to visualize a database based on a piece of SQL. In databases—as in so many areas—a picture is worth a thousand words. Consequently, database designers have become proficient at creating drawings of how database tables can be combined to make up a database model.

These images of databases are called entity-relationship diagrams (or *ERDs* in "geek-speak"). They outline in a lucid and visual way these two key elements that make up a database:

- The tables that contain the data (known as entities)
- The joins that link these tables (known as relationships)

This is, inevitably, only a high-level definition of what an ERD is. Indeed, a complete ERD can contain much more information about a database than this. However, this definition is enough to get you started for the moment.

Now that you have the theory, it is time for a practical application. So, in Figure 2.10, you can see the ERD for the PrestigeCars database.

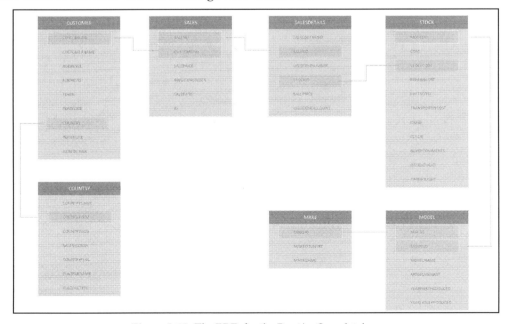

Figure 2.10. *The ERD for the PrestigeCars database*

If ever you are unsure of how the tables used in the SQL samples in this book join together, you can flip back to this diagram to get a better idea of how the tables relate one to another. You can also use this image as a visual representation of the code you saw in the previous section to join all the core tables in the PrestigeCars database.

2.7 Using Views to Memorize Complex Table Joins

The code that you saw in section 5 was both long and complicated. Yet you could need to reuse complex code like this frequently. As it could become very wearing to rewrite or copy and paste intricate code like this time and again, SQL Server has a solution that can make your life easier.

One solution that database developers apply is to memorize SELECT queries even, or indeed especially, if the queries contain multiple joins. This technique is called creating views. The outcome is that, instead of using multiple table names and complex joins, you simply use the view name in the FROM clause of the query.

The PrestigeCars database contains a view called SalesByCountry that contains all the tables you joined in section 5. So, if you wanted to use this view in the place of the seven tables and all the joins you used previously, the FROM clause would read as follows:

```
FROM        SalesByCountry
```

You will probably agree that this is a much simpler way of working.

For the moment, I only want to explain what views are and how you can use them instead of tables in certain circumstances.

For the moment, the important point to remember is that a view can be used in a SQL query just like a table can. A view is a way of remembering how the joins were set up to deliver analysis from multiple tables at once.

> **Note:** You need to be careful when using views instead of tables in SQL queries. This is because often you will want to display only a *subset* of data. So, be careful that using a view does not mean you are filtering out essential data from a query without meaning to do so.

Conclusion

This chapter explained how you can use the multiple tables that you will probably find in most databases as the basis for your analytics.

You saw how to join tables using a shared field to look at data in one or both the tables that you queried. Then you saw how to extend this approach to join several tables and pick out any fields that interested you in the tables you joined. You also learned how to remove duplicates from a result set and how to join tables on a range of values as well as on a specific element.

Although this chapter introduced you to the concept of table joins, it has not explained all that you will ever need to know to join tables in SQL Server. There is more still to learn on this subject, and you will see more on this in the following chapter.

Core Knowledge Learned in This Chapter

The following are the key elements you learned in this chapter:

Concept	Description
Joins	This is the technique used to link tables so that you can return data from multiple tables coherently.
Intermediate tables	These are tables that are used in joins but do not send any data back to the query.
INNER JOIN	This keyword lets you add another table to a query.
ON	This keyword allows you to tell SQL how two tables are to be joined and, more specifically, which fields provide the link between the two tables
AS	Just as you can alias fields, you can alias tables with the AS keyword.
DISTINCT	This keyword removes duplicate records from a result set.

CHAPTER 3
Using Advanced Table Joins

Joining tables to produce the data you want to see is key to creating the analyses that drive your business. In this chapter, you will build on the knowledge that you acquired in the previous chapter and further develop your SQL skills so that you can create more complex and powerful queries. This means learning further variations of the JOIN clause to help you shape the data that is output from the SQL queries that you write.

In this chapter, you will learn to create the following:

- Outer joins that let you return all the data from one table and only some of the data in a second table that you join to it

- Full joins that let you display all the data from both tables in a join

- Intermediate joins where you join multiple tables in a query, but not all the tables are used as data sources

- Self-joins where you join a table to itself to display hierarchical data

- Joins on data ranges when you need to map a value in one table to a range of values in another table

- Joins on multiple fields

- Cross joins that allow you to return all the data from both tables in a join

I realize that these concepts may seem more than a little abstract when you read about them for the first time. But don't worry, you will see how all these ideas have a thoroughly practical application to SQL queries and can be used in your day-to-day data analysis. Indeed, applying these more advanced techniques is often the only way to obtain clear and accurate results from your SQL queries.

3.1 Using Left Joins to Return All the Data in One Table but Not from the Other Table

The IT director is convinced that the PrestigeCars database needs some polishing. He is certain that there are makes of vehicles stored in the Make table for which there are no corresponding models. Rather than manually looking through all the MakeIDs in the Make table and comparing them with the MakeIDs in the Model table, you write the following piece of code to use SQL Server to find the missing values:

```
SELECT DISTINCT    MK.MakeName, MD.ModelName
FROM               Data.Make MK
LEFT OUTER JOIN    Data.Model MD
                   ON MK.MakeID = MD.MakeID
```

Running this query gives the result shown in *Figure 3.1*. You will need to scroll down the output to see all the data.

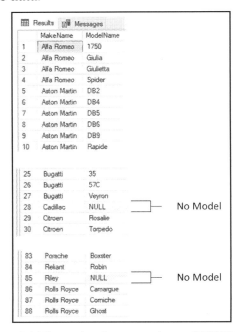

Figure 3.1: *The results of a query using an OUTER JOIN*

How It Works

This piece of SQL solves what at first sight appears to be a conundrum. How do you join two tables and show missing data given that joins only show data that is present in both tables?

The answer is to use a different type of join. This query did not use the INNER JOIN keyword that you learned to apply in the previous chapter. Instead, you used the LEFT OUTER JOIN keyword to join the tables. This keyword will return `all the records` from one of the tables (the first table in the join) but `only matching records` from the second table. This lets you visualize any missing information across the two tables.

More precisely, the query is constructed like this:

First:	Create a SELECT clause that returns the MakeName and ModelName fields. To make the results easier to read, you add the DISTINCT keyword to remove duplicates from the query result.
Second:	Add a FROM clause and enter the table name from which you want to return *all* the data, the Make table in this example.
Third:	You use the LEFT OUTER JOIN keyword. This tells SQL Server that you want to return *all* the data in the selected columns from the first table (the Make table, the one to the *left* of the join keyword).
Fourth:	You add the second table from which you want to return information. This table will only return records where the join field contains *identical values* in the two tables.
Finally:	You add an ON clause and specify which fields are used to "link" the two tables.

This query still joins the two tables on a specified field. However, all the contents from the Make table are returned, whether or not there are corresponding MakeIDs in the Model table.

To appreciate exactly what has happened here, you need to remind yourself that the INNER JOIN queries that you learned to use in the previous chapter returned data from tables that you joined only if there were corresponding values in the fields that were used in the ON clause of the query in both tables. If this was not the case, then `no records` were returned from either table.

If you want to reassure yourself that this query really returns different results with an INNER JOIN, then try running the following code snippet:

```
SELECT DISTINCT    MK.MakeName, MD.ModelName

FROM               Data.Make MK

INNER JOIN         Data.Model MD

                   ON MK.MakeID = MD.MakeID
```

I will not show the results here, but if you run the query and scroll down through the output, you will see that two makes are now "missing" from the result. These are Cadillac and Riley. This means that there are no NULL model names in this query output.

As this is a new and fairly powerful concept, let's imagine it in a more schematic way. *Figure 3.2* shows you how a LEFT OUTER JOIN works.

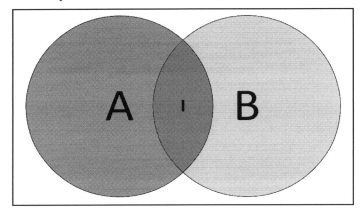

Figure 3.2. *The concept of a LEFT OUTER JOIN*

In this image:

- Circle A represents the table on the `left` of the LEFT OUTER JOIN keyword (the Make table in the code used previously). All data in this table (unless it is restricted in other ways that you will learn later in this book) is returned by the query.

- Circle B represents the table on the `right` of the LEFT OUTER JOIN keyword (the Model table in the code used previously). Only records that share values in the join fields provided in the ON clause will be returned.

- I represents the data from table on the right of the join that can be returned.

The result of using a LEFT OUTER JOIN is that all the data from table A is returned in the query output, but `only the matching records` from table B (shown as I in the image) are returned. Any records from table B where there is no corresponding data in the JOIN field are `not` present in the query result.

Tricks and Traps

I have a few comments to make about outer joins (and specifically about left outer joins).

- We used table aliases when writing this SQL because this approach makes the code easier to understand. This is not strictly necessary but does help you to write shorter code than if you had used full table names.

- You can write LEFT JOIN instead of LEFT OUTER JOIN if you prefer. Indeed, you may see this in code that you inherit or in examples from other sources. The result is strictly the same. However, I prefer to use the "complete" keyword in this book and will always show you these kinds of queries written as LEFT OUTER JOIN because this makes the point that you are using an `outer` join as opposed to an `inner` join. In other words, you are choosing not to restrict data in the output rather than aiming for a smaller result set.

- When actually writing LEFT OUTER JOINs, you may choose to adopt a style that places the first table `above` the second table (much as is the case with many of the query examples in this book). However, this still means that the first table (the one preceded by the FROM clause) is considered the left-hand table in the join.

- If there is no data in the table on the right of a left outer join, the data from the left-hand table will still be returned, even if nothing is returned from the right-hand table.

- If you are unsure whether applying an inner join or a left outer join will affect the result, then I suggest you run each type of query in turn and look at the number of records produced in each case.

3.2 Right Joins to Return All the Data in One Table but Not from the Other

There are several types of OUTER JOIN in SQL. Fortunately, they all follow a similar principle. That is, the OUTER keyword tells you that all the data from one or more tables will be returned by a query.

To show this, try running the following piece of SQL:

```
SELECT DISTINCT     MK.MakeName, MD.ModelName
FROM                Data.Model MD
RIGHT OUTER JOIN    Data.Make MK
                    ON MK.MakeID = MD.MakeID
```

I will not give the results of this query here because they are identical to those returned by the previous query. So, you can see the output in Figure 3.1. However, the result is only the same because the order of the tables in this query has changed in te query. AS you can see, the Make table is now on the `right` of the Model table.

How It Works

This query uses the Model table in the FROM clause and the Make table in the RIGHT OUTER JOIN. This means that the table order is now reversed compared to the previous query. However, using a right outer join tells SQL Server to take all the data from the table on the `right` of the JOIN clause and only use the data from the tables on the `left` of the JOIN where there are matching values in both tables for the field used on the ON clause.

A right outer join is a mirror image of the left outer join that you saw previously. This applies the same principles to a join, in that it ensures that all the records on one "side" of a JOIN keyword (the right table) are returned by the query, but only matching records from the table on the `left` of the join.

To get a more visual idea of this, take a look at Figure 3.3.

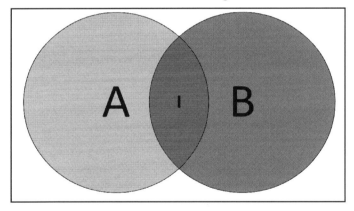

Figure 3.3. The concept of a RIGHT OUTER JOIN

This figure illustrates how a RIGHT OUTER JOIN takes all the data from the right-hand table and only records that share values in the "link" field from the left-hand table.

In this image:

- Circle A represents the table on the left of the RIGHT OUTER JOIN keyword (the Model table in the code used previously). Only records that share values in the join fields provided in the ON clause will be returned.

- Circle B represents the table on the right of the RIGHT OUTER JOIN keyword (the Make table in the code used previously). All data in this table (unless it is restricted in other ways that you will learn later in this book) is returned by the query.

- I represents the data returned from table A.

Finally, the choice between a RIGHT OUTER JOIN and a LEFT OUTER JOIN simply depends on the order in which you place the tables in the SQL you write.

Tricks and Traps

I have only a few comments to make about right outer joins.

- A RIGHT OUTER JOIN is a mirror image of a left outer join. Essentially it depends on which table you place before the OUTER JOIN keywords and which table you place after these keywords.

- You can write the SQL to place each table in a join on the same lines as the JOIN keywords or on separate lines; it is all the same to SQL.

- You can simply use the keyword RIGHT JOIN if you prefer to achieve the same result.

3.3 Full Joins to Return All the Data from Both Tables in a Join

The sales director wants to get an idea of all the customers who have ever bought a car from Prestige Cars and all the countries that the company either has sold to or might sell to one day. After a little thought, you come up with the following query:

```
SELECT          CT.CountryName, CT.SalesRegion, CS.*

FROM            Data.Country CT

FULL OUTER JOIN Data.Customer CS

                ON CS.Country = CT.CountryISO2

ORDER BY        CT.SalesRegion
```

Executing this piece of SQL gives the result shown in *Figure 3.4*.

	CountryName	SalesRegion	CustomerID	CustomerName	Address1	Address2	Town	PostCode	Country	IsReseller	IsCreditRisk
1	India	Asia	NULL	NULL	NULL	NULL	NULL	NULL	NULL	NULL	NULL
2	China	Asia	NULL	NULL	NULL	NULL	NULL	NULL	NULL	NULL	NULL
3	United Kingdom	EMEA	0078	Expensive Shine	89, Abbots Lane	NULL	Manchester	M17 3EF	GB	1	0
4	United Kingdom	EMEA	0079	Steve Docherty	5, Albemarle Avenue	NULL	Manchester	M7 9AS	GB	0	0
5	Germany	EMEA	0080	Rodolph Legler	SingerStrasse 89	NULL	Stuttgart	NULL	DE	0	0
6	United Kingdom	EMEA	0081	Pete Spring	53, Pimlico Square	NULL	Manchester	M3 4WR	GB	0	1
7	France	EMEA	0082	Khader El Ghannam	10, rue de Jemappes	4eme etage	Paris	NULL	FR	0	0
8	France	EMEA	0083	Jacques Mitterand	1 Quai des Pertes	NULL	Paris	NULL	FR	0	0
9	Switzerland	EMEA	0084	Francoise LeBrun	56, Rue Verte	NULL	Lausanne	NULL	CH	0	0
10	United Kingdom	EMEA	0085	Alex McWhirter	89, Harlequin Road	NULL	Newcastle	NE1 7DH	GB	0	0
11	France	EMEA	0086	Francois Chirac	2, Quai de l'Enfer	NULL	Paris	NULL	FR	0	0
12	United Kingdom	EMEA	0087	Andy Cheshire	7, Wedgewood Steet	NULL	Stoke	ST4 2OZ	GB	0	0
13	United Kingdom	EMEA	0088	Jimmy McFiddler	57, Smile Square	NULL	Glasgow	G15 1AA	GB	1	1
14	United Kingdom	EMEA	0001	Magic Motors	27, Handsworth Road	NULL	Birmingham	B1 7AZ	GB	1	0
15	United Kingdom	EMEA	0002	Snazzy Roadsters	102, Bleak Street	NULL	Birmingham	B3 5ST	GB	1	1

Figure 3.4. Applying a FULL OUTER JOIN to a query

How It Works

This query displays all the records from both tables. Here is how it works:

First:	The SELECT clause specifies the two columns from the Country table and *all* the columns from the Customer table. The table aliases are used to specify which fields are returned from which table. Indeed, to avoid spelling out all the field names from the Customer table, the alias CS is used followed by the *. This will return all the fields from the Customer table.
Then:	The FROM clause is used, followed by the first table in the join (the Country table) followed by an alias.
Next:	The FULL OUTER JOIN keyword is added.
Then:	The second table is specified (the Customer table). This table is aliased as CS.
Finally:	An ORDER BY clause is added.

You can see this in the data that is returned because there are two countries (India and China) where Prestige Cars does not yet have any customers. Nonetheless, the two country records from the Country table appear in the output. However, these two records do not contain any customer data because none is available. Equally, `all` the records from the Customer table are returned.

To continue with the conceptual illustration of how joins return data, take a look at *Figure 3.5*.

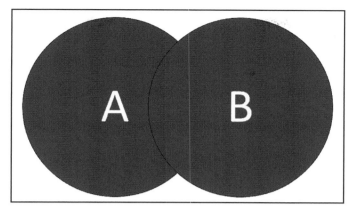

Figure 3.5. A conceptual view of the data returned from a FULL OUTER JOIN

This image makes the point that all the records from both tables will appear in the query result if you use a FULL OUTER JOIN. This also illustrates that, independently of the join type, you can select either one or more columns—or even all the columns—from any table in a join. More particularly, this query shows you that you can return a single column from one table (the CountryName field from the Country table) alongside `all` the fields from the Customer table in the SELECT statement by following the table name or alias with the * operator.

Tricks and Traps

I have a few comments to make about full outer joins.

- You can enter FULL JOIN rather than FULL OUTER JOIN if you prefer. The query will work in the same way. However, I nonetheless prefer to use the three-word definition as it reminds you—the query developer—that this is an `outer` join and so will not automatically limit the data that is returned.

- If you used the * operator `without` a table name or alias, the query would return all the fields from `both` tables, rather like the data you can see in *Figure 3.6.*

	CountryName	CountryISO2	CountryISO3	SalesRegion	CountryFlag	FlagFileName	FlagFileType	CustomerID	CustomerName	Address1	Address2	Town	PostCode	Country	IsReseller	IsCreditF
1	Belgium	BE	BEL	EMEA	NULL	NULL	NULL	0034	Diplomatic Carr	Rue Des Coteaux, 39	NULL	Brussels	NULL	BE	1	0
2	Belgium	BE	BEL	EMEA	NULL	NULL	NULL	0045	Stefan Van Helsing	Nieuwstraat 5	NULL	Brussels	NULL	BE	0	0
3	Belgium	BE	BEL	EMEA	NULL	NULL	NULL	0067	Flash Voitures	Place Anspach 85	NULL	Brussels	NULL	BE	1	0
4	France	FR	FRA	EMEA	NULL	NULL	NULL	0005	Casseroles Chromes	29, Rue Gigondas	NULL	Lyon	NULL	FR	1	0
5	France	FR	FRA	EMEA	NULL	NULL	NULL	0008	M. Pierre Dubois	14, Rue De La Hutte	NULL	Marseille	NULL	FR	0	0
6	France	FR	FRA	EMEA	NULL	NULL	NULL	0013	La Bagnole de Luxe	890 Place de la Concorde	Cedex 8	Paris	NULL	FR	1	0
7	France	FR	FRA	EMEA	NULL	NULL	NULL	0016	SuperSport S.A.R.L	210 Place de la Republique	NULL	Paris	NULL	FR	1	1
8	France	FR	FRA	EMEA	NULL	NULL	NULL	0028	Vive La Vitesse	56, Rue Nozatre	NULL	Marseille	NULL	FR	1	0
9	France	FR	FRA	EMEA	NULL	NULL	NULL	0035	Laurent Saint Yves	49, Rue Guacampox	NULL	Marseille	NULL	FR	0	0
10	France	FR	FRA	EMEA	NULL	NULL	NULL	0043	Le Luxe en Motion	37, Allee de la Paix	NULL	Paris	NULL	FR	1	0

*Figure 3.6. Using the * operator to return all the columns from all the tables in a join*

Inner Joins and Outer Joins

SQL has several definitions of all the types of join that you may, one day, end up using. However, when starting out on the road to data analysis with SQL, it is probably easiest to begin by noting the two essential types of join.

- **Inner joins** ensure that only data that shares the same values in the fields that are used to join a table is returned from the two tables.

- **Outer joins** return all the data from one—or even both—of the tables in the join.

The different types of join you can apply are called the `join condition` by SQL purists.

While users often use link fields or shared columns to refer to the field or fields that appear in the ON clause of a table join, the technical name for these fields is the join predicate.

- If using any specific field names in a query that uses more than one table, you can use the * operator without table aliases. This will return all the fields from all the tables in the query.

- Be aware that using FULL OUTER JOINs on large tables can mean very long-running queries.

3.4 Intermediate Table Joins

When you are analyzing data, there will almost certainly be times when you will need to join tables but not use any data from them. As an example, perhaps you want to look at the sales made in each separate country. Looking at the tables in the PrestigeCars database, you have discovered that the sales figures are in the Sales table, and the country names are in the Country table. However, these two tables have no common fields and so cannot be joined one to the other. However, these two tables both connect to the Customer table. If this seems a little strange, then take a look at *Figure 3.7.*

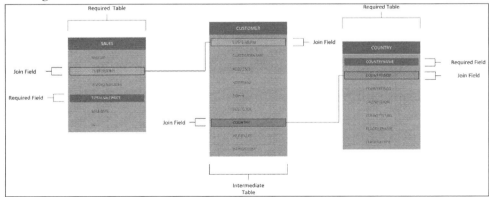

Figure 3.7. *Joining tables using an intermediate table*

So, you `can` join the Sales and Country tables if you add the Customer table as an intermediate (or link) table. The following SQL allows you to join these three tables:

```
SELECT      CO.CountryName, SA.TotalSalePrice

FROM        Data.Sales SA

INNER JOIN Data.Customer CS

            ON SA.CustomerID = CS.CustomerID

INNER JOIN Data.Country CO

            ON CS.Country = CO.CountryISO2
```

If you run this query, you should see the output in Figure 3.8.

	CountryName	TotalSalePrice
1	United Kingdom	65000.00
2	United Kingdom	220000.10
3	United Kingdom	19500.00
4	Germany	11500.00
5	France	19900.00
6	United Kingdom	29500.00
7	United Kingdom	49500.20
8	United Kingdom	76000.90
9	France	19600.00
10	United States	36500.00
11	United Kingdom	89000.00
12	United Kingdom	169500.00
13	France	8950.00
14	United Kingdom	195000.00
15	France	22950.00

Figure 3.8. *The output when using bridging tables to return data*

How It Works

This query returns the country from the table on the right (the Country table) and the sales figure from the table on the left (the Sales table) but nothing at all from the middle (the Customer table). Yet without the Customer table to provide the "bridge" between the two tables, it would not have been possible to link the two tables, which would have made it impossible to produce this data.

You can see that in the case of the Country table. the key field is `text`, not a numeric field, unlike the previous examples. This is perfectly normal in many databases. All that matters is that the database design allows you to specify the columns that join the tables.

> **Note: This query shows the full detail of each sale. You may want to see the aggregate result of all sales per country. This kind of query is explained in** *Chapter 7.*

3.5 Using Multiple Fields in Joins

Not all tables can be successfully joined using a single field. Sometimes you may find that you need to use two or more fields to join two tables.

As an example of this, let's suppose that the marketing director of Prestige Cars has just spent a large amount of money on some external data about clients. You need to join this new table called MarketingInformation to the existing Customer table. However, this new table does not have a customer ID, only the customer name andcountry. Fortunately, there are also customer name and country fields in the Customer table and SQL can join tables on multiple fields, as the following SQL snippet shows:

```
SELECT      CS.CustomerName, MI.SpendCapacity
FROM        Data.Customer CS
INNER JOIN  Reference.MarketingInformation MI
            ON CS.CustomerName = MI.Cust
            AND CS.Country = MI.Country
```

If you run this code, you will see the output shown in Figure 3.9.

	CustomerName	SpendCapacity
1	Magic Motors	Lots
2	Snazzy Roadsters	Some
3	Birmingham Executive Prestige Vehicles	None
4	WunderKar	Lots
5	Casseroles Chromes	Lots
6	Le Luxe en Motion	Lots
7	Eat My Exhaust Ltd	Lots
8	M. Pierre Dubois	None
9	Sondra Horowitz	Some
10	Wonderland Wheels	Immense
11	London Executive Prestige Vehicles	Some
12	Glittering Prize Cars Ltd	Lots
13	La Bagnole de Luxe	Immense
14	Convertible Dreams	Immense
15	Alexei Tolstoi	Some

Figure 3.9. Output from a multiple field join

How It Works

In this example, you created a table join just as you did previously. However, once you have specified the first field you will be using to join the two tables, you extended the join by doing the following:

First:	You added the AND keyword
Second:	You specified the second field from one of the tables that you need in the join.
Third:	You entered the equal (=) sign.
Finally:	You specified the second field from the other table that you need in the join.

You can imagine this kind of join more easily, perhaps, if you see it displayed graphically. *Figure 3.10* illustrates a join using multiple fields.

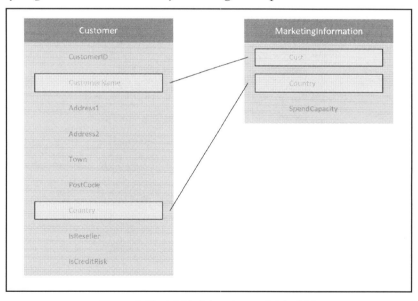

Figure 3.10. *A table join using multiple fields*

The reason for using multiple fields to join tables is that, sometimes, the data in a single column might not be sufficient to identify a record uniquely. Imagine that you are selling cars to a client with multiple sites in several countries. If each site has the same company name, the firm could exist several times in the table (the MarketingInformation table in this example). So, you need a further piece of information in the data that lets you uniquely identify each record. In this example, it is the Country field. The end result is that the combination of the elements in the fields used in the join defines a record without any risk of duplicate records being found.

Tricks and Traps

I have only a couple of comments to make here.

- You can extend this principle to join on three or more fields simply by introducing each pair of join fields with the AND keyword in the FROM clause of the SQL.
- When more than one field is required to identify a record uniquely then these fields make up what is called a `composite key`.

3.6 Joining a Table to Itself

The CEO has requested a quick list of staff so that she can produce an organization chart for the next board meeting. She has even reminded you that there is a table in the database (the Staff table) that contains all the staff and their managers. You can see this in *Figure 3.11.*

	StaffID	StaffName	ManagerID	Department
1	1	Amelia	NULL	NULL
2	2	Gerard	1	Finance
3	3	Chloe	1	Marketing
4	4	Susan	1	Sales
5	5	Andy	4	Sales
6	6	Steve	4	Sales
7	7	Stan	4	Sales
8	8	Nathan	4	Sales
9	9	Maggie	4	Sales
10	10	Jenny	2	Finance
11	11	Chris	2	Finance
12	12	Megan	3	Marketing
13	13	Sandy	11	Finance

Figure 3.11. The Staff table

Using this table (whose existence you had forgotten about), you produce the following SQL to show which staff member reports to which manager:

```
SELECT      ST1.StaffName, ST1.Department, ST2.StaffName AS
ManagerName

FROM        Reference.Staff ST1
```

```
INNER JOIN    Reference.Staff ST2
              ON ST1.ManagerID = ST2.StaffID
```

Running this short piece of code gives the result shown in *Figure 3.12.*

Results | Messages

	StaffName	Department	ManagerName
1	Gerard	Finance	Amelia
2	Chloe	Marketing	Amelia
3	Susan	Sales	Amelia
4	Andy	Sales	Susan
5	Steve	Sales	Susan
6	Stan	Sales	Susan
7	Nathan	Sales	Susan
8	Maggie	Sales	Susan
9	Jenny	Finance	Gerard
10	Chris	Finance	Gerard
11	Megan	Marketing	Chloe
12	Sandy	Finance	Chris

Figure 3.12. *Joining the Staff table to itself to display manager names*

How It Works

The Staff table contains a field that contains the manager for each staff member. Unfortunately, however, this reference is in the form of the staff ID number of the manager and not the manager's actual name. So, you can use the data in the table twice (once to get the staff member's name and once to return their manager's name). However, this means using the table `twice` in the FROM clause of the SQL.

Then the SQL joins the table to itself. This is what allows the manager ID to be used to refer to the manager name using the second application of the table. It works like this:

First:	You select the staff member's name from the Staff table. This is the standard and perfectly usual way of querying a table like this.
Second:	You add the staff table a second time to the query with an INNER JOIN. Each of the references to the Staff table uses a *different alias* (ST1 and ST2) so the SQL can differentiate between the two.
Third:	You add an ON clause that tells the SQL that the StaffID field from the first reference to the Staff table (ST1) is linked to the ManagerID field in the second reference to the Staff table (ST2).

Finally:	You use the table alias in the SELECT clause for every field reference. This allows the SQL to know whether you are referring to *staff details* (those in the first table reference to ST1) or to the *manager details* (those in the second table reference to ST2). You also alias any fields that are used more than once.

This kind of table join is also called a self-join. You can see this more graphically in *Figure 3.13*.

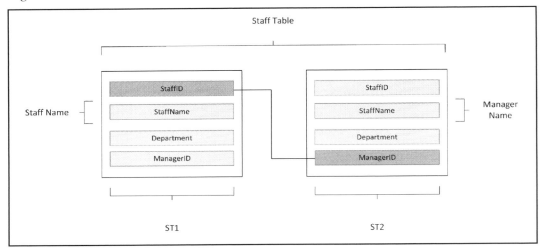

Figure 3.13. *Anatomy of a self-join*

Tricks and Traps

You need to be aware of the following key points when joining a table to itself:

- Be sure that you alias the two table references in the FROM clause so that you understand that you are using the information in the table twice to display different elements from the table. This means using a `different alias` each time that the same table is used in the join.

- It is vital to alias the fields that you use in the output that are used `twice` such as the StaffName field in this example. Otherwise, you will not know which piece of information is which.

- This approach is also known as a "Hierarchical Join".

3.7 Joining Tables on Ranges of Values

There are an infinite number of ways to store data, and you will probably encounter the need to analyze data in multiple tables where you cannot simply join one field in one table to another field in another table. An example of this is the SalesCategory table in the PrestigeCars database. This small table contains a company-specific set of reference information that allows the sales manager to categorize each car sold according to the sale price.

Now the sales manager wants you to use the data in the SalesCategory table to define the specific sales category of each vehicle sold. So, to begin with, you take a look at the table. You can see the data it contains in *Figure 3.14.*

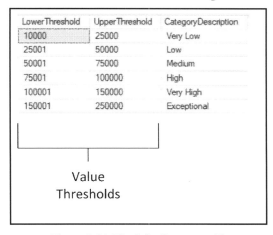

Figure 3.14. *The SalesCategory table*

The first thing you notice is that this table does not contain a unique value in a single column that you can link to a single value (the sale price) in another table. So, you need to find a way to map the **range** of values that are stored in the SalesCategory table to the SalePrice field in the SalesDetails table.

The following SQL shows you how this can be done:

```
SELECT
 MK.MakeName
,MD.ModelName
,SD.SalePrice
,CAT.CategoryDescription

FROM        Data.Stock ST
INNER JOIN  Data.Model MD
```

```
                ON ST.ModelID = MD.ModelID
INNER JOIN  Data.Make MK
                ON MD.MakeID = MK.MakeID
INNER JOIN  Data.SalesDetails SD
                ON ST.StockCode = SD.StockID
INNER JOIN  Reference.SalesCategory CAT
                ON SD.SalePrice BETWEEN
                        CAT.LowerThreshold AND CAT.UpperThreshold
```

Running this piece of SQL gives the result shown in Figure 3.15.

	MakeName	ModelName	SalePrice	CategoryDescription
1	Ferrari	Testarossa	65000.00	Medium
2	Ferrari	355	220000.00	Exceptional
3	Porsche	911	19500.00	Very Low
4	Porsche	924	11500.00	Very Low
5	Porsche	944	19950.00	Very Low
6	Aston Martin	DB4	29500.00	Low
7	Aston Martin	DB5	49500.00	Low
8	Aston Martin	DB6	76000.00	High
9	Porsche	911	19600.00	Very Low
10	Aston Martin	DB5	36500.00	Low
11	Aston Martin	DB6	45000.00	Low
12	Bentley	Flying Spur	80500.00	High
13	Ferrari	355	169500.00	Exceptional
14	Ferrari	Testarossa	195000.00	Exceptional
15	Mercedes	280SL	22950.00	Very Low

Figure 3.15. Joining tables on a range of values

How It Works

This query starts by joining the SalesDetails, Stock, Make, and Model tables using the techniques you have explored so far in this chapter. You need to link these four tables so that you can return the following information:

Make name:	From the Make table
Model name	From the Model table
Sale price	From the SalesDetails table

You are not actually returning any data from the Stock table. However, you need this table to act as a "link" table so that you can join the Model table to the SalesDetails table.

Once you have this core query in place, you can extend it by looking up the CategoryDescription value from the SalesCategory table. This is where you need to use the SalePrice field in the SalesDetails table and see into which category of the SalesCategory table each car falls.

More on Join Types

The joins you have used up until now in this chapter are called equijoins because they use the equal sign (which is known as an equality operator) to join fields. So, joins that use other operators to join tables are described by database geeks as non-equijoins.

You can also join tables using operators such as the following:

- < (less than)
- > (greater than)
- <= (less than or equal to)
- >= (greater than or equal to)
- <> (not equals to)

I feel, however, that the occasions when you might have to do this are extremely rare. Indeed, there are occasions when they are not best practice. So, I will not be giving any examples of these kinds of join in this chapter.

This operation is carried out in the final three lines of SQL in the query (shown in bold). This join says, "Use the SalePrice field and compare it to the two fields (UpperThreshold and LowerThreshold) in the SalesCategory table." If the SalePrice field is between the upper threshold value and the lower threshold value, then join the tables.

This "range join" introduces a new keyword combination. This is the BETWEEN… AND operator. This keyword combination can be used to look up a value between a lower threshold and an upper threshold.

First:	Add the table to the FROM clause of the SQL query.
Second:	Add the ON keyword to introduce the fields that will be used to link the tables.
Third:	Add the BETWEEN keyword and the field name from the linked table that contains the lower threshold value.

Finally:	Add the AND keyword and the field name from the linked table that contains the upper threshold value.

This allows you to look up the category description from the SalesCategory table for each sale price value.

Tricks and Traps

Joining tables on ranges of data is, admittedly, a fairly rare occurrence in practice. However, should you ever have to do this, it helps to be aware of the following points:

- Joining tables on a range of values is nearly always used—as was the case in this example—to look up data from a "reference" table. This kind of operation presumes that the ranges in the "lookup" table have been defined coherently and cannot overlap.

3.8 Cross Joins

The CEO wants a list of all countries that Prestige Cars sells to, with a list of all makes that the company has ever stocked. However, when you ask for more details, she says that she wants to see every make appear for every country because this allows her to galvanize the sales teams to sell every make in every country. After a little thought, you produce the following piece of SQL:

```
SELECT       CountryName, MakeName

FROM         Data.Country

CROSS JOIN   Data.Make
```

Running this SQL produces the result shown in *Figure 3.16*. This query produces some 260 records, so I am not displaying the entire output. However, if you scroll through the output, you can see that the makes of car are repeated for each country.

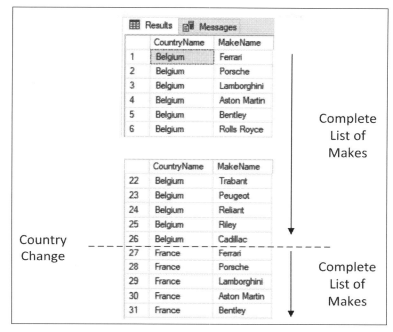

Figure 3.16. *The output from a CROSS JOIN*

How It Works

This query consists of four elements:

First:	The SELECT clause, where you list the fields that you want returned from the two tables
Second:	The first table that you want to return all the data from
Third:	The CROSS JOIN keyword
Finally:	The second table that you want to return all the data from

It really is that simple. A cross join query like this will return a collection of records where each record from each of the two tables will be paired up with each record in the other table.

Tricks and Traps

There is one vital point to be aware of if you ever start using cross joins in your queries—and a couple of minor points of interest—listed here:

- Cross joins can produce huge result sets. This is because they multiply all the rows in one table by the number of rows in the second table in the join. So, you should use them only when you need the specific kind of output that they deliver.

- A cross join does not have an ON clause because there is no link between any fields in the two tables.

- This kind of join is also known by SQL geeks as a Cartesian join.

3.9 Join Concepts

Learning about the various join types in SQL Server can seem a little daunting at first sight. To make your learning curve smoother, take a look at *Figure 3.17*, where the main types of joins are explained graphically.

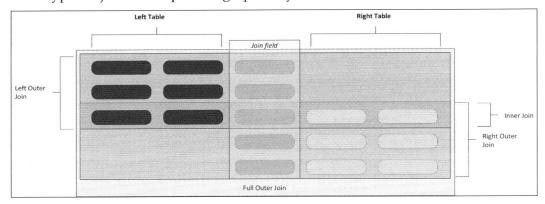

Figure 3.17. *Join concepts*

Conclusion

This chapter has extended the knowledge that you acquired in the previous chapter and has taken you further toward understanding some of the many techniques that you can apply when joining tables in SQL Server.

You have seen the difference between inner and outer joins and how using the LEFT and RIGHT keywords in a join can completely change the data that is returned by a query. While looking at types of joins, you saw how an OUTER join can be used to return all the data from both tables in a join as well as how a CROSS JOIN can return a complete cross mapping of every field in the two tables. You also learned how to use multiple fields in a table join as well as how to join tables on a range of data and not just on a single value. As a final flourish, you even saw how to join a table to itself when querying hierarchies of data.

However, for the moment, it is appropriate to move on to another subject. So, in the next chapter, you will begin learning about some of the techniques you can apply in SQL queries to filter your data.

Core Knowledge Learned in This Chapter

The following are the keywords and concepts you learned in this chapter:

Concept	Description
LEFT OUTER JOIN	This type of join returns all the data from the first (left-hand) table in a join and only matching data from the second (right-hand) table.
RIGHT OUTER JOIN	This type of join returns all the data from the first (right-hand) table in a join and only matching data from the second (left-hand) table
FULL OUTER JOIN	This kind of join returns all the data from both tables on either side of a join.
BETWEEN…AND	This operator can be used to join tables on a range of values.
CROSS JOIN	This keyword multiplies all the rows in the first table by all the rows in the second table.

CHAPTER 4
Filtering Data

All over the world the amount of data that people and organizations create and store is growing at an ever-increasing rate. "Seeing the wood for the trees" is becoming more and more difficult—but ever more necessary. So, you need to be able to filter your data to deliver relevant and useful information from the multitude of facts and figures in the many tables that make up your database.

Using SQL to Filter Data

This chapter introduces the core techniques that you will need to learn to extend your queries so that you are delivering only the information you want. As you might expect, filtering data has been around as long as databases have existed. Consequently, a variety of methods exist that you can apply to restrict the data that is returned by a query. Sometimes there could be several ways to get the same result. This is why I will occasionally give you alternative solutions to a problem. However, our primary focus is to introduce you to the core techniques that you can apply to your own queries to obtain a valid and reliable result.

To this end, you will take away the following key points from this chapter:

- Filtering data using table joins
- Finding records containing one or more pieces of text
- Finding rows that do not contain a specific piece of text

- Using numbers as thresholds to filter output
- Using ranges of numbers to filter results
- Finding records that match a yes/no criterion

Data scientists often talk about the "logic" of data. This is because databases are (most often) the result of logical design, and consequently querying them requires a coherent and structured approach. This does not mean you need an advanced degree in philosophy or mathematics to analyze data with SQL. All you really need is a little rationality and some practice. This chapter will encourage you to use both of these as you take your first steps in filtering data.

4.1 Filtering Data Using Inner Joins

I realize that you have spent the previous two chapters looking at ways of joining tables. Nonetheless, I have an extremely important point to make about joins in the context of filtering data.

First, you need to remember that an inner join acts as a filter. An inner join guarantees that `only` the data in the records containing matching values in the fields that are used to join tables will be returned in the query result. This provides an initial filter on the underlying data.

Second, you need to be aware that only a subset of data from one of the tables in an outer join will be returned (more precisely, this affects the data in the table on the right of the join in a left outer join and the data in the table on the left of the join in a right outer join). So, these two join types also filter data, if only partially.

It might be that table joins have already filtered your data and provided the result that you are looking for. However, if this is not the case, then you can extend the filter effect of joins with a myriad of other options that are the subject of both this chapter and the next.

4.2 Filtering Data Using Multiple Table Joins

Selling classy cars may be great fun, but sooner or later the finance director will need to know which makes and models the company has bought and stocked. The following query lets you show him a list displaying all the makes and models ever held in stock:

```
SELECT DISTINCT    MK.MakeName, MD.ModelName
FROM               Data.Stock ST
INNER JOIN         Data.Model MD
```

```
                    ON MD.ModelID = ST.ModelID
INNER JOIN          Data.Make MK
                    ON MK.MakeID = MD.MakeID
ORDER BY            MK.MakeName, MD.ModelName
```

Execute this query, and you should see the data in Figure 4.1.

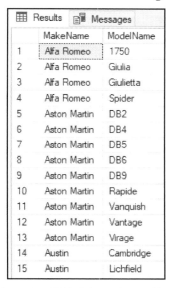

Figure 4.1. *Table joins acting as filters*

How It Works

This query joins the Make, Model, and Stock tables so that you can look up the make and model names for the vehicles in the Stock table. Indeed, this query is similar to the query you saw in section 2 in the previous chapter.

However, this is not the really important thing about this query. This example emphasizes a really fundamental aspect of SQL—that joining tables `actually filters` data.

First	This query applies *two* filters—one for each join clause.
Then	It applies the DISTINCT keyword to filter out any duplicate records (that is, any makes and models that appear more than once in the output).

So, even a simple query like this one is filtering data "out of the box," even though you have not applied any specific criteria.

To appreciate the filter effect produced by a join, you need to know that the Make table contains an exhaustive list of makes of classic cars. However, not all of these have ever been bought by Prestige Cars Ltd.—no Cadillacs have been bought so far, for instance. Yet if you scroll down the list of makes and models returned by this query, you will not see any Cadillacs. Yet the make Cadillac appears in the Make table. Equally, the Model table contains a couple of models that do not appear in the results from this query (the Lagonda 3 litre is an example). This is because the query is filtering the output so that **only** data that is in **all** the tables that are joined in a query is displayed. All other records in the tables that are used are excluded from the result.

To make this concept easier to grasp, take a look at the simple Venn diagram in *Figure 4.2*.

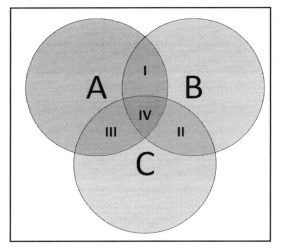

Figure 4.2. *Table filtering explained*

If you join tables A and B, you get the data outlined in I.

If you join tables B and C, you get the data outlined in II.

If you join tables A and C, you get the data outlined in III.

However, if you join tables A, B, and C, you get the data outlined in IV.

This aspect of database querying is so important that it needs to be repeated. When you join tables, `only the data that can be linked across all the tables will appear in the result`. If you take the principle explained in *Figure 4.2* (the Venn diagram) and show this as a set of tables, you can see what really happens when you join tables.

To get a clearer idea of how this works, take a look at *Figure 4.3*. This image shows how only a common subset of data is returned from multiple tables. This is because the common elements that make up each table join filter the query results.

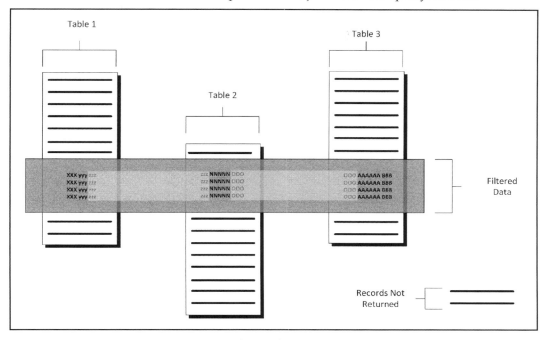

Figure 4.3. *Filtering data using table joins*

4.3 Filtering Data Output Using Intermediate Tables

Any business needs to see which products to sell. So, it is quite natural that the CEO should want to produce a list of all the models that Prestige Cars has ever sold and when they were sold.

The following SQL produces this list so that you can keep the CEO aware of the data that matters to her:

```
SELECT     MD.ModelName, SA.SaleDate, SA.InvoiceNumber
FROM       Data.Model AS MD
INNER JOIN Data.Stock ST
           ON ST.ModelID = MD.ModelID
INNER JOIN Data.SalesDetails SD
           ON ST.StockCode = SD.StockID
```

```
INNER JOIN Data.Sales SA
        ON SA.SalesID = SD.SalesID
ORDER BY   MD.ModelName
```

Running this query gives the output shown in *Figure 4.4*.

	ModelName	SaleDate	InvoiceNumber
1	135	2018-09-15 00:00:00.000	EURFR300
2	145	2018-09-15 00:00:00.000	GBPGB301
3	145	2017-04-05 00:00:00.000	EURES140
4	175	2018-09-15 00:00:00.000	EURIT302
5	1750	2018-04-15 00:00:00.000	EURFR241
6	1750	2018-06-03 00:00:00.000	GBPCH263
7	203	2018-01-05 00:00:00.000	EURFR211
8	203	2017-01-10 00:00:00.000	EURFR113
9	205	2018-01-10 00:00:00.000	EURBE218
10	205	2017-07-01 00:00:00.000	EURBE171
11	250SL	2017-08-04 00:00:00.000	USDUS179
12	250SL	2018-04-09 00:00:00.000	GBPGB238
13	280SL	2018-04-15 00:00:00.000	USDUS242
14	280SL	2018-07-25 00:00:00.000	GBPGB272
15	280SL	2017-06-01 00:00:00.000	GBPGB162

Figure 4.4. *Table joins acting as filters as well as simple joins*

How It Works

This short query joins the Model, Stock, SalesDetails, and Sales tables so that you can then select a detailed list of all the models that have been sold. As the SQL can seem a little dense, Figure 4.5 shows you in a more visual way exactly how the tables are linked.

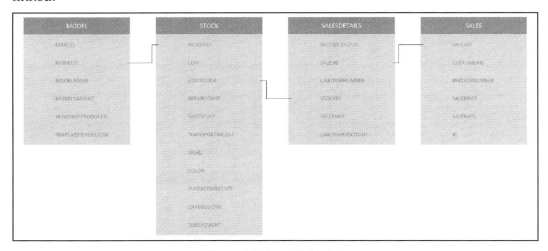

Figure 4.5. *A multitable join*

These are the reasons you need these four tables:

SalesDetails	Contains the stock number (the StockID field) of every car ever sold. However, it contains no details about the vehicle itself. To get these details, you need to join it to the Stock table.
Stock	Contains all vehicles that are in stock—or have ever been in stock. It does not indicate whether they have been sold. Also, it contains only a code for the model and not the model name, which is what you need. To get the full name of the model, you need to join it to the Model table.
Model	Contains the Model name.
Sales	Contains the date of sale and the invoice number. You can join this to the SalesDetails table on the SalesID field.

Once these four tables have been joined, you can display the model name (and other sales details) for every vehicle that is in the SalesDetails table—in other words, every car ever sold. It is important to note that even if you are **not** extracting data from the Stock table, you need to include it in the query so that you can join the Model table to the SalesDetails table. As the SalesDetails and Model tables have no direct connection, the only way to write the query is to join them using the Stock table as an intermediate join table.

This query also applies filters to the data. As this concept is vital to understanding SQL, I prefer to show a couple of examples to make it really clear. In this query, the filters are applied like this:

First	The Model table contains one or two models that Prestige Cars has never had in stock. However, even if you are selecting the list of models from the Model table, as you are doing here, you will not see *all* the models that are in the Model table because *only* models that are in the Stock table will appear in the output. This is because any table join will act as a filter and limit the data that is returned to data that is in *both* tables.
Second	The Stock table contains all vehicles that have ever been in stock. Yet this query only displays models that have been sold (if you want confirmation of this, you can see a Ferrari Testarossa in the Stock table that has not yet been sold—so it does not appear in the output from this query). Once again, the table join will act as a filter and limit the data that is returned to data that is in both tables.

However, no data is excluded when the Sales table is joined to the SalesDetails table. This is because the Sales table (which contains the data used to print the invoice header) contains a link to every item in the SalesDetails table. Equally, the SalesDetails table contains no SalesIDs that are not in the Sales table. So, in this case you are looking at a simple join that returns data from two tables, without filtering data. This is because these two tables are in a hierarchical—or parent to child—relationship.

As you can see from Figure 4.1 (and as I explained in Chapter 2), the names of many models appear several times. This is because the filter effect of a table join will nonetheless return `all the records from both tables` (after any selective filtering has been applied) based on the fields that are in the SELECT clause, irrespective of which table the fields come from. In this case, SQL Server returns the 348 records from the SalesDetails table—because the Model table does not contain any models that are absent from the Stock table, and the Stock table does not contain any vehicles that are not in the SalesDetails table. This is fortunate because otherwise Prestige Cars would be selling vehicles that it does not own.

4.4 Filtering Text

Imagine that a new marketing director has just arrived at Prestige Cars. The first thing that she wants to know is how the color of cars varies by model purchased. More precisely, she wants a report displaying all the models Prestige Cars has had in stock in a specific color. This means you can get off to a good start by applying some more specific filters to your data. As the Stock table contains a Color column, you can quickly see which models of what color the company has ever had in stock. The following short piece of SQL delivers this:

```
SELECT DISTINCT MD.ModelName, ST.Color
FROM            Data.Stock ST
INNER JOIN      Data.Model MD
                ON ST.ModelID = MD.ModelID
WHERE           ST.Color = 'Red'
```

Enter (or copy and paste) this query into the query window and run it. You should see a result something like in *Figure 4.6*.

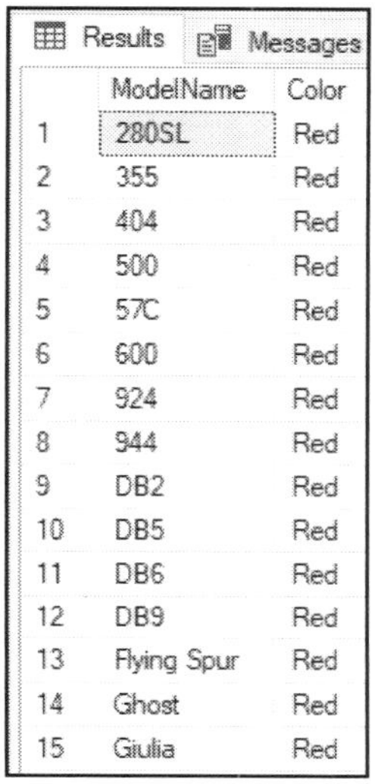

	ModelName	Color
1	280SL	Red
2	355	Red
3	404	Red
4	500	Red
5	57C	Red
6	600	Red
7	924	Red
8	944	Red
9	DB2	Red
10	DB5	Red
11	DB6	Red
12	DB9	Red
13	Flying Spur	Red
14	Ghost	Red
15	Giulia	Red

Figure 4.6. *A simple equality filter*

How It Works

This query introduces the WHERE clause, possibly the single most useful keyword in the SQL lexicon. A WHERE clause requires you to enter what data element you want to find in which column. Here that means saying that the Color field in the Stock table contains the element Red. This is done by specifying the following:

A field name	In this example, it is the Color column.
=	The equals operator tells SQL that you are looking for an exact match to an element.
The element to find	In this case, it is the color red.

Because you are looking for a text element (a color is not a number), you have to enclose the text that you are looking for in `single quotes`. This lets SQL Server know you are looking for a string of characters (text if you prefer) and not a number.

Finally, you need to add the DISTINCT keyword that you first encountered in Chapter 2. Using this keyword ensures that you see only one example of each red model—and avoid repeating records for any red models that have been sold several times.

Tricks and Traps

As this is the first time you applied a filter using the WHERE keyword, note the following important points:

- Any field contained in any of the tables that you have assembled in the FROM clause can be used to filter data. The field that appears in the WHERE clause does not have to be present in the SELECT clause.

- Although we humans can see instantly that a text is not a number, SQL does not find it so easy. So, you must remember always to enclose text in single quotes when writing SQL—and this is especially necessary when using a WHERE clause.

4.5 Applying Multiple Text Filters

The new marketing director liked your initial analysis of sales for a specific color. So, she has returned with a second request. She wants you to extend the previous query so that she can get an idea of all models ever stocked in red, green, or blue. The following SQL will d2o this for you:

```
SELECT      MD.ModelName, ST.Color
FROM        Data.Stock ST
INNER JOIN Data.Model MD
            ON ST.ModelID = MD.ModelID
WHERE       ST.Color IN ('Red', 'Green', 'Blue')
```

If you execute this query, you should see something like the output shown in *Figure 4.7*.

	ModelName	Color
1	Testarossa	Red
2	355	Blue
3	944	Red
4	Testarossa	Red
5	911	Blue
6	DB5	Blue
7	944	Blue
8	944	Green
9	Testarossa	Green
10	280SL	Red
11	Giulia	Red
12	944	Blue
13	TR5	Green
14	Flying Spur	Red
15	XK120	Red

Figure 4.7. Filtering on multiple criteria for a single column

How It Works

This query extends the WHERE clause by adding the new keyword IN. This keyword lets you enter a list of elements that you want to filter on—colors in this example. Each element must—if it is text—be in single quotes and then separated by a comma from each other element in the list. The entire list must then be enclosed in parentheses. There is no real limit to the number of elements that you can add to a list like this when filtering data. In this example, however, you only see vehicles that are red, green, or blue.

Tricks and Traps

It is probably worth noting the following important point:

- You can enter multiple elements in an IN clause over many lines if you prefer. So, the IN clause could have been written like this:

```
IN (
    'Red'
    ,'Green'
    ,'Blue'
    )
```

4.6 Excluding an Element

The marketing director is on a roll. The more she digs into the data, the more ideas she comes up with. Her latest intuition is to look at all sales except Ferraris. Fortunately, SQL lets you exclude an element from the results when filtering data, so you can output a list of all makes ever stocked except for a specific make of car. The following SQL snippet does just that:

```
SELECT     DISTINCT MK.MakeName
           FROM Data.Make AS MK
INNER JOIN Data.Model AS MD ON MK.MakeID = MD.MakeID
INNER JOIN Data.Stock AS ST ON ST.ModelID = MD.ModelID
INNER JOIN Data.SalesDetails SD ON ST.StockCode = SD.StockID
WHERE      MK.MakeName <> 'Ferrari'
ORDER BY   MK.MakeName
```

Running this code will return a list like the one in *Figure 4.8.*

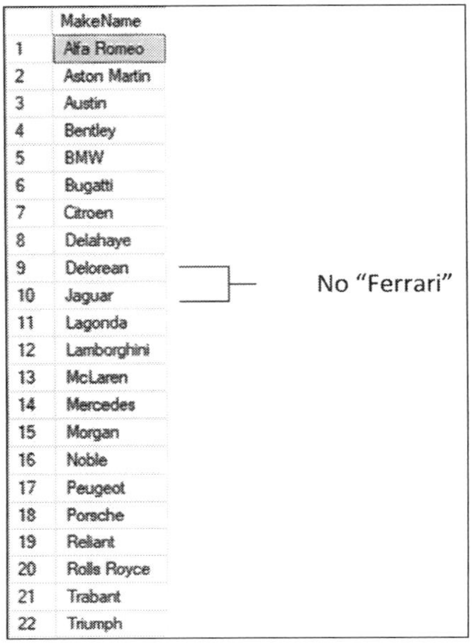

	MakeName
1	Alfa Romeo
2	Aston Martin
3	Austin
4	Bentley
5	BMW
6	Bugatti
7	Citroen
8	Delahaye
9	Delorean
10	Jaguar
11	Lagonda
12	Lamborghini
13	McLaren
14	Mercedes
15	Morgan
16	Noble
17	Peugeot
18	Porsche
19	Reliant
20	Rolls Royce
21	Trabant
22	Triumph

No "Ferrari"

Figure 4.8. *Applying an exclusion filter*

How It Works

In this query, you started by finding all vehicles sold. This meant linking the four tables (Make, Model, Stock, and SalesDetails) that contain the fields that interest you. Then you applied a filter on a field (Make in this example). This time, however, you specified that the filter is used to `exclude`, rather than include, the element that you specify. This is done by using the <> (or "not equal") operator. This operator is the exact opposite of the equal operator that you saw in the previous section and effectively means "anything but." It will exclude from the results any single item you specify—Ferrari in this example. Here again, any field in the tables that you have assembled in the FROM clause can be used to filter data.

As you can see, sorting the list in alphabetical order has helped you to understand the output. Equally, showing each make only once thanks to the judicious use of the DISTINCT keyword makes the result clearer and more comprehensible.

It is probably worth remembering that an initial filter has already been applied through joining the tables, as I mentioned at the start of this chapter. Because, in effect, the SalesDetails table contains a subset of the vehicles in the Stock table (those whose StockID is present), you will not see `all` the cars in stock in this query, only those in the SalesDetails table (that is, those that have been sold). The WHERE clause then filters this data set further by excluding Ferrari from the output.

Tricks and Traps

When excluding a single element from a list, there is one variation that you might find interesting—and one important reminder.

- As an alternative to using <>in the WHERE clause, you can use !=instead to signify "not equals"—and consequently exclude it from the output. Were you to use it, the WHERE clause in this example would look like this:

```
WHERE MakeName != 'Ferrari'
```

- Once again, any text that is used in a WHERE clause **must** be enclosed in single quotes. Numbers, however, should be entered without any quotes at all.

4.7 Using Multiple Exclusion Filters

An excited marketing director now wants even more data to power her research. This time she wants a list of all makes sold except Porsche, Aston Martin, and Bentley.

Luckily, it is also possible (and really not difficult) to exclude a selection of elements from a list in SQL. Take a look at the following code to see how to display a list of vehicles that excludes a specific list of makes:

```
SELECT     DISTINCT MK.MakeName
FROM       Data.Make AS MK
           INNER JOIN Data.Model AS MD ON MK.MakeID = MD.MakeID
           INNER JOIN Data.Stock AS ST ON ST.ModelID = MD.ModelID
           INNER JOIN Data.SalesDetails SD ON ST.StockCode = SD.StockID
WHERE      MK.MakeName NOT IN ('Porsche', 'Aston Martin', 'Bentley')
ORDER BY   MK.MakeName
```

If you run this code, you should see something like the output shown in *Figure 4.9.*

	MakeName
1	Alfa Romeo
2	Austin
3	BMW
4	Bugatti
5	Citroen
6	Delahaye
7	Delorean
8	Ferrari
9	Jaguar
10	Lagonda
11	Lamborghini
12	McLaren
13	Mercedes
14	Morgan
15	Noble

Figure 4.9. *Applying an exclusion filter using multiple criteria*

How It Works

As you can see (if you scroll through the query output), the cars that you specified in the NOT IN clause of this SQL are nowhere to be seen in the results.

This query is similar to the last one (and to some extent the one before that), so I will not explain the similarities, only the differences. In this query, the WHERE clause contains a list of elements (in parentheses, commA.separated and with each piece of text enclosed in single quotes), but the IN keyword has been extended to read NOT IN. The outcome is that any element in the list contained between the parentheses after NOT IN will not appear in the result set.

Tricks and Traps

I can think of only one main comment to make at this time.

- When you write queries to filter data, you will have to decide whether it is easier to include or exclude a specific list of elements in a dataset. In most cases, it is best to reduce coding to a minimum because this reduces the risk of error. So, if you have a shorter list of items to exclude than you have of items to include, then it is probably better to choose an exclusion list.

4.8 Filtering Numbers Over a Defined Threshold

Your reputation as an analytics guru is spreading through the company. Now it is the turn of the finance director to arrive at your desk with a request. He would like to get an idea of the higher-value cars that are in stock or have been sold; more specifically, he wants to see a list of all cars where the purchase price was more than £50,000.

This request is a reminder that filtering data is not always a question of defining exact matches. This is especially true where numbers are concerned. The following query will do this:

```
SELECT      ModelName, Cost

FROM        Data.Model

INNER JOIN  Data.Stock

            ON Model.ModelID = Stock.ModelID

WHERE       Cost > 50000
```

If you run this code, you should see something like the output in Figure 4.10, where all vehicle costs are more than £50,000:

	ModelName	Cost
1	Testarossa	52000.00
2	355	176000.00
3	Testarossa	176000.00
4	DB6	60800.00
5	Testarossa	172000.00
6	Flying Spur	64400.00
7	355	135600.00
8	Testarossa	156000.00
9	355	125200.00
10	Virage	98872.00
11	DB6	55600.00
12	355	127600.00
13	Testarossa	132000.00
14	Flying Spur	52712.00
15	355	125560.00

Figure 4.10. *Using a numeric comparison filter*

How It Works

In this example, you queried the Stock and Model tables using a WHERE clause on the Cost field, which applied the greater-than operator (>) followed by a value used in the comparison. This, in effect, told SQL to "give me the costs greater than 50000." As you can see, the figure used for the comparison is not formatted in any way.

> **Note:** What is possibly the most important thing to remember when using numbers to filter data is that a figure does *not* need to be enclosed in single quotes like text does.

Tricks and Traps

There is one specific thing to note about the greater-than operator.

- The greater-than operator (>) means exactly what it says. This query will not return any records where the vehicle cost is exactly £50,000—only those where the cost is at least £50,000.01, that is, greater than 50,000.

4.9 Filtering Numbers Under a Defined Threshold

As a variation on the previous example, let's imagine you want to take a look at any cars that are or have been in stock where the cost of any spare parts was below a certain threshold. The following piece of SQL returns this information:

```
SELECT     ModelName, Cost, PartsCost
FROM       Data.Model
INNER JOIN Data.Stock
           ON Model.ModelID = Stock.ModelID
WHERE      PartsCost < 1000
```

If you run this code, you should see something like the output in Figure 4.11, where the parts cost less than £1,000.

	ModelName	Cost	PartsCost
1	911	15600.00	0.00
2	924	9200.00	750.00
3	944	15960.00	500.00
4	DB4	23600.00	750.00
5	DB6	60800.00	750.00
6	Testarossa	172000.00	150.00
7	911	15680.00	500.00
8	DB5	29200.00	500.00
9	944	6800.00	225.00
10	DB6	36000.00	750.00
11	Flying Spur	64400.00	750.00
12	944	7160.00	750.00
13	280SL	18360.00	500.00
14	Giulia	6956.00	750.00
15	XK150	18392.00	150.00

Figure 4.11. *Using a less-than comparison filter*

How It Works

This example tweaks the previous one to apply a slightly different filter. This time you are looking at vehicles where the cost of spare parts was less than £1000. All this was done by using the field that you want to use as a basis for the comparison, the less-than operator (the < symbol), and a value.

Tricks and Traps

There are a couple of things to remember when filtering using numbers.

- You might have noticed that you did **not** need to include the parts cost in the output when filtering on this particular figure. However, it can be good practice to include the fields that you are using in a WHERE clause in the initial output as this enables you to "sanity check" the results of the query. Once you are satisfied that the results are accurate, you can always remove the field that you are filtering on from the SELECT clause.

- You must **never** format a number that you are using in the WHERE clause to filter output. That is, you always enter the number without a thousands separators or currency symbols. The number must be entered "raw" for the filter to work.

4.10 Filtering on Values Up to and Including a Specific Number

Still looking at our stock of vehicles—past and present—let's imagine that the finance director wants to take a look at all cars where the repair cost was up to and including £500.00. Writing the following SQL snippet will let you deliver the analysis that he wants to see:

```
SELECT     ModelName, RepairsCost
FROM       Data.Model
INNER JOIN Data.Stock
           ON Model.ModelID = Stock.ModelID
WHERE      RepairsCost <= 500
```

Running this code will deliver something like the output in Figure 4.12, where all repair costs are less than or equal to £500.

	ModelName	RepairsCost
1	924	500.00
2	DB4	500.00
3	944	250.00
4	Flying Spur	500.00
5	944	500.00
6	Giulia	400.00
7	XK150	390.00
8	XJS	290.00
9	944	140.00
10	TR4	500.00
11	TR5	320.00
12	924	360.00
13	Flying Spur	490.00
14	TR4	500.00
15	911	500.00

Figure 4.12. Using a less-than-or-equal-to comparison filter

How It Works

This example is a variation on the last one and shows that both the less-than and greater-than operators can be amended to make them "or equal to" by adding the equal sign. This will start the comparison with the figure (or letters) used in the comparison. As you can see from the results of the query, records containing the figure that is used as the upper threshold in the WHERE clause (500) are included in the result set.

Tricks and Traps

You might want to note the following trick with the greater-than or lesser-than operators:

- You can add the equal sign to either the greater-than (>) or lesser-than (<) operator to convert it to, respectively, greater than or equal to and lesser than or equal to.

4.11 Filtering on a Range of Values

You can also filter results so that a range of data is returned. Let's take a look at an example of this by setting up a query to show all vehicles where the parts cost is between a lower and an upper threshold. This lets you answer a request from the CEO for a list of all makes of car that Prestige Cars has stocked where the parts cost is between £1,000 and £2,000. The following is the SQL to do this:

```
SELECT      DISTINCT MK.MakeName
FROM        Data.Make AS MK INNER JOIN Data.Model AS MD
            ON MK.MakeID = MD.MakeID
INNER JOIN Data.Stock AS ST ON ST.ModelID = MD.ModelID
WHERE       ST.PartsCost BETWEEN 1000 AND 2000
ORDER BY    MK.MakeName
```

If you run this query, you will see the output shown in Figure 4.13.

Figure 4.13. Using a range comparison filter

How It Works

This query starts by joining the Stock, Model, and Make tables. It then adds a WHERE clause. In this example, the WHERE clause is in two parts.

First:	The BETWEEN operator followed by the figure for the *lower* threshold in your filter
Finally:	The AND operator followed by the figure for the *upper* threshold in your filter.

The overall result is that using the BETWEEN and AND operators in a WHERE clause lets you specify a range of data to filter on.

Tricks and Traps

The BETWEEN and AND operators are extremely powerful when applied to filters. However, there are several aspects of their use that require fairly close attention. These include the following:

- BETWEEN ... AND can also be used with text. If you use letters rather than numbers, you can limit the output across an alphabetical range.

- You must begin a BETWEEN…AND filter with the lower threshold and end with the upper threshold. If you reverse the thresholds, then the query will likely return nothing at all.

- As you can see from this example (and, indeed, is the case in any other code using a WHERE clause), you do not have to place the field used in the WHERE clause in the SELECT statement. Of course, you can repeat the "filter" field in the SELECT clause if you want to be really sure that no data has been returned that does not meet the criteria you have entered. In fact, it can be advisable to do this when developing and testing queries—and then remove it once you are sure you have the correct result.

- If you prefer, you can write this kind of WHERE clause using the <= (less than or equal to) and >= (greater than or equal to) operators. The WHERE clause in this example, rewritten using these operators, would look like this:

```
WHERE      PartsCost >= 1000 AND PartsCost <= 2000
```

As you can see, this approach requires you to repeat the field name in the clause. However, when you write a filter that defines a range to exclude using greater than or equal to and lesser than or equal to, you do **not** have to enter the lowest threshold value first. In other words, this piece of SQL would work equally well:

```
WHERE      PartsCost <= 2000 AND PartsCost >= 1000
```

- You saw the BETWEEN...AND keyword combination in the previous chapter when applied to range joins. However, I am applying it here in a slightly different context—as part of a WHERE clause rather than in a table join. This is just one example of how SQL can use the same keywords in different situations to achieve different results.

4.12 Using Boolean Filters (True or False)

Sometimes a table may contain a simple yes or no value. Depending on the tool you are using to view the data, this might be displayed as Yes/No, True/False, or even 1/0. Filtering on fields like this is easy—but it requires you to know that data like this is, in fact, stored as a one or a zero. In the Stock table, there is a field named IsRHD that is one of these fields. The following code snippet shows how you can use it to display all right-hand drive models that Prestige Cars has sold:

```
SELECT     DISTINCT MK.MakeName, MD.ModelName

FROM       Data.Make AS MK

INNER JOIN Data.Model AS MD ON MK.MakeID = MD.MakeID

INNER JOIN Data.Stock AS ST ON ST.ModelID = MD.ModelID

INNER JOIN Data.SalesDetails SD ON ST.StockCode = SD.StockID

WHERE      ST.IsRHD = 1

ORDER BY   MK.MakeName, MD.ModelName
```

If you execute this query, you will see the output shown in Figure 4.14:

	MakeName	ModelName
1	Alfa Romeo	1750
2	Alfa Romeo	Giulia
3	Alfa Romeo	Giulietta
4	Alfa Romeo	Spider
5	Aston Martin	DB2
6	Aston Martin	DB4
7	Aston Martin	DB5
8	Aston Martin	DB6
9	Aston Martin	DB9
10	Aston Martin	Rapide
11	Aston Martin	Vanquish
12	Aston Martin	Vantage
13	Aston Martin	Virage
14	Austin	Cambridge
15	Austin	Lichfield

Figure 4.14. *Using a Boolean filter in a WHERE clause*

How It Works

Here, again, we have joined the Stock and SalesDetails tables to get a list of vehicles sold. Then we have joined the Make and Model tables so that we can see the actual names of the make and model. To finish, we have added the DISTINCT keyword to ensure that no duplicates are returned—and the ORDER BY clause to output the result in alphabetical order to make it easier to read. The final tweak is to ensure that the WHERE clause only allows records that contain an IsRHD field with a value of 1—indicating that this vehicle is right-hand drive.

The really interesting aspect of this query is that it is adapted to a specific type of SQL data. The data type used in the IsRHD column is called a BIT data type. It will accept only a 1 or a 0 (true or false if you prefer).

It might, possibly, accept empty (or NULL) values as well. However, we will examine these subtleties in the following chapter.

Tricks and Traps

As I am introducing a new SQL concept, there are, inevitably, a few key points to retain.

- If you wanted to reverse this query to show only left-hand drive cars—which are stored in the SalesDetails table with the IsRHD column set to 0 (false)—you would tweak the WHERE clause to read as follows:

```
WHERE      IsRHD = 0
```

- In SQL, the value True is represented by a 1, and the value False is represented by a 0. So, when you are writing a SQL query on a true/false column, you **cannot** say =True or =False. You have to use a 1 or a 0.

- In geeky language, a yes/no filter like this is called a Boolean condition.

Conclusion

This chapter has taken you much further into the world of SQL querying. Where before you could select only tables and columns, now you can delve deep into the data itself and output only the parts that interest you.

First you saw how joining tables can filter the data that a query returns. Then you learned the importance of the WHERE clause and how to use the power of SQL Server to choose to display only the contents—or even part of the contents—of certain fields. You saw how to select text and numbers, including ranges of numbers and figures above or below a specified value.

Core Knowledge Learned in This Chapter

This has been quite a full and fairly intense chapter. The following are the keywords you saw in this chapter:

Concept	Description
WHERE	This essential keyword starts every clause that allows you to filter data in a query.
IN	This keyword lets you enter a series of words or numbers that must exist in a column if the data for a record is to be displayed.
<>	This operator selects data that is not equal to a specified word, phrase, or number.
!=	This operator also selects data that is not equal to a specified word, phrase, or number.
NOT IN	This keyword combination excludes any records where a column does not contain one of a series of words or numbers.
>	This operator filters on numbers or letters that are less than a specified figure.
<	This operator filters on numbers or letters that are more than a specified figure.
>=	This operator filters on numbers or letters that are more than or equal to a specified figure.
<=	This operator filters on numbers or letters that are less than or equal to a specified figure.
BETWEEN...AND	This operator allows you to set a range (usually of figures) that you use to filter a data set.

CHAPTER 5
Applying Complex Filters to Queries

Filtering data is at the heart of SQL. In many cases you will have to apply multiple filters at the same time to extract exactly what you are looking for. This means learning how to apply a little logic to filter criteria to achieve the desired result. The logic you need may be quite simple—or possibly quite advanced. However, it will always be built using the same approach and similar methods.

Advanced Filters

In this chapter, you will extend the knowledge that you acquired in the previous chapter by learning how to use SQL filters to

- Search for data on alternative criteria
- Apply separate criteria simultaneously to narrow down a search
- Use simple logic to apply multiple criteria in more complex searches
- Use wildcard data searches, that is, finding a value that is only part of a field
- Filter data on a specific part of a field
- Find NULL (or empty) data

5.1 Using Either/Or Filters

The CEO has just sent you an email. She needs to narrow down her analysis so that she can carry out an in-depth review of the sales of cars that are `either` red `or` Ferraris.

A request like this (however bizarre it may seem at first sight) makes the point that not all data searches are as simple as those you saw in Chapter 3. On many—if not most—occasions you will probably want to create more complex queries that require either one or another condition to be met. The following code snippet shows how to select data where either of two possible conditions is true:

```
SELECT     DISTINCT MK.MakeName, ST.Color

FROM       Data.Make AS MK

INNER JOIN Data.Model AS MD ON MK.MakeID = MD.MakeID

INNER JOIN Data.Stock AS ST ON ST.ModelID = MD.ModelID

INNER JOIN Data.SalesDetails SD ON ST.StockCode = SD.StockID

WHERE      ST.Color = 'Red' OR MakeName = 'Ferrari'
```

Executing this query will show something like the output in *Figure 5.1.*

	MakeName	Color
1	Alfa Romeo	Red
2	Aston Martin	Red
3	Austin	Red
4	Bentley	Red
5	Bugatti	Red
6	Ferrari	Black
7	Ferrari	Blue
8	Ferrari	British Racing Green
9	Ferrari	Dark Purple
10	Ferrari	Green
11	Ferrari	Night Blue
12	Ferrari	Red
13	Ferrari	Silver
14	Jaguar	Red
15	Mercedes	Red

Figure 5.1. Filtering on alternative criteria

How It Works

This example introduces a fundamental SQL keyword: OR. This keyword lets you apply alternative filter conditions. Here you have queried the Sales, SalesDetails, Stock, Make, and Model tables (so that you can see vehicles sold as well as the names—and not the codes—of the make and model) using a WHERE clause that filters on either a certain color or a specified make. This query shows you that when you are looking for elements in different columns, you need to use the OR keyword in the WHERE clause. You can see from the WHERE clause that you must always be extremely precise and indicate which column has which specific filter applied to it.

Tricks and Traps

When meeting a vital new concept for the first time, you need to take away a few key notions.

- By definition this kind of query will return more results than the more restrictive filters that you saw in Chapter 4 as it implies a wider search, given that it is an either/or selection.

- An OR query like this will return data when either of the two conditions is true or even when both of them are true. However, a record where both conditions are true (that is, where the make is Ferrari and the color is red) will not appear twice.

- Each part of the WHERE clause follows the logic you saw in Chapter 4. So, text is inside single quotes, as is normal when filtering on text data.

- The technical name for a filter like this is a logical or.

- You can add as many OR operators to a query as you want. However, you will have to repeat the column name for each different filter that you apply— even if the filters apply to the same column.

5.2 Using Multiple Separate Criteria Concurrently

The CEO now wants to build on your query results and carry out a much narrower search—she wants to look for red Ferraris only. You can deliver the required result with only a small tweak to the code that you just wrote.

```
SELECT DISTINCT   MK.MakeName, ST.Color

FROM              Data.Make AS MK
```

```
INNER JOIN        Data.Model AS MD ON MK.MakeID = MD.MakeID

INNER JOIN        Data.Stock AS ST ON ST.ModelID = MD.ModelID

INNER JOIN        Data.SalesDetails SD ON ST.StockCode = SD.StockID

WHERE             ST.Color = 'Red' AND MK.MakeName = 'Ferrari'
```

Running this query should show something like *Figure 5.2*.

Figure 5.2: Searching on simultaneous criteria

How It Works

This query is similar to the previous one. So, let's just look at the differences. In this example, OR has been replaced by AND. This tells SQL that both criteria must be met for a record to pass the filter. So, only records where the vehicle is a red Ferrari will appear in the output.

Tricks and Traps

You are likely to use the AND keyword frequently in your SQL career. So, it is worth noting the following right from the start:

- The AND operator will narrow down the search considerably, as both filter conditions have to be met for a record to be allowed through to the output.

- A query can have multiple criteria that are applied to filter the data. This means in practice that you can add as many AND clauses to the WHERE clause that you like.

- The technical name for a filter like this is a logical and.

5.3 Using Multiple Filters and an Exclusion

Up until now, when using multiple selection criteria, you have looked at fairly limited selections using only two elements. Now, however, you have been asked to find all makes except Bentleys where the cars are red, green, or blue. You are lucky that SQL can help you to create much more complex filters that can apply these kinds of criteria really easily. To see how this kind of complex query is written, take a look at the following piece of SQL:

```
SELECT      DISTINCT MK.MakeName, ST.Color
FROM        Data.Make AS MK
INNER JOIN Data.Model AS MD ON MK.MakeID = MD.MakeID
INNER JOIN Data.Stock AS ST ON ST.ModelID = MD.ModelID
INNER JOIN Data.SalesDetails SD ON ST.StockCode = SD.StockID
WHERE       ST.Color IN ('Red', 'Green', 'Blue')
            AND MK.MakeName != 'Bentley'
```

Running this query will return the output in *Figure 5.3*.

Figure 5.3: *Combining multiple selections with an exclusion*

How It Works

This query shows you that you can combine any of the filtering techniques that you have seen so far in this chapter and the previous one if they help you attain the required result. This filter mixes the IN operator to filter on a chosen selection of colors (red, green, or blue) but excludes all Bentleys from the result—whatever the color.

This query applies two conditions.

First:	It itemizes a list of colors that the vehicle can be.
Second:	It extends the criteria with an AND clause to add a second condition that excludes Bentley as the make.

The result is that you have a list of all makes except Bentley as long as the cars are red, green, or blue.

Tricks and Traps

I have only two points to make here.

- You can use either <> or != to exclude an element in a WHERE clause.

- I added the DISTINCT keyword to the SELECT clause to produce a shorter list of results by excluding any duplicates.

5.4 Filtering on Both Text and Numbers Simultaneously

Sometimes you could want to filter data so that a certain condition is always met, and then a second criterion has to be met as well—only the second criterion can apply different, alternative criteria to other fields. Take, for example, the request from the finance director to see a report containing all the red cars ever bought where their repair cost or the cost of spare parts exceeds £1,000.00. The following SQL snippet shows this type of query in action:

```
SELECT      MD.ModelName, ST.Color, ST.PartsCost, ST.RepairsCost

FROM        Data.Stock AS ST

INNER JOIN Data.Model AS MD


            ON ST.ModelID = MD.ModelID

WHERE       ST.Color = 'Red' AND (ST.PartsCost > 1000

            OR ST.RepairsCost > 1000)
```

Executing this piece of SQL will return a list like that shown in *Figure 5.4*.

	ModelName	Color	PartsCost	RepairsCost
1	355	Red	750.00	2000.00
2	355	Red	750.00	9250.00
3	57C	Red	457.00	5500.00
4	57C	Red	7500.00	9250.00
5	924	Red	750.00	1360.00
6	944	Red	500.00	1360.00
7	DB2	Red	750.00	2000.00
8	DB9	Red	750.00	1490.00
9	Mark X	Red	750.00	2175.00
10	Rapide	Red	750.00	1360.00
11	Testarossa	Red	1500.00	2175.00
12	Veyron	Red	2200.00	9250.00
13	Virage	Red	1500.00	3950.00
14	Wraith	Red	3150.00	3950.00
15	XK120	Red	500.00	1100.00

Figure 5.4: Nested criteria

How It Works

This query joins the Stock and Model tables and then specifies that only red cars must be output. Then it extends the filter with a second criterion to select data using another condition that must be met on `either` of two other columns.

The parentheses that are used to enclose the second part of the filter (after the AND operator) are an important part of the WHERE clause. Placing part of the WHERE clause inside parentheses like this means the following:

First:	Any of the conditions inside the parentheses have to be true.
Second:	The condition outside the parentheses must also be true.

So, the resulting filter is essentially in two parts.

Not only	The Color field must contain the "Red" text.
As well as	Either the parts cost must be over £1,000.00 or the repair cost must be over £1,000.00.

The filter is saying this: "For every red car, see whether either the parts cost or the repair cost is over 1,000." Only if both these criteria are met will the record containing this data appear in the result set.

Tricks and Traps

When writing queries that provide alternative filters, there are a few key points to take away.

- It is `vital` to place any alternative choices (in this example that means the cost of spares or the repair cost) inside parentheses. If you do not do this, then the query will be interpreted as "any red car or any repair cost over £1,000.00 or any parts cost over £1,000.00." This will return a completely different result set.

- If both the parts cost and the repair cost are over 1,000, then the filter will work, as it needs only one of them to match to function. Once one filter condition is met, SQL does not care if others are met or not. This does not, however, mean that a record that meets all the criteria will appear multiple times in the output. It just means that the minimal conditions for the row to be allowed through into the result set have been met.

- In this example we deliberately avoided using the DISTINCT keyword in the SELECT clause. This way the query output delivered the complete list of vehicles matching the required criteria.

5.5 Applying Complex Alternative Filters at the Same Time

There could be days in your career as a data analyst when you will wonder why (and how) people can possibly dream up the requests that they send you. Take, for instance, this suggestion from the finance director: "I want to see all red, green, or blue Rolls-Royce Phantoms—or failing that any vehicle where both the parts cost and the repair cost are over £5,500.00."

You are, yet again, in luck because SQL queries can be tailored to filter data down to an extremely fine level of detail. This query supposes you need to see either of the following categories of sales:

- Red, Green, or Blue Rolls-Royce Phantoms

- Sales where both the parts and repair costs are over 5,500

I realize that this may seem to be a strange thing to ask—but believe me, I have seen more peculiar requirements in the past. In any case, here is the code that can satisfy the request:

```
SELECT DISTINCT  MD.ModelName, ST.Color, ST.PartsCost, ST.RepairsCost

FROM             Data.Stock AS ST
```

```
INNER JOIN Data.Model AS MD

                ON ST.ModelID = MD.ModelID
WHERE           (ST.Color IN ('Red', 'Green', 'Blue')

            AND

            MD.ModelName = 'Phantom')

        OR

        (ST.PartsCost > 5500 AND ST.RepairsCost > 5500)
```

If you run this piece of SQL, you will see a data set like that shown in Figure 5.5.

	ModelName	Color	PartsCost	RepairsCost
1	57C	Red	7500.00	9250.00
2	F50	Silver	7900.00	9250.00
3	Phantom	Green	1500.00	5500.00
4	Phantom	Green	2200.00	1490.00
5	Phantom	Red	750.00	500.00

Figure 5.5: Complex nested criteria

How It Works

This piece of SQL has two parts—each one on either side of the central OR keyword. What the filter does is to apply both parts of the WHERE clause independently and then return any records that match either (or both) conditions. It is as if there are two separate filters in action where each one is independent of the other.

To ensure that each side of the OR clause does exactly what you want it to, it is vital that you enclose each side of the clause in parentheses. This way, the filter consists of these three elements:

A first condition:	That defines the acceptable color and model.
The OR operator:	That tells SQL to apply either the first criterion or the second.
A second condition:	That sets a specific cost threshold for either of two fields.

As this WHERE clause is a little more complex, you might want to take a look at *Figure 5.6*, which explains how it works in a more visual way.

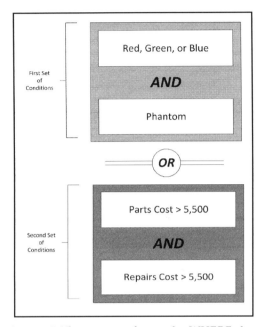

Figure 5.6. *The anatomy of a complex WHERE clause*

Tricks and Traps

These kinds of complex filters come with their own set of variations and caveats. You need to remember the following:

- You can write the WHERE clause as a single line if you prefer so that it reads as follows:

```
WHERE (Color IN ('Red', 'Green', 'Blue') AND ModelName =
'Phantom') OR (PartsCost > 1500 OR RepairsCost > 1500)
```

   This is purely a question of presentation. However, you may find that separating the WHERE clause over several lines makes it easier to read and to understand because a multi-line format enhances the fact that there are two separate aspects to the filter, each one on a separate side of the OR keyword.

- Once again, if both of the filter conditions are met, the filter will work because it needs only one of them to match to succeed. If one filter condition is met, SQL does not care if others are met or not.

5.6 Using Wildcard Searches

Returning a list of data is nearly always easy when everything (including the data) is perfect. In the real world, however, this is not always the case. Maybe the data has not been entered correctly, or perhaps you cannot remember how it was spelled. Sometimes it could be a combination of both these circumstances. You are reminded of this when the receptionist comes to your desk with a request for some help. She knows that Prestige Cars has a customer with Peter (or was that Pete?) somewhere in their name, and you need to find this person in the database. Fortunately, SQL has a few solutions to help you filter a little more approximately. One example is given in the following piece of SQL:

```
SELECT      CustomerName
FROM        Data.Customer
WHERE       CustomerName LIKE '%pete%'
```

Running this query will return the output in *Figure 5.7*.

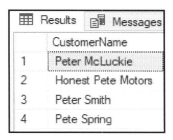

Figure 5.7. *Wildcard filtering*

How It Works

This piece of code searched the Customer table for any element in the CustomerName field that contains the characters pete. Consequently, it found Pete and Peter and would also have found Peteer, Pete's Sake—well, you get the idea!

This kind of search is called a `wildcard` filter, and it requires you to adhere to a few basic principles.

- Wildcard searches require you to use the LIKE operator.

- As I am searching inside a text field, the text has to be enclosed in single quotes, as was the case in all queries that you saw previously that searched on text-based fields.

- The percentage symbol (%) really means "any character or characters." This symbol is called a wildcard in this context.

- You must place any percentage symbols inside the `single quotes`.

In other respects, a wildcard search is very much like a filter applied to any text-based column. The only real difference is the use of the % character to widen the range of elements that SQL Server can return.

Tricks and Traps

Wildcard searches are powerful, but you do have to take care when using them. Here are some examples:

- When using these kinds of searches, it makes no difference if you enter the search text in uppercase or lowercase—or if the data in the table is in uppercase or lowercase. SQL will find all matching records no matter what the case of the search text or the data.

- If you want to locate a few characters anywhere inside a field, then you need to place the wildcard (the percentage symbol) on either side of the text that you are looking for.

- If you are certain the records you are looking for have a field that `begins` with the text that you are using to filter the result (pete in this example), then you can alter the WHERE clause so that it looks like this:

```
WHERE      CustomerName LIKE 'pete%'
```

As you can see, the wildcard is entered only `after` the search text. This, in effect, tells SQL that the field to look for begins with pete—and can have any text after this.

- If the records that you are looking for have a field that `ends` with the text that you are using to filter the result (pete in this example), then you can alter the WHERE clause so that it looks like this:

```
WHERE      CustomerName LIKE '%pete'
```

This code tells SQL to find records where the CustomerName field ends with pete—however many characters precede the text you are looking for.

- Wildcards will apply to letters, numbers, or even symbols; they are not limited to alphabetical letters. However, they are mostly used when filtering on text-based data.

5.7 Using Wildcards to Exclude Data

There could be occasions when you want to use wildcards to exclude data from the query output. Suppose, for instance, that you want to produce a list of all the customers `except` those with pete somewhere in their name. The following SQL extends the code from the previous example to do exactly this:

```
SELECT      CustomerName

FROM        Data.Customer

WHERE       CustomerName NOT LIKE '%pete%'
```

Running this query will show the kind of result that you can see in *Figure 5.8.*

Figure 5.8. Excluding data by applying a wildcard

How It Works

Preceding the LIKE operator with the NOT keyword reverses the filter logic. This means that—in this query at least—every customer will be displayed unless their name contains the characters pete. You can verify this by scrolling down through the result set. You will see that no customer with `pete` in their name is present.

5.8 Using a Specific Part of Text to Filter Data

Just as you were glancing at the clock at the end of the day, the finance director appears beside your desk with an apparently strange demand. He informs you that the account number field is structured in such a way that you can identify the country of sale from certain characters at a specific point in the field. So, he wants you to use this to isolate all the sales made to French customers.

Put another way, what he means is "I have a field where each character—or certain characters—has a specific meaning and the field always has the same number of characters with the same subgroups of meaningful characters." A bank account or certain Social Security numbers (or other identity codes) are examples of this kind of data. In these cases, you may well want to specify that a certain number of characters can be anything at all—but others (at a specific place in the field) have a meaning that you want to filter on.

The InvoiceNumber field of the Sales table is one of these fields. It is defined like this:

The left three characters	Indicate the currency of sale
Characters 4 and 5	Indicate the destination country
The last three characters	Provide a sequential invoice number

This approach is explained more graphically in *Figure 5.9.*

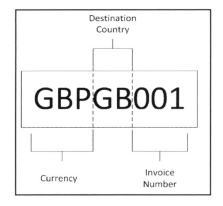

Figure 5.9: *Structured fields*

So, the invoice number GBPGB001 tells you that this sale was made in pounds sterling to a client in the United Kingdom—and is invoice No 001.

If you are faced with a structured field like this, you can search on `parts of the field` to isolate certain records. In this example, the following SQL returns only vehicles sold to France—whatever the currency and whatever the invoice number.

```
SELECT DISTINCT    MD.ModelName, SA.InvoiceNumber
FROM               Data.Make AS MK
INNER JOIN         Data.Model AS MD
                   ON MK.MakeID = MD.MakeID
```

```
INNER JOIN          Data.Stock ST
                    ON ST.ModelID = MD.ModelID
INNER JOIN          Data.SalesDetails AS SD
                    ON SD.StockID = ST.StockCode
INNER JOIN          Data.Sales AS SA
                    ON SA.SalesID = SD.SalesID
WHERE               SA.InvoiceNumber LIKE '___FR%'
```

Running this query (and specifically using three underscores in the WHERE clause before the FR%) will return the output in *Figure 5.10*.

Figure 5.10: *Wildcard searches in structured fields*

How It Works

This piece of SQL uses wildcards to filter a field. More precisely, it uses the underscore character as a single-character wildcard. So, the WHERE clause in this sample says this:

First:	Find any *three* characters on the left of the field (three underscores).
Then:	Filter on FR.
Finally:	Don't filter on any other characters to the end of the text (let anything through, no matter how many characters). This is represented by the percentage symbol.

When faced with structured coded texts like this one, it is vital to know what each subset of characters means in the field. Providing that you know this, you can then filter on any part of the text, as you did here.

Tricks and Traps

While filtering on a specific part of a field is not difficult, it helps to remember the following points when you do this:

- Where there is a strict coding scheme, such as a bank account number, you can use the underscore wildcard to replace a `single` character, or a specified number of characters. However, there must be one character at least if you use an underscore. This is unlike the percentage wildcard that means `zero to any number` of characters.

- You can use the underscore wildcard anywhere in a search pattern—and even use it several times. For instance, you could also have written this WHERE clause as follows:

```
WHERE       InvoiceNumber LIKE '___FR____'
```

This pattern will find any initial three characters, FR, and then any four final characters.

- Be warned that wildcard searches (using % or _) can be slow on large data sets. If your work will entail carrying out lots of searches like these on massive tables, then it could be worth talking to your database administrator to see if he or she can implement a way of speeding up searches like these. If you have no one to help you, then you can find plenty of advice on the Web that explains how to accelerate text searches in SQL Server.

5.9 Using NULLs, or Nonexistent Data

Finding data is fairly easy if the data is present. However, real-world databases can contain missing data elements. Indeed, the marketing director has noticed that the corporate database is missing postcodes (ZIP codes) for some clients. So, she has asked for a list of all customers without this vital piece of information.

Fortunately, SQL can handle empty data fields easily. So, you use the following short piece of SQL to deliver the report that will make the man from the marketing department very happy:

```
SELECT    CustomerName

FROM      Data.Customer

WHERE     PostCode IS NULL
```

Running this query will return the output shown in *Figure 5.11*.

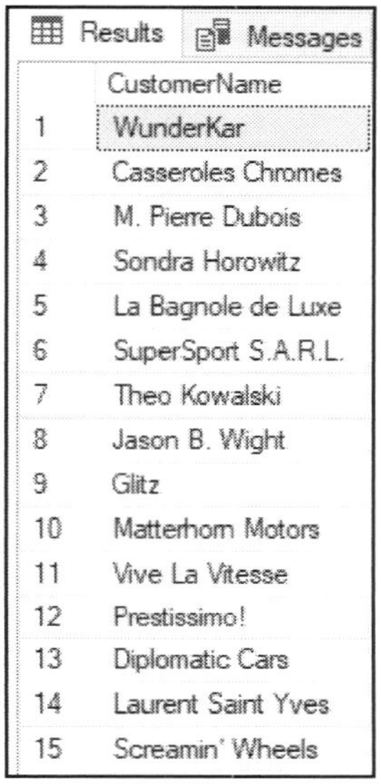

	CustomerName
1	WunderKar
2	Casseroles Chromes
3	M. Pierre Dubois
4	Sondra Horowitz
5	La Bagnole de Luxe
6	SuperSport S.A.R.L.
7	Theo Kowalski
8	Jason B. Wight
9	Glitz
10	Matterhorn Motors
11	Vive La Vitesse
12	Prestissimo!
13	Diplomatic Cars
14	Laurent Saint Yves
15	Screamin' Wheels

Figure 5.11: *Finding NULL fields*

How It Works

Nonexistent data is handled in specific ways in SQL because "empty" fields are considered special. Indeed, any missing or empty data element is even given a particular name; it is called a `NULL value` by SQL.

I have to be up-front with you and admit that dealing with NULL values can get tricky. So, rather than explain everything that you need to know about them in one fell swoop, I prefer to introduce the various techniques that you will need to know as required during the course of this book.

For now, you need to know that you can filter on NULL values using the IS keyword followed by the word NULL. This will allow you to isolate data on nonexistent elements.

Tricks and Traps

To begin your acquaintance with NULLs, you should take note of the following points:

- Although SQL Server Management Studio displays the word NULL in output from queries, this is only a way of indicating that the field is blank. The field itself contains nothing at all—and certainly not the word NULL.

- If you need to filter on records where there actually **is** data, you can use SQL like the following:

```
SELECT    CustomerName
FROM      Data.Customer
WHERE     PostCode IS NOT NULL
```

Here, as you can see, any nonempty elements can be displayed by negating the IS NULL command and instead writing IS NOT NULL.

- As SQL uses the equal operator for other filters, you could be tempted to write code like this:

```
WHERE     PostCode = NULL
```

However, you need to be aware that this will **not** work correctly. In fact, it will always return a blank record set. So, you could be lured into a false sense of security and end up believing that there are no empty items in a dataset when this is far from the case.

- Be warned, however, that NULL means a field that is empty. If users have entered spaces or even a couple of single quotes (which are invisible to the eye but mean that the field is not strictly empty), then these fields will not be caught by IS NULL.

- To find fields containing a space, you can use SQL like this:

```
WHERE     PostCode = ' '
```

- To find fields containing a blank, you can use SQL like this:

```
WHERE     PostCode = ''
```

Conclusion

This chapter took you much further into the world of SQL filtering. You saw how to apply either/or filters as well as define multiple cumulative conditions using the data from different fields in a SQL query. Moreover, you also saw how to apply more complex logic to force SQL Server to apply certain conditions but not others—or to combine conditions—to deliver the result you wanted. Finally, after learning how to carry out "fuzzy" searches using wildcards, you learned that you can apply filter conditions to certain parts of a field—and that you can even filter on nonexistent (or NULL) data.

Core Knowledge Learned in This Chapter

These are the keywords that you saw in this chapter:

Concept	Description
AND	This logical operator forces a filter to meet two conditions if a record is to be displayed in the output.
OR	This logical operator allows a filter to let data through to the result if either of two filter conditions is met.
NOT	is logical operator reverses the logic of a filter.
LIKE	This keyword lets you look for the partial contents of a column when filtering records.
%	This operator is used with the LIKE keyword to filter on the partial contents of a column and can represent any characters—or none.
_	This operator is used with the LIKE keyword to filter on the partial contents of a column. It represents any single character.
<>	This operator excludes an element from a query.
!=	This operator excludes an element from a query.

CHAPTER 6
Making Simple Calculations

SQL is not limited to merely finding, filtering, and eventually aggregating data. It can also carry out calculations that range from elementary math to relatively advanced statistical operations. It follows that an essential aspect of writing SQL queries consists of learning how to apply math to the core data to deliver increased insight and analysis.

Performing Calculations in SQL

In this chapter, I will show you how to perform simple math on the numeric data contained in SQL Server data tables. One you have mastered the basics, you should be able to build on this knowledge to enhance your own SQL queries to deliver all kinds of numerical analysis.

More specifically, you will see how to

- Perform basic arithmetic
- Create formulas that force SQL Server to perform calculations in the right order
- Identify numeric fields in tables
- Handle missing (or NULL) numeric data
- Use calculations to filter data

None of this is at all difficult, so now is the time to start learning to use SQL to practice your math.

6.1 Doing Simple Math

The finance director is fuming. He cannot find a spreadsheet that tells him what the exact cost of every car sold is, including any repairs, parts, and transport costs. Inevitably this becomes something that you have to deal with. So, let's see how to calculate the total cost of each vehicle sold. A quick look at the SalesByCountry view shows that there are four columns that itemize the cost elements, which are the purchase cost of the vehicle and the cost of repairs, parts, and transport. The following code snippet shows how you can add them together to produce the cost of sales on the fly in SQL:

```
SELECT    MakeName, ModelName

          ,Cost + RepairsCost + PartsCost + TransportInCost AS TotalCost

FROM      Data.SalesByCountry
```

Executing this code returns the output shown in *Figure 6.1.*

	MakeName	ModelName	TotalCost
1	Ferrari	Testarossa	56425.00
2	Ferrari	355	185650.00
3	Porsche	911	16410.00
4	Porsche	924	10600.00
5	Porsche	944	17970.00
6	Aston Martin	DB4	25000.00
7	Aston Martin	DB5	44150.00
8	Aston Martin	DB6	65550.00
9	Porsche	911	17220.00
10	Aston Martin	DB5	32200.00
11	Porsche	944	7425.00
12	Aston Martin	DB6	38550.00
13	Bentley	Flying Spur	66400.00
14	Ferrari	355	145250.00
15	Porsche	944	8560.00

Figure 6.1: Adding up the data from several columns

How It Works

This code snippet takes a view rather than a joined set of tables as the basis for the calculation. If you cast your mind back to Chapter 2, you will remember that a view like this is a way of memorizing a set of tables and all the joins required to link them. You could have replaced the single view in the FROM clause with several lines of SQL, but I am trying to keep things simpler for the moment so that you can concentrate on the math. In any case, using this view lets you access all the fields that you need to analyze the sales data.

As you can see, adding up the data in a set of columns is as simple as entering the columns as part of a SELECT clause with a plus (+) operator between each column name. The key element is that all the columns must contain numeric data.

So, although SQL Server is a database, it can perform a wide variety of calculations. These range from the elementary to the complex. While the math that you used to work out the cost of sales is not particularly demanding, it is a useful introduction to basic calculations that you can apply to your data using SQL.

Tricks and Traps

As I am introducing a new concept in SQL, there are—perhaps inevitably—a few key points to retain when carrying out elementary calculations.

- As a matter of principle, we have added an alias to the calculated column that is returned to avoid it being called "(No column name)"—as it would if you did not give it an alias.

- All in all, carrying out calculations in SQL Server is similar to carrying out arithmetical operations in Excel (or any other spreadsheet). Only in SQL you define the calculation once for a column or a set of columns rather than for a cell reference, and it will be applied to every row in the query output without you having to copy the formula down over hundreds—or even tens of thousands—of rows as you would have to in a spreadsheet.

- Remember that you can place commas at the start of fields or the end of fields when laying out your SQL. You can add them to the end of lines or the start of lines—it is all the same to SQL. This is why the second line of this example begins with a comma (and this is also why there is no comma at the end of the first line).

6.2 Examining Data Types in SQL Tables and Views

When using SQL to carry out calculations, it is `fundamental` that the columns you reference contain `numbers` and `not strings of characters`. It takes only a single column in a calculation to contain some text for the entire query to fail. Indeed, even if 99.99 percent of the data in a column is numeric and just one record contains text, then the query will fail if you try to use this column in a calculation.

It follows that you need to learn to be careful when choosing the columns that you can—and cannot—use when performing calculations in SQL. Fortunately, data tables do contain some reliable indications of which columns can be used to store only numbers. Columns like this are known as having numeric data types. Generally, database designers will have used them to contain numeric data that you can use in your calculations.

In section 10 of Chapter 1, you saw how to expand a table in SQL Server Management Studio to look at the columns in the table. This technique has the added advantage of letting you see what the data type of each column is so that you can build your calculations safely and reliably. You can also apply this approach to views, which is what you will learn how to do now:

1. In SQL Server Management Studio, expand the contents of the database containing the view that interests you (the PrestigeCars database in this example).

2. Expand the Views folder.

3. Click the plus symbol to the left of the view whose data types you want to examine (we will use the SalesByCountry view in this example).

4. Click the plus symbol to the left of the Columns folder. You should see something like *Figure 6.2.*

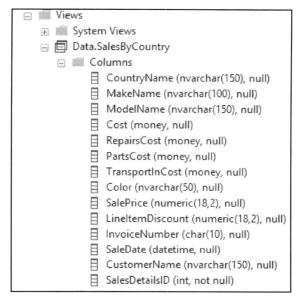

Figure 6.2: *Displaying the columns in a view and their data types*

You can see that the columns you used in the query in the previous section (Cost, RepairsCost, PartsCost, TransportInCost, SalePrice, and LineItemDiscount) are all one of the two following data types:

- Money
- Numeric

This is good news because these are two of SQL Server's numeric data types. The following are other numeric data types:

- Float
- Decimal
- Int
- Tinyint
- Bigint
- Smallint
- SmallMoney

As long as the columns you want to use in a calculation are any of these data types, then your calculation should not give you an error.

There are, inevitably, many other SQL Server data types, but I prefer to introduce them as the need arises rather than overwhelm you with technical details this early in your SQL querying career.

6.3 Isolating Sections of Formulas When Applying Math

Now let's return to the finance director's analysis of costs. He was pleased with your cost of sales calculation. However, he wants you to subtract this from the sale price to give the net margin. The piece of code that follows delivers exactly what he is looking for. As you can see, it groups certain elements inside parentheses to isolate parts of the formula so that they are calculated independently of the rest.

```
SELECT   MakeName, ModelName
         ,SalePrice - (Cost + RepairsCost + PartsCost + TransportInCost)
         AS GrossMargin
FROM     Data.SalesByCountry
```

If you run this code, you should get the output in *Figure 6.3*.

	MakeName	ModelName	GrossMargin
1	Ferrari	Testarossa	8575.0000
2	Ferrari	355	34350.0000
3	Porsche	911	3090.0000
4	Porsche	924	900.0000
5	Porsche	944	1980.0000
6	Aston Martin	DB4	4500.0000
7	Aston Martin	DB5	5350.0000
8	Aston Martin	DB6	10450.0000
9	Porsche	911	2380.0000
10	Aston Martin	DB5	4300.0000
11	Porsche	944	1075.0000
12	Aston Martin	DB6	6450.0000
13	Bentley	Flying Spur	14100.0000
14	Ferrari	355	24250.0000
15	Porsche	944	390.0000

Figure 6.3: *Nesting calculations to guarantee precedence in SQL math*

How It Works

Even simple arithmetic may require that certain elements of the calculation have to be worked out before others. Adding parentheses around the cost elements guarantees that the fields containing the vehicle costs will be added together before the resulting figure is subtracted from the sale price. I realize that this may seem obvious and that you are probably used to creating calculations like this in Excel. However, I prefer to make it clear from the start that all calculations in SQL Server can be "nested" in parentheses like this to force an order of precedence in your arithmetic. This way, certain parts of the calculation are carried out before others.

Tricks and Traps

As simple as the math is, here are a couple of key points to note:

- It is always safer to nest fields inside parentheses rather than to trust a computer to get things right every time. Not only that, but adding parentheses to "nest" calculation elements can help you to make your logic clearer, especially when you return to it weeks or even months later.

- Any calculation really should have a meaningful alias. This, too, can help you better understand the logic when you look at it again in days to come.

6.4 Calculating Ratios

The finance director is getting more and more excited at the thought that SQL can apply the math he needs for his analyses. So, now he wants you to give him a list containing the ratio of cost to sales (this is also known as the cost of goods sold ratio or the cost of sales to revenue ratio). As this is quite simply the gross profit (that you calculated in the previous section) divided by the sale price, the SQL for this is as follows:

```
SELECT    (SalePrice - (Cost + RepairsCost + PartsCost
          + TransportInCost))
          / SalePrice AS RatioOfCostsToSales
FROM      Data.SalesByCountry
```

When you run this code, SQL Server gives you the output shown in *Figure 6.4.*

	RatioOfCostsToSales
1	0.13192307692307692230
2	0.15613636363636363636363
3	0.15846153846153846153846615
4	0.07826086956521739131
5	0.09924812030075187960
6	0.15254237288135593222
7	0.10808080808080808080808
8	0.13750000000000000000
9	0.12142857142857142850
10	0.11780821917808219171
11	0.12647058823529411760
12	0.14333333333333333333
13	0.17515527950031055900
14	0.14306784660766961650
15	0.04357541899441340780

Figure 6.4: Calculating a ratio

How It Works

As you have already seen addition and subtraction, now is a good time to move on to simple division in SQL. This formula is a three-step process.

First:	It adds up the total costs per vehicle (the field names nested inside the inner parentheses).
Second:	It subtracts the cost of sales from the sale price. This calculation is contained in the outer parentheses and is the gross margin
Finally:	It divides the gross margin by the sale price to return the cost ratio per vehicle.

The result is that you see the ratio of costs to sale for every vehicle sold. For the moment, the result has no formatting applied, and consequently it looks much as it probably would in a spreadsheet. I fully realize that raw data can be hard to read. However, we will look at formatting output in Chapters 10 and 21so that you can concentrate on the calculation techniques for the moment.

6.5 Increasing Values by a Defined Percentage

To finish your tour of elementary math in SQL, let's imagine that the sales director wants to test the improvement in margins if you increased the sale prices by 5 percent but kept costs the same. The SQL formula that does this is shown here:

```
SELECT  (SalePrice * 1.05)
        - (Cost + RepairsCost + PartsCost + TransportInCost)
        AS ImprovedSalesMargins
FROM    Data.SalesByCountry
```

When you execute this code, you should get something like the result shown *Figure 6.5.*

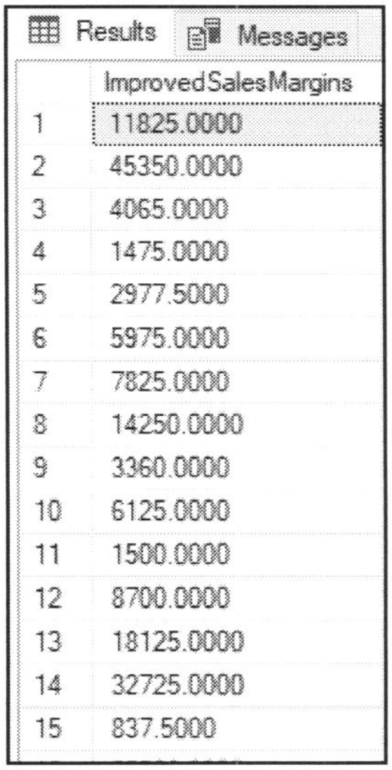

	ImprovedSalesMargins
1	11825.0000
2	45350.0000
3	4065.0000
4	1475.0000
5	2977.5000
6	5975.0000
7	7825.0000
8	14250.0000
9	3360.0000
10	6125.0000
11	1500.0000
12	8700.0000
13	18125.0000
14	32725.0000
15	837.5000

Figure 6.5: *"What if" calculations in SQL*

How It Works

This formula extends the gross margin calculation you created earlier and multiplies the sale price by 5 percent. It is, to all intents and purposes, a "what if" projection. In practice (and just as you would in a spreadsheet), this means the following:

First:	Take the existing formula and add the asterisk (*) as the multiplication operator after the SalePrice field.
Second:	Type in 1.05 to "hard-code" the 5 percent increase (100 and 5 percent, literally).
Third:	Nest this projected sale price calculation in parentheses to ensure that it is calculated correctly—and separately—from the rest of the formula.
Finally:	The cost elements are added together. These fields are also enclosed in parentheses to guarantee that this calculation is carried out independently of the remainder of the formula. Then the total cost is subtracted from the increased sale price to give the increased margin.

One other thing that this formula teaches you is that you can mix static values and fields in SQL formulas. To extend the spreadsheet analogy that we have been using so far in this chapter, you can mix references and values in a formula in SQL just as you can in Excel.

6.6 Ordering the Output of Calculations

Knowing even the most basic math in SQL can help you unlock real insights. As an example, let's see how using the knowledge—and SQL techniques—that you have seen so far in this chapter can be used to produce the list of the 50 most profitable sales in percentage terms. Here is the SQL to deliver this:

```
SELECT TOP 50 MakeName
         ,(SalePrice - (Cost + RepairsCost + PartsCost
           + TransportInCost))
         / SalePrice AS Profitability
FROM     Data.SalesByCountry
ORDER BY Profitability DESC
```

Executing this code should return the data shown in *Figure 6.6* (and if you scroll through the output, you will see that it contains only 50 records).

	MakeName	Profitability
1	Aston Martin	0.187014701998415353 4
2	Lamborghini	0.183921568627450980 3
3	Lamborghini	0.183191489361702127 6
4	Ferrari	0.181780821917808219 1
5	Bugatti	0.181641791044776119 4
6	Ferrari	0.181400000000000000 0
7	Aston Martin	0.180000000000000000 0
8	Ferrari	0.179899497487437185 9
9	Mercedes	0.179600000000000000 0
10	Bentley	0.179155672823218997 3
11	Aston Martin	0.178181818181818181 8
12	Aston Martin	0.178000000000000000 0
13	Rolls Royce	0.177653631284916201 1
14	Lamborghini	0.177142857142857142 8
15	Bugatti	0.177081159420289855 0

Figure 6.6: *Sorting on a calculated column*

How It Works

This formula combines many of the techniques you have seen in this chapter as well as previous chapters.

First:	It calculates the ratio of costs to sales as described previously.
Second:	It orders the output by this ratio (which you have aliased, which means that you can now use the alias to sort the results).
Third:	It finishes by limiting the number of rows returned to 50 using the TOP keyword.
Finally:	The ORDER BY keyword—with DESC to specify that the sort is from greatest to smallest figure—presents the data in descending order.

The useful trick here is to mix the TOP and ORDER BY keywords. As you are requesting that the data is output from the most profitable through to the least profitable sale, the top 50 will—by definition—be the 50 most profitable sales.

In this example, I have deliberately chosen not to display all the 50 records that the query returns. However, you can scroll through the result set in the query window if you want to check that only 50 records are displayed.

Tricks and Traps

There is one major point to note when you are sorting on the result of a calculation.

- When sorting the output in a query, you can—fortunately—sort on the column alias that you have applied to a calculation. If you do not apply an alias, you will have to `repeat the entire calculation in the ORDER BY clause` to sort on the calculation. In other words, if you had not specified that the calculated column was named Profitability, then you would have had to create an ORDER BY clause like this:

```
ORDER BY (SalePrice - (Cost + RepairsCost + PartsCost
            + TransportInCost))
         / SalePrice DESC
```

6.7 Handling Missing Data

The sales director has lost her sunny optimism. She has stormed over to your desk and asked how it can be possible that a top-of-the-range sports car can cost nothing. To prove her point, she scrolls down the output from the query that you wrote to calculate gross margin (in section 4) and points at the records shown in *Figure 6.7*.

	MakeName	ModelName	GrossMargin
315	Jaguar	Mark V	3223.0000
316	Jaguar	XK150	4340.0000
317	Jaguar	XK120	8500.0000
318	Triumph	TR5	500.0000
319	Triumph	TR5	380.0000
320	Triumph	TR4	300.0000
321	Aston Martin	DB9	10350.0000
322	Aston Martin	Virage	18800.0000
323	Aston Martin	DB9	16910.0000
324	Aston Martin	DB6	9091.0000
325	Trabant	600	-1082.0000
326	Triumph	TR5	900.0000
327	Alfa Romeo	Giulietta	390.0000
328	Citroen	Rosalie	-300.0000
329	Reliant	Robin	-1210.0000
330	Ferrari	Daytona	NULL	— Missing Value

Figure 6.7: The effect of NULLs on a calculation

NULLs

The calculations you have tried on the sample database have ideally worked smoothly. However, this may not always be the case in the real world of less than perfect data.

This is because we have up until now glossed over a database concept that lies in wait to trap the unwary. This potential problem is called NULL handling.

Put simply, fields (columns if you prefer) can contain no data at all in some cases. For instance, the RepairsCost column could be nothing for a particular vehicle. In this case, the value contained in the data table would be NULL. In database terms, this means "I don't know what this value is." It is a techie way of saying "nothing."

This in itself is not a problem. It simply means that there is no corresponding value and that NULL will be output for this particular column if you write a query that selects this record.

However, things get complicated if you try to perform a calculation on a record where one or more of the numeric values that you are using contains a NULL. If this is the case, then the entire calculation will return NULL. In effect, all the calculation is nullified, and nothing at all is calculated. It is almost as if a NULL has a contagious effect that infects the entire calculation that contains it.

This can be extremely disconcerting in practice because it is probably not what you are expecting. Indeed, if you are used to spreadsheet calculations where an empty cell makes virtually no difference (unexcept in a few cases), then this result probably comes as a most unwelcome surprise.

Unfortunately, this is the effect that a NULL has produced in a calculation. One car does not have a repairs cost. However, instead of ignoring this—or treating it as a zero—SQL invalidates the `whole calculation` for that record.

There is a safeguard that you can apply to your calculations to prevent NULLs from distorting the results you were expecting. The solution involves wrapping numeric fields inside the SQL ISNULL() function to convert any NULL values in a field to another value that you specify. When handling NULLs in calculations, this nearly always means replacing the NULL with a zero.

To show you how this can be done, here is the SQL from the previous section using the ISNULL() function to prevent errors from creeping into the calculation this time:

```
SELECT    MakeName, ModelName
          ,Cost + RepairsCost + ISNULL(PartsCost, 0)  + TransportInCost
          AS TotalCost
FROM      Data.SalesByCountry
```

This code returns the records shown in *Figure 6.8*.

327	Alfa Romeo	Giulietta	17560.00
328	Citroen	Rosalie	5800.00
329	Reliant	Robin	2160.00
330	Ferrari	Daytona	121900.00

Figure 6.8: *Using the ISNULL() function*

How It Works

This query uses the SalesByCountry view that you used previously to avoid having to join several tables. It is almost identical to the query from section 1; the only difference is that the PartsCost field (that contains NULL values) is wrapped in the ISNULL() function so that any NULLs will be converted to zeros—thus ensuring that the calculation will work correctly for every record (as a zero has no effect on an arithmetical calculation).

You have seen a few functions in previous chapters. The ISNULL() function works like the functions you have already met, with one major difference. The ISNULL() function needs you to place `two elements` inside the parentheses.

A field or value	In this case, it is the numeric field that can contain NULLs.
A replacement value	In this case, it is a 0 (zero).

When you enclose the PartsCost field inside the ISNULL() function, you are saying "If the PartsCost field contains a NULL, then use a zero instead." This way the calculation will add a zero to the costs that you are adding up instead of making the calculation fail for any record with a NULL in the PartsCost field.

Note: You can, of course, wrap any numeric field used in a calculation in the ISNULL() function as a simple precaution against SQL Server returning a NULL value rather than the result that you were expecting.

Tricks and Traps

As you will be using more and more SQL functions as you continue through this book, you need to be aware of a few core principles that underlie their use.

- The elements that are inside the parentheses of any function are called `parameters` that you pass in to the function. The first parameter that the ISNULL() function requires is the field that it must be applied to, and the second parameter (after the comma) is the number to apply if the field is NULL.

- In most cases, the parameters you use in functions are compulsory. That is, if you do not add a parameter, all you will get is an error message.

- Geeks call using a parameter in a function like this parameter passing.

6.8 Filtering on a Calculation

It is hard to argue with the idea that there is no more fundamental business metric than profitability. So, it will come as no surprise to learn that the CEO of Prestige Cars Ltd. wants to know what the net profit is on sales. She particularly wants to see a list of sales for all vehicles making a profit of more than £5,000.00. This SQL snippet shows you how to keep her happy:

```
SELECT      DISTINCT MK.MakeName, MD.ModelName, SD.SalePrice

FROM        Data.Make AS MK

INNER JOIN Data.Model AS MD ON MK.MakeID = MD.MakeID

INNER JOIN Data.Stock AS ST ON ST.ModelID = MD.ModelID

INNER JOIN Data.SalesDetails SD ON ST.StockCode = SD.StockID

WHERE       SD.SalePrice -

            (ST.Cost + ST.RepairsCost + ISNULL(ST.PartsCost, 0)

            + ST.TransportInCost) > 5000
```

If you execute this piece of SQL, you will see data similar to the output shown in *Figure 6.9*.

	MakeName	ModelName	SalePrice
1	Aston Martin	DB2	39500.00
2	Aston Martin	DB2	45000.00
3	Aston Martin	DB2	45950.00
4	Aston Martin	DB2	49500.00
5	Aston Martin	DB2	52500.00
6	Aston Martin	DB2	61500.00
7	Aston Martin	DB2	62500.00
8	Aston Martin	DB2	99990.00
9	Aston Martin	DB4	36500.00
10	Aston Martin	DB4	42500.00
11	Aston Martin	DB4	46900.00
12	Aston Martin	DB4	56850.00
13	Aston Martin	DB4	56950.00
14	Aston Martin	DB5	42950.00
15	Aston Martin	DB5	45000.00

Figure 6.9: Filtering on a calculation

How It Works

SQL can also use calculations in WHERE clauses to filter data. As our data does not contain the figure for the net profit, we must calculate this metric "on the fly" if we want to use it as a filter criterion.

This query shows how you can use calculated data to filter the data that is returned by a SQL query. The SQL calculates the net profit by adding up all the costs and then deducting this figure from the sale price. If the result exceeds 5000, then the record is displayed. As we want to show the make and model, we need to join the Make and Model tables, and as we want to see actual sales (and not stock), we need to join the SalesDetails table to the Stock table as well.

Tricks and Traps

The one point you need to take away from this example is this:

- You do not have to add the calculation used in a WHERE clause to a SELECT clause. However, it can be useful to start out by adding the calculation to the output so that you can verify the result.

6.9 Using Complex Calculated Filters

It is late in the day, and you are thinking of heading home. Just as your eyes drift toward the door, in rushes the sales director with a seemingly interminable request for data. She wants a list of all car makes and models sold where the profit exceeds £5,000.00 and the car is red and the discount greater than or equal to £1,000.00 or the repairs cost and the parts cost are greater than £500.00.

This query is an extension of the code used in the previous example. So, you can build on your previous experience and discover that even seemingly complex requests often require nothing more than a well-thought-out WHERE clause to deliver the required result. The code you need is given here:

```
SELECT     DISTINCT MK.MakeName, MD.ModelName
FROM       Data.Make AS MK
INNER JOIN Data.Model AS MD ON MK.MakeID = MD.MakeID
INNER JOIN Data.Stock AS ST ON ST.ModelID = MD.ModelID
INNER JOIN Data.SalesDetails SD ON ST.StockCode = SD.StockID
WHERE      (ST.Color = 'Red' AND SD.LineItemDiscount >= 1000
           AND (SD.SalePrice - (ST.Cost + ST.RepairsCost + ST.PartsCost
                          + ST.TransportInCost)) > 5000)
             OR (ST.PartsCost > 500 AND ST.RepairsCost > 500)
```

Running this query should show something like *Figure 6.10.*

	MakeName	ModelName
1	Alfa Romeo	Giulia
2	Alfa Romeo	Giulietta
3	Aston Martin	DB2
4	Aston Martin	DB5
5	Aston Martin	DB6
6	Aston Martin	DB9
7	Aston Martin	Rapide
8	Aston Martin	Vanquish
9	Aston Martin	Vantage
10	Aston Martin	Virage
11	Austin	Cambridge
12	Austin	Lichfield
13	Bentley	Arnage
14	Bentley	Brooklands
15	Bentley	Continental

Figure 6.10: *A complex query filtering on several fields and a calculation*

How It Works

This query starts by joining all the tables that we need either to display output (Make and Model) or to use in a filter (SalesDetails and Stock—or both). It then applies the WHERE clause to filter records where

Either	The color of the vehicle is red, the discount greater than £1,000.00, and the net profit over £5,000.00
Or	The parts and repair cost are greater than £500.00

As you can see, the focus of this query is on the WHERE clause. Inside this clause it is worth paying particular attention to the parentheses that are used. The filters on either side of the OR operator are enclosed in parentheses. This means all the conditions inside the parentheses must be true for the filter to be successful. Consequently, the parts cost must be more than 500 as must the repair cost for a sale to make the grade. Alternatively, all the three conditions for the other filter (red; discount of 1,000 or more; and profit of at least 5,000) must be met for the record to make it through to the final output.

The only potentially tricky aspect of this query is the way you have to "nest" criteria inside parentheses to obtain the result you are looking for. This can take a little practice, but the effort is well worth it. Of course, if you have any experience writing formulas using Microsoft Excel or Access, then you are probably used to this concept already. In any case, breaking down filter requirements into logical, isolated steps is a key part of learning to write efficient SQL.

Tricks and Traps

Complex WHERE clauses can become easier to understand and simpler to write if you remember the following points:

- When you have to produce complex WHERE clauses, it may help to begin by isolating the "levels" of the logic over several lines, as you can see in *Figure 6.11*.

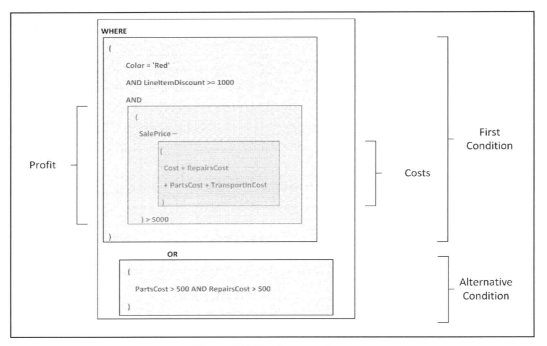

Figure 6.11: Nesting parentheses

- Even a complicated query is nothing more than a series of component parts that you assemble to apply a filter based on a set of criteria. Our advice when faced with complex queries is to try to break them down into their constituent elements and to try to understand what is required before you start writing SQL code.

- It can help if you first try to write out the filter as "pseudo-code"—that is, more as a description of the required logic than an exact and accurate piece of SQL. This can help you to understand the underlying requirements of the filter and how to

- o Create all the individual comparison elements that make up the whole
- o Group the filter elements so that they respect the final logic that is required
- In this query, we chose not to add the fields that were used in the WHERE clause to the query output. You can, of course, add them to check that the filter is working if you so desire.

The Query Window

By now you are probably getting used to using the SSMS query window to enter and modify queries. However, you can take several approaches when working with SSMS queries. You can do the following:

Delete the existing contents of the query window and enter a new query.

Close the query window (by selecting File➤Close or clicking the Close icon—the small X—to the right of the query window tab). Then open a new query window.

Open a new query window and enter the query into the blank query window. This way you can switch between the queries that you have written.

Enter a new query under the existing query and then `select the query text` before executing the query. This will execute `only` the code you have selected and not the entire query.

Save and reopen queries just like you would a document in Microsoft Word. Any queries created with SSMS will have the extension .sql.

The way you choose to work is up to you. The results will always be the same. You will be querying your data whichever approach you take.

Nonetheless, you might find it useful when learning SQL to open separate query windows. This will allow you to copy and paste queries into separate windows where you can extend and tweak the SQL—while keeping the original for reference or as a fallback should you need to revert to it.

It is worth noting that you can have multiple separate queries in the same query window. However, if you execute the SQL without selecting only part of the code first, you will be running `all the queries` that are in the window. There is nothing wrong with this, but it means you will return all the data from all the queries in the query output as multiple windows in the lower pane of the query window. This can get confusing until you are used to it. So, I advise, at least when beginning SQL, to apply the principle of one query per query window. This lets you focus on the SQL and not on the interface.

6.10 Writing Accurate SQL Code Faster

Producing good SQL requires a certain attention to detail. As you have probably noticed already, the slightest error will make your code not only refuse to deliver the results that you were expecting but also return extremely irritating error messages.

Fortunately, SQL Server Management Studio can help you face up to the challenge of avoiding basic coding errors. It can do this in these two ways:

- Letting you drag and drop table and field names from the database in the Object Explorer (left-hand) window into a query window

- Suggesting table and field names as you type them into a query

Suppose you want to show the country names from the Country table. One way to do this with very little typing is as follows:

1. Expand the PrestigeCars database in the Object Explorer window and then expand the Tables folder.

2. Expand the Data.Country table and then expand the Columns folder.

3. Open a new query window.

4. Enter SELECT and a space.

5. Drag the CountryName field from the Object Explorer window and drop it after the SELECT keyword. The field name will appear and will be enclosed in square brackets.

6. Click to the right of the CountryName field (or press the right arrow to unselect it).

7. Press the Return key to begin a new line and enter FROM.

8. Drag the Data.Country table from the Object Explorer window and drop it after the FROM keyword. The table name will appear and will be enclosed in square brackets. The query should look like it does in *Figure 6.12*.

Figure 6.12: Using drag and drop to create queries

9. Execute the query.

Alternatively, you can use the SSMS autocomplete feature to help you write SQL. Here is how to write the same code snippet but selecting the table and field names from those that SSMS will suggest for you:

1. Open a new query window.

2. Type SELECT followed by a space.

3. Press the Return key to begin a new line and enter FROM.

4. Enter a space and start typing the word Data. After a couple of characters, SSMS will start listing everything it can think of (including SQL keywords that you did not know even existed). The query should look like it does in *Figure 6.13*.

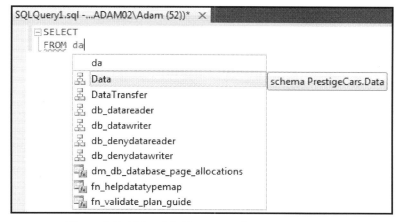

Figure 6.13: *Using SSMS autocomplete to create queries*

5. Click Data in the autocomplete menu.

6. Enter a period. The list of all the tables and views that are available to use in the Data schema will appear. You can see this in *Figure 6.14*.

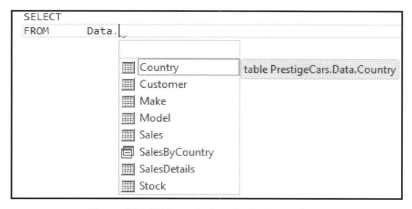

Figure 6.14: *Tables and views in the Data schema*

7. Double-click the Country table (or select it and press the Tab key).

8. Click after the SELECT keyword and type the letter C. Autocomplete will prompt you with a menu of all the column names that begin with C.

9. Double-click Country (or select it and press the Tab key).

You can add any number of fields or tables this way in an SSMS query window. All you have to do is to add the core SQL keywords (such as SELECT, FROM, INNER JOIN, and ON, for instance), and SSMS can then help you to craft your queries quickly and accurately.

Tricks and Traps

You need to remember these points when using SSMS to help you write your SQL:

- You may well be used to using autocomplete in other applications. However, in case it is new to you, remember that the more characters you enter when selecting tables or fields, the narrower the selection of available elements (or objects as they are known in technical circles) will be.

- When you drag and drop table or field names into the query window, SSMS automatically wraps them in square brackets. This has no effect on the query and is simply a way of ensuring that if table and field names do not contain any spaces or nonstandard characters, then the query is nonetheless likely to work correctly.

Conclusion

In this chapter, you saw some of the ways that SQL can be used to carry out simple arithmetic. You learned how to perform basic math using the data in fields as well as values that you add to your code to perform calculations across multiple rows and columns in a few lines of code.

You also saw how to pre-empt errors when the source data contains NULLs or when attempting to divide by zero in a calculation.

All in all, you have already made vast strides toward the basic analysis of SQL Server data. With this knowledge safely acquired, it is time to move on to the next step—aggregating data to deliver totals, subtotals, and other simple calculations. This is what you will be looking at in the next chapter.

Core Knowledge Learned in This Chapter

These are the fundamental keywords you have learned to use in this chapter:

Concept	Description
+	This is the arithmetical addition symbol; it adds two elements (fields or values).
-	This is the arithmetical subtraction symbol; it subtracts tw elements (fields or values).
*	This is the arithmetical multiplication symbol; it multiplies two elements (fields or values).
/	This is the arithmetical division symbol; it divides two elements (fields or values).
ISNULL()	This converts NULL (or empty) values into a value that can be used in your calculations.
Parentheses	Parentheses are used in calculations to force certain parts of a formula to be calculated before others.

CHAPTER 7
Aggregating Output

A nalyzing data consists of much more than just selecting records from a database. There is no denying that you have to start by choosing the right columns from the right tables, joining the tables correctly, and of course filtering the data accurately. However, SQL really starts to deliver true insights when you begin to aggregate data so that you can see the high-level figures that drive your business.

Aggregating Data in SQL

It is well worth looking at how SQL can aggregate metrics. This is because it is particularly good at returning totals, averages, and a multitude of analytical insights with little effort—and often in a short time. In this chapter, you will start to explore the basic techniques that you can use to apply aggregations to your data and to deliver real insight straight from the database. More specifically, you will learn how to

- Generate grand totals
- Group elements with aggregate totals
- Count categories of elements
- Find maximum and minimum values
- Calculate averages

- Select data using aggregated results
- Filter data on aggregated values

So, without further ado, it is time to discover how SQL can aggregate data in many different ways at multiple levels to deliver the analysis you need.

7.1 Calculating Table Totals

To begin with (and, you guessed it, following a call from the finance director), let's suppose that you want to calculate the total cost of all the vehicles that have ever been stocked by Prestige Cars Ltd. The SQL looks like this:

```
SELECT      SUM(Cost) AS TotalCost
FROM        Data.Stock
```

Running this query gives the results shown in *Figure 7.1.*

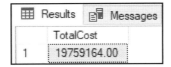

Figure 7.1: *Using the SUM() function to calculate the total for a field*

How It Works

Adding up a column of figures is easy to do in SQL. You can use the SUM() function on any numeric field in a table to get the total of the values in the column. In this example, the SUM() function was applied to the Cost field of the Stock table. The result is simply the total—the sum—of all the available figures in the Cost field (or column if you prefer) of the Stock table. What you did is to wrap up the name of the field that you wanted to add inside the parentheses that are part of the SUM function. This simple modification was all that SQL Server needed to return the `total`, rather than the detail for each record.

Tricks and Traps

As this is the first time you have used a function to aggregate data, you need to be aware of the following essential points:

- SUM() is what is known as an `aggregation` function—it returns a single value for a calculation across a set of values (a field in this case). This makes it different from the functions you have seen so far in this book. Up until now, any function was applied to each record in a table. Functions like

SUM() do not work at such a detailed level and cannot show the detail of each individual row. They exist only to provide a high-level aggregation of values.

- The SUM() function requires numeric values to work. If you try to calculate the total of a text field, then SQL Server will only return an error message.

- It is always a good idea to provide an alias for aggregation functions because SQL will never display a name for an aggregated column unless you provide one. Instead, it will add the column heading "no column name."

7.2 Using Calculated Aggregations

Muttering that he is too busy to copy formulas down over hundreds of records in a spreadsheet, the finance director has tasked you with extending the previous example to calculate the aggregate sales, cost, and gross profit for all vehicles sold. Fortunately, you can use multiple aggregate expressions in the same query. Here is the SQL to do this:

```
SELECT      SUM(ST.Cost) AS TotalCost
            ,SUM(SD.SalePrice) AS TotalSales
            ,SUM(SD.SalePrice) - SUM(ST.Cost) AS GrossProfit
FROM        Data.Stock ST
INNER JOIN  Data.SalesDetails SD
            ON ST.StockCode = SD.StockID
```

Executing this query gives the results displayed in *Figure 7.2*.

Figure 7.2: *Calculating the total for several fields using SUM()*

How It Works

This code snippet shows you that you can return the total for any numeric field from any table in a query. This piece of SQL is also a reminder that joining tables acts as a filter (as you saw in Chapter 3). In this example, the filter effect means you only see result where vehicles appear in both the Stock and SalesDetails tables—that is, you only see the totals for cars that have actually been sold. As a final touch, this piece of code calculates aggregations by subtracting the total purchase cost from the total sale price.

As the SQL makes clear, you can apply aggregation functions such as SUM() to several columns and then apply calculations to the aggregated value just as you did to nonaggregated fields in the previous chapter.

Tricks and Traps

There are a couple of cool features you will like when using aggregation functions. So, be aware of the following:

- One great feature of the SUM() function (and this applies to all the aggregation functions that you will meet in this chapter) is that it handles NULL values without affecting the result. If you remember, a NULL in a calculation will make the result of the calculation into NULL too. However, any number of NULLs in a column that you aggregate using SUM() will not cause any difficulties at all—unlike normal SQL math.

- It is important to wrap each numeric column inside its own SUM function when carrying out calculations on aggregated values. In theory, you could have expressed the calculation as follows:

  ```
  SUM(SD.SalePrice - ST.Cost)
  ```

This code may appear to work at first sight if you try it. However, it is **not guaranteed** to work in all circumstances. This is because NULL values in a column are handled without difficulty by the SUM() function only if `each column` is wrapped inside its own SUM(). So this approach could return an erroneous result if there are NULL values in a field.

7.3 Using Grouped Aggregations

The sales manager has just emailed you an apparently simple request for data. She wants the aggregate cost for each model of car. The next piece of SQL shows you just how easy this is to segment your data this way with SQL:

```
SELECT     MD.ModelName, SUM(ST.Cost) AS TotalCost
FROM       Data.Stock ST
INNER JOIN Data.Model MD ON MD.ModelID = ST.ModelID
GROUP BY   MD.ModelName
```

If you run this query, you should see the results shown in *Figure 7.3.*

	ModelName	TotalCost
1	135	20400.00
2	145	55200.00
3	175	28120.00
4	1750	10820.00
5	203	2560.00
6	205	5720.00
7	250SL	28440.00
8	280SL	216232.00
9	308	156000.00
10	350SL	109380.00
11	355	1078720.00
12	360	415600.00
13	400GT	116000.00
14	404	10356.00
15	500	4196.00

Figure 7.3: *Grouping aggregated results using GROUP BY*

How It Works

The previous two examples showed you that SQL can calculate the grand total for a column in one or more tables easily and quickly. In practice, however, you will probably want to analyze results broken down into separate categories. In this query, you joined the Model and Stock tables (so that you could see the model name, and not just a code) and output the model name and the total cost. Then you added a new keyword—GROUP BY—to the end of the SQL statement. Simply adding another field that is `not being aggregated` (usually a text field) to the GROUP BY clause is enough for SQL Server to calculate the total for each individual element in the field that is `not` wrapped in an aggregate function.

While not strictly necessary, it is normal—most of the time—to add the field that you are grouping on to the SELECT statement so that you can see which figure corresponds to which aggregated element.

Tricks and Traps

There is only one potential trap for the unwary in code that groups data.

- It is `vital` that any nonaggregated fields in the SELECT clause (the ones that are not enclosed in aggregation functions such as SUM) are repeated in the GROUP BY clause. If you do not do this, then SQL Server will complain by showing an error message such as this:

```
Msg 8120, Level 16, State 1, Line 1
Column 'Data.Model.ModelName' is invalid in the select list
because it is not contained in either an aggregate function or
the GROUP BY clause.
```

Fortunately, this is one of the more comprehensible error messages. It is simply telling you to make sure that any fields that you output have to be either in the GROUP BY clause or wrapped in an aggregation function if they are numeric.

7.4 Using Multiple Levels of Grouping

Fired up by the analysis you have provided so far, the finance director wants you to dig deeper into the data and compare the total purchase cost for every make and model of vehicle sold. This is easier than you might think, as the following code illustrates:

```
SELECT     MK.MakeName, MD.ModelName, SUM(ST.Cost) AS TotalCost
FROM       Data.Stock ST
INNER JOIN Data.Model MD ON MD.ModelID = ST.ModelID
INNER JOIN Data.Make AS MK ON MK.MakeID = MD.MakeID
GROUP BY   MK.MakeName, MD.ModelName
```

Executing this query should return the results in *Figure 7.4*.

	MakeName	ModelName	TotalCost
1	Delahaye	135	20400.00
2	Delahaye	145	55200.00
3	Delahaye	175	28120.00
4	Alfa Romeo	1750	10820.00
5	Peugeot	203	2560.00
6	Peugeot	205	5720.00
7	Mercedes	250SL	28440.00
8	Mercedes	280SL	216232.00
9	Ferrari	308	156000.00
10	Mercedes	350SL	109380.00
11	Ferrari	355	1078720.00
12	Ferrari	360	415600.00
13	Lamborghini	400GT	116000.00
14	Peugeot	404	10356.00
15	Trabant	500	4196.00

Figure 7.4: Grouping on multiple fields

How It Works

This SQL snippet shows you that you can extend the grouping principle by adding as many nonaggregated fields as you want to a query. Each field that you add to the SELECT clause (and also to the GROUP BY clause) will entail a deeper level of detail in the output—giving you a hierarchical analysis of your data.

As you can see in the results from the query, the total sales appear for each model by make. So, grouping data on multiple fields in effect creates a hierarchy in the output. This hierarchy corresponds to the order in which the fields are entered in the GROUP BY clause. In other words, the first field (MakeName) is the topmost level in the hierarchy, and then ModelName is the second level.

Tricks and Traps

Grouping on multiple fields comes easily with a little practice. Nonetheless, it can help to remember the following:

- It is important to add the fields you are aggregating in a coherent order in both the SELECT clause and the GROUP BY clause. This is because the output will be perceived as a logical hierarchy by your users. In practice, this means starting with the highest level on the left and working down through successive lower levels of data. This is because users probably expect a model to be a subdivision of a make of car—and not the reverse.

- Although you do not have to apply the same order for the fields you are using to segment data in the SELECT and GROUP BY clauses, it is generally best to keep them identical—for the sake of the person viewing the data. This is because it can become extremely confusing if you sort the data using one kind of sequence and then display the fields in another. In any case, the actual hierarchy is defined by the fields in the GROUP BY clause, whatever the sequence of the fields in the SELECT clause.

- Once again, it is best to add an alias to any field that is the result of an aggregation.

7.5 Calculating Averages

An essential business metric is the average cost of goods bought. So, it was inevitable that the finance director would want to see the average purchase price of every make and model of car ever bought. Fortunately, SQL makes this kind of calculation easy—as the following piece of code illustrates:

```
SELECT      MK.MakeName, MD.ModelName
            ,AVG(ST.Cost) AS AverageCost
```

```
FROM       Data.Make AS MK
INNER JOIN Data.Model AS MD ON MK.MakeID = MD.MakeID
INNER JOIN Data.Stock AS ST ON ST.ModelID = MD.ModelID
GROUP BY   MK.MakeName, MD.ModelName
```

Running this query should return the results shown in *Figure 7.5.*

	MakeName	ModelName	AverageCost
1	Delahaye	135	20400.00
2	Delahaye	145	27600.00
3	Delahaye	175	14060.00
4	Alfa Romeo	1750	5410.00
5	Peugeot	203	1280.00
6	Peugeot	205	1906.6666
7	Mercedes	250SL	14220.00
8	Mercedes	280SL	30890.2857
9	Ferrari	308	156000.00
10	Mercedes	350SL	21876.00
11	Ferrari	355	134840.00
12	Ferrari	360	103900.00
13	Lamborghini	400GT	116000.00
14	Peugeot	404	1726.00
15	Trabant	500	1398.6666

Figure 7.5: Calculating the average purchase price using the AVG() function

How It Works

This code snippet introduces another aggregation function: AVG(). As its name implies, the AVG() function calculates the average of the values in a column.

Once again, all the required tables are joined in the FROM clause of the query. Then any required fields that will be used to aggregate the data added to the SELECT and GROUP BY clauses. Finally, the AVG() function is "wrapped" around the Cost field from the Stock table to calculate the average purchase price of every make and model.

Tricks and Traps

One thing may surprise you when grouping and aggregating with SQL Server.

- Although you may see output that is sorted as you expect when using a GROUP BY clause there is no guarantee that this will always be the case. So, to be sure, you should always add an ORDER BY clause.

7.6 Counting Grouped Elements

The CEO has stated categorically that any business must be able to see at a glance how many items have been sold per product category. In the case of Prestige Cars Ltd., this means visualizing the number of cars sold by make and model. SQL can answer these kinds of questions with consummate ease, as the following SQL snippet shows:

```
SELECT      MK.MakeName, MD.ModelName
            ,COUNT(SD.SalesDetailsID) AS NumberofCarsSold
FROM        Data.Make AS MK
INNER JOIN  Data.Model AS MD ON MK.MakeID = MD.MakeID
INNER JOIN  Data.Stock AS ST ON ST.ModelID = MD.ModelID
INNER JOIN  Data.SalesDetails SD ON ST.StockCode = SD.StockID
GROUP BY    MK.MakeName, MD.ModelName
ORDER BY    MK.MakeName, MD.ModelName
```

Running this query should return the results in *Figure 7.6*.

	MakeName	ModelName	NumberofCarsSold
1	Alfa Romeo	1750	2
2	Alfa Romeo	Giulia	8
3	Alfa Romeo	Giulietta	7
4	Alfa Romeo	Spider	5
5	Aston Martin	DB2	8
6	Aston Martin	DB4	7
7	Aston Martin	DB5	6
8	Aston Martin	DB6	14
9	Aston Martin	DB9	15
10	Aston Martin	Rapide	4
11	Aston Martin	Vanquish	7
12	Aston Martin	Vantage	4
13	Aston Martin	Virage	12
14	Austin	Cambridge	1
15	Austin	Lichfield	2

Figure 7.6: Counting cars by model using the COUNT() function

How It Works

The SQL aggregation functions are not limited to just adding up columns of numbers. You can also count the number of records that make up a subset of data. So, this piece of SQL introduces the COUNT() aggregation function. As its name implies, it counts the number of rows in a group of records, rather than adding up any figures.

The trick in this piece of SQL is to use exactly the same grouping element in the GROUP BY clause as in the SELECT clause. So, as we have concatenated the make and model in the SELECT clause, we have to do the same in the GROUP BY clause.

Tricks and Traps

Although the COUNT() function works in a virtually identical way to the SUM() and AVG() functions you have already seen, there are nonetheless a few things to be aware of.

- Sometimes all you want to do is to find the total number of rows in a table. Perhaps you are looking at a large table and want an idea of its size. Should this be the case, then the SQL is extremely simple. Just use the following:

```
SELECT COUNT(*) FROM Data.Stock
```

- This will return the total number of records in a table.

- You could be tempted to use COUNT(*) when analyzing data, but I advise that you always add the name of the field that you are interested in between the parentheses when using the COUNT() function. This is because COUNT(*) will count all rows—whether they contain data or not. COUNT(Cost) will count only the records where there is a cost figure, and the two results could be different.

- The trick in SQL that counts the number of elements is to use exactly the same grouping elements in the GROUP BY clause as in the SELECT clause. So, as we have used the make and model in the SELECT clause, we have to use them in the GROUP BY clause as well.

- If you are dealing with really huge datasets and the result of a COUNT() operation could exceed 2 billion, then you will have to use the COUNT_BIG() function instead of COUNT() to avoid an error message.

- The COUNT() function can be applied to text fields as well as numeric fields.

7.7 Counting Unique Elements

There could be occasions when you need to analyze a dataset and deduce the number of specific and individual elements that it contains, as opposed to the total number of rows. You discovered this when the sales director appeared at your desk and asked for the number of different countries that Prestige Cars has ever sold vehicles to.

Fortunately, SQL makes this kind of high-level investigation really easy; it can be done in a couple of lines of code like in the following snippet:

```
SELECT   COUNT(DISTINCT CountryName) AS CountriesWithSales
FROM     Data.SalesByCountry
```

Running this query will show the results in *Figure 7.7*.

Figure 7.7: *Counting unique values in a list*

How It Works

In this query you are using the SalesByCountry view that you met earlier as the source of the data. Once again you are using the COUNT() function to return a number of records, and you are specifying that you want to see the number of records where the CountryName field contains data.

However, you have also added the DISTINCT keyword inside the parentheses for the COUNT() function, and this changes everything. Because now, instead of getting the total number of records where there is a country, you are returning the number of unique countries in the CountryName field.

7.8 Displaying Upper and Lower Numeric Thresholds

Data analysis is frequently about identifying limits and thresholds. At least, this is what the sales manager seems to think because she wants you to identify the largest and smallest sale prices for each model of car sold. SQL makes it easy to perform analyses of the limits of datasets, as you can see from the following piece of T-SQL:

```
SELECT       MD.ModelName
             ,MAX(SD.SalePrice) AS TopSalePrice
             ,MIN(SD.SalePrice) AS BottomSalePrice
FROM         Data.Model AS MD
INNER JOIN   Data.Stock AS ST ON ST.ModelID = MD.ModelID
INNER JOIN   Data.SalesDetails SD ON ST.StockCode = SD.StockID
GROUP BY     MD.ModelName
```

If you execute this query, you will see the results in *Figure 7.8.*

	ModelName	TopSalePrice	BottomSalePrice
1	135	25500.00	25500.00
2	145	39500.00	29500.00
3	175	12500.00	12500.00
4	1750	9950.00	3575.00
5	203	1950.00	1250.00
6	205	3950.00	950.00
7	250SL	22600.00	12950.00
8	280SL	62500.00	22500.00
9	350SL	33600.00	23500.00
10	355	220000.00	125950.00
11	360	135000.00	99500.00
12	400GT	145000.00	145000.00
13	404	3500.00	950.00
14	500	2500.00	1150.00
15	500SL	45000.00	30500.00

Figure 7.8: *Using the MAX()and MIN()functions to show the maximum and minimum values for a data group*

How It Works

The FROM clause in this query ensures that you are looking at sales data (and not just stock) and that you can access the model names. It does this by joining the SalesDetails, Stock, and Model tables. Then you use SELECT to specify the model name and the sale price (twice—once for each aggregation function). However, you have applied the MAX() and MIN() functions on the SalePrice field to calculate the maximum and minimum, respectively. Finally—and once again—any nonaggregated fields that you have placed in the SELECT clause are added to the GROUP BY clause.

Tricks and Traps

As simple as they are, the MAX() and MIN() functions necessitate a couple of comments.

- You can extend the principle by adding further fields to the SELECT and GROUP BY clauses to drill down into a finer level of analytical detail, as you saw previously in section 4.

- If you are applying a series of aggregation functions to the same field, you will have to repeat the field name for each function used.

7.9 Filtering Groups

The sales director was pleased with your ability to aggregate results using all the available data in a database. So, she wants you to push the envelope and filter the data so that she can see how many red cars have been sold. Of course, SQL will let you do this—and you can build on the knowledge that you have acquired so far in this book by applying any of the filtering techniques you saw in previous chapters.

As an example, here is how to count the cars sold in a specific color:

```
SELECT      MK.MakeName, COUNT(SD.SalePrice) AS CarsSold
FROM        Data.Make AS MK
INNER JOIN  Data.Model MD
            ON MK.MakeID = MD.MakeID
INNER JOIN  Data.Stock AS ST ON ST.ModelID = MD.ModelID
INNER JOIN  Data.SalesDetails SD ON ST.StockCode = SD.StockID
WHERE       ST.Color = 'Red'
GROUP BY    MK.MakeName
```

This code returns the output shown in *Figure 7.9.*

	MakeName	CarsSold
1	Alfa Romeo	1
2	Aston Martin	6
3	Austin	1
4	Bentley	2
5	Bugatti	3
6	Ferrari	2
7	Jaguar	5
8	Mercedes	1
9	Peugeot	1
10	Porsche	3
11	Rolls Royce	2
12	Trabant	3
13	Triumph	3

Figure 7.9: A calculated aggregation with a filter applied

How It Works

This code snippet returns the number of cars sold, using the technique you saw in section 8 of this chapter. What is new is the WHERE clause, which is applied just as you would use it in a "normal" (that is nonaggregated) query. What you have to remember is that the WHERE clause must be placed before the GROUP BY clause, or you will get an error message.

Tricks and Traps

I have only one point to make (again) here; it is an important one, so it bears repetition.

- Although I said it in the previous chapter, it is worth repeating that if you want to filter on a field, then the table containing the filtered field must be present in one of the tables in the FROM clause. As this query shows, this does not mean you have to add this field to the SELECT clause.

7.10 Filtering on Aggregated Results

As part of the company's worldwide sales drive, the sales director wants to focus Prestige Cars' marketing energies on the countries where you are making the most sales. This section shows you how to show the data only for countries where more than 50 cars have been sold. To start with, take a look at the following SQL snippet:

```
SELECT      CountryName, COUNT(SalesDetailsID) AS NumberofCarsSold

FROM        Data.SalesByCountry

GROUP BY    CountryName

HAVING      COUNT(SalesDetailsID) > 50
```

Running this code gives the output in *Figure 7.10.*

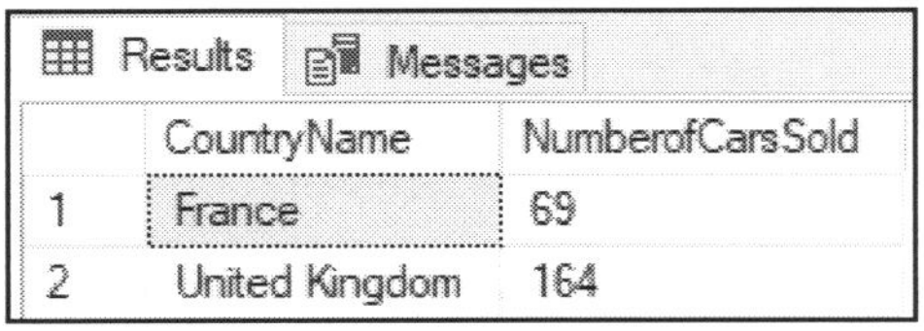

	CountryName	NumberofCarsSold
1	France	69
2	United Kingdom	164

Figure 7.10: Applying a filter to an aggregation

How It Works

There will be occasions when you will need to use an aggregation to filter data. That is, you want to calculate an aggregated value and use this metric to filter a dataset. In cases like these, you need to apply a filter that is not a straight comparison with a value stored in a table, as was the case in the preceding example.

This query uses the SalesByCountry view that joins all the main tables in the database. This is first to remind you that you can also query views and second to avoid swamping the query in a seven-table join clause. This way you can use all the fields from the Country, Make, Model, Sales, Stock, SalesDetails, and Customer tables without having to pay too much attention to a complex JOIN.

What is interesting in this query is the HAVING clause. It is here that the aggregate filter is applied. What this clause says is this: "Allow aggregated output into the result set only where there are more than 50 source records (that is, sales) in the aggregate source set." Put another way, it counts the number of sales (identified by the SalesDetailsID value of each individual sale) for each element in the GROUP BY clause (the country)—and then `only` returns rows where the country that you have grouped on has more than 50 sales.

The end result is that the HAVING clause acts like a filter. Only whereas a WHERE clause operates at the level of each individual record, the HAVING clause filters data on an aggregated value—the number of sales made for each aggregated element.

If you want to convince yourself that this technique really works, then run the query without the HAVING clause. This will return the number of sales for all countries.

7.11 Selecting Data Based on Aggregated Results as Well as Specific Filter Criteria

The sales director has surpassed herself. This time she has left a note with what looks like a complicated request. She wants to know who are the clients who have not only bought at least three cars but where each of the three vehicles generated a profit of at least £5,000.00. So, before getting anxious about it, let's consider what question is being asked. Her demand could be translated as follows: "Find all car sales making more than £5,000 in profit. Now group them by customer. Finally, display only those customers who have at least three cars making at least this much profit."

Believe us, this sounds more complicated than it really is. So, before your eyes glaze over, take a look at the following SQL:

```
SELECT     CU.CustomerName, COUNT(SD.SalesDetailsID) AS NumberofCarsSold
FROM       Data.Make AS MK INNER JOIN Data.Model AS MD
           ON MK.MakeID = MD.MakeID
INNER JOIN Data.Stock AS ST ON ST.ModelID = MD.ModelID
INNER JOIN Data.SalesDetails SD ON ST.StockCode = SD.StockID
INNER JOIN Data.Sales AS SA ON SA.SalesID = SD.SalesID
INNER JOIN Data.Customer CU ON SA.CustomerID = CU.CustomerID
WHERE      (SD.SalePrice
             - (
                 ST.Cost + ISNULL(ST.RepairsCost,0) + ST.PartsCost
```

```
        + ST.TransportInCost)
      ) > 5000
GROUP BY   CU.CustomerName
HAVING     COUNT(SD.SalesDetailsID) >= 3
```

Query Analysis

I cannot deny that SQL can get complicated sometimes. However, it is never more than an accumulation of techniques—and keywords—that must be applied to deliver a result. So, if you are faced with a seemingly difficult challenge, the approach should always be to break the question down into its smallest parts and then try a sequential approach, something like this:

What tables are needed?	Without the source data, there is nothing that you can do. So, it is best to begin with the FROM clause to ensure that you can access all the columns that you need from all the required tables.
What output is required?	Choose the columns that you want to see in the result—and set up any calculations that are needed.
What aggregations?	If you need aggregations, you should add them—and ensure that the GROUP BY clause contains any nonaggregated fields that you have placed in the SELECT clause.
How are you filtering data?	Then you should apply any filters that you need to exclude data that is not relevant to your analysis. Remember to break down the filter into its smallest parts and build it up slowly and coherently. Remember that you can filter at both a detailed and an aggregate level—and that joining tables can filter data.
Any aggregated filters?	Finally, use the HAVING clause if you are filtering on the result of an aggregation.

Running this code gives the output shown in *Figure 7.11*.

	CustomerName	NumberofCarsSold
1	Alexei Tolstoi	4
2	Alicia Almodovar	3
3	Antonio Maura	6
4	Birmingham Executive Prestige Vehicles	3
5	Casseroles Chromes	3
6	Convertible Dreams	4
7	Eat My Exhaust Ltd	3
8	Glittering Prize Cars Ltd	4
9	Glitz	4
10	Honest Pete Motors	7
11	King Leer Cars	6
12	Laurent Saint Yves	8
13	Le Luxe en Motion	4
14	Liverpool Executive Prestige Vehicles	3
15	M. Pierre Dubois	3

Figure 7.11: *A calculated aggregation with both a HAVING clause and a WHERE clause*

How It Works

Once again, the FROM clause merely guarantees that you can access all the fields that are needed to answer the query. The SELECT clause merely says that you want to list the customer name and the number of vehicles sold to that customer. As this is an aggregation query, the field you are using to break down the data (customer name) must also appear in the GROUP BY clause.

The power of this query resides in using two types of filter that are applied in sequence.

- A classic WHERE clause for a nonaggregate filter
- An aggregate filter in a HAVING clause

Each of these performs a separate and distinct function in the query in a specific order.

First:	The WHERE clause calculates the individual margin for each sale and allows only those records that match this criterion through to the next (grouping) stage.
Finally:	The HAVING clause takes the resulting filtered records that have been grouped and aggregated and applies a second level of filter. This time only groups that have at least three elements (that is, three cars making more than £5,000.00 profit) are let through into the query output.

The main thing to remember with queries like this one is that there is a strict filter priority that is applied by SQL. It will apply a WHERE clause before it will apply a HAVING clause.

Tricks and Traps

As you are meeting a new concept—and a new keyword—for the first time, you need to be wary of a couple of potential issues that have to be managed carefully when you are using the HAVING clause.

- Note that we used the ISNULL() function that was described in the previous chapter when calculating the profit for each car sold. Had we not used this function, SQL Server would have returned a NULL rather than the profit for any car with a NULL value in the RepairsCost field.

- The order of the clauses in the SQL statement is extremely important when you are applying a HAVING clause to the code. You must always place the HAVING clause after the GROUP BY clause—and before the ORDER BY clause (if there is one).

7.12 Sorting by Aggregated Results

The CEO wants to see what drives the company's bottom line. More specifically, she wants to isolate the three most lucrative models sold so that she can focus sales efforts around those brands. Aggregation queries can, of course, be used to help you to analyze and prioritize your data. A classic example is when you want to see what brings in the most money. The following short piece of SQL illustrates this:

```
SELECT      TOP (3) MK.MakeName

FROM        Data.Make AS MK

INNER JOIN  Data.Model AS MD ON MK.MakeID = MD.MakeID

INNER JOIN  Data.Stock AS ST ON ST.ModelID = MD.ModelID

INNER JOIN  Data.SalesDetails SD ON ST.StockCode = SD.StockID

GROUP BY    MK.MakeName

ORDER BY    SUM(SD.SalePrice) DESC
```

Executing this code snippet gives the output shown in *Figure 7.12.*

***Figure 7.12:** Using TOP, ORDER BY, and GROUP BY to segment data*

How It Works

This query groups the output data by make and shows you that you can also add an ORDER BY clause to sort the output. What is interesting is that you can sort by an aggregated field—whether it is present in the SELECT clause or not. What is more, the TOP keyword can be used in aggregation queries too.

To encourage you to persevere with SQL, just consider the potential value of the information returned by such a concise and efficient query. You can see where your company is really making money. This, after all, is worth a little effort on the SQL learning curve.

Conclusion

This chapter has introduced you to the vast potential of SQL to calculate aggregations. You saw how to group data into separate segments and return totals, counts, maxima, and minima for these segments in a few lines of code.

Then you learned how to use calculations alongside aggregations to perform deeper analyses. You also saw how to filter data using aggregation functions to isolate certain data elements.

Finally, you saw how to combine aggregation functions with some of the functions that you saw in previous chapters to deliver in-depth commercial analysis.

Core Knowledge Learned in This Chapter

The following are the keywords you learned in this chapter:

Concept	Description
SUM()	This function returns the total for a column of numbers. It will also calculate the total for or for each segment of data where grouping is applied.
GROUP BY	This phrase tells SQL Server that you want to segment results into groups of elements.
COUNT()	This function tells you how many records there are in a table or for each segment of data.
COUNT(DISTINCT)	This function tells you how many individual records there are in a table.
MAX()	This function returns the largest value in a column of numbers for each segment of data.
MIN()	This function returns the lowest value in a column of numbers for each segment of data.
HAVING	This clause filters the data on aggregate values (unlike the WHERE clause, which filters individual records).

CHAPTER 8

Working with Dates in SQL Server

Most data analysis has a time component. You could want to look at sales for a certain day, month, or year. Perhaps you need to compare margins with the previous year or the preceding month. Indeed, the list of possible questions that need answering when it comes to analyzing data over time is virtually infinite. It follows from this that it can be really important to understand how SQL Server handles dates. Indeed, it can rapidly become essential to master the techniques that you need to apply when adding a time element to your analyses.

Analyzing Data over Time

Fortunately, SQL Server delivers a range of solutions when it comes to analyzing data over time. The possibilities are as far reaching as the analytical requirements that you could face. This chapter introduces how to deal with dates in data analysis because this will prepare you for the real-world challenges you may face when analyzing data over time.

Handling time analysis (or querying dates in databases if you prefer) is a vast subject. As you are still taking your first steps with SQL, I will not attempt to provide answers to every imaginable question on this subject in one chapter. I will, however, try to provide you with a basic understanding of how SQL Server databases can be used as the basis for deep insights into how data evolves over time.

This involves learning how to

- Filter by a specific date
- Filter by a range of dates
- Isolate data by year, month, week, and day
- Aggregate values over time
- Handle SQL date data types and avoid common pitfalls

I would like to make clear from the start that—for the moment at least—I am using date and time as interchangeable concepts for the most part in this chapter. For the moment, I will be dealing only with dates as you learn to analyze data over time. InChapter 20, you will see how to deal with the hours and minutes that make up the time element of certain data elements. For the moment, however, what matters is bringing the date element to the fore when analyzing data.

8.1 Filtering Records by Date

Suppose that the sales director wants to see the list of cars bought on July 25, 2015. The following SQL does just that:

```
SELECT      MK.MakeName, MD.ModelName, ST.DateBought
FROM        Data.Make AS MK
INNER JOIN Data.Model AS MD
            ON MK.MakeID = MD.MakeID
INNER JOIN Data.Stock AS ST
            ON ST.ModelID = MD.ModelID
WHERE       ST.DateBought = '20150725'
```

Run this code and you will see the output in *Figure 8.1.*

	MakeName	ModelName	DateBought
1	Porsche	944	2015-07-25
2	Aston Martin	DB6	2015-07-25
3	Jaguar	XJS	2015-07-25

Figure 8.1: Using dates in a WHERE clause

How It Works

Once you have joined the necessary tables (Make, Model, and Stock) to output all the details of vehicles that have been bought, you can filter on the field that shows when a car was bought. You do this by applying a WHERE clause—just as you would do for text or numbers. The interesting thing is how you represent the data in the WHERE clause. There are two main aspects to this.

Quotes:	The date is enclosed in single quotes as if it were text.
Date specification:	The date is best specified as YYYYMMDD—that is, four digits for the year, then two digits for the month (including a leading zero for months 1–9), and then two digits for the day (including a leading zero for days 1–9). No separator elements are required (that is, no hyphens or slashes are needed to separate the year from the month or the day).

Otherwise, this is a pretty standard WHERE clause. It uses the equal operator to specify that you are looking to filter data on a specific date.

Tricks and Traps

As you are just beginning to learn how to handle dates in SQL queries, there are inevitably key elements that you have to retain. The following are the major starting points:

- There are many other ways of representing dates in SQL. However, most of them depend on the date format matching the local settings of your SQL Server instance. To avoid complications, I therefore prefer to use dates in the YYYYMMDD format when querying, as this is independent of the SQL Server configuration. In practical terms, it means that queries that use this method of specifying a date should work in nearly all circumstances. I will be showing you some other ways of entering dates later in this chapter. However, you need to be aware that most other date formats that you can use to specify a date will depend on the local language settings of your SQL Server. Consequently, other ways of entering dates cannot be guaranteed to work in all situations and contexts.

- You can use other operators besides the equal operator (=) when entering dates. For instance, you can use >= (greater than or equal to) to list all records from—and including—a specific date. To list data up to and including a specific date, you can use the <= (less than or equal to) operator. For dates before or after a given date, you can use the < (less than) or > (greater than) operator.

8.2 Using a Range of Dates to Filter Data

Pleased with your initial answer to her request, the sales director now wants a list of all the cars bought between June 30, 2016, and July 31, 2016. The following SQL shows how to do this:

```
SELECT      MK.MakeName, MD.ModelName
FROM        Data.Make AS MK INNER JOIN Data.Model AS MD
            ON MK.MakeID = MD.MakeID
INNER JOIN Data.Stock AS ST ON ST.ModelID = MD.ModelID
WHERE       ST.DateBought BETWEEN '2018.08.30' AND '2018.08.31'
```

Figure 8.2 shows the output from this piece of SQL.

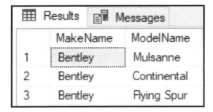

Figure 8.2: *Filtering on a range of dates using the BETWEEN operator*

Date Data Types

A filter like the one that you applied in the previous section will work correctly only if the field (or fields) that you are using for date filters is in one of SQL Server's date data types. If the field is a string (text, that is), you will have to enter the date exactly as it is typed in the table—and hope that there are no typos in any of the data, or the query will not work properly.

Fortunately, the fields that contain date information in the PrestigeCars database have been designed correctly, and they can only contain dates. However, when you are querying other databases, you are probably best advised to check the data types of any fields that look like they hold dates or date and time data.

To check the data type of a field, you can expand the list of columns that make up a table or a view in SQL Server Management Studio. You can use a database field for date filters and calculations if you see any of the following data types:

- Date
- Datetime
- Datetime2
- Smalldatetime

How It Works

Once again (with the FROM clause duly configured to include all the required tables), you can apply a WHERE clause to filter on dates, this time outputting `all the records` where the sale date was in the range specified in the WHERE clause. In this example, I chose to enter the dates in the YYYY-MM-DD format as it is easier to read. This format works with most language versions of SQL Server too and so will avoid nearly all potential errors when entering dates. In any case, if a date filter does not work when you use the YYYY-MM-DD format, you can always adjust the query so that the date is in the YYYYMMDD format.

Tricks and Traps

Dealing with date ranges means you have to be precise, specifically as far as the following are concerned:

- When you use the BETWEEN and AND keywords, SQL will include the start and end dates in the range that you define. In the case of this particular query, that means from June 30, 2015, to July 31, 2015, inclusive.

- If you are using BETWEEN...AND in a date range query it is really important that you `place the start date before the end date` and not vice versa. If you reverse these elements and write the filter as follows:

```
WHERE DateBought BETWEEN '20150731' AND '20150630'
```

it will return no results, even if you are certain that there are records for the date range you have specified.

- If you want another way to enter a date that will work under any circumstances—that is, whatever the language settings of your SQL Server— you can use the DATEFROMPARTS() function. It is a little more long-winded than a simple date as text, but the following code will also let you enter July 31, 2015, wherever you need to specify a date:

```
DATEFROMPARTS(2015, 7, 31)
```

The DATEFROMPARTS() function takes three parameters.

  o The year—entered as two or four figures

  o The month—entered as one or two figures

  o The day—entered as one or two figures

Fortunately, you do not need to add a leading zero to the figure for the month or the day if either of these is less than 10.

All you need to remember to use this function is that the year, month, and day must be entered in exactly that order and separated by commas.

o   You can also enter date ranges using the <= and >= operators if you prefer. Using these, the WHERE clause for the query in this example would be as follows:

```
WHERE DateBought >= '20150731' AND DateBought <= '20150630'
```

If you are using the <= and >= operators, you can enter the upper and lower threshold values in any order.

8.3 Finding the Number of Days Between Two Dates

The finance director is keen to make sure that cars do not stay on the firm's books too long—he says that they tie up expensive capital. So, he wants a list of the makes and models and the number of days that each vehicle remained, unsold, on the lot. After a few minutes you deliver the following piece of code:

```
SELECT
          MK.MakeName
          ,MD.ModelName
          ,ST.DateBought
          ,SA.SaleDate
          ,DATEDIFF(d, ST.DateBought, SA.SaleDate) AS DaysInStock
FROM      Data.Make AS MK
INNER JOIN Data.Model AS MD
          ON MK.MakeID = MD.MakeID
INNER JOIN Data.Stock AS ST ON ST.ModelID = MD.ModelID
INNER JOIN Data.SalesDetails SD ON ST.StockCode = SD.StockID
INNER JOIN Data.Sales SA ON SA.SalesID = SD.SalesID
```

Executing this code snippet gives the output shown in *Figure 8.3*.

	StockCode	MakeName	ModelName	DateBought	SaleDate	DaysInStock
1	B1C3B95E-3005-4840-8CE3-A7BC5F9CFB3F	Ferrari	Testarossa	2015-01-01	2015-01-02 08:00:00.000	1
2	A2C3B95E-3005-4840-8CE3-A7BC5F9CFB5F	Ferrari	355	2015-01-10	2015-01-25 00:00:00.000	15
3	558620F5-B9E8-4FFF-8F73-A83FA9559C41	Porsche	911	2015-01-29	2015-02-03 10:00:00.000	5
4	72443561-FAC4-4C25-B8FF-0C47361DDE2D	Porsche	924	2015-02-14	2015-02-16 08:00:00.000	2
5	2189D556-D1C4-4BC1-B0C8-4053319E8E9D	Porsche	944	2015-01-01	2015-01-02 10:33:00.000	1
6	C1459308-7EA5-4A2D-82BC-38079BB4049B	Aston Martin	DB4	2015-03-05	2015-03-14 00:00:00.000	9
7	E6E6270A-60B0-4817-AA57-17F26B2B8DAF	Aston Martin	DB5	2015-03-15	2015-03-24 00:00:00.000	9
8	CEDFB8D2-BD98-4A08-BC46-406D23940527	Aston Martin	DB6	2015-03-26	2015-03-30 00:00:00.000	4
9	6081DBE7-9AD6-4C64-A676-61D919E64979	Porsche	911	2015-04-04	2015-04-06 00:00:00.000	2
10	D63C8CC9-DB19-4B9C-9C8E-6C6370812041	Aston Martin	DB5	2015-04-02	2015-04-04 00:00:00.000	2

Figure 8.3: Using the DATEDIFF() function to calculate the difference in days between two dates

How It Works

This SQL introduces the DATEDIFF() function. This function allows you to calculate the number of days (or even weeks, months, or years—among many other possibilities) between two dates. The DATEDIFF() function needs `three` elements (or parameters—to give them their technical name) to work properly.

First:	The date element that you want to calculate (day, week, and so on). In this example you want the number of days, so you just enter a d (the other date elements are given in *Table 8.1*). This parameter must *not* be entered in quotes.
Second:	The start date for the calculation. This means defining the initial date in the calculation, which is the DateBought field from the Sales table in this example. This must be in a format that SQL Server can recognize as a date.
Finally:	The end date for the calculation. In this example, you want to end the period with the date that the vehicle is sold. This means using the SaleDate field from the Stock table. This parameter, too, has to be in a format that SQL Server can recognize as a date.

Naturally, if you are using these fields, you need the tables that contain them (SalesDetails, Sales and Stock) in the FROM clause. Indeed, as the SELECT clause also requires the make and model, the FROM clause has to join the Make and Model tables as well.

As you can see in *Figure 8.3*, the DateBought field contains only a date, whereas the SaleDate field contains both a date and the time of day. This is because the DateBought field has been defined as being a DATE data type and the DateBought field is defined as a DATETIME data type. You will be looking at how these data types can affect date queries a little later in this chapter.

Tricks and Traps

The DATEDIFF() function is not difficult to apply to SQL queries. However, you do need to be aware of a few key aspects of its use.

- You can enter the d for days in uppercase or lowercase in the DATEDIFF() function to specify that you want the date difference expressed in days; it makes no difference to SQL.

- DATEDIFF() can count more than just days. It can also count days, weeks, months, quarters, years—or even hours and minutes. *Table 8.1* shows you the code you must use in the DATEDIFF() function to return these elements. Technically, these various date and time aspects of a date are called date parts.

Date Part	Abbreviations
Year	yy (or yyyy)
Quarter	qq (or q)
Month	mm (or m)
Day of year	dy (or y)
Day	dd (or d)
Week	wk (or ww)

Table 8.1: *Date Parts Used in the DATEDIFF() Function*

- The dates you use in the DATEDIFF() function must also be entered in a way that lets SQL Server recognize them as being dates. In other words, they must be entered as a valid date data type. This can be YYYYMMDD, YYYY-MM-DD, or indeed any date that your version of SQL Server recognizes.

- You need to add an alias to the function as SQL Server will never try to guess a column name when a function is used. If you do not add an alias, the column will be entitled "No column name."

- You can test the DATEDIFF() function independently of the rest of the query in a code snippet or use a fixed date as one or both of the date parameters that you apply to the function like this:

```
SELECT DATEDIFF(d, '20150701', '20150815')
```

This code will return the number of days between the two dates you specify.

8.4 Aggregating Data over a Date Range

Suppose your sales manager wants to know the average monthly purchasing spend over a six-month period. After a few minutes of thought, you come up with the following code snippet:

```
SELECT      SUM(ST.Cost)
            / DATEDIFF(m, '20150701', '20151231')
              AS AverageMonthlyPurchase
FROM        Data.Make AS MK INNER JOIN Data.Model AS MD
            ON MK.MakeID = MD.MakeID
INNER JOIN Data.Stock AS ST ON ST.ModelID = MD.ModelID
WHERE       ST.DateBought BETWEEN '20150701' AND '20151231'
```

You can see how this code works in *Figure 8.4.*

	AverageMonthlyPurchase
1	153404.00

Figure 8.4: *Calculating an average using the number of months between two dates with the DATEDIFF() function*

How It Works

You just saw that SQL Server can determine the number of days between two dates—and this can be extended to calculate the average purchase price over a period of months. To achieve this objective, this query begins by defining all the tables that are required to provide the necessary data in the FROM clause. This means the Make, Model and Stock tables.

Then the SQL used here filters the date range used for the calculation to the period from July 1, 2016, to December 31, 2016. This date range is defined in the WHERE clause.

Then the SQL applies the SUM() function to the SELECT clause to calculate the total cost of all vehicles. This will apply only to vehicles bought between the two dates specified in the WHERE clause. Then, the DATEDIFF() function is used again in the SELECT clause to calculate the number of months between the two dates. Finally, the SQL divides the total purchase price by the number of months. The result is then displayed as the single figure that the query returns.

Once again, the DATEDIFF() function is used to calculate the number of days between two dates. The two dates, this time, are "hard-coded" into the DATEDIFF() function.

The start date:	is entered as 20150701 because in this example you want to start the evaluation period on July 1, 2016.
The end date:	is entered as 20161231 because you want to end the evaluation period on December 31, 2016.

Tricks and Traps

There is one vital point to make here.

- Make sure that the date period used in the WHERE clause matches the dates specified in the DATEDIFF() function or the result will not be correct because you will, in effect, have not calculated the same number of months in the WHERE clause as there are in the SELECT clause.

8.5 Eliminating the Time Element in a Date Filter

Some databases are designed to store dates and times of certain events in case the time element is important too. If you need to remind yourself of this, then take another look at Figure 8.3, where you can see a field with only a date element (date bought) as well as a field with a date and time element (SaleDate). While undeniably useful in certain cases, this can cause potential issues when filtering on dates alone. This is because when you enter just a date (as you did in the previous sections), SQL presumes you mean that the event took place a fraction of a second after midnight on the date you entered. No other time of day will count when filtering the data. The consequence of this is that if a sale is made during normal office hours for a single date (or for the final date in a range), SQL will not find the sale because the exact time was not specified when filtering on the date—and the hours until midnight when the next day begins are excluded from the output.

As mishandling the time element of a date can seriously distort the results, it follows that there will be occasions when you will need to strip out the time part of any fields that contain both date and time elements. Doing this will guarantee that only the date part is used in the filter and that the time part will not skew the results. The following SQL gives an example of this:

```
SELECT     MK.MakeName, MD.ModelName
FROM       Data.Make AS MK INNER JOIN Data.Model AS MD
           ON MK.MakeID = MD.MakeID
```

```
INNER JOIN Data.Stock AS ST ON ST.ModelID = MD.ModelID
INNER JOIN Data.SalesDetails SD ON ST.StockCode = SD.StockID
INNER JOIN Data.Sales AS SA ON SA.SalesID = SD.SalesID
WHERE       CAST(SA.SaleDate AS DATE) = '20160228'
```

You can see this code in action in *Figure 8.5.*

Figure 8.5: *Filtering on the date in a DATETIME field using the CAST() function*

How It Works

In this query you apply the CAST() function to a DATETIME field (one that contains both the date and time elements for an event) to remove the time part. This, in effect, means that you are comparing a date (June 30 in this example) to the `date part only` of the field. So, whatever the time of the sale, only the `date` is used in the filter. This makes the time irrelevant and prevents the query from returning erroneous results.

The CAST() function can seem a little peculiar, but it is saying this:

First:	Enter the field name that contains the date and time.
Then:	Enter AS DATE keywords.

This way, the SaleDate field—that is defined in the database to use the DateTime data type—will be converted to a Date data type. This conversion removes the time element from the field and prevents possible errors in the query.

Tricks and Traps

Understanding the difference between date and datetime fields can be a little daunting when you start writing time-based queries. To help you in this, try remembering the following:

- When beginning to use SQL—and when dealing with a database that you do not yet know inside out—you may well wonder exactly how you can be sure that you have a field that contains both date and time parts. The simple solution is to carry out a simple SELECT on the field in question. If you see only the date (whatever the format), then you have a date field. If you see time elements after the date, then the field is a datetime data type.

As you can see, the DateBought field contains only the date, whereas the SaleDate field contains both date and time elements.

- If you are not sure whether a field is a date or a date and time, then you can always apply the CAST function to the field that you are not sure about. Doing this cannot cause any harm and will not cause a filter on a date field (that is, one without a time element) to go wrong.

8.6 Filtering by Year

As Prestige Cars has been selling cars for several years, the finance director wants to isolate the records for a specific year. SQL makes this easy, as the following code shows:

```
SELECT      MK.MakeName, MD.ModelName, YEAR(SA.SaleDate) AS YearOfSale
FROM        Data.Make AS MK INNER JOIN Data.Model AS MD
            ON MK.MakeID = MD.MakeID
INNER JOIN Data.Stock AS ST ON ST.ModelID = MD.ModelID
INNER JOIN Data.SalesDetails SD ON ST.StockCode = SD.StockID
INNER JOIN Data.Sales AS SA ON SA.SalesID = SD.SalesID
WHERE       YEAR(SA.SaleDate) = 2015
ORDER BY    MK.MakeName, MD.ModelName
```

Running this SQL delivers the output shown in *Figure 8.6*.

	MakeName	ModelName	YearOfSale
1	Alfa Romeo	Giulia	2015
2	Aston Martin	DB4	2015
3	Aston Martin	DB5	2015
4	Aston Martin	DB5	2015
5	Aston Martin	DB6	2015
6	Aston Martin	DB6	2015
7	Aston Martin	DB6	2015
8	Aston Martin	Virage	2015
9	Bentley	Flying Spur	2015
10	Ferrari	355	2015
11	Ferrari	355	2015
12	Ferrari	Testarossa	2015
13	Ferrari	Testarossa	2015
14	Jaguar	XJS	2015
15	Jaguar	XJS	2015

Figure 8.6: Using the YEAR() function on a date field

Local Date Formats

SQL Server allows you to enter a date in the local language of the server. It would take up too much space to show every possible way of entering a date in every language and culture, so I will show you examples only in British English here.

For July 25, 2018, for instance, you could enter the following:

'25.Jul 2018'

'25.July 2018'

'25.Jul 18'

'25.July 18'

Remember that you will always need to enter a date in single quotes.

How It Works

This query uses the YEAR() function to extract the year from the date in the WHERE clause so that you can then specify which year to filter on. Although it is perhaps not strictly necessary, we have added this same function to the SELECT clause as well so that you can then confirm, visually, that the year that interests you is being returned by the query. As you can observe, the YEAR() function extracts the year element from a date field, irrespective of the month and day of the month. As is the case with all SQL functions, you can use this function in any part of the query. Applying it to the WHERE clause means that it is used to filter on the year.

We also added an ORDER BY clause to this piece of SQL merely to add some structure to the output—and to remind you that this can be done whatever the type of query that you are writing.

Tricks and Traps

There are only a couple of points to make here.

- The YEAR function outputs (or returns in geek-speak) the year as a number. This means that when using YEAR in a query, you do not need to enter the year in single quotes.

- You can always begin by adding any fields that you are using in the WHERE clause to the SELECT clause when you are writing and testing the query. Once you are satisfied that the SQL is working correctly, you can then remove these fields from the SELECT clause unless you really need to display the data.

8.7 Filtering Records over a Series of Years

Now that he has the sales lists for 2015, the finance director wants to compare these results with those for 2016. Fortunately, SQL does not limit you to analyzing data for a single year, as the following query makes clear:

```
SELECT DISTINCT  MK.MakeName, MD.ModelName, YEAR(SA.SaleDate)
                 AS YearOfSale
FROM             Data.Make AS MK INNER JOIN Data.Model AS MD
                 ON MK.MakeID = MD.MakeID
INNER JOIN       Data.Stock AS ST ON ST.ModelID = MD.ModelID
INNER JOIN       Data.SalesDetails SD ON ST.StockCode = SD.StockID
INNER JOIN       Data.Sales AS SA ON SA.SalesID = SD.SalesID
WHERE            YEAR(SA.SaleDate) IN (2015, 2016)
ORDER BY         YEAR(SA.SaleDate), MakeName, ModelName
```

Run this query and you will get the output shown in *Figure 8.7*. You will have to scroll down the output to see the change in the year of sale.

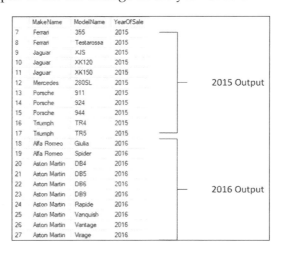

Figure 8.7. Filtering on a series of years using the IN keyword

How It Works

Once you have defined the FROM clause to join all the tables that are needed to access the Make, Model, and SaleDate columns, you only have to add a WHERE clause that tells SQL Server to filter the results so that only data for 2014 to 2015 is returned. This is done using an IN keyword—just as you did in Chapter 3. As was the case with the previous queries that used the IN keyword, each separate filter element is separated by a comma from the other elements, and the complete list is enclosed in parentheses.

Finally, the results are sorted by year, make, and model. However, to sort by the year, you need, once again, to apply the YEAR() function to the SaleDate field in the ORDER BY clause.

Tricks and Traps

I hope that you did not find this kind of query difficult. To make things easier when you are writing your own queries to isolate data over time, you may want to pay attention to the following key points:

- You can enter as many years as you like in an IN function—just remember to separate each year with a comma (,). As was the case when filtering on a single year, the YEAR() function uses figures, so no single quotes are needed.

- You can enter the years in an IN function in any order.

- For a wide range of years you might prefer to avoid entering each year individually and use the BETWEEN…AND syntax in the WHERE clause to specify a range of years, like this:

```
WHERE YEAR(SaleDate) BETWEEN 2013 AND 2016
```

- You need to repeat the YEAR() function in a SQL query `every time` you need to extract the year from a date or datetime field. This kind of function can be applied to most parts of SQL queries.

8.8 Isolating Data for a Specific Year and Month

The CEO is convinced that some months are better for sales than others. She has asked for the sales for July 2015 to check out her hunch. Fortunately, SQL lets you be as precise as you like when querying for data. If you want to list the vehicle sales for a certain month in a given year, you could use code like the following:

```
SELECT     MK.MakeName, MD.ModelName, SA.SaleDate
FROM       Data.Make AS MK INNER JOIN Data.Model AS MD
           ON MK.MakeID = MD.MakeID
INNER JOIN Data.Stock AS ST ON ST.ModelID = MD.ModelID
INNER JOIN Data.SalesDetails SD ON ST.StockCode = SD.StockID
INNER JOIN Data.Sales AS SA ON SA.SalesID = SD.SalesID
WHERE      YEAR(SA.SaleDate) = 2015
           AND MONTH(SA.SaleDate) = 7
```

Execute this code snippet, and you will see the cars that are displayed in *Figure 8.8.*

	MakeName	ModelName	SaleDate
1	Aston Martin	DB6	2015-07-25 00:00:00.000
2	Alfa Romeo	Giulia	2015-07-12 10:00:00.000
3	Jaguar	XK150	2015-07-15 00:00:00.000
4	Jaguar	XJS	2015-07-25 00:00:00.000

Figure 8.8: Using the YEAR() and MONTH() functions to filter output

How It Works

The MONTH() function isolates the month part of a date. More precisely, it returns—or filters on—the number of the month in the year. So, January is 1, February is 2, and so on, until 12 (December). As you can combine both the YEAR() and MONTH() functions in a WHERE clause, limiting the output data to a specific month and year is not difficult. However, you do have to filter on the year and the month separately. This is why the query required you to say "I want the year 2015 and the month of July."

8.9 Finding Data for a Given Quarter

The CEO was disappointed about the sales in July 2015, so now she wants to see sales for the entire third quarter of 2015. SQL can recognize calendar quarters (or trimesters) too, as the following code snippet makes clear:

```
SELECT      MK.MakeName, MD.ModelName
FROM        Data.Make AS MK INNER JOIN Data.Model AS MD
            ON MK.MakeID = MD.MakeID
INNER JOIN Data.Stock AS ST ON ST.ModelID = MD.ModelID
INNER JOIN Data.SalesDetails SD ON ST.StockCode = SD.StockID
INNER JOIN Data.Sales AS SA ON SA.SalesID = SD.SalesID
WHERE       DATEPART(q, SA.SaleDate) = 3
            AND YEAR(SA.SaleDate) = 2015
```

Figure 8.9 shows you what happens when you run this code.

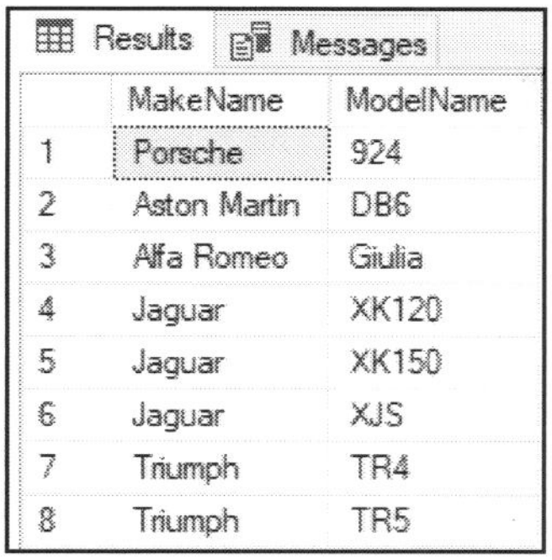

Results | Messages

	MakeName	ModelName
1	Porsche	924
2	Aston Martin	DB6
3	Alfa Romeo	Giulia
4	Jaguar	XK120
5	Jaguar	XK150
6	Jaguar	XJS
7	Triumph	TR4
8	Triumph	TR5

Figure 8.9: *Filtering on the calendar quarter with the DATEPART() function*

How It Works

The DATEPART() function can isolate (among other things) the calendar quarter of the year. Consequently, the months of January through March are quarter 1, the months of April through June are quarter 2, the months of July through September are quarter 3, and the months of October through December are quarter 4. The number of the quarter can then be used in a WHERE clause. In this example, the result is that only sales for the third quarter of 2015 are returned.

The DATEPART() function needs two parameters to be applied.

First:	The part of the date you want to extract—the quarter in this example. This is represented (or passed in to the function in geek-speak) as the letter q.
Second:	The field containing the date.

In this query, the DATEPART() function is applied to the SaleDate field. Consequently, it returns the calendar quarter for each sale. This will inevitably be a number between 1 and 4. Then the WHERE clause looks for the `third` quarter of the date of sale, or, more precisely, says this: "The quarter of the SaleDate field equals three." So, you will see sales for the third quarter only. As you want to limit the result to the third quarter of a specific year (and not just any third quarter of every year for which there is data), you have to extend the WHERE clause by specifying the year to filter on as well.

Tricks and Traps

The DATEPART() function is really simple to use. The following are the only things to remember:

- The DATEPART function will work only if the field that you apply to the DATEPART() function is one of the date data types.

- You do not have to specify a year, of course, but it is probably rare not to want to narrow down the search to sales for a specific year.

- There are many other ways that the DATEPART function can be used to filter and output data. You will see some of them in the following sections.

8.10 Filtering Data by Weekday

When analyzing sales, you may well want to isolate all purchases for a given weekday to find the most profitable day of the week for your business. SQL can do this using code like this:

```
SELECT      MK.MakeName, MD.ModelName
FROM        Data.Make AS MK INNER JOIN Data.Model AS MD
            ON MK.MakeID = MD.MakeID
INNER JOIN Data.Stock AS ST ON ST.ModelID = MD.ModelID
INNER JOIN Data.SalesDetails SD ON ST.StockCode = SD.StockID
INNER JOIN Data.Sales AS SA ON SA.SalesID = SD.SalesID
WHERE       DATEPART(dw, SA.SaleDate) = 6
            AND YEAR(SA.SaleDate) = 2016
```

Running this code snippet produces output similar to that in *Figure 8.10*.

	MakeName	ModelName
1	Ferrari	Testarossa
2	Ferrari	355
3	Porsche	911
4	Porsche	944
5	Porsche	944
6	Porsche	944
7	Aston Martin	DB5
8	Aston Martin	DB6
9	Aston Martin	DB9
10	Aston Martin	Virage
11	Aston Martin	Rapide
12	Bentley	Continental
13	Jaguar	XK120
14	Jaguar	XK120
15	Triumph	TR4

Figure 8.10: Finding all the vehicles sold on a specific day of the week

How It Works

The DATEPART() function also lets you isolate the weekday for a date. It returns the weekday as a number, where 1 is Monday, 2 is Tuesday, 3 is Wednesday, 4 is Thursday, 5 is Friday, 6 is Saturday, and 7 is Sunday. Knowing this allows you to use DATEPART() in a WHERE clause to filter by day of the week.

Once again, you have narrowed down the search to a specific year as a separate part of the WHERE clause.

Tricks and Traps

There are only a small number key points to note here.

- You can enter the first parameter—dw in this example—in either uppercase or lowercase. This holds true for all the DATEPART() parameters, whichever one that you use. You must **not**, however, enclose the first parameter in quotes as it is part of the function itself and not a text element.

- The definition of the way that the weekdays are numbered can vary according to the settings of the SQL Server instance you are using. In many countries, Monday is considered the first day of the week. In other countries, however, it may be Sunday.

- If you need to know which day SQL Server has set for Sunday, just execute the following code:

```
SELECT  @@DATEFIRST
```

If you see a 1 returned by this code, then the server considers that Monday is the first day of the week, so the code in this section will work correctly. If you see a 7, it means that Sunday is day 1, and Saturday is day 7. In this case, you will have to alter the WHERE clause so that it reads as follows:

```
WHERE      DATEPART(dw, SA.SaleDate) = 7

           AND YEAR(SA.SaleDate) = 2016
```

8.11 Finding Records for a Specific Week of the Year

The sales director has announced that she would like to look at the sales for a specific week. SQL helps you to do this by filtering data by week. You can see an example of this in the following SQL:

```
SELECT     MK.MakeName, MD.ModelName

FROM       Data.Make AS MK INNER JOIN Data.Model AS MD

           ON MK.MakeID = MD.MakeID

INNER JOIN Data.Stock AS ST ON ST.ModelID = MD.ModelID

INNER JOIN Data.SalesDetails SD ON ST.StockCode = SD.StockID

INNER JOIN Data.Sales AS SA ON SA.SalesID = SD.SalesID

WHERE      DATEPART(wk, SA.SaleDate) = 26

           AND YEAR(SA.SaleDate) = 2017
```

Execute this code, and you will get the results shown in *Figure 8.11.*

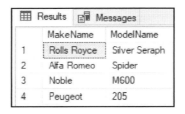

Figure 8.11: *Using the DATEPART() function to isolate the week of the year*

How It Works

This code sample selects all records where the sale took place in the 26th week of the year. Once again, you used the DATEPART() function, but this time you used WK as the first parameter to indicate that you wanted to extract the week of the year from the date. As this function is used in a WHERE clause, you are filtering the data so that only sales records for week 26 are returned.

Tricks and Traps

As you have seen, for most of the basic ways that you can use DATEPART(), you only really have to remember the following point:

- DATEPART() can be used virtually anywhere in a SQL query. This means you can apply it in the SELECT clause, for instance, if you want to see the weeks or weekdays when sales took place.

8.12 Aggregating Data by the Day of Week in a Given Year

The HR manager needs to see how sales vary across days of the week. He has explained that he needs to forecast staff requirements for busy days. So, let's suppose he wants to see, overall, which were the weekdays where Prestige Cars made the most sales in 2015. This piece of SQL does just that:

```
SELECT     DATEPART(dw, SA.SaleDate) AS DayOfWeek

           ,SUM(SD.SalePrice) AS Sales

FROM       Data.Make AS MK INNER JOIN Data.Model AS MD

           ON MK.MakeID = MD.MakeID

INNER JOIN Data.Stock AS ST ON ST.ModelID = MD.ModelID

INNER JOIN Data.SalesDetails SD ON ST.StockCode = SD.StockID

INNER JOIN Data.Sales AS SA ON SA.SalesID = SD.SalesID

WHERE      YEAR(SA.SaleDate) = 2015

GROUP BY   DATEPART(dw, SA.SaleDate)

ORDER BY   SUM(SD.SalePrice) DESC
```

If you run this code, you will get the table shown in *Figure 8.12*.

	DayOfWeek	Sales
1	1	403695.00
2	5	306950.00
3	6	231140.00
4	3	186000.00
5	7	154150.00
6	2	107100.00
7	4	31940.00

Figure 8.12: *Grouping output by day of week using the DATEPART() function*

How It Works

This code returns the seven days of the week and the aggregate sales per weekday. It uses the DATEPART() function in two ways in this query.

First:	The DATEPART() function is used in the SELECT query. This time, however, the *dw* date part is used as the first parameter to specify that it is the number of the day of the week that you want to isolate in the query.
Finally:	The DATEPART() function is used again in the GROUP BY clause. This ensures that the data is aggregated at the level of the day of the week.

The WHERE clause filters on a specific year (2015 in this example). Finally, for good measure, the query sorts the aggregated output by sales value from highest to lowest. This way it is clear which days have the greatest sales over a year.

Tricks and Traps

Analyzing data over time does have its traps, as well as a few things that you might need to know.

- You can group output on a function—such as DATEPART—just as you would on any field. You could also sort on a function like this if you needed.

- You saw a few of the principal DATEPART() parameters that specify the type of date element that you are looking for—weekdays, weeks, or quarters—in the last few pages. There are, however, several more date element types that can be used. These are given in *Table 8.2*. The same parameters can be used with the DATENAME() function.

Element	Definition	Example
yy	Year	DATEPART(yy, SaleDate)
mm	Month	DATEPART(mm, SaleDate)
dd	Day	DATEPART(dd, SaleDate)
qq	Quarter	DATEPART(qq, SaleDate)
dw	Day of Week	DATEPART(dw, SaleDate)
dy	Day of year	DATEPART(dy, SaleDate)

Table 8.2:. DATEPART() Elements

8.13 Grouping Data by the Full Weekday

The HR manager liked the information that you just gave him. However, he would prefer to see the days of the week written out in full and not just have them appear as numbers in the output. After a couple of simple modifications, your SQL now looks like this:

```
SELECT      DATENAME(dw, SA.SaleDate) AS DayOfWeek

            ,SUM(SD.SalePrice) AS Sales

FROM        Data.Make AS MK INNER JOIN Data.Model AS MD

            ON MK.MakeID = MD.MakeID

INNER JOIN Data.Stock AS ST ON ST.ModelID = MD.ModelID

INNER JOIN Data.SalesDetails SD ON ST.StockCode = SD.StockID

INNER JOIN Data.Sales AS SA ON SA.SalesID = SD.SalesID

WHERE       YEAR(SA.SaleDate) = 2015

GROUP BY    DATENAME(dw, SA.SaleDate)

            ,DATEPART(dw, SA.SaleDate)

ORDER BY    DATEPART(dw, SA.SaleDate)
```

If you execute this code, you will get the table shown in *Figure 8.13*.

	DayOfWeek	Sales
1	Sunday	403695.00
2	Monday	107100.00
3	Tuesday	186000.00
4	Wednesday	31940.00
5	Thursday	306950.00
6	Friday	231140.00
7	Saturday	154150.00

Figure 8.13: Grouping output by day of week using the DATEPART() function

How It Works

Displaying the day of the week as a number can be a little brutal. So, SQL has a function that can "humanize" the output if you want. So, to display the actual weekday, you can tweak the first line of the query so that it looks like this:

```
SELECT      DATENAME(dw, SaleDate) AS DayOfWeek
```

By using the DATENAME() function, the weekday appears as the text of the weekday. As you can see, the DATENAME() function also takes two parameters—the type of date that is to be converted and the DATENAME() function itself.

Once again, any field that is used in the SELECT or ORDER BY clause that is not an aggregate function must also be present in the GROUP BY clause. So, both the DATENAME() and DATEPART() functions must appear here, as well.

Tricks and Traps

There are only a few points to make here.

- Fortunately, the DATENAME() function uses the same elements when converting numbers to text as when describing date elements, so you can use refer to *Table 8.2* for them, too.

- Sorting on the DATEPART() function makes the days of the week appear in the traditional order of the days of the week. If you were to sort on the DATENAME() function, the weekdays would appear in alphabetical order.

8.14 Displaying Cumulative Data over 90 Days Up to a Specific Date

The HR manager has emailed another request. He needs to calculate the final bonus of a salesperson who is leaving the company and consequently needs to see the accumulated sales made by this staff member up to July 25, 2015. SQL can do this (and we will imagine here that it is for the salesperson who sells Jaguars for Prestige Cars). So, to see her sales for the 90 days up to the specified date, you would write SQL like this:

```
SELECT      SUM(SD.SalePrice) AS CumulativeJaguarSales
FROM        Data.Make AS MK INNER JOIN Data.Model AS MD
            ON MK.MakeID = MD.MakeID
INNER JOIN Data.Stock AS ST ON ST.ModelID = MD.ModelID
INNER JOIN Data.SalesDetails SD ON ST.StockCode = SD.StockID
INNER JOIN Data.Sales AS SA ON SA.SalesID = SD.SalesID
WHERE       SA.SaleDate BETWEEN DATEADD(d, -90, '20170725')
            AND '20170725'
            AND MK.MakeName = 'Jaguar'
```

Run this piece of SQL, and you will see the output shown in *Figure 8.14*.

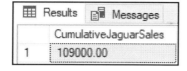

Figure 8.14: Using the DATEADD() function to specify a time period relative to a date

How It Works

As you can see, this piece of SQL returns the total sales for Jaguars. However, what is new is the way that a time period is defined in the WHERE clause. There is no need to reach for a calendar and work out exactly what was the exact date 90 days previously; SQL can do this for you using the DATEADD() function.

The DATEADD() function needs three elements—or parameters—to work.

First:	The increment (or decrement) that you want—days, months, quarters, years, and so on. In this case, you want to see a number of days, so a d is used.
Second:	The actual number of days (or whatever you are using in your query). If you are going back in time—as we are here, to look back over 90 days—you need to enter *-90* (preceding the figure with a minus sign) to make it clear to SQL that the date is in the past.
Third:	The date for the number of days to be added to—or subtracted from. Once again, it is more reliable to enter this in the YYYYMMDD format—and always in single quotes.

Using the DATEADD function in the WHERE clause means that you are saying this: "Filter on a date range between a specified date (July 25, 2015) and 90 days previous to that date."

Tricks and Traps

As you would probably expect, DATEADD() does come with a couple of important points that you need to remember when you are using it.

- Do not be confused by the fact that you are using the AND keyword twice. The first time it is as part of the BETWEEN…AND function. The second time it is to apply a second filter to the WHERE clause.

- Forgetting the minus sign before the number of days in the DATEADD() function would show the sales for the 90 days `after` the specified date.

- The DATEADD() function can calculate time periods using more than just days. If you need it to, you can define that number as being in months, quarters, or years. *Table 8.3* shows the main elements that you add as the first parameter of a DATEADD() function to specify the type of time period you are using.

Element	Definition	Example
yy	Year	`DATEADD(d, -1, '20170725')`
mm	Month	`DATEADD(d, -2, '20170725')`
dd	Day	`DATEADD(d, -90, '20170725')`
qq	Quarter	`DATEADD(d, -1, '20170725')`
dw	Day of Week	`DATEADD(d, -1, '20170725')`

Table 8.3: DATEADD() Elements

8.15 Displaying the Data for the Previous Three Months

Now suppose you want to see the rolling sum of car sales for each make sold during the previous three months up to and including the current date. This piece of SQL can do it for you:

```
SELECT     MK.MakeName, SUM(SD.SalePrice) AS CumulativeSales
FROM       Data.Make AS MK INNER JOIN Data.Model AS MD
           ON MK.MakeID = MD.MakeID
INNER JOIN Data.Stock AS ST ON ST.ModelID = MD.ModelID
INNER JOIN Data.SalesDetails SD ON ST.StockCode = SD.StockID
INNER JOIN Data.Sales AS SA ON SA.SalesID = SD.SalesID
WHERE      CAST(SA.SaleDate AS DATE)
           BETWEEN DATEADD(m, -3, CAST(GETDATE() AS DATE))
           AND CAST(GETDATE() AS DATE)
GROUP BY   MK.MakeName
ORDER BY   MK.MakeName ASC
```

Run this code, and you will see the output shown in *Figure 8.15*.

	MakeName	CumulativeSales
1	Alfa Romeo	25000.00
2	Aston Martin	49500.00
3	BMW	5500.00
4	Ferrari	405000.00
5	Lamborghini	480000.00
6	Mercedes	100275.00
7	Noble	55000.00
8	Porsche	84750.00
9	Rolls Royce	165000.00
10	Triumph	39500.00

Figure 8.15: Returning sales for a time period up to a specific date

How It Works

This code snippet introduces another new date function, the GETDATE() function. All this function means in SQL is "now." So, this query will always display data relative to the day that it is run. If you run it today, you will see data up to today's date. Run it tomorrow and the data will be different because the rolling total now ends on a different date.

This query does the following:

First:	It aggregates the total sales for each make, using a SUM on the SalePrice field and a GROUP BY on the MakeName field so that you see the total sales by make. This requires joining five tables so that the necessary fields can be used in the query.
Second:	It limits the data to the last three months using the DATEADD() function that was introduced in the previous section and specifies that the period covers "now until three months subtracted from now"—using the BETWEEN... AND function. What can make this WHERE clause seem a little complex at first is the fact that it also applies the CAST() function. If you remember from earlier in this chapter, some dates also have time elements, which can make results go awry on certain occasions. So, you have to remove the time element to ensure that everything will work cleanly. What is important to know is that the GETDATE() function includes the time of day. So, a query that you run at 9 a.m. could give a different result than one you run at 6 p.m. Therefore—and to be absolutely certain that you are looking at the whole day when querying— you have to wrap GETDATE() in the CAST function to ensure that the query will always return the same results.
Third:	It presents the results in alphabetical order of make using the MakeName field in the ORDER BY clause.

8.16 Finding the Current System Date

If all you want to do is to check the current date and time, then a single line of SQL can do this for you.

```
SELECT GETDATE()
```

Running this code will return the date that your Oracle server assumes to be the current date.

How It Works

This short piece of code uses the DUAL table you saw in Chapter 3 as the "dummy" data source. From this, you return the current system date using the SYSDATE function.

Tricks and Traps

I have just one point to make here.

- It can be useful to check the system date before carrying out date calculations. After all, you should never trust a computer!

Conclusion

This chapter has taken you on a whirlwind tour of the core date functions that you will need to analyze how data evolves over time. You have discovered how to query data for a specific date or a range of dates. You have seen, too, that you can look at data over years, quarters, weeks, months, or days. Indeed, you learned how to analyze data "to date" and how to compare data with previous time periods.

Analyzing data over time is such a vast subject that we have been able only to scratch the surface in a single chapter of all that you can do. However, you can rest assured that you will be seeing many more ways of handling date and time data in Chapter 20.

Core Knowledge Learned in This Chapter

These are the keywords that you learned in this chapter:

Concept	Description
DATEDIFF()	This function finds the number of days, months, years, and so on, between two given dates.
CAST()	This function converts a datetime data type to a date.
YEAR()	This function isolates the year part of a date.
MONTH()	This function isolates the month part of a date.
DAY()	This function isolates the day part of a date.
DATEPART()	This function returns the quarter, weekday, and so on, for a date.
DATENAME()	This function displays the name of part of the date such as the month or weekday.
DATEADD()	This function adds or subtracts a number of days, months, years, and so on, to or from a given data and finds the date in the future or the past.
GETDATE()	This function finds the current date.

CHAPTER 9

Formatting Text in Query Output

A large part of SQL code is written purely to delve into mounds of data and return carefully chosen and filtered output. However, this is not the whole picture. Sometimes you will need your SQL skills to tweak the presentation of the data you are delivering. This chapter explains how to take the text that is returned by a query and make the output easier to read as well as more meaningful.

Enhancing the Output from SQL Queries

So, after the logical and technical focus of the previous chapters, it is time to learn some presentation techniques. You may not need these approaches on all occasions, but there are bound to be times when you will need to select not just a column of data but part of a column. Perhaps you will need to amalgamate two or more columns into one. Maybe you will need to convert the contents of a column to lowercase or simply add some extra text to the concents of a column.

Presenting your data is, then, the subject of this chapter. After all, delivering clear and comprehensible analysis is your aim. It follows that knowing how to polish the final delivery is every bit as fundamental as the initial analysis.

9.1 Adding Text to the Output

On some occasions you may want not just to list some data but to add repetitive text to the output. Suppose, for instance, that you want to add the word Customer: before each customer name in a query. You can do this using the following code:

```
SELECT 'Customer: ' + CustomerName AS Customer

FROM   Data.Customer
```

Executing this piece of code will give you a result similar to that shown in *Figure 9.1.*

Figure 9.1: *Adding text to the output from a column*

How It Works

Any text that you like can be added to the data in an output column. However, so that SQL knows that what you are adding is extra text—and not a SQL keyword of some kind—you need to place the additional text in single quotes. Then you use the plus (+) operator to append the column containing the variable data. Of course, you can start with the column name and then add some fixed text afterward if you prefer.

Tricks and Traps

Although this technique is relatively simple, there are nonetheless a couple of things you should know.

- You do not need to add an alias when adding text to a single field because SQL Server will use the name of the field you are adding text to as the column header. Of course, you can add an alias if you want.

- You can use most printable characters (such as spaces) in the text that you add to a column name. Just ensure that any text is inside the single quotes.

- If you want to add a single quote to the complementary text, then you will need to double up on any quotes used. So, to add the text Yesterday's Sales, the SQL will look like this:

```
SELECT 'Yesterday''s Sales for ' + CUSTOMERNAME

FROM    Data.SalesByCountry
```

9.2 Adding Text to Numbers

Occasionally numbers are just not enough. You need to enhance them by adding some explanatory text. SQL, of course, can let you do this. The following short snippet shows how:

```
SELECT 'Sold For:' + STR(SalePrice)

FROM    Data.SalesDetails
```

Running this SQL will return the output in *Figure 9.2*, which is what you expect to see.

	(No column name)
1	Sold For: 65000
2	Sold For: 220000
3	Sold For: 19500
4	Sold For: 11500
5	Sold For: 19950
6	Sold For: 29500
7	Sold For: 49500
8	Sold For: 76000
9	Sold For: 19600
10	Sold For: 36500
11	Sold For: 8500
12	Sold For: 80500
13	Sold For: 169500
14	Sold For: 8950
15	Sold For: 195000

Figure 9.2: Adding text to a numeric field

How It Works

The SQL STR() function takes a numeric field and converts it to a character string. Then the resulting string can be concatenated (added if you prefer) to any text you want.

Be warned, however, that if all you do is try to add text to the data from a column in a table when creating a query, you will see an error message that begins as follows:

```
Error converting data type...
```

This means the column of data to which you want to add text contains a number. More precisely, the database developer set the column to hold a specific numeric or date data type.

So, if you write the following code, you will get an error message:

```
SELECT  'Sold For: ' + SalePrice AS SalePrice
FROM    Data.SalesDetails
```

This is because you are trying to add text to a number, and SQL Server cannot do this. So, you always have to convert numeric date to a string before appending or prepending text to a number.

Tricks and Traps

Using the STR() function does mean remembering this key point:

- The STR() function will work only if you use it on a numeric column. If you try to use it on a date or a string of characters, SQL Server will return an error message.

> Note: I deliberately avoided providing an alias for the column in this example. As you can see, SQL Server provided the column header "(No column name)."

9.3 Amalgamating Columns

Relational databases—by definition—fragment data into small, independent pieces. That is a key factor in their success and the way they work. Yet when you want to output data, you frequently need to join data from two or more columns into one piece of information. This technique is called concatenation and can be applied to any column containing any type of data.

Take a look at the following code snippet:

```
SELECT CustomerName, Address1 + ' ' + Town + ' '
       + PostCode AS FullAddress
FROM   Data.Customer
```

Executing this code returns the output in *Figure 9.3*.

	CustomerName	FullAddress
1	Magic Motors	27, Handsworth Road Birmingham B1 7AZ
2	Snazzy Roadsters	102, Bleak Street Birmingham B3 5ST
3	Birmingham Executive Prestige Vehicles	96, Aardvark Avenue Birmingham B2 8UH
4	WunderKar	NULL
5	Casseroles Chromes	NULL
6	Le Luxe en Motion	Avenue des Indes, 26 Geneva CH-1201
7	Eat My Exhaust Ltd	29, Kop Hill Liverpool L1 8UY
8	M. Pierre Dubois	NULL
9	Sondra Horowitz	NULL
10	Wonderland Wheels	57, Grosvenor Estate Avenue London E7 4BR
11	London Executive Prestige Vehicles	199, Park Lane London NW1 0AK
12	Glittering Prize Cars Ltd	46, Golders Green Road London E17 9IK
13	La Bagnole de Luxe	NULL
14	Convertible Dreams	31, Archbishop Ave London SW2 6PL
15	Alexei Tolstoi	83, Abbey Road London N4 2CV

Figure 9.3: *Concatenating data from several columns*

How It Works

Using the plus (+) operator takes the data from another column and appends it to the end of the column that you have already added to a SELECT clause. You then add any separator text (spaces, commas, and so on) that you want to add to make the result more readable. As you saw in the previous section, any text you add to a query must be in single quotes.

Tricks and Traps

Here are some of the tricks and trap you need to know:

- If you are amalgamating (concatenating to use the technical term) fields that are numeric or dates, then you need to use the STR() function that you saw in the previous section or you will get an error message. As an example, suppose you want to blend the data in the Make, Model, and SalePrice columns of the SalesByCountry table. You will need to write this:

```
SELECT  MakeName + ', ' + ModelName + ': ' + STR(SalePrice)
FROM    Data.SalesByCountry
```

This will convert the sale price to text and then join the data from all three columns—with the appropriate spaces and punctuation.

- As you are, by definition, using data from several fields, SQL cannot know what name to give to the resulting column. So, you should probably add an alias when concatenating data.

9.4 Concatenating and Grouping

The sales director now wants a list of all the different make and model combinations that have ever been sold with the total sale price for each combination. However, this time she wants to display the make and model in the same column. As she is hovering near your desk, you quickly produce the following piece of SQL to deliver what she wants:

```
SELECT    MK.MakeName + ', ' + MD.ModelName AS MakeAndModel
          ,SUM(SD.SalePrice) As TotalSold
FROM      Data.Stock ST
INNER JOIN Data.Model MD
          ON ST.ModelID = MD.ModelID
INNER JOIN Data.Make MK
          ON MD.MakeID = MK.MakeID
INNER JOIN Data.SalesDetails SD
          ON ST.StockCode = SD.StockID
INNER JOIN Data.Sales SA
          ON SD.SalesID = SA.SalesID
GROUP BY  MK.MakeName + ', ' + MD.ModelName
```

Running this query produces the output in *Figure 9.4.*

	MakeAndModel	TotalSold
1	Alfa Romeo, 1750	13525.00
2	Alfa Romeo, Giulia	89695.00
3	Alfa Romeo, Giulietta	92190.00
4	Alfa Romeo, Spider	48100.00
5	Aston Martin, DB2	456440.00
6	Aston Martin, DB4	281700.00
7	Aston Martin, DB5	300340.00
8	Aston Martin, DB6	1019095.00
9	Aston Martin, DB9	959500.00
10	Aston Martin, Rapide	302500.00
11	Aston Martin, Vanquish	361040.00
12	Aston Martin, Vantage	343500.00
13	Aston Martin, Virage	1078640.00
14	Austin, Cambridge	22500.00
15	Austin, Lichfield	30100.00

Figure 9.4: Grouping on concatenated fields

How It Works

It is vital when you are using a GROUP BY clause to include all the fields that are in the SELECT clause in the GROUP BY clause—if these fields are not part of an aggregation function such as SUM(). This means you generally have to copy the fields from the SELECT clause to the GROUP BY clause, as we did in this example.

Tricks and Traps

There is one variation on a theme you can use when grouping on aggregated fields, noted here:

` • You do not need to add the fields that are used in the SELECT clause exactly as they appear. That is, you could write the GROUP BY clause like this:

```
GROUP BY    MakeName, ModelName
```

9.5 Avoiding NULLs in Text-Based Data

If you take a closer look at the output shown in *Figure 9.3*, you will see a large number of records that only show NULL as the result of joining the Address, Town, and PostCode fields. Yet if you look at the data in these fields in the Customer table, you will notice that there is data for at least one of these fields for clients such as WunderKar—and yet when the fields are concatenated, they show nothing at all.

Fortunately, SQL has a solution to this problem. Take a look at the following SQL snippet that is adapted from the initial code in the previous example:

```
SELECT CustomerName, ISNULL(Address1, '') + ' ' + ISNULL(Town, '') + ' '
                    + ISNULL(PostCode, '') AS FullAddress
FROM    Data.Customer
```

The result will now look like the record set shown in *Figure 9.5.*

	CustomerName	FullAddress
1	Magic Motors	27, Handsworth Road Birmingham B1 7AZ
2	Snazzy Roadsters	102, Bleak Street Birmingham B3 5ST
3	Birmingham Executive Prestige Vehicles	96, Aardvark Avenue Birmingham B2 8UH
4	WunderKar	AlexanderPlatz 205 Berlin
5	Casseroles Chromes	29, Rue Gigondas Lyon
6	Le Luxe en Motion	Avenue des Indes, 26 Geneva CH-1201
7	Eat My Exhaust Ltd	29, Kop Hill Liverpool L1 8UY
8	M. Pierre Dubois	14, Rue De La Hutte Marseille
9	Sondra Horowitz	10040 Great Western Road Los Angeles
10	Wonderland Wheels	57, Grosvenor Estate Avenue London E7 4BR
11	London Executive Prestige Vehicles	199, Park Lane London NW1 0AK
12	Glittering Prize Cars Ltd	46, Golders Green Road London E17 9IK
13	La Bagnole de Luxe	890 Place de la Concorde Paris
14	Convertible Dreams	31, Archbishop Ave London SW2 6PL
15	Alexei Tolstoi	83, Abbey Road London N4 2CV

Figure 9.5: Adding the ISNULL() function to avoid NULL propagation

How It Works

A NULL value in any field—even if it is a text field—will "propagate" a NULL value into all the other fields you concatenate it with. This will result in a NULL being output. This is to all intents and purposes the same effect as you saw for numbers in Chapter 3. However, I imagine that this is not what you expected—and certainly not what you want to see in the result.

The solution is the same for both letters and numbers. If you suspect that a column contains NULLs, then you are best advised to enclose the field name in the ISNULL() function. This function requires the following:

First:	The field containing possible NULL values you want to trap and replace with another character.
The replacement character:	That can be a blank space or an empty character (as it is in this example) in which case two single quotes will do the trick.

Tricks and Traps

Make sure you retain the following point when using the ISNULL() function, as it is important:

- If you are applying ISNULL() to a text field, you **must** set the replacement character to be text too. So, even if you are replacing NULL with a number, this must be in single quotes.

9.6 Adding Multiple Pieces of Text to Numbers

Occasionally you may want to output data from text and numeric fields joined together in a single element. You could, for instance, want to add the word Sales before the sale price and a currency indicator afterward. The following SQL shows you how this can be done:

```
SELECT      CONCAT('Sales: ', TotalSalePrice ,' GBP')

            AS SalePriceInPounds

FROM        Data.Sales
```

Running this code gives the results shown in *Figure 9.6.*

	SalePriceInPounds
1	Sales: 65000.00 GBP
2	Sales: 220000.10 GBP
3	Sales: 19500.00 GBP
4	Sales: 11500.00 GBP
5	Sales: 19900.00 GBP
6	Sales: 29500.00 GBP
7	Sales: 49500.20 GBP
8	Sales: 76000.90 GBP
9	Sales: 19600.00 GBP
10	Sales: 36500.00 GBP
11	Sales: 89000.00 GBP
12	Sales: 169500.00 GBP
13	Sales: 8950.00 GBP
14	Sales: 195000.00 GBP
15	Sales: 22950.00 GBP

Figure 9.6: Adding text to the output from a numeric field using the CONCAT() function

How It Works

As you saw previously, SQL will not let you just assemble the contents of various fields by stringing them together—or even to add descriptive text to numbers—

without a little tweaking. Another way to output dates or numbers with standard text is to use the CONCAT() function. This lets you join together multiple fields and/or text to produce the output that you want. The result is the same as if you had used the STR() function to convert a number to a string before you concatenate it. However, if you have multiple fields to join together, then the CONCAT() function can be much easier to use. Just make sure you separate each text or field with a comma and that you place all text in single quotes.

Tricks and Traps

The CONCAT() function can really be incredibly useful. You can really take advantage of it if you bear the following points in mind:

- Normally you don't worry about formatting numbers in SQL like you do in Excel or reporting software. Indeed, you nearly always have to leave numbers unformatted because otherwise they will be considered text by SQL Server. However, there could be cases where you need to format numbers (albeit to a limited extent). One way to do this is to append text to a number.

- Note that you can include spaces inside the single quotes around the text you are appending to the figures (the GBP) to enhance the final appearance of the output.

- This example shows only three elements inside the CONCAT() function, but there you can add several more fields and text if you want.

- The CONCAT() function will also handle date data types and convert them to strings.

- A final—but extremely useful—advantage of using the CONCAT() function is that it handles NULLs flawlessly. So, even if one or more of the fields that you apply it to contain a NULL, this will not cause the final output to become a NULL.

9.7 Converting Text to Uppercase

SQL Server can store alphabetical data in either uppercase or lowercase characters. However, the sales director wants a list of all the customer names in uppercase for a mailmerge operation. As there will inevitably be times when you want to standardize the output without having to worry about how the data itself is stored, SQL can, of course, do this for you:

```
SELECT      UPPER(CustomerName) AS Customer

FROM        Data.Customer
```

Running this query gives the results shown in *Figure 9.7*.

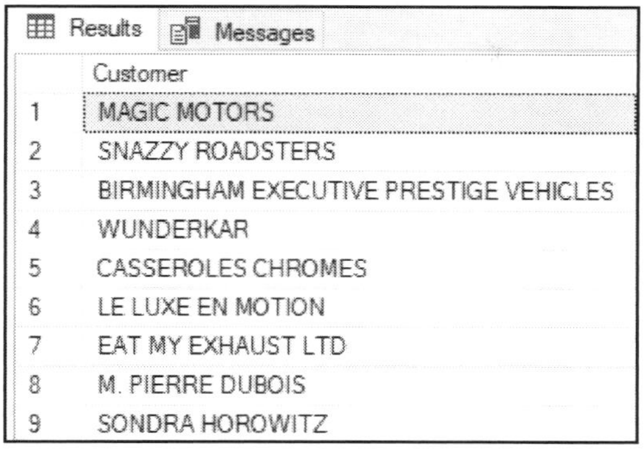

	Customer
1	MAGIC MOTORS
2	SNAZZY ROADSTERS
3	BIRMINGHAM EXECUTIVE PRESTIGE VEHICLES
4	WUNDERKAR
5	CASSEROLES CHROMES
6	LE LUXE EN MOTION
7	EAT MY EXHAUST LTD
8	M. PIERRE DUBOIS
9	SONDRA HOROWITZ

Figure 9.7: *Converting the text in a field to uppercase using the UPPER() function*

How It Works

Applying the UPPER() function to the CustomerName field ensures that every customer name that is output by the query will appear in uppercase. The UPPER() function requires at least one field as its parameter.

Tricks and Traps

These are a few suggestions of things you might need to be aware of when using the UPPER() function:

- Using a function—any function—means that SQL will not deduce the column name (even if it seems obvious). So, you will have to add an alias if you want the query output not to say "No column name" for any columns you are converting to uppercase.
- This function will have no effect on any nonalphabetic characters in a field. So, numbers and punctuation will not change.
- This function is purely "decorative" and has no effect whatsoever on the underlying data. If the customer name is stored in lowercase in the database, it will stay that way.
- You can apply the UPPER() function to multiple fields at once if you need to do so. So, you could write SQL like this:

```
SELECT     UPPER(CustomerID + ' ' + InvoiceNumber)
FROM       Data.Sales
```

9.8 Converting Text to Lowercase

Just as you can convert text (or strings, to give them their technical definition) to uppercase, you can convert them to lowercase. Take a look at the following code:

```
SELECT      LOWER(ModelName) AS Model

FROM        Data.Model
```

Executing this query gives the output shown in *Figure 9.8.*

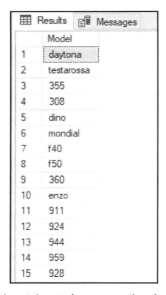

Figure 9.8: Converting strings to lowercase using the LOWER() function

How It Works

Applying the LOWER() function to the ModelName field ensures that every vehicle model that is output by the query will appear in lowercase. This will not affect the way that the original data is stored and will produce the same result whether the original data in the source table is in lowercase, uppercase, or a mixture of the two. As you can see, numbers are not affected by this function.

9.9 Extracting the First Few Characters from a Field

Sometimes text can be just too long. At least this is what the marketing director thinks, as she wants to show the make names as acronyms using the first three letters of each make in a catalog of products. Fortunately, SQL lets you choose to output only a few characters of longer text—as you can see in the next code excerpt:

```
SELECT      ModelName + ' (' + LEFT(MakeName, 3) + ')' AS MakeAndModel

FROM        Data.Make

INNER JOIN Data.Model

ON          Make.MakeID = Model.MakeID
```

Running this query gives the results in *Figure 9.9.*

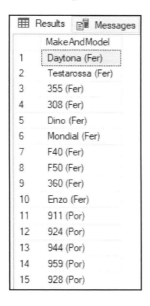

Figure 9.9: Using the LEFT() function to extract a
specific number of characters from the left of a string

How It Works

Not only does this SELECT clause concatenate strings from two fields (ModelName and Make), it adds brackets to the result. The LEFT() function ensures that only the three leftmost characters from the Make field are used when creating the make and model composite name.

The LEFT() function works like this:

First:	Enter LEFT and a left parenthesis.
Second:	Enter the field name containing the data you want to extract a few characters from, followed by a comma.
Third:	Enter the number of characters to extract from the field as the second part of the LEFT() function.
Finally:	Add a right parenthesis to end the LEFT() function.

Tricks and Traps

When using functions like this one, you need to be mindful of the following:

- Functions like LEFT() that require more than one parameter require that each parameter inside the parentheses is separated by a comma.

- The LEFT() function requires you first to specify the `field` you are extracting characters from and then the `number` of characters you want to display. It is important to respect the order of these two elements (field first and then number of characters) when you use the LEFT() function.

- Text functions are frequently used as part of a more complex formatting requirement. As you go through this chapter, remember that you can combine multiple text functions in many ways to get the output you are looking for.

- Like most functions, LEFT() really requires an alias because it will not deduce the column name in the output header row.

- You can not alias tables when using small tables containing only a few columns.

9.10 Displaying the Three Characters at the Right of Text

On some occasions you may have to isolate a series of characters from the right of a field. In Prestige Cars' system, for instance, the finance director wants you to select only the three characters at the right of the invoice number as these indicate the sequential number for the invoice. The SQL to do this is as follows:

```
SELECT      RIGHT(InvoiceNumber, 3) AS InvoiceSequenceNumber
FROM        Data.Sales
ORDER BY    InvoiceSequenceNumber
```

Running this query returns results similar to *Figure 9.10.*

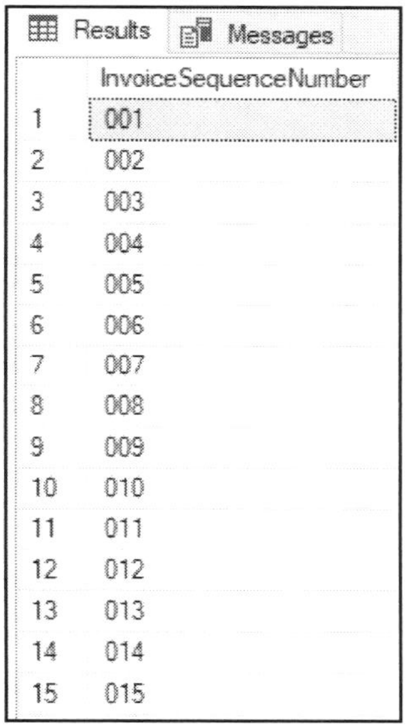

	InvoiceSequenceNumber
1	001
2	002
3	003
4	004
5	005
6	006
7	007
8	008
9	009
10	010
11	011
12	012
13	013
14	014
15	015

Figure 9.10: *Extracting characters from the right of a string using RIGHT()*

How It Works

The RIGHT() function ensures that only a specified number of characters from the right of the InvoiceNumber field are displayed. Any characters to the left of these characters (however many there are) are discarded. The RIGHT() function is pretty much like the LEFT() function—only it operates at the other end of the text in a field. You specify the field that you are using as the base data and then give the number of characters to extract from the right of the field.

One other thing that you did here is to sort the data on the output from the RIGHT() function. There are two ways of doing this.

Either:	Specify the same function—RIGHT(InvoiceNumber, 3)—that you used in the SELECT statement in the ORDER BY clause.
Or:	Use the alias in the ORDER BY clause as we did here.

Tricks and Traps

Our comments on using functions like RIGHT()—or LEFT() for that matter—largely concern sorting the data.

- Using the alias to sort data is often a lot simpler than rewriting the function that produced the output data.
- If you are sorting the data by a subset of the contents of a field, then you `must` either use the alias from the SELECT clause or rewrite the function in the ORDER BY clause. If you use the field name on its own you will probably not get the output you are expecting.

9.11 Displaying a Given Number of Characters at a Specific Place in Text

In the Prestige Cars IT system, the fourth and fifth characters of the invoice number indicate the country where the vehicles were shipped. Knowing this, the sales director wants to extract only these characters from the invoice number field in order to analyze destination countries. Here is the SQL to do this:

```
SELECT      SUBSTRING(InvoiceNumber, 4, 2) AS DestinationCountry
FROM        Data.Sales
```

If you execute this query, you will see the data that is shown in *Figure 9.11*.

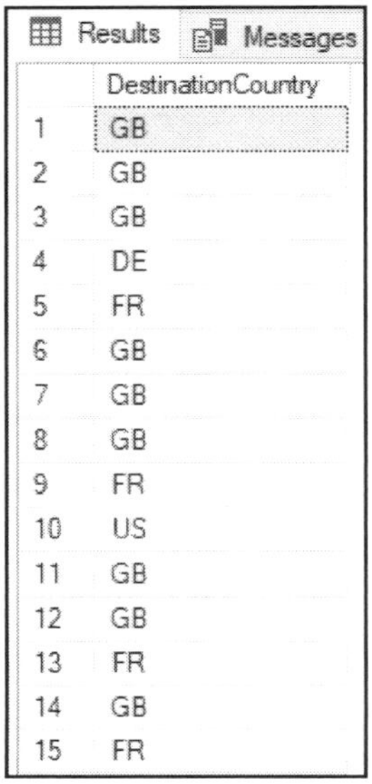

	DestinationCountry
1	GB
2	GB
3	GB
4	DE
5	FR
6	GB
7	GB
8	GB
9	FR
10	US
11	GB
12	GB
13	FR
14	GB
15	FR

Figure 9.11: *Extracting a fixed number of characters from inside a field using SUBSTRING()*

How It Works

If you are always extracting a fixed number of characters from the same starting point in the text of a field, then SUBSTRING() is the function to use. However, this function takes three parameters (or needs three pieces of information) to work correctly.

First:	Indicate the field you are working on.
Second:	Give the number of characters in from the left where you want to start extracting text.
Finally:	Provide the number of characters to extract commencing at the starting point defined in the preceding parameter.

As with all functions, each parameter is separated from the others by a comma.

As this function can seem unwieldy at first glance, *Figure 9.12* explains it more visually.

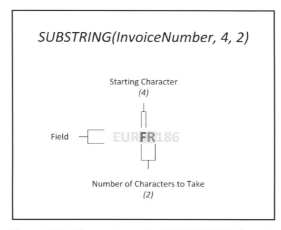

Figure 9.12. The anatomy of a SUBSTRING() function

Tricks and Traps

There are a couple of important points to retain here.

- It is vital to respect the order that you enter the parameters (starting point and number of characters) when using the SUBSTRING function, or you are likely to get only gibberish returned.

- Only a few functions require more than one or two parameters to be supplied, so SUBSTRING is fortunately more an exception than a rule.

9.12 Filtering Records Based on Part of a Field

In the Prestige Cars database, the invoice number field always begins with three characters that indicate the currency of payment (even if all the invoices are in pounds sterling). This allows you to produce a list of sales in a specified currency—which is great as the sales director has requested a list of sales where the invoice was paid in euros. The SQL that can do this is mercifully simple.

```
SELECT      InvoiceNumber, TotalSalePrice
FROM        Data.Sales
WHERE       LEFT(InvoiceNumber, 3) = 'EUR'
```

Executing this query gives the results in *Figure 9.13*.

	InvoiceNumber	TotalSalePrice
1	EURDE004	11500.00
2	EURFR005	19900.00
3	EURFR009	19600.00
4	EURFR013	8950.00
5	EURFR015	22950.00
6	EURFR018	75500.00
7	EURFR031	2550.00
8	EURDE036	71890.00
9	EURFR037	39500.00
10	EURDE043	99500.00
11	EURFR047	49580.00
12	EURFR048	5500.00
13	EURFR051	174650.00
14	EURES058	79500.00
15	EURIT059	14590.00

Figure 9.13: Using a string function in a WHERE clause

How It Works

This approach allows you to filter the InvoiceNumber field and output only those records where the three leftmost characters are EUR.

Here you are using a string function in the WHERE clause of a SQL query. This function is applied just as it would be in a SELECT clause. In this particular case, the LEFT() function is used. The first parameter is the field from which you want to extract part of the data (the InvoiceNumber field). The second parameter is the number of characters to extract (three in this case). The value that is returned from the function is then used to filter the data.

Tricks and Traps

Note the following:

- You can use a function in a WHERE clause without using it in the SELECT clause.

- You can use the "full" field that you are filtering on in the SELECT clause without affecting the WHERE clause in any way.

- You might want to add the function that you are using in the WHERE clause to the SELECT clause initially (with or without the filter) so that you can see whether the function is giving the result you expect.

9.13 Filtering Data Using Specific Characters at a Given Position Inside a Field

The sales director now wants to see all the cars shipped to France but made in Italy. Fortunately, the invoice number definition used by Prestige Cars guarantees that the fourth and fifth characters of the invoice number contain the two-character code of the country where the car was shipped. So, you can use this information to extract a list of vehicles delivered to one country—and use another field to add a second field to restrict the country of manufacture. The SQL to do this is as follows:

```
SELECT      SA.InvoiceNumber, SA.TotalSalePrice

FROM        Data.Make AS MK INNER JOIN Data.Model AS MD

            ON MK.MakeID = MD.MakeID

            INNER JOIN Data.Stock AS ST ON ST.ModelID = MD.ModelID

            INNER JOIN Data.SalesDetails SD ON ST.StockCode =
SD.StockID

            INNER JOIN Data.Sales AS SA ON SA.SalesID = SD.SalesID

WHERE       SUBSTRING(SA.InvoiceNumber, 4, 2)  = 'FR'

            AND MK.MakeCountry = 'ITA'
```

Running this query gives the results that you can see in *Figure 9.14.*

	InvoiceNumber	TotalSalePrice
1	EURFR186	155000.00
2	EURFR254	269500.00
3	EURFR151	255950.00
4	EURFR235	310000.00
5	EURFR121	365000.00
6	EURFR122	395000.00
7	EURFR107	169500.00
8	EURFR189	235000.00
9	EURFR031	2550.00
10	EURFR194	62700.00
11	EURFR241	9950.00

Figure 9.14. Using SUBSTRING() and a standard comparison operator in a WHERE clause

How It Works

The point of this example is to make it clear that a WHERE clause can contain multiple criteria—both straight comparisons and more complex filters using functions. Here you are using a WHERE clause to filter the InvoiceNumber field where the fourth and fifth characters are FR (to isolate cars delivered to France), as well as using a different field (country of make) to specify that the car was built in Italy.

The WHERE clause of this query is where the action takes place. Its anatomy is as follows:

First:	The SUBSTRING() function is applied. The first parameter (the field name) is InvoiceNumber in this example. The second parameter—the number of characters from the left where the extraction will begin—is set to four. Then the number of characters to extract at this point in the text is set to two. The filter is then defined as being the two characters FR (for France).
Second:	An AND operator is added to the WHERE clause to add a second filter element to the query.
Finally:	The MakeCountry field is set to ITA (for Italy). Of course, this means knowing that the MakeCountry field uses ISO three-character acronyms to represent countries—but this is part and parcel of the need to know your data before you can use it.

Conclusion

This chapter gave you an overview of some of the core techniques you can apply to your code to adjust the presentation of text-based data. You saw how to extract part of a column of text and convert text from uppercase to lowercase, and vice versa. You also learned how to mix text and numbers in a single column.

These techniques enable you to use and shape the data so that you can go beyond merely listing columns of data. Armed with the knowledge you have acquired in this chapter, not only can you query SQL Server data but you can present it in a more meaningful and comprehensible way to your users.

Core Knowledge Learned in This Chapter

These are the keywords and concepts you learned in this chapter:

Concept	Description
UPPER()	This function converts any text into uppercase characters. Numbers and symbols are not affected by this function.
LOWER()	This function converts any text into lowercase characters. Numbers and symbols are not affected by this function.
LEFT()	This function extracts a defined number of characters from the left of a string.
RIGHT()	This function extracts a defined number of characters from the right of a string.
STR()	This function converts a number to text so that it can be used as a string of characters in a piece of SQL.
SUBSTRING()	This function extracts a defined number of characters from a string, beginning at a specified number of characters from the left of the string.
Concatenation	This technique joins the output from two or more columns into a single output field.

CHAPTER 10

Formatting Numbers and Dates

SQL will always attempt to present numbers at the most detailed level possible. This could mean displaying more decimals than you actually need. Equally it will display dates in a way that you (or the users you deliver the output to) find a little clunky. So, you need to be able to format both numbers and dates in ways that make the data more readable and intuitively comprehensible. This chapter covers a range of techniques that will help you acieve these aims.

Presenting Numbers and Dates

While learning to query data so that you always return the exact data you need is a science, presenting the results in a way that both you and your users understand is an art. You may want to remove the decimals from the output or apply a specific number format, for instance. Alternatively, you could need to display a date in a certain way—much as you would in Excel.

This chapter introduces the basic formatting techniques you should find essential when you are enhancing the presentation of your query results. So, while these techniques do not alter the accuracy of the output, they can make it considerably easier to understand.

Note: Formatting dates and numbers converts them into text. This means SQL will probably no longer be able to carry out any calculations on the formatted date or number. So, you should always format data once you are sure that this is the final result of a query.

10.1 Removing the Decimals from the Output

In some reports you just don't need decimals. So, SQL lets you remove them from output data really easily. Just take a look at the following snippet, which applies this technique to the Sale Price field:

```
SELECT     TotalSalePrice, FLOOR(TotalSalePrice) AS
SalePriceRoundedDown

FROM       Data.Sales
```

Applying this query gives the results in Figure 10.1. I have kept the original "untouched" data as well as the output from the FLOOR function so that you can see the difference when the function is applied.

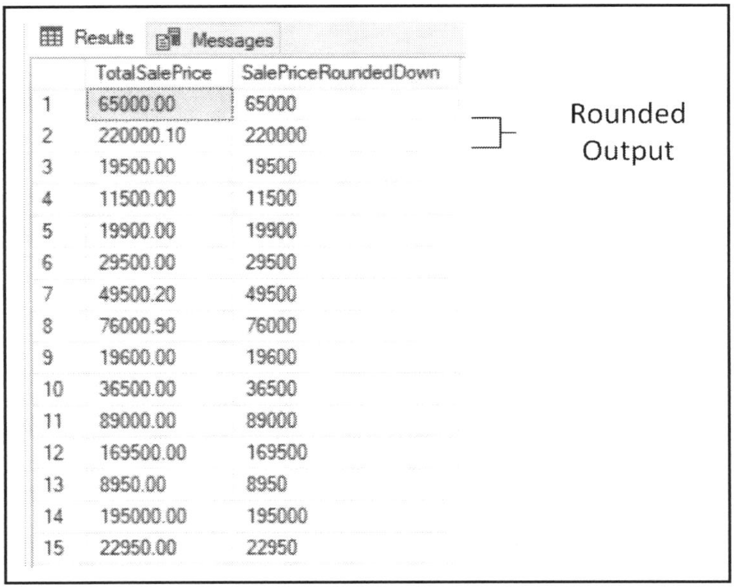

	TotalSalePrice	SalePriceRoundedDown
1	65000.00	65000
2	220000.10	220000
3	19500.00	19500
4	11500.00	11500
5	19900.00	19900
6	29500.00	29500
7	49500.20	49500
8	76000.90	76000
9	19600.00	19600
10	36500.00	36500
11	89000.00	89000
12	169500.00	169500
13	8950.00	8950
14	195000.00	195000
15	22950.00	22950

Figure 10.1: *Truncating decimals from a number using the FLOOR() function*

How It Works

The FLOOR function can be used to round down the decimals from a column of figures. No rounding is applied—the numbers are simply stripped of the decimal part. If the number does not contain any decimals, then it simply stays the same.

Tricks and Traps

You must remember one main factor when applying the FLOOR() function.

- The FLOOR function can be applied only to numeric data types.

10.2 Rounding a Field Up to the Nearest Whole Number

Just as you can round numbers down, you can also round them up in SQL. The following code snippet shows you how to do this to the TotalSalePrice field:

```
SELECT     TotalSalePrice, CEILING(TotalSalePrice) AS
SalePriceRoundedUp

FROM       Data.Sales
```

Running this query gives the results in *Figure 10.2*.

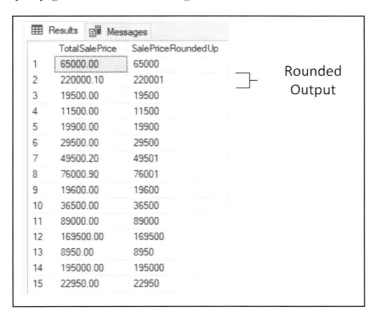

Figure 10.2: *Rounding up a decimal number to the nearest whole number using the CEILING() function*

How It Works

The CEILING() function removes the decimals from the figures that you are outputting but rounds the number up to the nearest whole number (or integer if you prefer the term). I have included the original data in the output so that you can compare the two versions of the numbers. In the real world, you would probably display only one version of the data.

Tricks and Traps

As was the case with the FLOOR() function, the following is true:

- The ceiling function can be applied only to numeric data types.

10.3 Rounding a Value to the Nearest Whole Number

If you want to round decimals up or down to the nearest whole number, SQL Server has the ROUND() function to do this, as the following SQL snippet makes clear:

```
SELECT      TotalSalePrice, ROUND(TotalSalePrice, 0) AS
SalePriceRounded

FROM        Data.Sales
```

Running this query shows you both the original and rounded values, as you can see in *Figure 10.3*.

	TotalSalePrice	SalePriceRounded
1	65000.00	65000.00
2	220000.10	220000.00
3	19500.00	19500.00
4	11500.00	11500.00
5	19900.00	19900.00
6	29500.00	29500.00
7	49500.20	49500.00
8	76000.90	76001.00
9	19600.00	19600.00
10	36500.00	36500.00

Figure 10.3. *Applying the Round function to numeric output*

How It Works

The ROUND() function finds the nearest whole number—be it higher or lower than the numeric value that you want to output. As you can see from Figure 10.12 (where you can compare the sale price to the rounded sale price), this can mean rounding down, just like it can mean rounding up.

The ROUND() function needs you to add a parameter that indicates how many decimal places the number is rounded to. Using a 0 as the second parameter means no decimals—effectively removing the decimals from the field that is used as the first parameter.

Tricks and Traps

I have only one comment to make here.

- Exporting a rounded output to a spreadsheet and then calculating the total for the column can produce rounding errors (compared to calculating the total for a column where no rounding has been applied), as the decimals have been limited or removed definitively.

10.4 Rounding a Value Up or Down to the Nearest Thousand

When you are dealing with really large figures, you may want to round up or down to hundreds or even tens of thousands. SQL can do this easily, as the following code snippet shows:

```
SELECT     TotalSalePrice, ROUND(TotalSalePrice, -3)

           AS SalePriceRoundedUp

FROM       Data.Sales
```

Executing this query gives you the original data and the rounded output, as you can see in *Figure 10.4*.

	TotalSalePrice	SalePriceRoundedUp
1	65000.00	65000.00
2	220000.10	220000.00
3	19500.00	20000.00
4	11500.00	12000.00
5	19900.00	20000.00
6	29500.00	30000.00
7	49500.20	50000.00
8	76000.90	76000.00
9	19600.00	20000.00
10	36500.00	37000.00
11	89000.00	89000.00
12	169500.00	170000.00
13	8950.00	9000.00
14	195000.00	195000.00
15	22950.00	23000.00

Figure 10.4. *Rounding to the nearest thousand*

How It Works

The ROUND() function takes two parameters:

First:	The numeric field whose output you want to modify.
Second:	The type of rounding to be applied. This can be a positive or negative number. A positive number affects the number of decimals, and a negative number affects the integer values (the whole number).

In this example, the SalesDate field is rounded to the nearest thousand. This happens because the second parameter used in the ROUND() function is negative. Consequently, the rounding is applied to the nearest tens, hundreds, or thousands in this particular case. You can even extend this to millions and billions if you want.

The negative number you use as the second parameter indicates how the number is rounded. You apply the number shown in the left column of *Table 10.1* as the second parameter of the ROUND() function to obtain the result described in the right column.

Element	Comments
-1	Rounds to the nearest 10
-2	Rounds to the nearest 100
-3	Rounds to the nearest 1,000
-4	Rounds to the nearest 10,000
-5	Rounds to the nearest 100,000

Table 10.1: Rounding Up Numbers

You can continue and round to millions or billions if you really want, but ideally you get the idea—the parameter represents the number of zeros that you will get in the rounded result. If you are looking only at rounding to a decimal value, then you simply make the second parameter of the ROUND() function a positive number—just as you did in the previous section.

10.5 Displaying a Value in a Specific Currency

The sales director is in a hurry and says that she will not have the time to format the data you send her. As a consequence, she wants you to output a list of vehicle sales that can be immediately presented to the CEO.

It is worth noting that if you are using SQL output directly—that is, not as a source for another program like Excel or PowerBI—then you may want to produce formatted output that is easier for your public to understand. You can do this, too, as the following short SQL example shows:

```
SELECT     FORMAT(TotalSalePrice, 'C', 'en-gb') AS SterlingSalePrice
FROM       Data.Sales
```

Running this query gives the results in *Figure 10.5*, where the result appears in pounds sterling.

	Sterling Sale Price
1	£65,000.00
2	£220,000.10
3	£19,500.00
4	£11,500.00
5	£19,900.00
6	£29,500.00
7	£49,500.20
8	£76,000.90
9	£19,600.00
10	£36,500.00
11	£89,000.00
12	£169,500.00
13	£8,950.00
14	£195,000.00
15	£22,950.00

Figure 10.5. Formatting numbers as dollars

How It Works

As of SQL Server 2012, you can apply output formats to numbers. You do this by applying the FORMAT() function to a numeric field. The FORMAT function requires three parameters.

The field to format:	This is the numeric field you want to display with the format applied.
The format code:	This is the format code—chosen from a specific list, some of which you can see in *Table 10.2*—that indicates the format you want to apply.
The culture code:	This is the language and culture of the formatting. Setting this to en-gb, for instance, will apply the British pound symbol (£). This is also known as the locale, or localization code.

Table 10.2 outlines a few of the most useful format codes. The list of possible cultures is fairly extensive, so we cannot repeat them all here. You are probably best searching for these online should you need them.

Element	Definition	Example	Comments
C	Currency	`FORMAT(SalePrice, 'C', 'en-gb)`	The currency indicator will depend on the culture setting.
E	Exponential or scientific notation	`FORMAT(SalePrice, 'E')`	This is also called the scientific format, and it can be a little hard to read.
F	Fixed number of decimals	`FORMAT(SalePrice, 'F5')`	Adding a number after the F sets the number of decimals that will be displayed.
G	General	`FORMAT(SalePrice, 'G')`	This format chooses the most compact of either fixed-point or scientific notation.

Table 10.2: Currency Formats

Tricks and Traps

It is important to remember that SQL is at its heart a query language and not a presentation tool. So, you need to take the following into consideration when delivering formatted output:

- This function was not available in versions of SQL Server prior to SQL Server 2012. So, you will get an error if you try to use it with older versions.

- You need to be careful if you are formatting numbers in T-SQL. This is because using the FORMAT function will convert the number to a string. This can make it difficult (if not impossible) to use the formatted number in a further calculation.

- It is probably obvious, but I prefer to mention anyway that there is no exchange rate conversion taking place here. All that happens is that the figures are formatted in dollars—just as you would in Excel, for instance.

10.6 Defining Your Own Number Formats

If the built-in number formats that SQL Server provides "out of the box" do not let you display a column as you would like, then you can create your own number formats. The following SQL snippet gives you an example of how you can do this to give the CEO a list of "Excel-style" sales figures with decimals and thousands separators:

```
SELECT     FORMAT(SalePrice, '#,#0.00') AS FormattedSalePrice

FROM       Data.SalesDetails
```

Running this piece of SQL will produce the output in *Figure 10.6*.

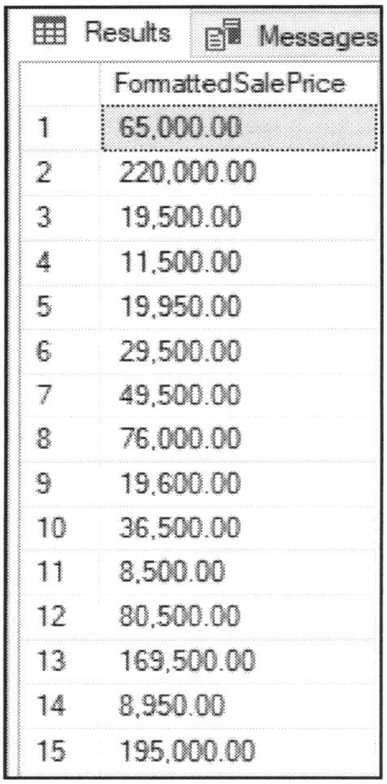

	FormattedSalePrice
1	65,000.00
2	220,000.00
3	19,500.00
4	11,500.00
5	19,950.00
6	29,500.00
7	49,500.00
8	76,000.00
9	19,600.00
10	36,500.00
11	8,500.00
12	80,500.00
13	169,500.00
14	8,950.00
15	195,000.00

Figure 10.6: *Applying a custom number format*

How It Works

In this example, the "raw" output from the SalePrice field is made more presentable using the FORMAT() function. This function takes two parameters.

First:	The field to format.
Second:	The code that specifies the format. This is a hand-crafted "composite" code that must be enclosed in single quotes. These codes are virtually identical to the codes that Excel uses, so you will (ideally) not find them too difficult.

The codes used in this example are explained in *Figure 10.7.*

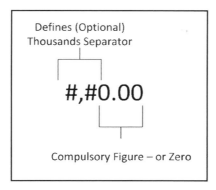

Figure 10.7: *Formatting codes*

Tricks and Traps

This example gave you a specific format that can be applied. Custom formats can be assembled using a series of placeholder elements.

- *Table 10.3* contains some of the most useful formatting codes that you can use to construct your own number formats.

Element	Description	Comments
0	The zero placeholder	Adds a zero even if no number is present.
#	The digit placeholder	Represents a number if one is present.
.	The decimal character	Sets the character that will be used before the decimals.
,	The thousands separator	Defines the thousands separator. This is repeated for millions, billions, and so on.
%	Percentage symbol	Adds a percentage symbol.
E0	Exponential indicator	Adds an exponential indicator.

Table 10.3: *Custom Number Formats*

- Formatting codes must be applied to numeric or (as you will see in a few pages) date fields. They will have no effect on text fields.

10.7 Outputting a Date in the ISO Date Format

Suppose you need to send a list of data to the CEO that contains a date, and you need that date to be in the specific format that she has requested (year, month, and day in figures in this occurrence). The following SQL will do that for you:

```
SELECT      InvoiceNumber

            ,CONVERT(DATE, SaleDate, 113) AS SaleDate

FROM        Data.Sales
```

Running this query gives the results shown in *Figure 10.8.*

	InvoiceNumber	SaleDate
1	GBPGB001	2015-01-02
2	GBPGB002	2015-01-25
3	GBPGB003	2015-02-03
4	EURDE004	2015-02-16
5	EURFR005	2015-01-02
6	GBPGB006	2015-03-14
7	GBPGB007	2015-03-24
8	GBPGB008	2015-03-30
9	EURFR009	2015-04-06
10	USDUS010	2015-04-04
11	GBPGB011	2015-04-30
12	GBPGB012	2015-05-10
13	EURFR013	2015-05-20
14	GBPGB014	2015-05-28
15	EURFR015	2015-06-04

Figure 10.8: Outputting a date in a specific format using the CONVERT() function

How It Works

The CONVERT() function is one of the rarer T-SQL functions that takes three input parameters.

First:	The output data type—DATE in this example
Second:	The field you want to convert
Third:	The internal code that indicates the output format

As with all functions, you just need to make sure you enter the parameters (or elements if you prefer) in the right order, from left to right.

The CONVERT() function takes a field and alters (if necessary) its data type to another specific data type. If the output data type is a DATE type (as is the case here), then the function can also force the result to be presented in one of the standard date formats that SQL Server can deliver.

Table 10.4 lists some of the possible date formats.

Element	Description	Example
1	U.S. date format	07/25/95
101	U.S. date format with four-digit year	10/31/2012
3	French or British date format	25/07/95
103	French or British date format with four-digit year	31/10/2012
4	German date format	25.07.95
104	German date format with four-digit year	31.10.2012
5	Italian date format	21.10.95
105	Italian date format with four-digit year	21.10.1995
12	ISO date format	120127
112	ISO date format with four-digit year	20120127

Table 10.4: Date Formats

Don't worry about ever trying to learn these codes. In all probability you will only ever need a couple of them, and you will almost certainly end up by remembering the ones you use most often. If you need a complete list of all the possible codes, then they are available on the Microsoft website.

Tricks and Traps

There are just a couple of things to note here.

- This approach will work only if the field is—or can be converted to—a date. If this is not the case, the code will fail, and SQL will display an error message.

- It may seem strange to convert a date type to a DATE, but this is because the CONVERT() function can format output only if it is in the appropriate data type. So, it ensures this by converting the original data to the destination type first—even if this is technically superfluous. The big difference between the two is that FORMAT() will turn a date into a string (a text). CONVERT() will keep a date as a date.

10.8 Applying a Format to a Date

If you want to display a date in a wider range of possible formats and you have SQL Server 2012 or a later version, you can also use the FORMAT() function to display dates in the precise format you require. The following piece of SQL shows an example of this:

```
SELECT      FORMAT(SaleDate, 'D', 'en-us') AS SaleDate

FROM        Data.Sales
```

Running this query gives the results in *Figure 10.9*.

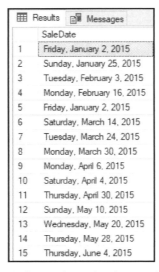

Figure 10.9: *Outputting a date in a specific format*

How It Works

The FORMAT() function takes a date field and presents it according to the format code that you have entered as the second parameter in the function.

The FORMAT() function takes the same three parameters for a date as it does for numbers—as you saw in section 10.17. Just as a reminder, these are the field to format, a date code, and the localization code.

In case this function seems complex at first sight, *Figure 10.10* explains it a little more visually.

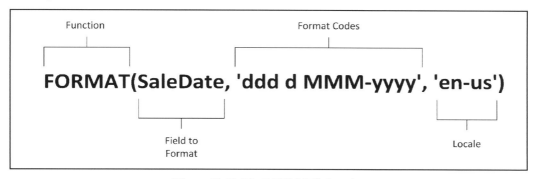

Figure 10.10: The FORMAT() function

Table 10.5 lists the built-in codes that you can use to choose a date format. I suggest that you try these codes for yourself, as they will produce varying results depending on the settings of your SQL Server version.

Element	Description	Comments
d	Short date	Formats the date using figures only
D	Long date	Formats the date with the month as text—and possibly the day of the week
f	Date and short time	Formats the date with the month as text and the hour and minutes of the day
F	Date and long time	Formats the date with the month as text and the hour and minutes and seconds of the day
M or m	Month and day	Displays only the day and the month for the date
Y or y	Year and month	Displays only the month and the year for the date

Table 10.5: Custom Format Codes

Tricks and Traps

When using the FORMAT() function on dates, just remember the following:

- The field you apply the FORMAT() function to must be one of the SQL date data types for this to work.

10.9 Defining Your Own Date Format

If the list of predefined formats that SQL Server provides is insufficient for your specific needs, then you can always hand-craft a date format—as the following short SQL snippet shows:

```
SELECT      FORMAT(SaleDate, 'ddd d MMM-yyyy', 'en-us')

            AS SaleDate

FROM        Data.Sales
```

Running this query gives the results in *Figure 10.11.*

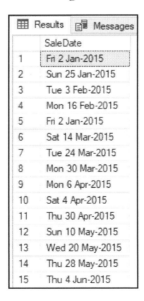

Figure 10.11: *Outputting a date in a user-defined format*

How It Works

If the built-in date formats do not satisfy your needs, you can write your own date format. This is done by assembling the composite elements of a date (weekday, day, month, and year) in the order that you want and applying the presentation you require.

Table 10.6 lists the codes that you can use to assemble a date format.

Element	Description	Example
d	The day of the month	'd MMM yyyy' produces "2 Jan 2016"
dd	The day of the month with a leading zero when necessary	'd MMM yyyy' produces "2 Jan 2016"
ddd	The three-letter abbreviation for the day of the week	'ddd d MMM yyyy' produces "Sat 2 Jan 2016"
dddd	The day of the week in full	'dddd dd MMM yyyy' produces "Saturday 02 Jan 2016"
M	The number of the month	'dd M yyyy' produces "02 1 2016"
MM	The number of the month with a leading zero when necessary	dd MM yyyy' produces "02 01 2016"
MMM	The three-letter abbreviation for the month	'dd MMM yyyy' produces "02 Jan 2016"
MMMM	The full month	dd MMMM yyyy' produces "02 January 2016"
YY	The year as two digits	'd MMM yy' produces "2 Jan 16"
YYYY	The full year	'MMMM yyyy' produces "January 2016"

Table 10.6: *Custom Date Formats*

Tricks and Traps

Here, too, there are a couple of points to take away.

- It is vital that you respect the capitalization of the format codes when you write your own output formats for dates. For instance, using a lowercase m for the month or an uppercase D for the day in a date format will simply not work.

- If you use the FORMAT() function, you are, in effect, converting the date to text. Consequently, you will no longer be able to carry out date calculations once the field has been formatted.

Conclusion

This chapter showed you some of the core techniques you can use to alter the way that numbers and dates are output from a SQL query. You learned how to round numbers both up and down—as well as rounding by tens, hundreds, and even thousands. Finally, you saw how to present both dates and numbers in a variety of ways using both predefined and custom formats.

Core Knowledge Learned in This Chapter

The following are the keywords and concepts you learned in this chapter:

Concept	Description
CAST()	This function converts one data type to another data type, where possible.
CONVERT()	This function converts one data type to another data type, where possible, and can format numbers and dates in predefined ways.
FLOOR()	This function rounds numbers down to the nearest integer.
CEILING()	This function rounds numbers up to the nearest integer.
ROUND()	This function rounds numbers to integers—and factors of 10.
FORMAT()	This function applies an output format to numbers and dates either from a predefined list or according to a user-defined format.

CHAPTER 11
Using Basic Logic to Enhance Analysis

Accurate data selection is a good first step in effective analysis. However, there may be times when you are faced with so much data that it is difficult to detect the nuggets of information hidden in all the columns and rows of facts and figures. To prevent you from missing key details, SQL Server can highlight the records that stand out from the rest—and give you greater control over your data.

Applying SQL Logic

Applying logic in a SQL query generally involves testing data for the characteristics that interest you and either flagging any records that need to be investigated further or handling the output in specific ways depending on the result of a logical process. This can mean applying different scenarios depending on the values in a field or excluding data based on a logical test.

Logic tests are, essentially, limited only by your requirements and imagination. So, in this chapter, I will introduce you to some of the techniques you can apply to use SQL to do some of the "heavy lifting" when analyzing data.

11.1 Generating an Alert When a Value Is Too High

Keeping track of costs is an essential part of any business. Let's suppose that the finance director of Prestige Cars Ltd. wants a report that flags any car ever bought where the parts cost was greater than the cost of repairs. The following code does this by adding an extra column to the list of parts and repairs costs that draws your attention to any potential anomalies:

```
SELECT      Cost, RepairsCost, PartsCost

            ,IIF(PartsCost > RepairsCost, 'Cost Alert!', NULL)

            AS CostAnalysis

FROM        Data.Stock
```

Running this query gives the results in *Figure 11.1*.

	Cost	RepairsCost	PartsCost	CostAnalysis
1	52000.00	2175.00	1500.00	NULL
2	176000.00	5500.00	2200.00	NULL
3	15600.00	660.00	0.00	NULL
4	9200.00	500.00	750.00	Cost Alert!
5	15960.00	1360.00	500.00	NULL
6	176000.00	1000.00	3150.00	Cost Alert!
7	23600.00	500.00	750.00	Cost Alert!
8	39600.00	2500.00	1500.00	NULL
9	60800.00	3250.00	750.00	NULL
10	172000.00	750.00	150.00	NULL
11	15680.00	890.00	500.00	NULL
12	29200.00	1950.00	500.00	NULL
13	6800.00	250.00	225.00	NULL
14	36000.00	1250.00	750.00	NULL
15	64400.00	500.00	750.00	Cost Alert!

Figure 11.1: Using conditional logic and the IIF() function to test output

How It Works

This short piece of SQL introduces the IIF() function. This function is another of the "three-parameter" functions in SQL, and it requires the following:

First:	A test to be carried out. Normally this consists of comparing the data in a column with either a fixed value or the data in another column. In this example, the test sees whether the data in the PartsCost column is of a higher value than the data in the RepairsCost column for each record.
Second:	A result that is displayed if the test proves *true* (in this example that means a parts cost greater than the repair cost). This can be text, a number, a calculation, or nothing at all. In this example, you are displaying the text "Cost Alert!" Because the result is a text in this case, it has to be in single quotes.
Finally:	A result that appears if the test proves *false* (in this example, that means a parts cost less than or equal to the repair cost). This part of the function can also be text, a number, a calculation, or indeed nothing at all. In this example, you want to show nothing, so the NULL keyword is used because that means "nothing" in this context.

Figure 11.2: shows you how this works in a more graphic way.

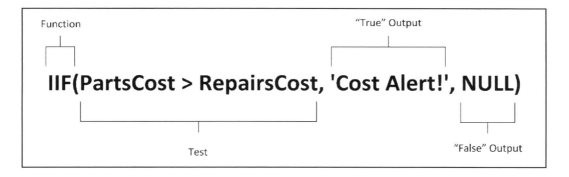

Figure 11.2: The anatomy of an IIF() expression

Tricks and Traps

IIF() expressions can be a powerful addition to your SQL armory. However, when using them, you will always have to bear these key points in mind:

- If you wanted to show something other than a blank cell in the output (the word OK, for instance), you could use the IIF() function in the following way instead:

```
IIF(PartsCost > RepairsCost, 'Alert', 'OK')
```

- You can consider the "test" that is the first parameter of an IIF() function as being a mini WHERE clause to some extent. This is because you apply the same sort of comparative logic in the test parameter as you would in a WHERE clause. Only in this case the result must return an outcome that can be interpreted by SQL as `true or false`.

- An IIF() function is not limited to just displaying text. It can also carry out calculations in the second and third parts of the function.

- The IIF() keyword is not available in versions of SQL Server before SQL Server 2012. So, if you are using an older version of the database, attempting to use this function will display an error message.

- You may already have seen the IIF() function in Microsoft Access or even the IF() function in Excel. If this is the case, then you can breathe easily because the SQL Server IIF() function works in virtually the same way that it does in these two other applications.

11.2 Shortening Text and Adding Ellipses to Indicate Truncation

The sales director wants some customer feedback. She knows that the sales database has comments from clients in it, but she does not need—or want—to display all the text. All she wants is to show only the first few characters and then use ellipses to indicate that the text has been shortened. This way she can always extract the full comment at a later date. Applying SQL logic to your output can do just this, as the following code snippet shows:

```
SELECT     Cost, RepairsCost, PartsCost

           ,IIF(

                LEN(BuyerComments) < 25

                ,BuyerComments

                ,LEFT(BuyerComments, 20) + ' ...'

           ) AS Comments

FROM       Data.Stock
```

Running this query gives the results in *Figure 11.3*.

	Cost	RepairsCost	PartsCost	Comments
1	52000.00	2175.00	1500.00	Superb Car! Wish I c ...
2	176000.00	5500.00	2200.00	NULL
3	15600.00	660.00	0.00	An absolute example ...
4	9200.00	500.00	750.00	NULL
5	15960.00	1360.00	500.00	NULL
6	176000.00	1000.00	3150.00	NULL
7	23600.00	500.00	750.00	NULL
8	39600.00	2500.00	1500.00	FAbulous motor!
9	60800.00	3250.00	750.00	NULL
10	172000.00	750.00	150.00	NULL
11	15680.00	890.00	500.00	NULL
12	29200.00	1950.00	500.00	NULL
13	6800.00	250.00	225.00	NULL
14	36000.00	1250.00	750.00	NULL
15	64400.00	500.00	750.00	NULL

Figure 11.3: Applying conditional logic to alter output using the IIF() function

How It Works

Here an IIF() function tests the contents of a column. However, instead of comparing one value with another, it calculates the number of characters in the column for each record, using the LEN() function. This function quite simply calculates the number of letters or numbers in a string. In this example, if there are less than 25 characters in the field, then it is output in full. If not, then only the first 20 characters are allowed through into the result, but with three dots (an ellipsis) appended to them. This way, you can be certain that you will never see more than 25 characters when displaying the buyer comments.

The point of this example is to make it clear that the output from an IIF() function need not just be hard-coded text as you saw previously. An IIF() function will let you use database fields as the output for both the true and false parameters.

11.3 Designing Complex Calculated Alerts

This time the sales director has left you astounded. She wants you to look at the profit on each car sold and flag any sale where the profit figure is less than 10 percent of the purchase price—while at the same time the repair cost is at least twice the parts cost! However abstruse at first sight, this request illustrates the fact that you will frequently need to isolate specific cases from the rest of the data when analyzing datasets.

In practice, this often means that any tests that you apply to your data can be more complex than those that you have seen so far in this chapter. It is possible to use functions—like IIF()—to carry out quite complex logical tests and to return a value depending on the outcome of those tests. The following SQL is an example of this:

```
SELECT      ST.Cost, ST.RepairsCost, ST.PartsCost
            ,IIF(
                (SD.SalePrice -
                  (ST.Cost + SD.LineItemDiscount
                          + ST.PartsCost
                          + ISNULL(ST.RepairsCost, 0)
                          + ST.TransportInCost
                  )
                )

                < (SD.SalePrice * 0.1)
                AND (ST.RepairsCost * 2) > ST.PartsCost
            ,'Warning!!'
            ,'OK'

            ) AS CostAlert
FROM        Data.Stock ST
            INNER JOIN Data.SalesDetails SD ON ST.StockCode =
SD.StockID
```

Executing this SQL gives the results in *Figure 11.4.*

	Cost	RepairsCost	PartsCost	Cost Alert
1	52000.00	2175.00	1500.00	Warning!!
2	176000.00	5500.00	2200.00	Warning!!
3	15600.00	660.00	0.00	OK
4	9200.00	500.00	750.00	OK
5	15960.00	1360.00	500.00	OK
6	23600.00	500.00	750.00	OK
7	39600.00	2500.00	1500.00	Warning!!
8	60800.00	3250.00	750.00	Warning!!
9	15680.00	890.00	500.00	OK
10	29200.00	1950.00	500.00	Warning!!
11	6800.00	250.00	225.00	OK
12	36000.00	1250.00	750.00	OK
13	64400.00	500.00	750.00	OK
14	135600.00	5500.00	2200.00	OK
15	7160.00	500.00	750.00	Warning!!

Figure 11.4: More complex logical tests using IIF()

How It Works

Here, the IIF() function tests the sales and costs for every vehicle sold and flags any sales where the profit is less than 10 percent of the purchase price and **also** where the repair costs are at least double the parts cost. All this is done in the first part of the IIF() function.

If anything, this example shows you that an IIF() function can be as complex as you need it to be and that it can include nested parentheses just like a WHERE clause.

In a complex IIF() function, it is the first parameter—the test—that is usually complex. The actual output can be quite simple. In this example, the test is in two parts.

First:	The net profit is calculated (as you have done previously in this book) by subtracting the total of all the cost elements from the sale price.
Second:	Ten percent of the sale price is calculated. This, too, is enclosed inside its own set of parentheses.
Third:	The SQL then compares the net profit to 10 percent of the sale price.

Finally:	The code then multiplies repair costs by a factor of two (which is isolated from the rest of the test through being placed in parentheses) and compares this to the parts cost.

Only if both these tests are true will the IIF() function display "Warning" as its output.

Tricks and Traps

When designing complex tests using the IIF() function, it can help to remember the following:

- If you want to try a complex IIF() function, you can always start by using the "test" part of the IIF() statement in the WHERE clause. This will allow you to see the filter effect of the test code. Then, once you are sure the code does exactly what you want, you can place it inside an IIF() function in the SELECT statement.

- Using parentheses efficiently can be a real boon when building complex tests (that is, the first parameter of an IIF() function) in SQL. More specifically, they can help you to isolate separate aspects of the test so that you can concentrate on each "unit" separately.

- Because the test acts like a small WHERE clause, it can use the same logical operators—AND, OR, and NOT—that you first saw in Chapter 4.

- As the final output does not show the profit figure, you may want to add this to the output—at least when testing the query. This will let you ensure that the logic is correct.

11.4 Creating Key Performance Indicators

As a final flourish for the dashboard that she wants to present to the board of directors, the sales manager wants to create a set of key performance indicators (KPIs). This involves defining the output from the analysis as Good, Bad, or Acceptable.

This kind of request illustrates the fact that not all tests on your data can give simple "black or white" results. Sometimes you may require a more nuanced answer. You may well have to output three or more states that categorize the output.

The following piece of SQL is designed for precisely this kind of eventuality:

```
SELECT      ST.Cost, ST.RepairsCost, ST.PartsCost
           ,IIF(
                (SD.SalePrice -
```

```
                  (ST.Cost + SD.LineItemDiscount - ST.PartsCost

                     + ST.RepairsCost + ST.TransportInCost)
               ) < SD.SalePrice * 0.1
               ,'Warning!!'
          ,IIF(
               (SD.SalePrice -
                    (ST.Cost + SD.LineItemDiscount - ST.PartsCost
                     + ST.RepairsCost + ST.TransportInCost)
                 ) < SD.SalePrice * 0.5, 'Acceptable', 'OK'
               )
          ) AS CostAlert
FROM      Data.Stock ST
          INNER JOIN Data.SalesDetails SD ON ST.StockCode =
SD.StockID
```

Running this query gives the results in *Figure 11.5.*

	Cost	RepairsCost	PartsCost	CostAlert
1	52000.00	2175.00	1500.00	Acceptable
2	176000.00	5500.00	2200.00	Warning!!
3	15600.00	660.00	0.00	OK
4	9200.00	500.00	750.00	OK
5	15960.00	1360.00	500.00	OK
6	23600.00	500.00	750.00	Acceptable
7	39600.00	2500.00	1500.00	Acceptable
8	60800.00	3250.00	750.00	Warning!!
9	15680.00	890.00	500.00	OK
10	29200.00	1950.00	500.00	Warning!!
11	6800.00	250.00	225.00	Acceptable
12	36000.00	1250.00	750.00	OK
13	64400.00	500.00	750.00	Acceptable
14	135600.00	5500.00	2200.00	OK
15	7160.00	500.00	750.00	Acceptable

Figure 11.5: Nested logic tests using IIF()

How It Works

This type of query probably looks more complicated than it really is. It is called a nested IIF() statement because you are placing one IIF() function inside another. What it does is this:

First:	It calculates the sale price minus all the associated costs (the net margin) and then compares the result to the sale price multiplied by 10 percent. If the margin is *lower* than 10 percent of the sale price, the function displays "Warning" and goes no further.
Then:	If the costs are *higher* than the calculated sale price, it calculates the net margin and then compares the result to the sale price multiplied by 150 percent. If the margin is lower than 50 percent of the sale price, the function displays "Acceptable." This is realistic, as by definition the margin is already more than 10 percent of the costs at least—but less than 50 percent. If not (which means that we have a margin of more than 50 percent), it displays "OK."

A nested IIF() function like this is extremely logical and will try to stop the tests as fast as possible. So, when writing them, you want to ensure that you have defined a clear progression through the various parts of the test. This nearly always means beginning with the lowest value for the comparison (110 percent in this example) and then progressing to the next level in the comparison (150 percent here), and so on. If you make the succession of tests coherent and progressive, they will probably be easier to write as well as both simpler to understand and easier to correct if there are errors. It will also make it easier to update the test if you come back to it weeks—or even months—later.

Figure 11.6 makes this concept clearer. It shows the progression through the tests from the lowest to the highest value.

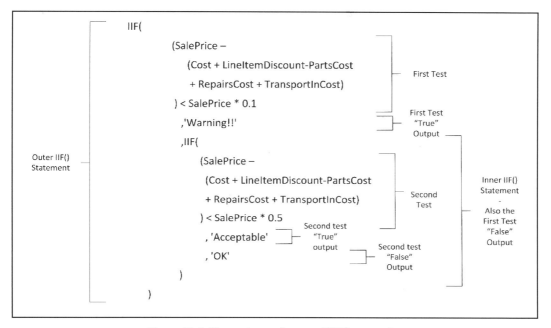

Figure 11.6: *The anatomy of a nested IIF() expression*

Tricks and Traps

Designing successive nested tests in SQL is both an art and a science. With this in mind, you might want to consider the following points:

- The really hard part to writing nested IIF statements is getting the parentheses right. This can take a little practice, so be patient if you are starting out down this particular route.

- If you have spent any time writing nested IF statements in Excel—or nested IIF statements in Access for that matter—then you are probably used to this particular technique because it is similar in SQL.

- You can nest only `ten` IIF statements at the most. However, at this level of logical complexity, it can become hard to write the SQL correctly, so I advise you to move on to using CASE statements (described in the following section) if your requirements become so challenging that they require this many levels of nesting.

11.5 Classifying a Series of Elements Without the Necessary Categories Present in Your Data

The finance director needs to manage exchange rate risk. So, he wants you to add each client's currency area to a printout. Unfortunately, the database does not have a field that holds the currency area. Moreover, you are not able to modify the data structures to add a new category to the database. The following SQL shows how you can carry out this kind of operation to extend your analysis by superposing an ad hoc categorization on an existing dataset:

```
SELECT      CountryName
            ,CASE CountryName
                WHEN 'Belgium' THEN 'Eurozone'
                WHEN 'France' THEN 'Eurozone'
                WHEN 'Italy' THEN 'Eurozone'
                WHEN 'Spain' THEN 'Eurozone'
                WHEN 'United Kingdom' THEN 'Pound Sterling'
                WHEN 'United States' THEN 'Dollar'

                ELSE 'Other'
            END AS CurrencyRegion
FROM        Data.Country
```

Running this query gives the results in *Figure 11.7.*

	CountryName	CurrencyRegion
1	Belgium	Eurozone
2	France	Eurozone
3	Germany	Other
4	Italy	Eurozone
5	Spain	Eurozone
6	United Kingdom	Pound Sterling
7	United States	Dollar
8	China	Other
9	India	Other
10	Switzerland	Other

Figure 11.7: Using a CASE statement to add categories

How It Works

The PrestigeCars database may not contain currency areas, but it does contain the countries for each client. Fortunately, there are not too many of them. This means you can write some SQL to check the country name and then, depending on the country, output one of the following:

- Eurozone

- Pound sterling

- Dollar

You do this with a CASE statement. This statement does the following:

First:	Define the field to test by adding it after the word CASE. In this example, the test is extremely succinct—it is simply CASE CountryName. That is all that is required.
Second:	List all the possible outcomes, by saying "If the country is [whatever the country], then output the following...." This is done by entering the WHEN keyword followed by the output you want to see. In this example, the output is text, so it is enclosed in single quotes. What is more, you can add as many WHEN clauses as you want to a CASE statement.
Third:	Say what is to happen if none of the tests is true—in other words, what must be output if the database contains a country not in your list? This is done by entering the ELSE keyword, followed by the output you want to see in this case.
Finally:	Add the END keyword—and provide a column alias if you want.

This example is carrying out a simple equality test. All you are doing is comparing the contents of a field with a list you enter and telling SQL what to do when a match is found.

To make this a little clearer, take a look at *Figure 11.8.*

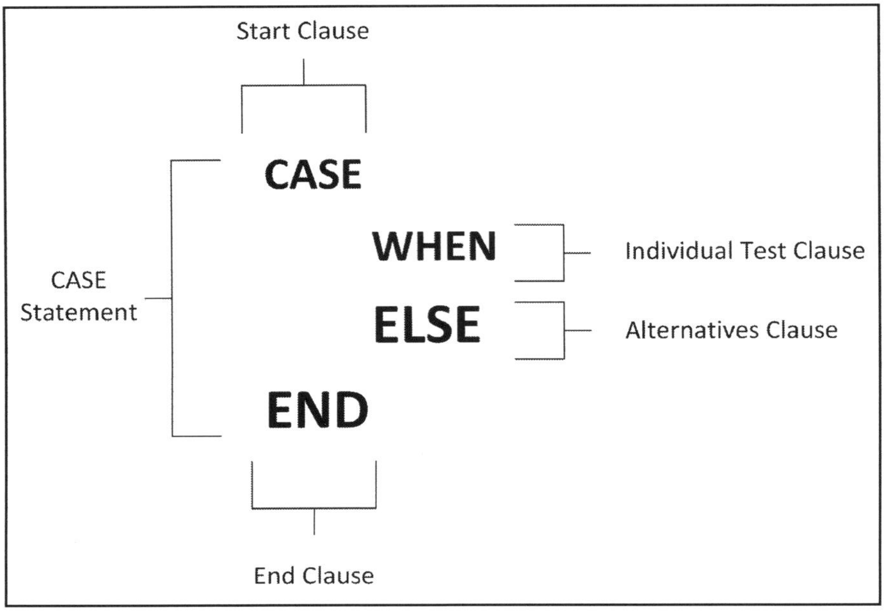

Figure 11.8: *The anatomy of a CASE expression*

Tricks and Traps

You need to bear the following in mind when using CASE statements:

- A CASE statement (a bit like a nested IIF() statement) will "exit" (that is, return an output value) at the first possible opportunity. So, if there are several elements in your list that can cause the statement to match a value, it will take only the first one that it comes to when going down through the list. Any others will **not** count and will not be applied to the data.

11.6 Creating Ad Hoc Category Groupings

The finance director is overjoyed that you solved his previous conundrum and were able to add currency areas to the output. So, now he wants to take this one step further and has asked you for a report that counts the makes of car according to the geographical zone where they were built.

Fortunately, you can extend the use of CASE statements to group and aggregate data even when you are adding categories that do not exist in the underlying database—as the following piece of SQL illustrates:

```
SELECT    CASE
            WHEN MK.MakeCountry IN ('ITA', 'GER', 'FRA') THEN
'European'
            WHEN MK.MakeCountry = 'GBR' THEN 'British'
            WHEN MK.MakeCountry = 'USA' THEN 'American'
            ELSE 'Other'
          END AS SalesRegion
          ,COUNT(SD.SalesDetailsID) AS NumberOfSales
FROM      Data.Make AS MK INNER JOIN Data.Model
          AS MD ON MK.MakeID = MD.MakeID
          INNER JOIN Data.Stock AS ST ON ST.ModelID = MD.ModelID
          INNER JOIN Data.SalesDetails SD ON ST.StockCode =
SD.StockID
GROUP BY  CASE
            WHEN MK.MakeCountry IN ('ITA', 'GER', 'FRA') THEN
'European'

            WHEN MK.MakeCountry = 'GBR' THEN 'British'
            WHEN MK.MakeCountry = 'USA' THEN 'American'
            ELSE 'Other'
          END
```

Executing this query gives the output that you can see in *Figure 11.9.*

Figure 11.9: *Using a CASE function to group data*

How It Works

This code snippet lets you add a custom grouping element that is not contained in the source data. However, at its heart it uses the same, identical CASE statement twice.

First:	In the SELECT clause to output the new grouping element (European, British, American, or Other)
Second:	In the GROUP BY clause to group and aggregate the output using the same categorization

The way that the CASE statement is structured is nonetheless slightly different from how it is used in the previous example. This time the field that is being tested appears in each WHEN clause and not once only after the CASE keyword. Although this may seem a little more long-winded, it is actually much simpler to apply. As you can see, you no longer have to detail every possible individual comparison separately as you can now use the IN function to enter lists of alternatives. This makes for shorter code that is easier to understand and maintain—even if you have to repeat the name of the field that you are testing.

Otherwise, this SQL is quite normal—it uses a COUNT() function to give the total number of sales using the Make, Model, Stock, and Sales tables as the data source. A standard FROM clause joins the Make, Stock, Model, and SalesDetails tables so that you can access all the fields that you need in the rest of the query.

Tricks and Traps

There is one key point to note when using CASE statements (in either the SELECT or GROUP BY clause).

- As in the previous example, the CASE statement ends with an ELSE clause (to handle any categorizations that you have not thought of) and with the END keyword (to tell SQL that the CASE statement is finished).

11.7 Applying Multiple Ad Hoc Categories

Applying categories that no one thought of when the database was being built is pretty normal in the world of SQL. However, there are times when users request quite complex analyses that can require you to provide some clever SQL. As a case in point, the sales director wants you to create a category that is built on two complementary analyses, categorizing purchasers by both type and geography. The following SQL does exactly this, if you want to take a look:

```
SELECT    CustomerName
          ,CASE
          WHEN IsReseller = 0 AND Country
                                IN ('IT', 'DE', 'FR', 'ES', 'BE')
                  THEN 'Eurozone Retail Client'
          WHEN IsReseller = 0 AND Country IN ('GB')
```

```
                THEN 'British Retail Client'
        WHEN IsReseller = 0 AND Country IN ('US')
                THEN 'American Retail Client'
        WHEN IsReseller = 0 AND Country IN ('CH')
                THEN 'Swiss Retail Client'
        WHEN IsReseller = 1 AND Country
                              IN ('IT', 'DE', 'FR', 'ES', 'BE')
                THEN 'Eurozone Reseller'
        WHEN IsReseller = 1 AND Country IN ('GB')

                THEN 'British Reseller'
        WHEN IsReseller = 1 AND Country IN ('US')
                THEN 'American Reseller'
        WHEN IsReseller = 1 AND Country IN ('CH')
                THEN 'Swiss Reseller'

    END AS CustomerType
FROM     Data.Customer
```

If you run this query, you should see the output in *Figure 11.10*.

	CustomerName	CustomerType
1	Magic Motors	British Reseller
2	Snazzy Roadsters	British Reseller
3	Birmingham Executive Prestige Vehicles	British Reseller
4	WunderKar	Eurozone Reseller
5	Casseroles Chromes	Eurozone Reseller
6	Le Luxe en Motion	Swiss Reseller
7	Eat My Exhaust Ltd	British Reseller
8	M. Pierre Dubois	Eurozone Retail Client
9	Sondra Horowitz	American Retail Client
10	Wonderland Wheels	British Reseller
11	London Executive Prestige Vehicles	British Reseller
12	Glittering Prize Cars Ltd	British Reseller
13	La Bagnole de Luxe	Eurozone Reseller
14	Convertible Dreams	British Reseller
15	Alexei Tolstoi	British Retail Client

Figure 11.10: Complex evaluation using CASE statements

How It Works

This code analyzes two separate fields to decide whether a client is a reseller and if so (or if not) which geographical area they belong to. It does this using a CASE statement, but this `must` be structured in the "second" way that you saw in this chapter—that is, you have to specify `each` of the fields that you are using to test data every time in `each` WHEN clause. This approach may seem a little laborious, but its key advantage is that `every individual WHEN clause` can contain its `own specific logic` that is completely separate from the other WHEN clauses. In this example, the combinations of reseller status and country are used to define a series of overall categories: Eurozone Retail Client, British Retail Client, American Retail Client, Eurozone Reseller, British Reseller, American Reseller, and Other.

Tricks and Traps

Complex case statements like this one entail being aware of the following key points:

- If tracking all these variations on a theme becomes difficult, then you can organize CASE statements into nested subgroups, as you can see in the following section.

- You can format the WHEN clause as you see fit. We placed the WHEN… THEN clauses on separate lines to make the code easier to understand. However, there is nothing to stop you writing the following, for instance, with all the SQL on a single line:

```
WHEN IsReseller = 1 AND Country IN ('USA') THEN 'American
Reseller'
```

- When there is only a single element to test in the WHEN clause, you can use equal (=) rather than IN.

11.8 Categorizing Data Using Nested Classifications

The sales director wants you to flag various customers by their credit status and geographical region. The following piece of SQL explains how to do that, but in a slightly different way from the one you saw in the previous example. In fact, to make custom categorizations easier to understand, you can nest the elements you are examining into structured hierarchies to make the concept—and the code—easier to comprehend.

```
SELECT     CustomerName
           ,CASE
               WHEN IsCreditRisk = 0 THEN
                       CASE
                           WHEN Country IN ('IT', 'DE', 'FR'
                                               ,'ES', 'BE')
                               THEN 'Eurozone No Risk'
                           WHEN Country IN ('GB')
                               THEN 'British No Risk'
                           WHEN Country IN ('US')
                               THEN 'American No Risk'
                           WHEN Country IN ('CH')
                               THEN 'swiss No Risk'
                       END
               WHEN IsCreditRisk = 1 THEN
                       CASE
                           WHEN Country IN ('IT', 'DE', 'FR'
                                               ,'ES', 'BE')
                               THEN 'Eurozone Credit Risk'
                           WHEN Country IN ('GB')
                               THEN 'British Credit Risk'
                           WHEN Country IN ('US')
                               THEN 'American Credit Risk'
                           WHEN Country IN ('CH')
                               THEN 'swiss Credit Risk'
                       END
           END AS RiskType
FROM       Data.Customer
```

Running this query gives the results in *Figure 11.11*.

	CustomerName	RiskType
1	Magic Motors	British No Risk
2	Snazzy Roadsters	British Credit Risk
3	Birmingham Executive Prestige Vehicles	British No Risk
4	WunderKar	Eurozone No Risk
5	Casseroles Chromes	Eurozone No Risk
6	Le Luxe en Motion	Swiss Credit Risk
7	Eat My Exhaust Ltd	British No Risk
8	M. Pierre Dubois	Eurozone No Risk
9	Sondra Horowitz	American No Risk
10	Wonderland Wheels	British No Risk
11	London Executive Prestige Vehicles	British Credit Risk
12	Glittering Prize Cars Ltd	British No Risk
13	La Bagnole de Luxe	Eurozone No Risk
14	Convertible Dreams	British No Risk
15	Alexei Tolstoi	British No Risk

Figure 11.11: Nested CASE statements

How It Works

This SQL query has an outer and an inner group of CASE statements.

First:	The outer statement looks at the IsCreditRisk field. It begins by saying the following: "When the credit risk is absent, move on to the inner CASE statement (and carry out further tests on the country). Then, if the customer poses a credit risk (that is, the field is true or contains a 1 for this kind of field), continue processing with another, separate CASE statement and test the country."
Then:	The inner statement in either case looks at the country and applies separate tests. Only if the outer and inner tests give a positive result (for instance, if a customer is not a credit risk and the country is Britain) will one of the outcomes be returned—"British No Risk" in the event of a British risk-free customer.

Tricks and Traps

I have only a couple of comments to make about nested CASE statements.

- There is a technical limitation to nesting CASE statements, which is that you can nest them only up to ten levels deep. However, this limit is rarely a problem in practice.

- In this example, the "inner" CASE statements were nearly identical—they both contained the same tests on the country. This approach is specific to this particular example and will not always be the case in practice.

11.9 Placing NULLs at the Start or End of a List

The sales director has presented you with a quandary. She requested a list of sales by increasing value of discounts, which you duly delivered. However, as there were a large quantity of sales where no discount was applied, SQL Server began the list with the NULL values for the LineItemDiscount field because NULLs are considered to be smaller than any numerical value.

However, this is not what the sales director wants. She wants a list that begins with the smallest values and places any empty (nondiscounted) sales at the bottom of the list.

This is where a little SQL logic can assist you, as the following code snippet shows:

```
SELECT      *
FROM        Data.SalesByCountry
ORDER BY    CASE WHEN LineItemDiscount IS NULL THEN 1 ELSE 0 END
            ,LineItemDiscount
```

Running this code will return the output in *Figure 11.12*.

	CountryName	MakeName	ModelName	Cost	RepairsCost	PartsCost	TransportInCost	Color	SalePrice	LineItemDiscount	InvoiceNumber	SaleDate	CustomerName	SalesDetailsID
1	France	Porsche	944	7160.00	500.00	750.00	150.00	Green	8950.00	25.00	EURFR013	2015-05-20 00:00:00.000	M. Pierre Dubois	14
2	Belgium	Peugeot	205	750.00	500.00	750.00	150.00	British Racing Green	950.00	25.00	EURBE218	2018-01-10 00:00:00.000	Stefan Van Helsing	237
3	United Kingdom	Porsche	944	7840.00	500.00	750.00	150.00	Canary Yellow	9800.00	35.00	GBPGB236	2018-03-19 00:00:00.000	Pierre Blanc	258
4	United Kingdom	Peugeot	404	1996.00	500.00	750.00	150.00	Canary Yellow	2495.00	45.00	GBPGB253	2018-05-03 00:00:00.000	Silver HubCaps	276
5	United Kingdom	Porsche	944	6800.00	250.00	225.00	150.00	Blue	8500.00	50.00	GBPGB011	2015-04-30 00:00:00.000	Wonderland Wheels	11
6	United Kingdom	Porsche	911	18360.00	500.00	750.00	150.00	Black	22950.00	50.00	GBPGB025	2015-11-10 00:00:00.000	Convertible Dreams	27
7	France	Alfa Romeo	Giulia	2040.00	500.00	750.00	150.00	British Racing Green	2550.00	50.00	EURFR031	2016-01-07 00:00:00.000	M. Pierre Dubois	33
8	United Kingdom	Porsche	944	6000.00	500.00	750.00	150.00	British Racing Green	7500.00	75.00	GBPGB084	2016-05-06 00:00:00.000	Birmingham Executive Prestige Vehicles	91
9	United Kingdom	Alfa Romeo	Giulia	6356.00	400.00	750.00	150.00	Red	9695.00	95.00	GBPGB016	2015-07-12 00:00:00.000	Convertible Dreams	17
10	United Kingdom	Porsche	944	7040.00	140.00	750.00	150.00	Blue	8800.00	500.00	GBPGB042	2016-04-30 00:00:00.000	Silver HubCaps	45
11	United States	Triumph	TR4	4400.00	500.00	750.00	150.00	Night Blue	5500.00	500.00	USDUS019	2015-08-20 00:00:00.000	Theo Kowalski	21
12	United Kingdom	Bentley	Flying Spur	64400.00	500.00	750.00	750.00	British Racing Green	80500.00	500.00	GBPGB011	2015-04-30 00:00:00.000	Wonderland Wheels	12
13	United States	Porsche	944	10120.00	500.00	750.00	150.00	Night Blue	12650.00	500.00	USDUS033	2016-01-09 00:00:00.000	Jason B. Wright	35
14	Germany	Ferrari	360	79600.00	500.00	750.00	750.00	Black	99500.00	500.00	EURDE043	2016-04-30 00:00:00.000	Glitz	46
15	United Kingdom	Alfa Romeo	Giulia	14000.00	1360.00	225.00	150.00	Green	17500.00	500.00	GBPGB044	2016-04-30 11:27:00.000	Silver HubCaps	47

Figure 11.12: Using a CASE statement to place NULL values at the end of a list

How It Works

The trick to handling NULL values in a sort order is to add an initial sort key that deals with the NULL values and then sorts the non-NULL values afterward.

This is what the ORDER BY clause has done here:

First:	An initial sort element is applied using a CASE statement. In this example, this piece of logic says, "If the LineItemDiscount field contains a NULL, consider it to contain a 1; otherwise, consider any value as a 0." So, the first sort key is, effectively, a 1 or a 0, meaning that NULLs are 1s and so appear after all the 0s (in effect after any numeric values).
Second:	The ORDER BY clause sorts on the LineItemDiscount field once the sort on the NULL fields has been applied.

Tricks and Traps

I have only one comment to make about these kind of CASE statements.

- You can place the NULL values at the top or bottom of the output simply by switching the 1 and 0 values in the CASE statement. So, to place the NULLs at the top of the list, you would write the following:

```
ORDER BY    CASE WHEN LineItemDiscount IS NULL THEN 0 ELSE 1 END
```

11.10 Classifying Data by Impromptu Categories

Sometimes, just sometimes, you may have to categorize data from a custom list. Suppose the sales director wants to make it clear in which season a vehicle is sold. None of the SQL built-in functions can do this. So, you need to tell SQL to map the month to a specific list that you have defined. The following code does this:

```
SELECT

MONTH(SaleDate) AS MonthNumber

,CHOOSE(MONTH(SaleDate), 'Winter', 'Winter', 'spring', 'spring',
'summer', 'summer','summer','summer','Autumn','Autumn',
'Winter','Winter') AS SalesSeason

FROM      Data.Sales
```

Running this query gives the results in *Figure 11.13*.

	MonthNumber	SalesSeason
1	1	Winter
2	1	Winter
3	2	Winter
4	2	Winter
5	1	Winter
6	3	Spring
7	3	Spring
8	3	Spring
9	4	Spring
10	4	Spring
11	4	Spring
12	5	Summer
13	5	Summer
14	5	Summer
15	6	Summer

Figure 11.13: Using CHOOSE() to return elements from a custom list

How It Works

This code finds the number of the month using the MONTH() function that you saw in Chapter 7. It then uses the number to select the "Nth" element in the list of seasons. This list contains 12 elements, so month 1 (January) maps to the first element in the list Winter. Month 2 (February) maps to Winter too. However, the third month—March—maps to the third element, which is Spring. The process then continues for all the elements in the list.

Tricks and Traps

You need to be aware that the CHOOSE() function comes with a few minor restrictions.

- The CHOOSE() keyword is not available in versions of SQL Server before SQL Server 2012.

- If the list contains fewer elements than the figure that is used to select an element, then SQL just returns NULL—that is, nothing. It does not warn you that something might not be working as you would expect.

- More generically, the CHOOSE() function can be used to map any number to the corresponding element in a list. However, the first parameter in the CHOOSE() function **must** be a number—it cannot be text.

Conclusion

In this chapter you saw how to classify data according to criteria that you set. You also learned how to use SQL to apply logical tests to data. This meant using unctions ike IIF() and CASE to evaluate logical conditions. This technique implied testing the contents of one or more fields in order to decide on an outcome.

Core Knowledge Learned in This Chapter

This chapter showed you how to test data for exceeding thresholds that you define or for showing unexpected characteristics. You saw that a little logic applied to a query can help you to see through a mountain of data and focus your attention on the outliers and anomalies that can be of real interest.

You learned the following keywords in this chapter:

Concept	Description
IIF()	This function allows you to test output and apply one or another outcome.
CASE	This function can test multiple data states and apply a choice of outcomes.
WHEN	This keyword is used with a CASE statement where it lets you apply a test to data.
ELSE	This keyword is used with a CASE statement where it lets you apply an outcome for any untested cases.
CHOOSE()	This selects an element from a list based on an initial number.
LEN()	This function detects the length of a string of text.

CHAPTER 12
Subqueries

In the first eleven chapters of this book you have learned the basics of SQL. Now it is time to move on and start resolving some more complex analytical challenges. The first step on this path is to learn how you can use independent SQL queries inside other queries. This technique is called using subqueries. It is particularly useful in data analysis as it allows you (among other things) to include aggregated data in detailed rowsets, for instance, or to compare a whole dataset with subsets of data.

What Are Subqueries?

Subqueries are more of a new technique than a new set of SQL keywords. In fact, you can write subqueries using only the SQL knowledge that you have acquired in the previous chapters. Nonetheless, learning to use subqueries to solve data challenges is a key part of your SQL apprenticeship. Once you master the art of the subquery, you are able to produce clear, concise, and in-depth analytics quickly and efficiently.

I want to convince you that subqueries are not an abstract database concept but an analytical skill that helps you dig deep into your data and unearth the insights that keep you ahead of the competition. In this chapter you learn how to

- Compare categories of data to the whole dataset and calculate percentages

- Isolate top and bottom elements in a dataset and use them as a basis for filtering records
- Filter data by comparing records to averages and overall thresholds

These—and many more analytical solutions—are made possible through the application of subqueries in your SQL. Let's now move on to some real-world examples that illustrate how subqueries can turn raw data into meaningful information.

12.1 Adding Aggregated Fields to Detailed Data Sets

Data analysis often means comparing individual elements to either all or a part of a dataset. As a first step, suppose that you want to count the number of cars sold per country and that you also want to see the total car sales for all vehicles, whatever their country, in the same query. Here is the SQL that lets you do this:

```
SELECT      CO.CountryName
            ,COUNT(SD.StockID) AS CarsSold
            ,(SELECT COUNT(SalesDetailsID)
              FROM Data.SalesDetails) AS SalesTotal
FROM        Data.SalesDetails SD
INNER JOIN Data.Sales AS SA ON SA.SalesID = SD.SalesID
INNER JOIN Data.Customer CU ON SA.CustomerID = CU.CustomerID
INNER JOIN Data.Country CO ON CU.Country = CO.CountryISO2
GROUP BY    CO.CountryName
```

Running this query gives the results that you can see in *Figure 12.1.*

	CountryName	CarsSold	SalesTotal
1	Belgium	10	351
2	France	69	351
3	Germany	13	351
4	Italy	18	351
5	Spain	27	351
6	Switzerland	18	351
7	United Kingdom	165	351
8	United States	31	351

Figure 12.1: Using a subquery

How It Works

Inevitably there are occasions in your analytical career when you want to see how a part of a set of data relates to a whole dataset. This approach frequently allows you to relativize values and to put them in a wider context.

This query exists to help you add perspective to the data. At its heart, it is a simple aggregation of sales by country. Once the Sales, SalesDetails, Customer, and Country tables have been joined, the SQL groups the data on the Country field and uses the COUNT() function to return the total number of sales for each country. Then—and this is where you are moving on to new territory—it adds a subquery to the SELECT clause to return the total number of sales without any grouping. In effect, this returns the total for all sales as a separate column alongside the number of cars sold. However, the SQL is carrying out this calculation for every row in the query output so that you can see—and possibly use—the total in every row.

To get a more visual idea of how a subquery works, take a look at *Figure 12.2*. The outer query "hosts" the separate inner query, yet both queries run at the same time and output their results together.

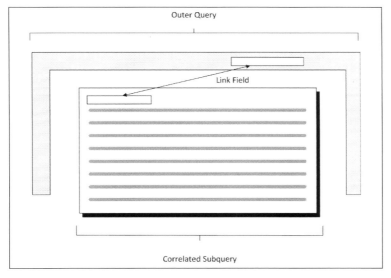

Figure 12.2: *A conceptual view of subqueries*

The code shows you how SQL Server lets you mix separate queries in a single output using a technique called a `subquery`. The principle characteristics of a subquery are

- It is included in the SELECT, WHERE, or HAVING clause of the "main" (outer) query, just as a normal field name would be.

- It is enclosed in parentheses.

- It is a `complete, separate query` with—at a minimum—its own SELECT and FROM clauses.

- If used in the SELECT clause it can only return `one value` (that is, you cannot output more than one field from the subquery).

- In the SELECT clause the subquery is separated from the other fields by acomma just like a normal field.

Tricks and Traps

A new concept like this implies a few key points that you need to remember:

- You do not have to use an alias for the name of the field returned by a subquery—but it `is` easier to understand the results if you do use aliases. You may also find that using a meaningful alias helps you understand the query better when you return to it at a later date.

- Any subquery can be executed independently of the main/outer query. This means that you can select the text that makes up the subquery (but not including the parentheses that contain it) and run it by pressing F5 or by clicking the toolbar Execute button at any time. In this example, you select the following code:

```
SELECT COUNT(SalesDetailsID) FROM Data.SalesDetails
```

Running this code returns a dataset like the one shown in *Figure 12.3*.

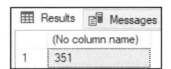

Figure 12.3: Executing a subquery independently

- Although you can only output a single value from a subquery, you can make the value that is returned the result of a calculation in the subquery if you need to, as you will discover in the next section.

- The subquery can be as simple or as complex as your requirements demand and can contain its own independent WHERE or GROUP BY clauses.

12.2 Displaying a Value as the Percentage of a Total

Calculating `ratios`—or percentages of a whole—is a core requirement in data analysis. Let's imagine that the sales director has put in a request for a list of sales by make of car sold that also displays the percentage of the total sales that the value for each make represents. Subqueries can help you do this easily and simply, as the following SQL snippet shows:

```
SELECT      MK.MakeName
            ,SUM(SD.SalePrice) AS SalePrice
            ,SUM(SD.SalePrice) / (SELECT SUM(SalePrice)
                            FROM Data.SalesDetails) AS SalesRatio
FROM        Data.Make AS MK
INNER JOIN Data.Model AS MD ON MK.MakeID = MD.MakeID
INNER JOIN Data.Stock AS ST ON ST.ModelID = MD.ModelID
INNER JOIN Data.SalesDetails SD ON ST.StockCode = SD.StockID
GROUP BY    MK.MakeName
```

Running this query gives the results that you can see in *Figure 12.4*.

	MakeName	SalePrice	SalesRatio
1	Alfa Romeo	243510.00	0.011044
2	Aston Martin	5102755.00	0.231444
3	Austin	64500.00	0.002925
4	Bentley	1689240.00	0.076618
5	BMW	60500.00	0.002744
6	Bugatti	1915500.00	0.086880
7	Citroen	101080.00	0.004584
8	Delahaye	107000.00	0.004853
9	Delorean	99500.00	0.004512
10	Ferrari	5540850.00	0.251314
11	Jaguar	882955.00	0.040047
12	Lagonda	218000.00	0.009887
13	Lamborghini	1727150.00	0.078337
14	McLaren	295000.00	0.013380
15	Mercedes	471115.00	0.021368

Figure 12.4: Using a subquery to calculate a ratio

How It Works

This query works like this:

First:	It joins the tables (Make, Model, Stock, and SalesDetails) that are required to return the make as well as the selling price for each vehicle sold.
Second:	It groups on the MakeName field and selects this field as well as the SUM() of the sale price to aggregate the selling price per make.
Finally:	It adds a new calculated field that divides the sum of the sale price by the total sale price of all vehicles sold. The "grand total" for all sales is defined using a subquery. In effect, this field (SalesRatio) divides the aggregate total for each make by the overall total and so calculates the percentage of total sales that each make represents.

Tricks and Traps

We are pushing the concept of subqueries quite a bit further in this example. Note that

- SQL frequently forces you to repeat a calculation if you need its output more than once. In this example, you can see that you need the total of vehicles sold **twice** to calculate the percentage of total sales: once for each make and once to calculate the overall total. Consequently, you have to repeat the formula

  ```
  SUM(SalePrice)
  ```

  This means that SQL is not like a spreadsheet where you can "chain" cells using cell references to produce ripple-through calculations. It follows that it is perfectly normal to repeat a calculation several times in a piece of SQL each time you need it.

- Percentages are expressed as a decimal value when they are calculated, just as they are in a spreadsheet. You may prefer to multiply the result by 100 to obtain a more comprehensible result:

  ```
  SUM(SalePrice) / (SELECT SUM(SalePrice)

                   FROM Data.SalesDetails) * 100 AS SalesRatio
  ```

If you use SQL like this in the lines that appear in bold earlier, you get the output in *Figure 12.5*.

	MakeName	SalePrice	SalesRatio
1	Alfa Romeo	243510.00	1.104400
2	Aston Martin	5102755.00	23.144400
3	Austin	64500.00	0.292500
4	Bentley	1689240.00	7.661800
5	BMW	60500.00	0.274400

***Figure 12.5:** Multiplying a percentage calculation to deliver a more comprehensible result*

- If you want to format the result as a percentage, you can use the following SQL in the third line of the code snippet:

```
FORMAT(SUM(SalePrice) / (SELECT SUM(SalePrice)

FROM Data.SalesDetails), '#0.00%') AS SalesRatio
```

Doing so gives you the kind of output that you can see in *Figure 12.6*.

	MakeName	SalePrice	SalesRatio
1	Alfa Romeo	243510.00	1.10%
2	Aston Martin	5102755.00	23.14%
3	Austin	64500.00	0.29%
4	Bentley	1689240.00	7.66%
5	BMW	60500.00	0.27%

***Figure 12.6:** Formatting a percentage output*

As you can see, if you are formatting the output, you do not need to multiply the result by 100.

- The main query in both this example and the previous one is an aggregate query. In practice the outer and inner queries can apply different levels of aggregation. This means that you can use aggregated subqueries inside simple list queries as well as in list-style subqueries inside aggregate outer queries.

Note: It is *vital* to remember that the two queries are completely independent of each other. This is why the SalePrice field has an alias in the "main" query but does not need an alias in the subquery.

12.3 Using a Subquery to Filter Data

Prestige Cars' new marketing director is convinced that some colors of car sell better than others. She wants you to find the color—or colors—of the most expensive vehicles sold. Here is the SQL that can do this:

```
SELECT     ST.Color

FROM       Data.Stock AS ST

INNER JOIN Data.SalesDetails SD ON ST.StockCode = SD.StockID

WHERE      SD.SalePrice = (SELECT MAX(SalePrice) FROM Data.
SalesDetails)
```

Running this query gives the results you can see in *Figure 12.7.*

Figure 12.7: Using a subquery in the WHERE clause of a query

How It Works

This query is really in two parts.

A subquery	This short piece of code finds the sale price for the most expensive vehicles sold.
The main query	Uses the figure calculated by the subquery as the criterion for returning the color (or colors) of any vehicles sold at this price from the main query

The main query itself simply selects the Color field from the Stock table and joins this table to the SalesDetails table so that the sale price can be used in the WHERE clause as a filter criterion.

What this example shows is that subqueries are not restricted to being used in a SELECT clause. As you can see here, you can also use them in a WHERE clause to restrict the results returned from the main/outer query.

Tricks and Traps

I only have one comment to make about this kind of subquery:

- Technically this piece of SQL is a single query. However, I prefer to describe it as a main query and a subquery purely because I feel that this helps you understand the code more easily.

Selecting the subquery and running it gives you the result you can see in *Figure 12.8.*

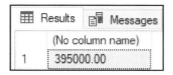

Figure 12.8: *The output from a subquery*

This is the value that is used by the main query to filter the query output.

12.4 Using a Subquery as Part of a Calculation to Filter Data

As part of a company cost containment exercise, you have been asked to take a closer look at any vehicles whose repair cost is significantly over the average for all the vehicles in stock. Specifically, the finance director wants to see a list of all vehicles whose repair cost is more than three times the average repair cost. The following SQL snippet does just this:

```
SELECT     MK.MakeName, MD.ModelName, ST.RepairsCost
FROM       Data.Make AS MK
INNER JOIN Data.Model AS MD ON MK.MakeID = MD.MakeID
INNER JOIN Data.Stock AS ST ON ST.ModelID = MD.ModelID
WHERE      ST.RepairsCost
           > 3 * (SELECT AVG(RepairsCost) FROM Data.Stock)
```

Running this query gives the results that you can see in *Figure 12.9.*

	MakeName	ModelName	RepairsCost
1	Ferrari	Testarossa	6000.00
2	Ferrari	355	5500.00
3	Ferrari	355	5500.00
4	Ferrari	355	9250.00
5	Ferrari	355	9250.00
6	Ferrari	355	9250.00
7	Ferrari	Dino	5500.00
8	Ferrari	Dino	9250.00
9	Ferrari	F40	5500.00
10	Ferrari	F50	5500.00
11	Ferrari	F50	9250.00
12	Ferrari	360	9250.00
13	Ferrari	360	5500.00
14	Ferrari	Enzo	9250.00
15	Ferrari	Enzo	9250.00

Figure 12.9: Applying a calculation and a subquery in the WHERE clause

How It Works

This query shows how you can use a subquery in a calculation to highlight certain records in a dataset. The main/outer query simply selects the cost of repairs for all makes and models of vehicle in the database using the Make, Model, and Stock tables. The clever part is placing a subquery in the WHERE clause. What this subquery does is

First:	It calculates the average repair cost. This is £1533.14 for the Prestige Cars dataset. You can verify this by selecting and running only the SQL for the subquery.
Then:	It multiplies this average repair cost by a factor of three.
Finally:	It compares this to the repair cost for each vehicle and only displays those where the repair cost is greater than three times the average repair cost—that is, over £4,599.42.

You may be thinking that it is a little strange to refer to the same table—the Stock table, in this example—twice in the same query. After all, it is already used in the outer query, so why would you need it in the subquery, too?

The reason is that you are looking at the data in two different ways:

| The outer query | Looks at the data at a *detailed level*, where each record is processed individually. |
| The subquery | Looks at the *whole table* to calculate the average repair cost for all records in the table. |

Because each query is completely independent of the other, both have separate SELECT clauses no matter which tables and fields are used.

The technical term for these two ways of looking at data is `granularity`. In effect, a SQL query can look at either the `detail` (that is, at a granular level) or `groups` of records (a higher level of granularity) or even the whole dataset—but it cannot combine multiple levels of focus at the same time in the same query. So, if you need to mix the whole with the parts, you need to use more than one query, even if the queries combine their results in a single output.

To see this more clearly, take a look at *Figure 12.10*. This is a visual representation of how granularity works in datasets.

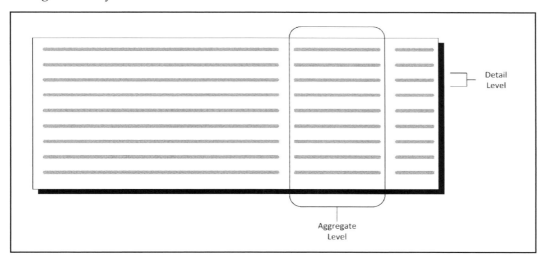

Figure 12.10: Data granularity

Using subqueries enables you to look at data at two or more separate levels of detail. Indeed, you **need** subqueries to return data at different levels of granularity in a single query.

Tricks and Traps

Here are a couple of useful points that you may need to remember when applying this kind of query:

- If you want to check that the calculation of the average cost of repairs really is the figure that I quoted, all you have to do is `select the SQL in the subquery and execute it`. This means running the following short piece of code that you can see in the WHERE clause of the SQL at the start of this section:

```
SELECT AVG(RepairsCost) FROM Data.Stock
```

You should see the result shown in *Figure 12.11*. This is the average repair cost for all vehicles in the Stock table.

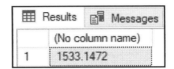

Figure 12.11: *The output from a subquery*

- It is perfectly normal to query the same table or tables in both a main query and a subquery. This only proves that the two queries are strictly independent of each other.

12.5 Filtering on an Aggregated Range of Data Using Multiple Subqueries

A further aspect of the finance director's corporate cost control project is to analyze all sales in which repair costs are within 10 percent of the average repair cost for all stock. The following SQL does this for you:

```
SELECT      MK.MakeName, MD.ModelName, ST.Cost, ST.RepairsCost
FROM        Data.Make AS MK
INNER JOIN Data.Model AS MD ON MK.MakeID = MD.MakeID
INNER JOIN Data.Stock AS ST ON ST.ModelID = MD.ModelID
WHERE       RepairsCost BETWEEN
                    (SELECT AVG(RepairsCost) FROM Data.Stock) *
0.9
                        AND
                    (SELECT AVG(RepairsCost) FROM Data.Stock) *
1.1
```

Running this query gives the results that you can see in *Figure 12.12*.

Results | Messages

	MakeName	ModelName	Cost	RepairsCost
1	Aston Martin	DB6	55600.00	1490.00
2	Bentley	Flying Spur	52712.00	1490.00
3	Porsche	959	53200.00	1490.00
4	Aston Martin	DB9	63600.00	1490.00
5	Rolls Royce	Phantom	95680.00	1490.00
6	Rolls Royce	Phantom	79600.00	1490.00
7	Rolls Royce	Silver Shadow	68000.00	1490.00
8	Delorean	DMC 12	79600.00	1490.00
9	Aston Martin	DB9	62000.00	1490.00
10	Rolls Royce	Silver Seraph	79960.00	1490.00
11	Bentley	Arnage	79960.00	1490.00
12	Aston Martin	Virage	82920.00	1490.00
13	Rolls Royce	Ghost	79160.00	1490.00
14	Porsche	959	71600.00	1490.00
15	Aston Martin	DB6	66072.00	1490.00

Figure 12.12: *Using multiple subqueries in the WHERE clause*

How It Works

You can use as many subqueries as you need in a SQL query. A practical use for this is when you need to isolate a dataset that falls between a range of values—such as when you are using a BETWEEN…AND operator in the WHERE clause.

This query selects the make, model, cost, and repair cost for all vehicles. It then filters the data in the WHERE clause. However, since the WHERE clause uses the BETWEEN…AND technique to select a range of values—and this approach requires a lower and an upper limit to the range—it needs `two` subclauses to calculate the average repair cost.

The range boundaries are defined like this:

The lower limit	Takes the overall average repair cost and multiplies by 0.9 to get the figure for 90 percent of the average value (£1,379.83).
The upper limit	Takes the overall average repair cost and multiplies by 1.1 to get the figure for 110 percent of the average value (£1,686.46).

These two range limits are then used by the BETWEEN…AND elements of the WHERE clause to filter the rows that are returned by the main query. This way only vehicles whose repair cost is plus or minus 10 percent of the average repair cost are displayed.

So, once again, you need to write a separate and independent subquery to return a specific result. You can even include multiple subqueries to apply multiple calculations across many different data tables.

Tricks and Traps

I need to make a couple of points here:

- In cases like these, you have to repeat the subquery and make sure that you have made both subqueriesdo exactly what is required of them in their separate contexts.

- Remember that when using the BETWEEN … AND technique, you must always begin with the lower threshold (90 percent in this example) and end with the higher threshold (110 percent in this example).

12.6 Filtering on Aggregated Output Using a Second Aggregation

On certain occasions your analysis may lead you to compare an aggregate from one dataset with a completely separate aggregate. This can happen, for instance, when salespeople request a list of the average sale price of all makes whose average sale price is over twice the average sale price. SQL allows you to compare data in this way, too, as the following SQL snippet shows:

```
SELECT      MK.MakeName, AVG(SD.SalePrice) AS AverageUpperSalePrice

FROM        Data.Make AS MK

INNER JOIN Data.Model AS MD ON MK.MakeID = MD.MakeID

INNER JOIN Data.Stock AS ST ON ST.ModelID = MD.ModelID

INNER JOIN Data.SalesDetails SD ON ST.StockCode = SD.StockID

GROUP BY    MK.MakeName

HAVING      AVG(SD.SalePrice) > 2 * (SELECT AVG(SalePrice)
                                     FROM    Data.SalesDetails)
```

Running this query gives the results that you can see in *Figure 12.13*.

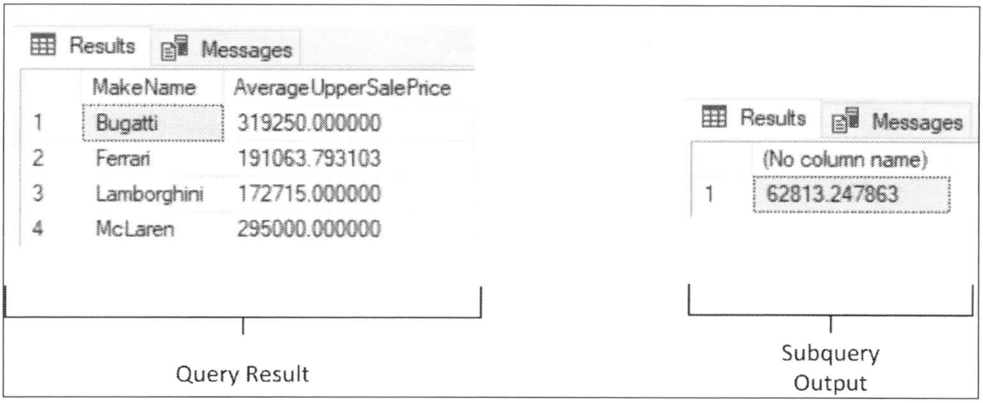

Figure 12.13: *Applying a calculation and a subquery in the HAVING clause*

How It Works

You can also use a subquery in the HAVING clause of an SQL query. As you might remember from Chapter 3 the HAVING clause operates at the level of the aggregation that has been applied to a dataset rather than at the level of individual records. So, when you apply a subquery to an aggregate query's HAVING clause, you are filtering the data on a total, an average, or any other aggregated value.

In this example

First:	The outer query calculates the average sale price for each make.
Next:	The subquery calculates the overall average sale price for all vehicles sold.
Then:	The subquery then multiplies this average by two and compares it to the average sale price by make for all the makes of car sold.

The result is that any make with an average sale price over twice the overall average sale price is then listed in the query output.

Tricks and Traps

When using calculations to filter data, you need to be aware that

- There are several ways of carrying out the calculation used in the query. If you prefer, you can use arithmetic like this:

```
HAVING AVG(SD.SalePrice) / 2 < (SELECT AVG(SalePrice)
                                FROM   Data.SalesDetails)
```

This code gives exactly the same result as the SQL at the start of this example. It is a simple choice between two arithmetical approaches.

12.7 Using Multiple Results from a Subquery to Filter Data

The sales director has asked you to find all the sales for the top five bestselling makes. A request like this illustrates that some data analysis challenges require you to output a set of records that uses the result of a second set (a derived table) as a filter.

The (slightly more complex) SQL to solve this problem is as follows:

```
SELECT     MKX.MakeName, SDX.SalePrice
FROM       Data.Make AS MKX
INNER JOIN Data.Model AS MDX ON MKX.MakeID = MDX.MakeID
INNER JOIN Data.Stock AS STX ON STX.ModelID = MDX.ModelID
INNER JOIN Data.SalesDetails SDX ON STX.StockCode = SDX.StockID
WHERE      MakeName IN (
                       SELECT     TOP (5) MK.MakeName
                       FROM       Data.Make AS MK
                       INNER JOIN Data.Model AS MD
                                  ON MK.MakeID = MD.MakeID
                       INNER JOIN Data.Stock AS ST
                                  ON ST.ModelID = MD.ModelID
                       INNER JOIN Data.SalesDetails SD
                                  ON ST.StockCode = SD.StockID
                       INNER JOIN Data.Sales SA
                                  ON SA.SalesID = SD.SalesID
                       GROUP BY   MK.MakeName
                       ORDER BY   SUM(SA.TotalSalePrice) DESC
                       )
ORDER BY   MKX.MakeName, SDX.SalePrice DESC
```

Running this query gives the results that you can see in Figure 12.14, where you can also see the output from the subquery. Although this list contains five makes (Aston Martin, Bentley, Bugatti, Ferrari, and Lamborghini), it is, nonetheless, fairly long. You have to scroll through the output to ensure that only these five makes are displayed.

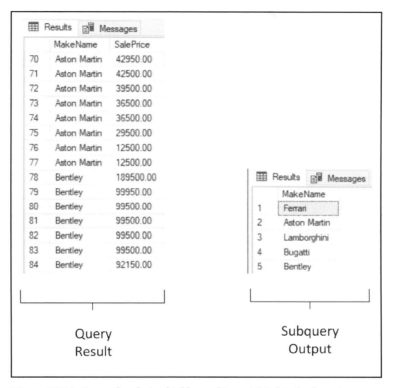

Figure 12.14: *A complex derived table used to restrict data in the outer query*

How It Works

Here you can see how data analysis can be a multistep process. This example shows you how to

First:	Use a subquery to find the top five bestselling makes by sale value.
Then:	Use this data to filter the results from a simpler "outer" query.

This example is another one of those times when a subquery can be a lot more complex—and powerful—than the rest of the query that uses it. Once again, most of the work is done by the subquery, so it makes sense to look at this first.

The subquery	Joins a series of tables so that you can return the make and sale price. It then aggregates sales by make, calculates the total sale price for each make, and finally returns only the top five makes.
The main query	Uses this result as a filter as it joins to the derived table on the MakeName field.

It is worth noting that the two queries—subquery and outer query—can be different types of query. In this example, the subquery is an aggregate query, whereas the outer query is a simple "list" (or detail-level) query.

> **Note:** When a subquery returns more than one record you *must* use the IN operator in the WHERE clause. If you do not, you will get an error message.

Tricks and Traps

Handling complex queries like this one inevitably introduces some key points to take away:

- This example introduces something new—but it is so subtle that it is easy to miss. Here the subquery returns `more than one record`. In fact, it returns precisely five elements—the top five bestselling makes of car.

- When solving complex analytical problems like this one, you may well find yourself beginning with the subquery and then moving on to the outer query.

- You should be able to run any subquery independently of the outer query. So, you can select the subquery and execute it at any time, just as you would execute the entire query.

- You can begin a complex query like this by writing the subquery first, if you prefer. That way, you can be sure that it returns the data you need to filter the outer query correctly.

- You can create a subquery using many separate tables that are joined together, just as you would any "ordinary" query.

- You can see in this code that we use different aliases in the inner and outer queries, even when the same tables are used. This is not strictly necessary, because the two queries are totally separate. However, I prefer to do this for a couple of reasons:
    - o It highlights the fact that you are dealing with two separate queries.
    - o It is less confusing to read because you can easily see which field comes from which table.
    - o More complex subqueries like this one can take longer to run, so do not be surprised if it takes a few seconds for the results to appear.

12.8 Complex Aggregated Subqueries

After all the work that you did for the sales director, your reputation as an analyst has hit new heights. Now it is the CEO's turn to request some assistance. She wants to know which makes are generating the most sales, and specifically, how many cars have been sold for the top three bestselling makes. The following code snippet lets you impress her with your SQL abilities:

```
SELECT      MK.MakeName

            ,COUNT(MK.MakeName) AS VehiclesSold

            ,SUM(SD.SalePrice) AS TotalSalesPerMake
FROM        Data.Make AS MK
INNER JOIN Data.Model AS MD ON MK.MakeID = MD.MakeID
INNER JOIN Data.Stock AS ST ON ST.ModelID = MD.ModelID
INNER JOIN Data.SalesDetails SD ON ST.StockCode = SD.StockID
WHERE       MakeName IN (
                    SELECT      TOP (3) MK.MakeName
                    FROM        Data.Make AS MK
                    INNER JOIN Data.Model AS MD
                            ON MK.MakeID = MD.MakeID
                    INNER JOIN Data.Stock AS ST
                            ON ST.ModelID = MD.ModelID
                    INNER JOIN Data.SalesDetails SD
                            ON ST.StockCode = SD.StockID
                    INNER JOIN Data.Sales AS SA

                            ON SA.SalesID = SD.SalesID
                    GROUP BY    MK.MakeName
                    ORDER BY    COUNT(MK.MakeName) DESC
                    )
GROUP BY   MK.MakeName
ORDER BY   VehiclesSold DESC
```

Running this query gives the results that you can see in *Figure 12.15.*

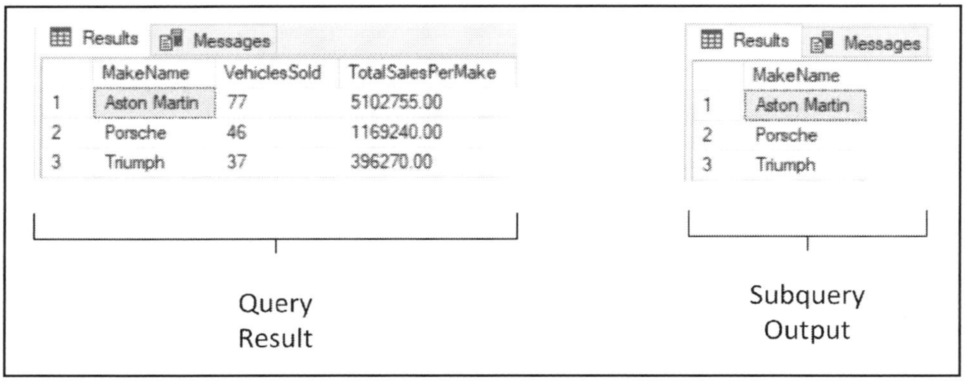

Figure 12.15: Using a complex subquery as a filter in an aggregated query

How It Works

Some queries are really two queries in one. In these cases, subqueries unlock the real power of SQL to allow you to carry out complex filtering that then becomes the basis of further analysis. This example extends the code from the previous example to show that the two queries that generate the final result are—and have to be—`totally independent` of one another. Even though the subquery counts the sales per make, you cannot pass this value back to the outer query. You have to count the number of vehicles sold `twice`: once in the `subquery` to act as a filter and once in the `outer query` to display the result.

Otherwise this query is very similar to the previous one. The subquery finds the top three makes sold by quantity. Then these three makes are used as the filter by the outer query.

Tricks and Traps

There are a couple of points to note here:

- In this example, both queries (outer query and subquery) aggregate data. As you saw in the previous example, this does not necessarily need to be the case.

- This code applies the `same aliases` for the tables in both the outer query and the subquery. This reinforces the point that the two queries are `completely separate` and that the aliases in the outer query only refer to tables in the outer query and the aliases in the inner query only refer to tables in the inner query—even if the same aliases are used in both queries.

12.9 Using a Subquery to Filter a Percentage of a Dataset

Investigating trends and patterns in data often means looking at the data that makes up a specific area of data. Finding attributes of least (and most) profitable sales is an example of this kind of analysis. As a specific example, the sales director wants you to find all colors for cars sold for the least profitable 5 percent of sales. Take a look at the following SQL snippet to see how this is done:

```
SELECT      DISTINCT STX.Color
FROM        Data.Stock STX
INNER JOIN  Data.SalesDetails SDX
            ON STX.StockCode = SDX.StockID
WHERE       SDX.SalesID IN (
                SELECT     TOP 5 PERCENT SalesID
                FROM       Data.Stock AS ST
                INNER JOIN Data.SalesDetails SD
                           ON ST.StockCode = SD.StockID
                ORDER BY   (SD.SalePrice -
                                (Cost + ISNULL(RepairsCost,
0)


                                + PartsCost +
TransportInCost)
                           ) ASC
                )
```

Running this query gives the results that you can see in Figure *12.16*.

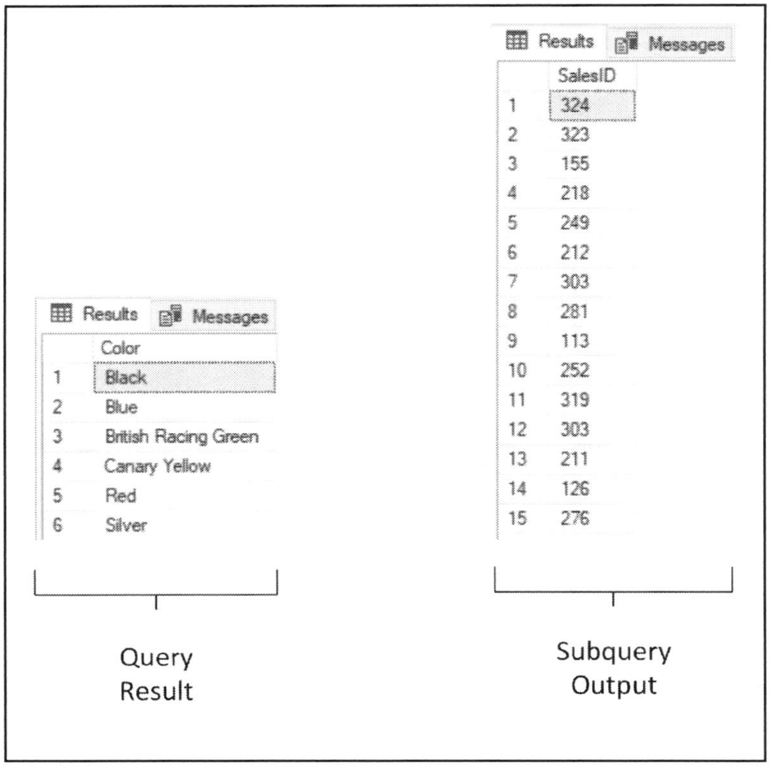

Figure 12.16: Using a subquery to filter a percentage of a dataset

How It Works

Once again, the subquery is the central part of this overall piece of SQL. It joins the Stock table to the SalesDetails table so that only cars sold are taken into consideration by the query. Then it calculates the net profit per car sold. Finally, it sorts this data set from lowest to highest—that is, from the smallest to the greatest profit. Adding the TOP 5 PERCENT to the SELECT clause ensures that only the initial 5 percent of sales records are returned.

The outer query then lists the colors of the vehicles whose SalesIDs are passed up to the outer query's WHERE clause as a filter. As a final touch, the outer query's SELECT clause uses the DISTINCT keyword to avoid duplication of colors, even if the same color appears several times in the top 5 percent of sales per make.

This query looks quite dense, yet it delivers some extremely efficient analysis. The art (as is so often the case) is to work out how to break down the requirement into its component parts so that you can then design and write the appropriate SQL.

Tricks and Traps

When using subqueries as filters, you need to remember that

- Even though the subquery uses the TOP keyword, it is really returning the bottom percentage. This is because the sort order is set to ascending—that is, from smallest to largest. So, the top 5 percent, starting at the smallest figure, in effect returns the lowest sales figures—that is, the bottom five percent.

12.10 Nested Subqueries

The only downside to making senior managers happy is that it generates even more work for you. This time the sales director wants you find the top five vehicles sold by value in the color of the most expensive car sold. The following piece of SQL does exactly this:

```
SELECT      TOP 5 MK.MakeName, MD.ModelName, SD.SalePrice
FROM        Data.Make AS MK
INNER JOIN Data.Model AS MD ON MK.MakeID = MD.MakeID
INNER JOIN Data.Stock AS ST ON ST.ModelID = MD.ModelID
INNER JOIN Data.SalesDetails SD ON ST.StockCode = SD.StockID
INNER JOIN Data.Sales AS SA ON SA.SalesID = SD.SalesID

WHERE       Color IN (SELECT     ST.Color
                      FROM       Data.Model AS MD
                      INNER JOIN Data.Stock AS ST
                                 ON ST.ModelID = MD.ModelID
                      INNER JOIN Data.SalesDetails SD
                                 ON ST.StockCode = SD.StockID
                      WHERE      SD.SalePrice =
                                 (
                                  SELECT      MAX(SD.SalePrice)
                                  FROM        Data.SalesDetails
SD
                                  INNER JOIN  Data.Sales SA
                                  ON SA.SalesID = SD.SalesID
                                  )
                      )
ORDER BY    SD.SalePrice DESC
```

Running this query gives the results that you can see in *Figure 12.17*.

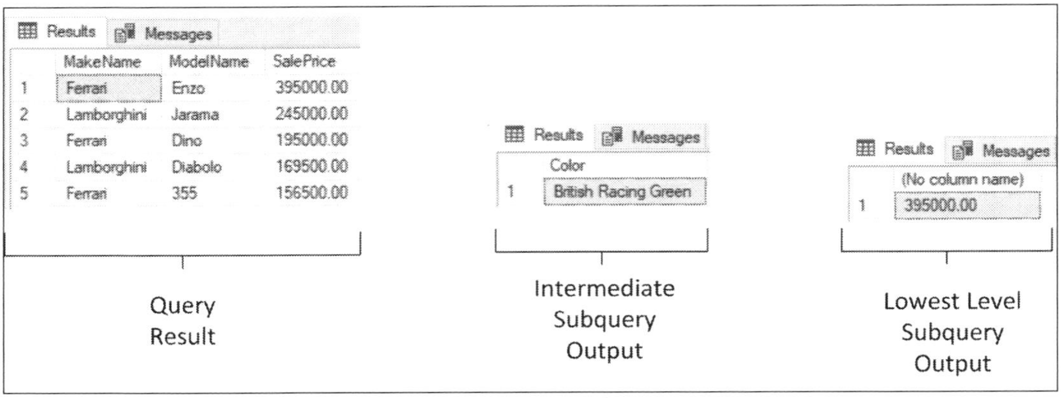

Figure 12.17: A query containing nested subqueries

How It Works

Answering some questions can require more complex queries. This is where SQL Server's ability to "nest" subqueries inside subqueries can help you find a solution to even quite tricky problems. This query is an example of this kind of approach because it contains a subquery inside another subquery. As is often the case with subqueries, it is easiest to start on the inside with the deepest nested subquery and then work outward to explain the SQL.

The innermost query (at the lowest level):	Joins the Sales and SalesDetails tables and returns the highest sale price for a vehicle sold.
The middle (or intermediate) subquery:	Uses the sale price from the deepest nested subquery as a filter (in its WHERE clause) to find any vehicles that have been sold at this price. It then returns the colors of this vehicle, or vehicles.
The outer query:	Lists the Make, Model, and Sale Price for all the vehicles sold in the color returned by the middle subquery. Note that the WHERE clause uses IN and not = (equals) because there is potentially *more than one vehicle* of this color returned by the intermediate query.

When faced with a challenge such as "Find the Top Five Vehicles Sold for the Bestselling Color by Value," the hard part can be to analyze the question and then break the solution down into separate parts that can then be answered as separate SQL queries. In these cases, our advice is to look hard at the question before starting to write any SQL. Often the code itself is easier than the analysis—and if the initial analysis is correct, then you are likely to write simpler and better SQL.

Because the concept of using nested subqueries can seem a little daunting at first glance, take a look at *Figure 12.18*. Here you can see how each query uses the output from the query at a lower level to filter the data that it, in turn, passes up to the query above it. Finally, the topmost query returns the required result.

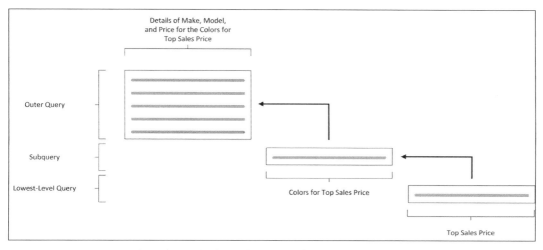

Figure 12.18: *Using subqueries to filter data progressively*

Tricks and Traps

This approach is best applied when you bear the following points in mind:

- There is a theoretical limit of 32 levels of nested subqueries in SQL Server. In practice, however, it is rare when you need to use more than 3 or 4 levels, so it is unlikely that you will hit the limit.

- As you can see in this example, you can easily end up repeating table joins in nested subqueries. This is perfectly normal considering that—as I have mentioned—each query is completely independent of the others.

12.11 Using Subqueries to Exclude Data

Some analysis requires you to examine data that lies outside a certain range or category. For instance, at Prestige Cars, the CEO wants a report that shows sales by make for all vehicles sold that are not in the sales made to the bottom four countries by value. Subqueries can often be the solution to these requirements, as the following SQL illustrates:

```
SELECT    MK.MakeName, SUM(SA.TotalSalePrice) AS TotalSales
FROM      Data.Make AS MK INNER JOIN Data.Model AS MD
```

```
              ON MK.MakeID = MD.MakeID
INNER JOIN Data.Stock AS ST ON ST.ModelID = MD.ModelID
INNER JOIN Data.SalesDetails SD ON ST.StockCode = SD.StockID
INNER JOIN Data.Sales AS SA ON SA.SalesID = SD.SalesID
INNER JOIN Data.Customer CU ON SA.CustomerID = CU.CustomerID
INNER JOIN Data.Country CO ON CU.Country = CO.CountryISO2
WHERE       CountryName NOT IN (
                                SELECT     TOP 4 CO.CountryName
                                FROM       Data.Sales AS SA
                                INNER JOIN Data.Customer CU
                                    ON SA.CustomerID = CU.CustomerID
                                INNER JOIN Data.Country CO
                                    ON CU.Country = CO.CountryISO2
                                GROUP BY   CountryName
                                ORDER BY   SUM(SA.TotalSalePrice) ASC
                                )
GROUP BY    MK.MakeName
```

Running this query gives the results that you can see in *Figure 12.19*.

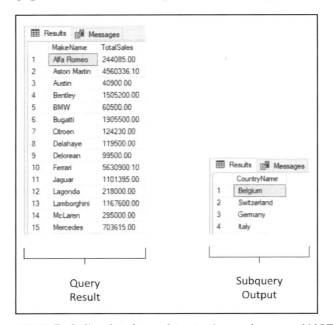

Figure 12.19: Excluding data from a dataset using a subquery and NOT IN

How It Works

This query extends the concepts that you have seen so far in this chapter. It also tries to show that what appears to be complex or convoluted SQL is, in fact, quite simple.

If you look at the preceding SQL, you can see that it breaks down into two main elements:

First:	Create a subquery that uses the tables required to aggregate sales by countries. This subquery then isolates the bottom four countries by sales by sorting the resulting data from lowest to highest
Second:	The outer query joins a series of tables so that you can use the make, customer country, and sales price fields. Even if you are only displaying the make and sales price fields, you are using the customer country field in the WHERE clause to use the subquery as a filter. So, the code must make the country field accessible by joining the table that contains this data to the query.

Once you have defined these queries, it is simply a question of using the output from the subquery (the top four countries for vehicle sales) and `excluding` it from the result that the outer query returns. You do this by using the NOT IN operator in the WHERE clause of the outer query. So, what you have done is say, "find me makes and sales where the sales are `not` made to the bottom four least-performing countries."

So, a query that seems long and complex is, in fact, relatively simple once you break it down into its constituent parts. Here, as in most SQL, it is largely a question of ensuring that a query or subquery can access `all` the required fields by ensuring that all the necessary tables are joined in the FROM clause of each query and the fields used to include or exclude records in the outer query are available in both inner and outer queries.

Tricks and Traps

To finish this introduction to simple subqueries, you should take note of the following:

- Once again, if a subquery is returning potentially more than one element—and because we are asking for four countries, we hope that more than one element is returned—you `cannot` use equals or not equals (=, !=, or <>); you have to use the IN keyword. Then you make it negative by adding NOT to the IN. This way you are excluding from the outer query an element returned from the subquery.

12.12 Filtering across Queries and Subqueries

In your analytical career you will probably have to produce reports that do not look at a dataset in its entirety. The following SQL snippet returns each make sold in 2015, along with the total sales figure per make for 2015, and the percentage that this represents of the total sales for that year only.

```
SELECT      MK.MakeName

            ,SUM(SD.SalePrice) AS SalePrice

            ,SUM(SD.SalePrice) /

                        (SELECT      SUM(SD.SalePrice)

                         FROM        Data.SalesDetails SD

                         INNER JOIN Data.Sales AS SA

                                    ON SA.SalesID = SD.SalesID

                         WHERE       YEAR(SaleDate) = 2015

                        ) AS SalesRatio

FROM        Data.Make AS MK

INNER JOIN Data.Model AS MD ON MK.MakeID = MD.MakeID

INNER JOIN Data.Stock AS ST ON ST.ModelID = MD.ModelID

INNER JOIN Data.SalesDetails SD ON ST.StockCode = SD.StockID

INNER JOIN Data.Sales AS SA ON SA.SalesID = SD.SalesID

WHERE       YEAR(SA.SaleDate) = 2015

GROUP BY    MK.MakeName
```

Running this query gives the results that you can see in *Figure 12.20*—where you can also see the result of the subquery.

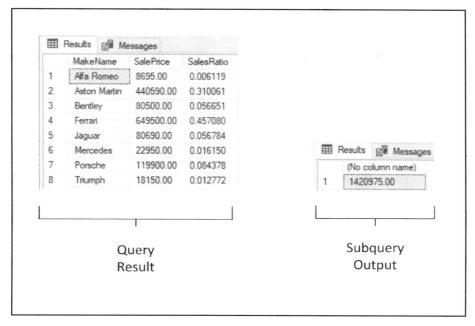

Figure 12.20: Applying filters to subqueries

How It Works

As you saw earlier in this chapter, a classic analytical requirement is comparing the whole with its constituent parts. Sometimes, however, you need to compare a subset of data with another subset. You do this by applying separate filters to both the main/outer query and the subquery (which some people call the inner query). So even if this query does provoke a sense of Déjà vu nonetheless, there is a major difference. Each query has a separate WHERE clause.

The subquery	Finds the figure for the total sales for 2015.
The outer query	Finds the sales per make for 2015. It then divides this by the total sales figure for the same year to display the percentage sales per make for the year.

I prefer to explain the subquery first, since SQL queries nearly always work from the inside to the outside, and not the other way around. The subquery is calculated first, and it returns the total sales for 2015. This query merely provides the total figure with no subsetting of data at all. It joins the necessary tables (only Sales and SalesDetails are needed to find the annual total) and calculates the SUM() of the sale price field. The outer query finds the sales for each make for the same year and then divides the sales for each make by the yearly total, giving the percentage of sales by value for each make. The outer query needs to return not only the sales total (from the

SalesDetails table) but also the year (from the Sales table); it also needs to return the makes of car sold. Consequently, it needs to add joins to the Stock and Make tables.

The really important thing to take away from this example is that each query is truly independent of the other. So, if you want to compare the sales by make for a given year with the total sales for the same year, you must apply an `identical` filter (that is, set the year to be 2015) in both queries.

Tricks and Traps

Obviously, you need to bear a few key points in mind when filtering multiple data sets like this:

- The subquery shown here follows all the same rules and restrictions as the subqueries that you saw earlier in this chapter.

- The fact that the queries are completely independent can work to your advantage by making querying really fluid. For instance, if you want to compare the sales per make for a given year to the total for all vehicles ever sold, all you have to do is omit the WHERE clause from the subquery. The subquery then calculates the value of all cars ever sold by the company, which you still use in the outer query to calculate the percentages of sales per make.

- Remember to test the subquery and to ensure that it gives the result that you expect before you rely blindly on the output that it sends up to the outer query.

- If you are filtering inner and outer queries, you need to pay particular attention to the filters that you apply and ensure that you are using similar filters in both queries if you are attempting to analyse comparable datasets.

12.13 Applying Separate Filters to the Subquery and the Main Query

"Like for Like" comparisons are a mainstay of business analysis. Like most companies that make their margin by buying and selling, Prestige Cars needs to see if sales are up or down compared to previous years. Specifically, the CEO wants to see the difference in sale price for each car sold compared to the average price for the previous year. As the following SQL snippet shows, year-on-year sales comparisons are not overly difficult:

```
SELECT      MK.MakeName
            ,MD.ModelName
```

```
        ,SD.SalePrice AS ThisYearsSalePrice

        ,SD.SalePrice

          - (SELECT    AVG(SD.SalePrice)

            FROM        Data.Stock ST

            INNER JOIN Data.SalesDetails SD

                        ON ST.StockCode = SD.StockID

            INNER JOIN Data.Sales AS SA

                        ON SA.SalesID = SD.SalesID

            WHERE       YEAR(SA.SaleDate) = 2015)

                                    AS DeltaToLastYearAverage

FROM        Data.Make AS MK INNER JOIN Data.Model AS MD

            ON MK.MakeID = MD.MakeID

INNER JOIN Data.Stock AS ST ON ST.ModelID = MD.ModelID

INNER JOIN Data.SalesDetails SD ON ST.StockCode = SD.StockID

INNER JOIN Data.Sales AS SA ON SA.SalesID = SD.SalesID

WHERE       YEAR(SA.SaleDate) = 2016
```

Running this query gives the results that you can see in Figure *12.21*.

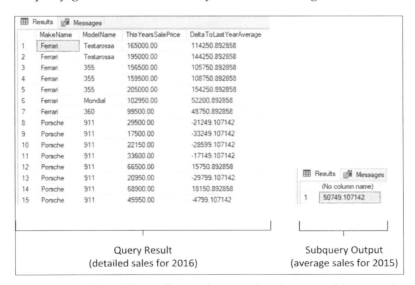

Figure 12.21: *Using different filters and aggregations in outer and inner queries*

How It Works

Being able to use completely independent queries together is particularly useful when you want to compare data over time. This time the subquery (or the inner query, if you prefer) calculates the average vehicle sale price for **2015**. The outer query, however, filters on **2016**—the following year.

When the outer query returns the list of makes sold in 2016, it calculates for each make the difference between the sale price for 2016 (returned by the outer query) and the average sale price for 2015 (returned by the inner query). This way you can compare data from two separate years.

The fact that the two queries can work together, while remaining completely independent, allows you to see how sales evolve over time from one year to the next.

Tricks and Traps

One important point to remember when applying different filters to queries and subqueries is this:

- Another indication of the fact that subqueries are completely independent of the query that contains them is given by the fact that you can use different filters in each query. In this example, for instance, the outer queryfilters on one year, whereas the subqueryfilters on another year.

Conclusion

In this chapter, you saw how you can nest queries inside queries to deliver far-reaching analytics. As you have learned, a subquery is nothing more than a standard SQL query in its own right. However, the ability to return two or more independent datasets inside a single query opens up the road to much more advanced comparative analysis of your data. You can compare data at different levels of aggregation and calculate percentages of a total with a minimum of effort. Subqueries also let you isolate data in many subtle and surprising ways and can, consequently, help you deliver deeper insights into your data.

Core Knowledge Learned in This Chapter

The concepts that you have seen in this chapter are

- A subquery is completely independent of the outer query.

- You can refer to the subquery in the SELECT, WHERE, or HAVING clauses of the outer query.

- You must enclose a subquery in parenthesis.

- A subquery must include a SELECT clause and a FROM clause.

- A subquery can include optional WHERE, GROUP BY, and HAVING clauses.

- You can include an ORDER BY clause only when a TOP clause is included.

- If a subquery returns more than one record, then you have to use the IN operator in the WHERE or HAVING clause of the outer query.

- You can nest subqueries inside other subqueries.

CHAPTER 13
Derived Tables

Some analytical challenges require you to combine different types of query to get the result that you are looking for. You may need to compare data at different levels of aggregation or carry out calculations that mix and match different ways of grouping data. For these types of problem, SQL has a clear answer—derived tables.

What Is a Derived Table?

Derived tables let you focus on producing complex datasets inside a single query. You can then use this data to solve your analytical conundrum. As you see during the course of this chapter, whenever you are faced with a challenge that seems to require different types of SQL queries at the same time, it can help to think in terms of derived tables. This is not only because they deliver a technical answer; they also help you analyze a problem by breaking it down into smaller, separate components. This, in turn, assists you in constructing the code that can produce the result that you need.

A derived table is, in many ways, a subquery. However, it is also often the "engine room" where most of the hard work is done. After the work is complete, the derived query may pass its output to the outer query that shapes and presents the final dataset.

Indeed, trying to carry out certain kinds of calculations and aggregations without a derived table is extremely difficult—both conceptually and practically. So, in this chapter, you learn how to use derived tables to

- Define calculated metrics that you can reuse several times without having to redefine the calculation each time

- Create your own ad-hoc classifications that you can use to group data

- Analyze ratios for subgroups of data

- Mix different data sources that have differing levels of data aggregation, such as monthly budgets and daily sales

- Compare values across years

- Isolate maximum, minimum, and average values and use them to analyze data that you have classified

- Filter data based on the first or last records output from a derived table

The aim of this chapter is to enhance and extend the knowledge that you have already acquired so far in this book. I also hope to introduce you to ways of juggling data that not only extend your SQL skills but also start you on the road to thinking in datasets as a way of solving analytical challenges.

13.1 Using a Derived Table to Create Intermediate Calculations

There is no point in being in business unless you are making a profit—at least that is what the boss of Prestige Cars maintains. She wants a printout of the sales, costs, and gross and net profit for every car sold. Fortunately, SQL Server makes delivering this kind of output easy, as the following code shows:

```
SELECT
 MakeName
,ModelName
,SaleDate
,SalePrice
,Cost
,SalePrice - DirectCosts AS GrossProfit
,SalePrice - DirectCosts - ISNULL(LineItemDiscount, 0) AS NetProfit
FROM
```

```
(
  SELECT
   MK.MakeName
  ,MD.ModelName
  ,SA.SaleDate
  ,SD.SalePrice
  ,ST.Cost
  ,LineItemDiscount
  ,(ISNULL(ST.RepairsCost, 0) + ISNULL(ST.PartsCost, 0)
  + ST.TransportInCost) AS DirectCosts
  FROM      Data.Make AS MK INNER JOIN Data.Model
            AS MD ON MK.MakeID = MD.MakeID
            INNER JOIN Data.Stock AS ST ON ST.ModelID = MD.ModelID
            INNER JOIN Data.SalesDetails SD ON ST.StockCode
                                        = SD.StockID
            INNER JOIN Data.Sales AS SA ON SA.SalesID = SD.SalesID
  ) DT
ORDER BY  MakeName, ModelName, SaleDate
```

Running this query gives the results that you can see in *Figure 13.1*.

	MakeName	ModelName	SaleDate	SalePrice	Cost	GrossProfit	NetProfit
1	Alfa Romeo	1750	2018-04-15 00:00:00.000	9950.00	7960.00	8550.0000	8550.0000
2	Alfa Romeo	1750	2018-06-03 00:00:00.000	3575.00	2860.00	2175.0000	1425.0000
3	Alfa Romeo	Giulia	2015-07-12 10:00:00.000	8695.00	6956.00	7395.0000	7300.0000
4	Alfa Romeo	Giulia	2016-01-07 00:00:00.000	2550.00	2040.00	1150.0000	1100.0000
5	Alfa Romeo	Giulia	2016-02-17 00:00:00.000	6000.00	4800.00	4600.0000	4600.0000
6	Alfa Romeo	Giulia	2016-04-30 11:27:00.000	17500.00	14000.00	15765.0000	15265.0000
7	Alfa Romeo	Giulia	2016-07-06 00:00:00.000	12500.00	10000.00	11100.0000	10350.0000
8	Alfa Romeo	Giulia	2017-11-01 19:35:00.000	25000.00	20000.00	22740.0000	21240.0000
9	Alfa Romeo	Giulia	2017-11-06 21:36:00.000	10500.00	8400.00	9100.0000	9100.0000
10	Alfa Romeo	Giulia	2018-07-10 00:00:00.000	6950.00	5560.00	5250.0000	4000.0000
11	Alfa Romeo	Giulietta	2017-02-09 17:01:00.000	21500.00	17200.00	20350.0000	20350.0000
12	Alfa Romeo	Giulietta	2017-05-16 16:16:00.000	6500.00	5200.00	5100.0000	5100.0000
13	Alfa Romeo	Giulietta	2018-01-05 00:00:00.000	11550.00	9240.00	10150.0000	10150.0000
14	Alfa Romeo	Giulietta	2018-03-05 00:00:00.000	5690.00	4552.00	4290.0000	3540.0000
15	Alfa Romeo	Giulietta	2018-06-25 00:00:00.000	18500.00	14800.00	17100.0000	17100.0000

Figure 13.1. A derived table that creates intermediate calculations

How It Works

It sometimes gets a little laborious to carry out financial analysis using SQL. The speed at which SQL Server can perform calculations on a large set of data is rarely a problem. However, as you have probably seen when practicing SQL, because you are required to repeat field names over and over as you create intermediate and final calculations, the process can get rather wearing.

Fortunately, there is a convenient way to minimize the repetitive use of field names. Start by creating a core query that carries out any basic analysis. You can then use the results of these calculations in the outer query without having to repeat the initial arithmetic.

In this example, the derived table (which has the alias DT in the preceding code) calculates the direct costs associated with a sale by adding up the total for the cost of repairs, parts, and transport. This inner query also ensures that any NULLs in the data are handled at the source to avoid them falsifying the results. It does this by enclosing any "suspect" field names in the ISNULL() function. The derived table joins all the tables that we need to output the make, model, date of sale, selling price, and vehicle cost. To see this more clearly, take a look at *Figure 13.2*, which displays part of the output from the derived table.

	MakeName	ModelName	SaleDate	SalePrice	Cost	LineItemDiscount	DirectCosts
1	Ferrari	Testarossa	2015-01-02 00:00:00.000	65000.00	52000.00	2700.00	4425.00
2	Ferrari	355	2015-01-25 00:00:00.000	220000.00	176000.00	60000.00	9650.00
3	Porsche	911	2015-02-03 00:00:00.000	19500.00	15600.00	NULL	810.00
4	Porsche	924	2015-02-16 00:00:00.000	11500.00	9200.00	NULL	1400.00
5	Porsche	944	2015-01-02 10:33:00.000	19950.00	15960.00	NULL	2010.00
6	Aston Martin	DB4	2015-03-14 00:00:00.000	29500.00	23600.00	1250.00	1400.00
7	Aston Martin	DB5	2015-03-24 00:00:00.000	49500.00	39600.00	2450.00	4550.00
8	Aston Martin	DB6	2015-03-30 00:00:00.000	76000.00	60800.00	5500.00	4750.00
9	Porsche	911	2015-04-06 00:00:00.000	19600.00	15680.00	NULL	1540.00
10	Aston Martin	DB5	2015-04-04 00:00:00.000	36500.00	29200.00	2500.00	3000.00

Figure 13.2: The output from a derived table

As you can see, the columns that are returned are not the same in the derived table as they are in the outer query. Nonetheless, the columns in the derived table are the basis for any data that is output by the outer query.

In cases like this, a derived table is a `query in a query`. More precisely, it is a `completely independent piece of SQL` that feeds its output into an outer query that wraps around the derived table. In this example, you can see that the outer query has a FROM clause that does not directly use a table or a set of joined tables.

Instead, the outer query refers to a self-sufficient query (the derived table or inner query) to isolate a dataset. This dataset is then used as the data source for the outer query.

The outer query is a straightforward list of the fields that are in the SELECT clause of the derived table. These fields are then extended with a couple of simple calculations to deliver both the gross profit and the net profit.

You could achieve the final calculation of gross and net profit without using a derived table. However, in this case, the query that returns the gross and net profit looks like this:

```
,SD.SalePrice - (ISNULL(ST.RepairsCost, 0)
            + ISNULL(ST.PartsCost, 0) + ST.TransportInCost)
                AS GrossProfit
,SD.SalePrice - (ISNULL(ST.RepairsCost, 0) + ISNULL(ST.PartsCost, 0)
            + ST.TransportInCost + LineItemDiscount) AS NetProfit
```

Although this code is not difficult to write, it is more laborious and certainly more repetitive; it is also possibly a greater source of potential errors precisely because of its repetitive nature. Defining a derived table not only removes the need to repeat fields (as well as their NULL handling code), it also makes any additional calculations you have to apply to these fields easier.

This technique is similar to the way you might use a spreadsheet to perform financial arithmetic. In a spreadsheet, you carry out basic arithmetic in multiple cells to get an intermediate result that you then use for other calculations. The principle is similar when you use a derived table in SQL:

First:	You carry out any essential calculations in a derived table and give the result an alias.
Then:	You use the derived table as the basis for any further calculations in the outer query.

The derived table we use in this example shows the two basic techniques used to define a derived table:

Enclosed in parentheses	A derived table *must* be enclosed in parentheses. If you forget the parentheses, you get an error message. Think of them as isolating and enclosing the derived table and making it into a separate self-contained table.
Must have an alias	A derived table *must* have an alias. In this example, the derived table is given the alias DT. You can use this alias just as you would use the alias for any "normal" table in a SQL query.

Visualizing a concept can often make it easier to understand, so take a look at *Figure 13.3* to see how a derived table works from a high level.

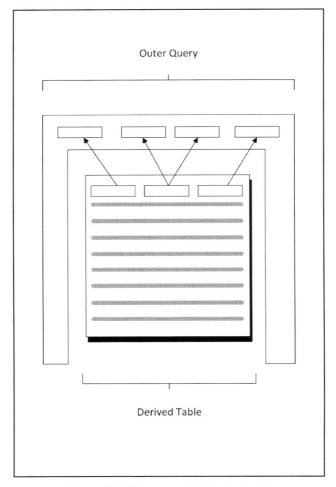

Figure 13.3; *The concept of a derived table*

Tricks and Traps

Derived tables are a fundamental concept in SQL, so there are, perhaps inevitably, several key points to remember when you begin to use them in your analysis:

- When you use a derived table in a FROM clause, you `must include all the fields that you wish to return from the outer query in the SELECT clause of the inner derived table`. This is because the derived table is the source of all the data that is accessible to the outer query. Consequently, you must ensure that every field that you want to output from the overall code is part of the inner SELECT clause. If you forget to include a field in the derived table and then try to select it in the main query, SQL Server returns an error message. Adding the field to the derived table normally solves this problem.

• Another advantage of beginning with a derived table when calculating metrics is that you only have to handle potential NULLs once—in the derived table at the heart of the query.

• Another factor that argues in favor of using a derived table to simplify calculations is that if a core calculation changes, you only make the change once in the derived table (just like in a spreadsheet). Any modifications ripple up through the rest of the query. Without a derived table, you have to make the change every time the calculation is repeated in the query.

• It is important to ensure that every field in a derived table has a name. SQL Server does not add a name (such as "Column 1") if you forget to add an alias. Indeed, the query does not work if any calculated fields (such as SalePrice and GrossProfit in this example) are not given aliases.

• The AS keyword that introduces the derived table alias is not strictly necessary, but it is good practice to use it, so we have kept it, even if the query would work without it.

13.2 Grouping and Ordering Data Using a Custom Classification

Suppose the CEO decides that she wants you to classify all your customers by spend. You realize that what she really wants is five categories of customer (tiny, small, medium, large, and megA.rich) according to a series of thresholds of total sales per customer. Then she wants the total spend for customers in each of these spending brackets.

This sounds complicated. Yet we can do it with only a few lines of SQL and the clever use of a derived table:

```
SELECT      DT.CustomerClassification
            ,COUNT(DT.CustomerSpend) AS CustomerSpend
FROM
            (
            SELECT      SUM(SD.SalePrice) AS CustomerSpend
            ,SA.CustomerID
            ,CASE
```

```
                WHEN SUM(SD.SalePrice) <= 100000 THEN 'Tiny'
                WHEN SUM(SD.SalePrice) BETWEEN 100001 AND 200000
                      THEN 'Small'
                WHEN SUM(SD.SalePrice) BETWEEN 200001 AND 300000
                      THEN 'Medium'
                WHEN SUM(SD.SalePrice) BETWEEN 300001 AND 400000
                      THEN 'Large'
                WHEN SUM(SD.SalePrice) > 400000 THEN 'Mega Rich'
                END AS CustomerClassification
                FROM       Data.SalesDetails SD
                           INNER JOIN Data.Sales AS SA
                           ON SA.SalesID = SD.SalesID
                GROUP BY   SA.CustomerID
           ) AS DT
GROUP BY    DT.CustomerClassification
ORDER BY    CustomerSpend DESC
```

Running this query gives the results that you can see in *Figure 13.4.*

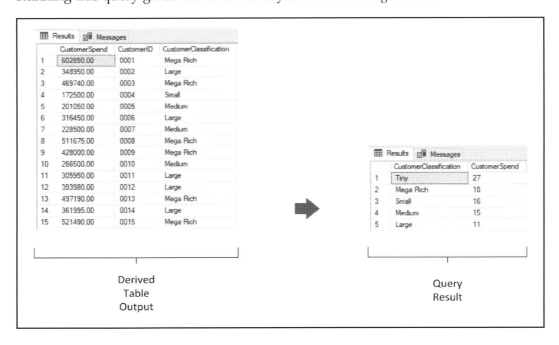

Figure 13.4: *An aggregated derived table feeding into a separate outer aggregation*

How It Works

It is said that a problem shared is a problem halved. In the case of SQL queries, a problem broken down into smaller parts is often a problem that has become much easier to solve. Using derived tables is a fundamental technique for breaking down seemingly complex challenges into smaller and more comprehensible solutions. This piece of SQL is an example of how a derived table can help you break down analytical tasks into their component parts.

Consequently (as is the case with much SQL), the logic of this code begins at the center and works its way outward. The overall query does two things:

The inner query	Takes the data from the Sales and SalesDetails tables and finds the total value of sales per customer. This query then uses a CASE statement to test the total value of sales for each customer and places each one in one of five custom categories—from the tiny customers to the megA.rich ones. In this kind of statistical query, we do not need to see the customer name because we are not interested in detail-level analysis. We can group on the CustomerID field from the SalesDetails table, and we do not need to refer to the Customer table for any customer data.
The outer query	Aggregates the results of the derived table by counting the number of customers in each category and grouping on the category itself (the field that has been given the alias CustomerClassification). Finally, it sorts the categories in descending order of the number of customers per classification.

As you can see, the main element in this piece of code is the derived table (the inner query), where the core aggregation is carried out. Indeed, you can run the derived table separately if you wish. You can do this by selecting only the SQL inside the parentheses, from SELECT SUM(SA.SalePrice) to GROUP BY SA.CustomerID. This way, you can check that the inner query gives you the result that you expect—something like the output from the derived table shown earlier in *Figure 13.4*.

Now that you can see the output from the derived table, hopefully you have a clearer understanding of the way that the overall query works. The derived table has let you create a classification of your entire customer base where each customer is categorized. The main query then groups and sorts this data to produce the final result set that shows the spend for customers in each classification "bucket."

13.3 Joining Derived Tables to Other Tables

When you are buying and selling, it can help to see how an article compares to others in its category. Specifically, say you have decided that you want to look at the purchase and selling price of each vehicle that has been sold and see how this data maps to the average cost and sale price for every similar model. This is all in a day's work for SQL.

```
SELECT    ST.DateBought, MK.MakeName, MD.ModelName, ST.Color
          ,ST.Cost, SD.SalePrice, DT.AveragePurchasePrice
          ,DT.AverageSalePrice
FROM
      (
      SELECT      MK1.MakeName
                  ,MD1.ModelName
                  ,AVG(ST1.Cost) AS AveragePurchasePrice
                  ,AVG(SD1.SalePrice) AS AverageSalePrice
      FROM        Data.Make AS MK1
                  INNER JOIN Data.Model AS MD1 ON MK1.MakeID = MD1.MakeID
                    INNER JOIN Data.Stock AS ST1 ON ST1.ModelID =
                                                          MD1.ModelID
                  INNER JOIN Data.SalesDetails SD1
                  ON ST1.StockCode = SD1.StockID
      GROUP BY    MK1.MakeName, MD1.ModelName
      ) AS DT
      INNER JOIN Data.Make AS MK
      INNER JOIN Data.Model AS MD ON MK.MakeID = MD.MakeID
      INNER JOIN Data.Stock AS ST ON ST.ModelID = MD.ModelID
      INNER JOIN Data.SalesDetails SD ON ST.StockCode = SD.StockID
      ON MK.MakeName = DT.MakeName
      AND MD.ModelName = DT.ModelName
ORDER BY   ST.DateBought, MK.MakeName, MD.ModelName
```

Running this query gives the results that you can see in *Figure 13.5*.

	DateBought	MakeName	ModelName	Color	Cost	SalePrice	AveragePurchasePrice	AverageSalePrice
1	2015-01-01	Ferrari	Testarossa	Red	52000.00	65000.00	139200.00	174000.000000
2	2015-01-10	Ferrari	355	Blue	176000.00	220000.00	136165.7142	170207.142857
3	2015-01-29	Porsche	911	British Racing Green	15600.00	19500.00	29357.1428	36696.428571
4	2015-02-14	Porsche	924	British Racing Green	9200.00	11500.00	12448.00	15560.000000
5	2015-02-27	Porsche	944	Red	15960.00	19950.00	9818.4615	12273.076923
6	2015-03-05	Aston Martin	DB4	Night Blue	23600.00	29500.00	32194.2857	40242.857142
7	2015-03-15	Aston Martin	DB5	Black	39600.00	49500.00	40045.3333	50056.666666
8	2015-03-26	Aston Martin	DB6	Canary Yellow	60800.00	76000.00	58234.00	72792.500000
9	2015-04-04	Porsche	911	Blue	15680.00	19600.00	29357.1428	36696.428571
10	2015-04-12	Aston Martin	DB5	Blue	29200.00	36500.00	40045.3333	50056.666666
11	2015-04-15	Porsche	944	Blue	6800.00	8500.00	9818.4615	12273.076923
12	2015-04-30	Aston Martin	DB6	Night Blue	36000.00	45000.00	58234.00	72792.500000
13	2015-05-04	Bentley	Flying Spur	British Racing Green	64400.00	80500.00	60350.2222	75437.777777
14	2015-05-15	Ferrari	355	Black	135600.00	169500.00	136165.7142	170207.142857
15	2015-05-26	Porsche	944	Green	7160.00	8950.00	9818.4615	12273.076923

Figure 13.5: A derived table that is part of a complex join clause

How It Works

SQL Server considers derived tables to be just like any "ordinary" tables that exist in a database. This means that you can collate or aggregate data from one or more tables to obtain a derived table and then join the result to another table, or tables, just as you would for any table.

This is particularly useful when you need to aggregate data and include the aggregated result in a query that contains nonaggregated data. This example shows how a single query can show—for every sale—the average selling price for that model of car. This opens up a whole spectrum of analytical possibilities that allow you to put each sale into perspective and see how it compares to other, similar sales.

This example differs from those that you have seen so far in this chapter in that it does not have an inner and outer query structure. Instead, it contains a series of table joins, which are

Standard joins	Using regular database tables to return the cost and sale price for every model of car sold.
A derived table join	Where a derived table is joined to existing tables in the query.

The derived table is interesting because it operates on a different level of data granularity than the other tables. More precisely, the derived table is an aggregation that calculates the average cost and selling price of each model of car. The derived table is then joined to the Make and Model tables in the query perfectly normally.

Because the SQL that underlies this example is a little complex at first sight, take a look at *Figure 13.6,* which is a visual representation of the joins—including the joins to the derived table.

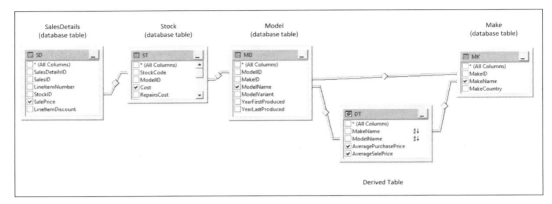

Figure 13.6: *Visualizing a complex join using a derived table*

To help you understand how this works, take a look at *Figure 13.7.* In it, you can see the output from the derived table (aliased as DT in the SQL code that you used to obtain this output).

	MakeName	ModelName	AveragePurchasePrice	AverageSalePrice
1	Delahaye	135	20400.00	25500.000000
2	Delahaye	145	27600.00	34500.000000
3	Delahaye	175	10000.00	12500.000000
4	Alfa Romeo	1750	5410.00	6762.500000
5	Peugeot	203	1280.00	1600.000000
6	Peugeot	205	1960.00	2450.000000
7	Mercedes	250SL	14220.00	17775.000000
8	Mercedes	280SL	30890.2857	38612.857142
9	Mercedes	350SL	23940.00	29925.000000
10	Ferrari	355	136165.7142	170207.142857

Figure 13.7: *The output from an aggregated derived table*

What is really interesting here is that because the derived table isolates data by **two** fields (make **and** model), it needs to join to the other tables using **both** these fields. Consequently, the derived table **has** to contain both these fields in its SELECT clause; otherwise you cannot join the derived table to the outer query.

The trick, in these cases, is to establish the join as you normally would. However, when you link a table to two tables at the same time, you start with an ON clause, as you would normally, and then you continue adding further field joins using the AND keyword.

The query then outputs fields from any or all of the tables that make up the FROM clause. It is in all other respects a perfectly standard query. However, using the derived table to calculate the average cost and average sale price allows you to show these aggregated figures in the query output and make some interesting comparisons.

Tricks and Traps

When joining derived tables, you need to remember the following:

- We chose to use independent table aliases in the derived query (ST1 for the Stock table, for instance) even if it is possible to use the same aliases in the derived table subquery as those we used in the main query's FROM clause. This is because it is generally easier to understand and debug queries when all the component elements are identifiable separately and uniquely.

13.4 Joining Multiple Derived Tables

Continuing with the theme of comparisons, let's suppose that you want to see which colors are purchased the most. Indeed, you want not only to produce this kind of analysis but also find the percentage of cars purchased by value for each color of vehicle. The following SQL does this for you:

```
SELECT

TOT.PurchaseYear

,AGG.Color

,(AGG.CostPerYear / TOT.TotalPurchasePrice) * 100 AS
PercentPerColorPerYear

FROM

    (

    SELECT        STX.Color

                  ,SUM(STX.Cost) AS CostPerYear

                  ,YEAR(STX.DateBought) AS YearBought

    FROM          Data.Stock AS STX ON STX.ModelID = MDX.ModelID

    GROUP BY      STX.Color

                  ,YEAR(STX.DateBought)

    ) AGG

INNER JOIN
```

```
(
    SELECT       YEAR(DateBought) AS PurchaseYear, SUM(Cost)
                 AS TotalPurchasePrice
    FROM         Data.Stock
    GROUP BY     YEAR(DateBought)
) TOT
ON TOT.PurchaseYear = AGG.YearBought
ORDER BY TOT.PurchaseYear, PercentPerColorPerYear DESC
```

Running this query gives the results that you can see in Figure 13.8.

	PurchaseYear	Color	PercentPerColorPerYear
1	2015	Black	24.38
2	2015	Red	16.76
3	2015	British Racing Green	12.68
4	2015	Blue	11.56
5	2015	Night Blue	10.56
6	2015	Silver	10.28
7	2015	Green	8.53
8	2015	Canary Yellow	5.20
9	2016	Black	29.10
10	2016	Red	12.04
11	2016	Blue	11.32
12	2016	British Racing Green	9.25
13	2016	Green	9.05
14	2016	Silver	7.66

Figure 13.8: Using two separate derived tables in a query

How It Works

This query requires you to produce two completely different aggregations and then use them together to deliver the final result.

The first aggregation	Is the total cost of vehicles purchased for each year for each color
The second aggregation	Is the total cost of purchases per year

Using derived tables allows you to handle each aggregation as a separate derived table. Before going any further, it is probably worth taking a look at the output from each of the derived tables so that you can see what each one is doing. *Figure 13.9* illustrates how multiple derived tables relate to an outer query. Once again, I hope that this simple illustration makes the concept clearer.

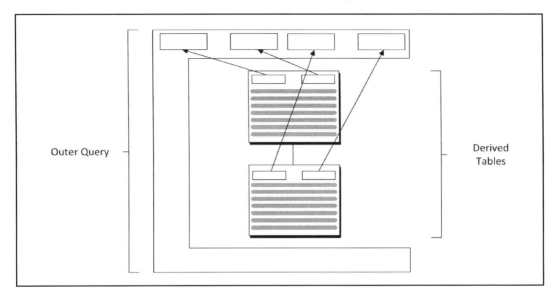

Figure 13.9: *Derived tables and the outer query*

Data Visibility

As I have already noted—but it bears repeating—one important aspect of derived tables is that they only allow access to the data that you specify. So, if you want the outer query to be able to access a field from the derived table, you **must** include the field name in the SELECT clause of the derived table.

"Self-contained" also means "locked away" as far as the data in a derived table is concerned. It does not matter if a table is part of the derived table definition; none of its fields are accessible to the rest of the code outside the derived table unless they are made visible in the SELECT clause.

The first derived table (aliased as AGG in this example) shows the year, color, and cost per year for each color of vehicle bought. If you select just the SQL for the first of the two derived tables, you see output similar to that in *Figure 13.10.*

	Color	CostPerYear	YearBought
1	Black	494944.00	2015
2	Blue	234720.00	2015
3	British Racing Green	257400.00	2015
4	Canary Yellow	105600.00	2015
5	Green	173280.00	2015
6	Night Blue	214392.00	2015
7	Red	340196.00	2015
8	Silver	208800.00	2015
9	Black	1275128.00	2016
10	Blue	496240.00	2016

Figure 13.10: *The output from an aggregated derived table*

This derived table needs three database tables to be joined to return the required data: Make, Model, and Stock. Then all it does is aggregate the result by year and color and return the total vehicle cost for all available combinations of these two fields.

Running the second of the derived table queries (aliased as TOT in the SQL code for this section) shows you the data that you can see in *Figure 13.11.*

	PurchaseYear	TotalPurchasePrice
1	NULL	NULL
2	2015	2029332.00
3	2016	4380988.00
4	2017	7083824.00
5	2018	6265020.00

Figure 13.11: *The output from a high-level aggregated derived table*

This high-level aggregated derived table only needs the Stock table to produce the annual cost of cars that have been purchased.

These two derived tables both output the Year field. Consequently, the overall query can use this field to join the two derived tables. Once the derived tables are constructed and joined, you can treat this query just like any other query and use the fields it contains to analyze your data.

In this specific example, the year and color fields are output and the cost per color for each year is divided by the total cost for the same timeframe to return the percentage cost of each color for each year.

Finishing the query with an ORDER BY clause allows you to list the result first by year and second in descending order of sales per color. This makes it easy to see which color tops the sales charts each year.

Once again, we use derived tables to break down the problem into component parts. The challenge is to produce two sets of data that aggregate at different "levels." One requires the year and the color, the other only the year. We build the query to handle these different requirements using the flexibility that derived tables bring to analysis with SQL.

What is interesting here is that the query uses nothing but derived tables to carry out its analysis. Once again, each derived table is a completely separate entity that works independently of the other parts of the overall query.

Tricks and Traps

One point needs to be made about joining derived tables:

- Because derived tables are `always` independent entities in a query, you can reuse "base" tables in separate derived tables. Here, for instance, the Stock table is used twice—once in each derived table. Each derived table makes use of the Stock table separately and in different ways.

13.5 Using Multiple Derived Tables for Complex Aggregations

Good analysis is about seeing the wood for the trees. This is where SQL really shines. The following code lets you create a report for the CEO that lists sales per customer by volume and value. Not only that, but the output is broken down by country and sorted to make it clear who the best customers are in each country. All of this is possible in a single query that produces an analysis of sales ratios per customer per country—as you can see in the following code:

```
SELECT
 DT2.CountryName
,DT2.CustomerName
,DT2.NumberOfCustomerSales
,DT2.TotalCustomerSales
,CAST(DT2.NumberOfCustomerSales AS NUMERIC)
```

```
        / CAST(DT1.NumberOfCountrySales AS NUMERIC)
            AS PercentageOfCountryCarsSold
,DT2.TotalCustomerSales / DT1.TotalCountrySales
            AS PercentageOfCountryCarsSoldByValue
FROM
(
    SELECT       CO.CountryName
                 ,COUNT(*) AS NumberOfCountrySales
                 ,SUM(SD.SalePrice) AS TotalCountrySales
    FROM         Data.Stock AS ST
    INNER JOIN Data.SalesDetails SD ON ST.StockCode = SD.StockID
    INNER JOIN Data.Sales AS SA ON SA.SalesID = SD.SalesID
    INNER JOIN Data.Customer CU ON SA.CustomerID = CU.CustomerID
    INNER JOIN Data.Country CO ON CU.Country = CO.CountryISO2
    GROUP BY     CO.CountryName
) AS DT1
INNER JOIN
(
    SELECT       CO.CountryName
                 ,CU.CustomerName
                 ,COUNT(*) AS NumberOfCustomerSales
                 ,SUM(SD.SalePrice) AS TotalCustomerSales
    FROM         Data.Stock AS ST
    INNER JOIN Data.SalesDetails SD ON ST.StockCode = SD.StockID
    INNER JOIN Data.Sales AS SA ON SA.SalesID = SD.SalesID
    INNER JOIN Data.Customer CU ON SA.CustomerID = CU.CustomerID
    INNER JOIN Data.Country CO ON CU.Country = CO.CountryISO2
    GROUP BY     CO.CountryName, CU.CustomerName
) AS DT2
ON DT1.CountryName = DT2.CountryName
ORDER BY DT2.CountryName, NumberOfCustomerSales DESC
```

Running this query gives the results that you can see in *Figure 13.12*.

	CountryName	CustomerName	NumberOfCustomerSales	TotalCustomerSales	PercentageOfCountryCarsSold	PercentageOfCountryCarsSoldByValue
1	Belgium	Stefan Van Helsing	6	80900.00	0.600000000000000000	0.259419
2	Belgium	Diplomatic Cars	3	224000.00	0.300000000000000000	0.718294
3	Belgium	Flash Voitures	1	6950.00	0.100000000000000000	0.022286
4	France	Vive La Vitesse	13	1269600.00	0.1884057971014492753	0.215815
5	France	Laurent Saint Yves	11	1343950.00	0.1594202898550724637	0.228453
6	France	SuperSport S.A.R.L.	9	509630.00	0.1304347826086956521	0.086630
7	France	M. Pierre Dubois	8	511675.00	0.1159420289855072463	0.086977
8	France	Capots Reluisants S.A.	6	583115.00	0.0869565217391304347	0.099121
9	France	La Bagnole de Luxe	6	497190.00	0.0869565217391304347	0.084515
10	France	Casseroles Chromes	4	201050.00	0.0579710144927536231	0.034175
11	France	Mme Anne Duport	3	162650.00	0.0434782608695652173	0.027648
12	France	Khader El Ghannam	2	50500.00	0.0289855072463768115	0.008584
13	France	Wladimir Lacroix	2	55100.00	0.0289855072463768115	0.009366
14	France	Le Luxe en Motion	1	255950.00	0.0144927536231884057	0.043508
15	France	Jean-Yves Truffaut	1	1950.00	0.0144927536231884057	0.000331

Figure 13.12: *A complex use of derived tables to apply different levels of aggregated calculation*

How It Works

Given the size of this query, it is probably easier to understand what it does if you begin by looking at the output from the two derived tables that are the core of the SQL.

The first derived table (DT1) shows the number of sales per country and the total value of sales per country, as you can see in *Figure 13.13*.

	CountryName	NumberOfCountrySales	TotalCountrySales
1	Belgium	10	311850.00
2	France	69	5882810.00
3	Germany	13	873040.00
4	Italy	18	1215280.00
5	Spain	27	1693060.00
6	Switzerland	18	839415.00
7	United Kingdom	165	9236375.00
8	United States	31	1995620.00

Figure 13.13: *An aggregate derived table to produce high-level totals*

The second derived table (DT2) goes into greater detail and shows the value and number of sales per customer for each country, as you can see (partially, at least) in *Figure 13.14*.

	CountryName	CustomerName	NumberOfCustomerSales	TotalCustomerSales
1	United Kingdom	Alex McWhirter	1	17850.00
2	United Kingdom	Alexei Tolstoi	9	521490.00
3	Spain	Alicia Almodovar	7	382090.00
4	United Kingdom	Andrea Tarbuck	2	454500.00
5	United Kingdom	Andy Cheshire	2	174500.00
6	Spain	Antonio Maura	9	550330.00
7	Spain	Autos Sportivos	1	65890.00
8	United Kingdom	Beltway Prestige Driving	2	54875.00
9	United Kingdom	Birmingham Executive Prestige Vehicles	6	469740.00
10	France	Bling Bling S.A.	1	345000.00

Figure 13.14: An aggregate derived table that produces detail-level totals

As a whole, the query builds on the data that is returned from the two derived tables. It joins the derived tables on the country field so that it can then list countries, clients, the number of sales made per client, and the value of those sales. So far, then, it is just an extension of the derived table DT2. However, once the aggregate data at country level is added to the query, it allows you to see the percentage of both the value of sales and the number of sales that each customer represents. This is done simply by dividing the totals for number of sales and sale value) by country in the derived table DT1 by the number of sales and sale value for each customer in the derived table DT2.

Because the SQL that creates and uses an aggregated derived table can seem a little dense at first sight, taking a look at a more graphic representation, like the one shown in *Figure 13.15*, might help you understand how it works.

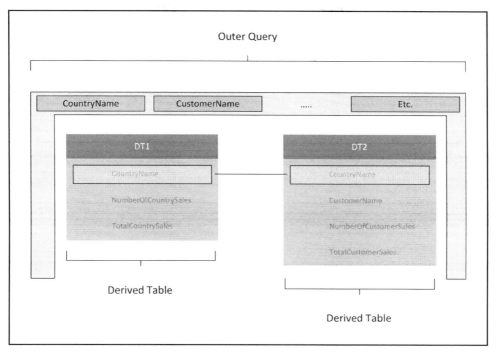

Figure 13.15: *Joining on derived tables*

Tricks and Traps

When creating complex analyses using multiple derived tables, you need to remain aware of the following key points:

- In this example, we left the figures as "raw" numbers without any formatting. You can use the FORMAT() function to display the percentages in a more readable way if you prefer.

- When calculating the percentage of cars sold per country, we had to force the count function to treat its output as NUMERIC—and, consequently, to include the decimals. This is because the COUNT() function always returns a whole number, and SQL takes this to be an INTEGER data type. This is not a problem until you divide an integer by an integer. When this happens, the result is considered to be an integer as well. This means that the percentage is then displayed as an integer, too—a zero. This is not only counterintuitive, it is highly disconcerting. However, if you use the CAST() function to force SQL Server to consider the result of the COUNT() a decimal number, then it can display the percentage as a decimal number as well.

13.6 Using Derived Tables to Join Unconnected Tables

A well-managed business almost certainly defines budgets and then tracks them over time. Fortunately, SQL can be very efficient at monitoring budgets and comparing and forecasts. So, when the financial director comes to your desk requesting a report that compares sales to the budget for each country by year and month, you know there is nothing to worry about. The following SQL is an example of this:

```
SELECT      CO.CountryName
            ,SUM(SD.SalePrice) AS Sales
            ,SUM(CSQ.BudgetValue) AS BudgetValue
            ,YEAR(SA.SaleDate) AS YearOfSale
            ,MONTH(SA.SaleDate) AS MonthOfSale
            ,SUM(CSQ.BudgetValue)
            - SUM(SD.SalePrice) AS DifferenceBudgetToSales
 FROM       Data.SalesDetails SD
INNER JOIN Data.Sales AS SA ON SA.SalesID = SD.SalesID
INNER JOIN Data.Customer CU ON SA.CustomerID = CU.CustomerID
INNER JOIN Data.Country CO ON CU.Country = CO.CountryISO2
INNER JOIN              (
                        SELECT      BudgetValue, BudgetDetail, Year,
                                    Month
                        FROM        Reference.Budget
                        WHERE       BudgetElement = 'Country'
                ) CSQ
            ON CSQ.BudgetDetail = CO.CountryName
            AND CSQ.Year = YEAR(SaleDate)
            AND CSQ.Month = MONTH(SaleDate)
GROUP BY CO.CountryName, YEAR(SA.SaleDate), MONTH(SA.SaleDate)
ORDER BY CO.CountryName, YEAR(SA.SaleDate), MONTH(SA.SaleDate)
```

Running this query gives the results that you can see in *Figure 13.16*.

	CountryName	Sales	BudgetValue	YearOfSale	MonthOfSale	DifferenceBudgetToSales
1	Belgium	125000.00	100000.00	2016	8	-25000.00
2	Belgium	12500.00	15500.00	2017	2	3000.00
3	Belgium	86500.00	100000.00	2017	3	13500.00
4	Belgium	45950.00	137850.00	2017	7	91900.00
5	Belgium	34000.00	68000.00	2017	11	34000.00
6	Belgium	950.00	950.00	2018	1	0.00
7	Belgium	6950.00	6950.00	2018	6	0.00
8	France	19600.00	19600.00	2015	4	0.00
9	France	8950.00	8950.00	2015	5	0.00
10	France	22950.00	22950.00	2015	6	0.00
11	France	75500.00	151000.00	2015	7	75500.00
12	France	2550.00	2550.00	2016	1	0.00
13	France	39500.00	39500.00	2016	2	0.00
14	France	49580.00	49580.00	2016	5	0.00
15	France	180150.00	720600.00	2016	6	540450.00

Figure 13.16: A derived table used to join otherwise unconnected tables

How It Works

Even a well-thought-out database model can have some tables that simply do not link in any conventional way to the core data tables that you are using. Budget data is frequently an example of this. Yet you can use the budget data stored in your database and compare it to the other data that you use to compare sales and budget data and highlight any differences. This only works, however, if you shape the budget data in a way that allows it to be joined to other tables.

This query joins the tables that contain the essential data for make, model, stock, sales details, and sales that you have used so far in this book. Then it also joins data from a new table—the Budget table—to the query so that you can also display data from this source.

The Budget table `cannot be joined directly to the other tables that contain sales and stock data`, however. This is because it contains budget data for many different elements (countries, makes of vehicle, etc.). Moreover, the data it contains is at a different level of granularity to the data for sales. As a result, you have to query this table and select only the data that you need. In this example, you need to filter the table on the Budget element to limit it to budgets for country sales.

If you highlight and run the SELECT query for the derived table, then you will see what the data is like (it is shown in *Figure 13.17*).

Results | Messages

	BudgetValue	BudgetDetail	Year	Month
1	100000.00	Belgium	2016	8
2	15500.00	Belgium	2017	2
3	100000.00	Belgium	2017	3
4	45950.00	Belgium	2017	7
5	34000.00	Belgium	2017	11
6	950.00	Belgium	2018	1
7	6950.00	Belgium	2018	6
8	19950.00	France	2015	2
9	19600.00	France	2015	4
10	8950.00	France	2015	5
11	22950.00	France	2015	6
12	75500.00	France	2015	7
13	2550.00	France	2016	1
14	39500.00	France	2016	2
15	49580.00	France	2016	5

Figure 13.17: *A derived table that filters source data*

As you can see from Figure 13.17 the budget data is for country, year, and month. To join the derived table to the other tables in the query, you must perform a complex join using three fields—country, year, and month of sale. This is why the join for the derived table uses the YEAR() and MONTH() functions to isolate these elements from the SaleDate field that is used to join in the SalesDetails table to the derived table of budget data.

Finally, the elements that are output from the outer query have to be grouped and aggregated. This is because the data from the tables used in the outer query is at a much more detailed level than the budget data used in the subquery. Mixing data at different levels of detail (or granularity, as it is also called) almost never produces coherent results. It is up to you to ensure that the data from all your tables is at the same level of granularity.

Tricks and Traps

I have a couple of points to stress here:

- It is interesting that in the outer query, you have to aggregate the budget value that is returned from the derived query (that is, the figure for each month's projected sales per country), even if the value is already at an aggregate level. This is because the outer query is an aggregate query, and so every value that is used must be used as part of an aggregate function such as SUM(), even if this does not alter the value since there is only one value per country per month.

- Unless you extract the year and month elements from the SalesDate field, the join to the derived tables cannot work correctly because it attempts to match a year (or a month) to a full date. This means that no data matches between the two tables and, consequently, no records are returned by the query.

13.7 Compare Year-on-Year Data Using a Derived Table

As part of a relentless focus on profitability, the CEO wants to look at all vehicle sales in 2016 and see how each sale compares to the best price achieved in the previous year for the same model of car. All this can be done with one piece of SQL:

```
SELECT      MK.MakeName
            ,MD.ModelName
            ,SD.SalePrice
            ,CSQ.MaxSalePrice - SD.SalePrice
                AS PriceDifferenceToMaxPrevYear
FROM        Data.Make AS MK
INNER JOIN Data.Model AS MD ON MK.MakeID = MD.MakeID
INNER JOIN Data.Stock AS ST ON ST.ModelID = MD.ModelID
INNER JOIN Data.SalesDetails SD ON ST.StockCode = SD.StockID
INNER JOIN Data.Sales AS SA ON SA.SalesID = SD.SalesID
INNER JOIN  (
                SELECT      MAX(SDX.SalePrice) AS MaxSalePrice
                            ,YEAR(SAX.SaleDate) AS SaleYear
                            ,MKX.MakeName
                FROM        Data.Make AS MKX
                INNER JOIN Data.Model AS MDX
                            ON MKX.MakeID = MDX.MakeID
                INNER JOIN Data.Stock AS STX
                            ON STX.ModelID = MDX.ModelID
                INNER JOIN Data.SalesDetails SDX
                            ON STX.StockCode = SDX.StockID
```

```
            INNER JOIN Data.Sales AS SAX

                       ON SAX.SalesID = SDX.SalesID

            WHERE      YEAR(SAX.SaleDate) = 2015

            GROUP BY   YEAR(SAX.SaleDate)

                       ,MKX.MakeName

      ) CSQ

      ON CSQ.MakeName = MK.MakeName

WHERE      YEAR(SA.SaleDate) = 2016
```

Running this query gives the results that you can see in *Figure 13.18*.

	MakeName	ModelName	SalePrice	PriceDifferenceToMaxPrevYear
1	Ferrari	Testarossa	165000.00	55000.00
2	Ferrari	Testarossa	195000.00	25000.00
3	Ferrari	355	156500.00	63500.00
4	Ferrari	355	159500.00	60500.00
5	Ferrari	355	205000.00	15000.00
6	Ferrari	Mondial	102950.00	117050.00
7	Ferrari	360	99500.00	120500.00
8	Porsche	911	29500.00	-6550.00
9	Porsche	911	17500.00	5450.00
10	Porsche	911	22150.00	800.00
11	Porsche	911	33600.00	-10650.00
12	Porsche	911	66500.00	-43550.00
13	Porsche	911	20950.00	2000.00
14	Porsche	911	68900.00	-45950.00
15	Porsche	911	45950.00	-23000.00

Figure 13.18: Applying different filters to a query and a derived table

How It Works

In this chapter, you have seen that a derived table is a completely independent dataset relative to the rest of the query. You can use this to your advantage when comparing virtually identical datasets.

In this code the main query is the part of the query that is not a derived table. It lists the makes and models of car sold in 2016 along with their sale price.

The derived table does something fairly similar. It, too, finds makes, models, and sale price, only it finds the maximum sale price for each model for a `different` year to the outer query—the previous year (2015), in fact. The output from this inner query (if you run it separately) is shown in *Figure 13.19*.

	MaxSalePrice	SaleYear	MakeName
1	8695.00	2015	Alfa Romeo
2	123590.00	2015	Aston Martin
3	80500.00	2015	Bentley
4	220000.00	2015	Ferrari
5	22990.00	2015	Jaguar
6	22950.00	2015	Mercedes
7	22950.00	2015	Porsche
8	12650.00	2015	Triumph

Figure 13.19: Output from a derived table query

As you can see, the derived table shows the maximum sale price per model for one year, yet a close examination of the code shows that the outer query looks at the data for another year. The trick is to join the derived table to the rest of the query using the make as the join element.

You can then output not only the details for sales in 2016, but also the maximum value of each make sold in the previous year. In this example, the current sale price is subtracted from the maximum sale price for the previous year. You can then analyze the difference to compare sales growth from year to year.

Tricks and Traps

I have a single comment for you to take away when using derived tables for data comparison:

- This type of query is extremely extensible and can become a basis for many varied types of comparative analysis. For instance, you cannot ever use a year in the WHERE clause of the derived table and compare the current sale price to the maximum sale price. The fact that the derived table and the outer query are completely independent makes derived queries ideal for comparing certain types of data over time.

13.8 Synchronizing Filters between a Derived Table and the Main Query

Clever buying strategies can make or break a business. Because of this, the finance director wants to ensure that Prestige Cars is not spending too much when buying stock. The following piece of SQL compares the purchase price of every car bought in 2016 with the average price of cars of the same color in 2015.

```
SELECT     ST.Color, ST.DateBought, ST.Cost, CSQ.MinPurchaseCost
FROM       Data.Stock ST
INNER JOIN
           (
           SELECT     Color, MIN(Cost) AS MinPurchaseCost
                      ,YEAR(DateBought) AS PurchaseYear
           FROM       Data.Stock
           WHERE      YEAR(DateBought) = 2016
           GROUP BY   Color, YEAR(DateBought)
           ) CSQ
           ON ST.Color = CSQ.Color
           AND YEAR(ST.DateBought) = CSQ.PurchaseYear - 1
```

Running this query gives the results that you can see in *Figure 13.20;* you can also see the output from the derived table.

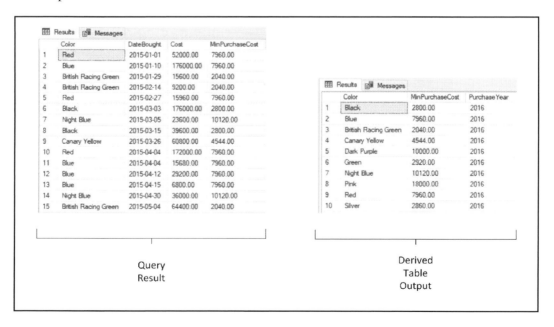

Figure 13.20: *Extending the JOIN clause for a derived table*

How It Works

This SQL is essentially two pieces of code:

A derived table	That calculates the minimum price for each car bought for every year of available data
An outer query	That displays the key stock information for all the cars bought in 2016

The interesting tweak is the way that the outer query and the inner derived table are joined. As the grouping for the derived table is by color and year, these are the fields that must be used in the JOIN clause. However, as the derived table contains data for all years, you can tweak the JOIN clause so that the data from the derived table is mapped not to a year that is specified in the WHERE clause of the outer query, but to a year that is defined in the ON clause that joins the outer query to the derived table. This is done simply by specifying

```
AND YEAR(ST.DateBought) = CSQ.PurchaseYear - 1
```

This filters the data returned from the outer query so that only data for the previous year is returned.

Of course, you could have specified the year to filter on in the outer query, but this approach is more fluid and extensible because it automatically finds data from the `previous` year in the outer query—whatever year is defined in the WHERE clause of the derived table.

Tricks and Traps

To end your introduction to derived tables, I suggest that you remember the following points:

- This particular technique can be used in JOIN clauses whenever the fields that are used in a join are numeric.

- It is particularly useful when comparing data across years. It also makes the point that the fields used in a JOIN can themselves be calculated if necessary.

Conclusion

In this chapter, I introduced you to ways of combining data that allow you to answer some tough analytical questions. We did all of this using derived tables—a technique that lets you assemble complex datasets "on the fly" inside other queries.

These virtual tables let you aggregate, filter, and slice data in-depth and then use the results to carry out all sorts of queries. Moreover, derived tables help you think in terms of sets of data and, consequently, learn to adapt your way of tackling datA. based problems so that you can handle more complex data analysis. Derived tables also let you aggregate and filter data so that you can join otherwise incompatible datasets.

Core Knowledge Learned in This Chapter

The concepts that you have seen in this chapter are

Concept	Description
Derived tables	When creating complex joins, you can define any or all of the component tables to be derived tables—that is, SQL that returns a dataset.
Multiple join fields	You can join derived tables to ther tables using several fields if you need to.

CHAPTER 14

Common Table Expressions

The previous two chapters have shown you that SQL is all about creating the datasets that allow you to deliver the analysis that you need. As you have probably surmised while reading this book, SQL imposes on its practitioners a particular way of thinking. More specifically, it is a language that wants you to adopt its world view and to think in terms of sets of data that become the building blocks of your analysis. "Thinking in datasets" can, nonetheless, be a skill that takes a while to acquire. Moreover, the way that some SQL solutions nest queries inside other queries can make for complex code that seems to hide—rather than expose—the true simplicity of the approach. The time has come to demonstrate a powerful way to simplify working with complex datasets.

Simplifying Complex Queries with Common Table Expressions

Once again SQL Server can come to the rescue if an analytical challenge seems too daunting at first sight. This is because SQL can not only help you create the code that delivers the analysis, it can also help you define the analytical approach and focus on how you structure the datasets based on the underlying tables. This can be accomplished using a technique known as Common Table Expressions (CTEs).

I admit that the name sounds cryptic and gives little indication of the power of this approach. Yet CTEs (as they are normally called) can help you

- Create datasets outside the core of a query to help you think a problem through.

- Reuse datasets so that you do not have to rewrite or copy SQL code several times.

- Create CTEs that use the output from other CTEs. This allows you to break down an analytical challenge into a sequence of coherent steps in which the results created by one CTE ripple through other CTEs in a query to deliver the final output.

Let's now see how CTEs can help you tame even the most complex SQL queries.

14.1 A Basic Common Table Expression

In sales and marketing, it is essential that you understand what your customers want. A first step to this knowledge can be analyzing what they have bought in the past. The following code snippet lets you prepare a report for the CEO of Prestige Cars that displays the make, model, and color combinations of every vehicle sold in 2015.

```
WITH Sales2015_CTE
AS
(
SELECT     MK.MakeName, MD.ModelName, ST.Color
FROM       Data.Make AS MK
INNER JOIN Data.Model AS MD ON MK.MakeID = MD.MakeID
INNER JOIN Data.Stock AS ST ON ST.ModelID = MD.ModelID
INNER JOIN Data.SalesDetails SD ON ST.StockCode = SD.StockID
INNER JOIN Data.Sales AS SA ON SA.SalesID = SD.SalesID
WHERE      YEAR(SA.SaleDate) = 2015
)
SELECT     MakeName, ModelName, Color
FROM       Sales2015_CTE
GROUP BY   MakeName, ModelName, Color
ORDER BY   MakeName, ModelName, Color
```

Running this query gives the results that you can see in *Figure 14.1*.

	MakeName	ModelName	Color
1	Alfa Romeo	Giulia	Red
2	Aston Martin	DB4	Night Blue
3	Aston Martin	DB5	Black
4	Aston Martin	DB5	Blue
5	Aston Martin	DB6	Canary Yellow
6	Aston Martin	DB6	Silver
7	Aston Martin	Virage	Black
8	Bentley	Flying Spur	British Racing Green
9	Ferrari	355	Black
10	Ferrari	355	Blue
11	Ferrari	Testarossa	Green
12	Ferrari	Testarossa	Red
13	Jaguar	XJS	Red
14	Jaguar	XJS	Silver
15	Jaguar	XK120	Red

Figure 14.1. *A simple CTE*

How It Works

This code snippet takes a two-phased approach to finding all the existing make, model, and color combinations of cars sold in 2015.

First:	An independent initial query—a `CTE`—joins the Make, Model, Stock, SalesDetails, and Sales tables. It then selects the MakeName, ModelName, and Color fields from these tables. Since the query contains joins to the two tables (Sales and SalesDetails) that contain data for actual sales, the output only shows details of cars that have been sold. It also filters on the SaleDate field.
Then:	The output from this CTE is then used as the data source in the FROM clause of the subsequent SQL statement.

A CTE is really nothing more than a kind of derived table, like those that you saw in the previous chapter. It is a perfectly normal SELECT query that you build to isolate a subset of data. As you can see from this example, a CTE is composed of the following:

A CTE name	A CTE must have a name. In this example, it is called "Sales2015_CTE." The name can be a single character or something more complex that explains more clearly what the CTE does.
A WITH clause	Begins the CTE.

A query	This is the core of the CTE. It must be a valid SQL SELECT query. It can be as complex as your needs require. The query *must* be enclosed in parentheses.
A use for the CTE	By this I mean that you must do something using the CTE—such as using the SELECT data from it as we do in this example.

You can see how a CTE can be imagined in *Figure 14.2.*

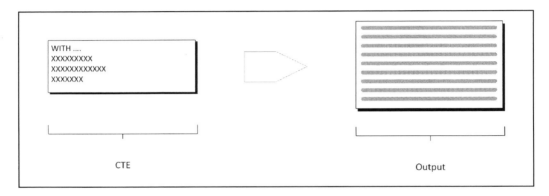

Figure 14.2: Conceptualizing a CTE

If you are looking at this example a little quizzically and thinking, "I am sure that I could have done this just by grouping the data without even needing a CTE," then you are right. The CTE that we apply here is not `strictly` necessary. Either approach delivers the required result. However, as you will see in this chapter, CTEs can be extremely useful in many different ways. I prefer to make the first one as easy as possible so it is as comprehensible as possible. However, there is more to using CTEs than just resolving coding challenges. A CTE like this helps you break down a problem into its component parts. In this specific example, this means

First:	Defining the list of data that you want to aggregate (this is the query inside the CTE).
Finally:	Grouping the data subset from the CTE to achieve the desired result.

So using CTEs is more than merely a variation on a theme; it can also help you think through a problem and enable you to separate out the building blocks that SQL uses to provide a solution in a clear and sequential way.

Tricks and Traps

With a new concept come a few key points to remember:

- You do not have to include the acronym CTE in a Common Table Expression name; however, I have chosen to adopt this approach in this book so that you can identify CTEs more easily among all the other SQL objects that we use.

- The nameof a CTE can be up to 128 characters.

- If you decide to use a CTE to isolate a subset of data, then you have to apply the CTE in some way. In other words, you cannot "declare" a CTE (as they say in the world of SQL programming) and then not use it. Indeed, if you do not use a CTE that you have created, then your code will **not** work.

- It is generally easier to avoid spaces and special characters in the names of CTEs. This way you avoid having to enclose the CTE name in square brackets everywhere in your code.

- The query that makes up a CTE is completely independent of the rest of the query that uses the CTE, so you can always test the CTE by first selecting the SQL inside the parentheses that enclose the query that makes it up, and by then executing it. *Figure 14.3* shows the results for the code in the CTE in this example.

	MakeName	ModelName	Color
1	Ferrari	Testarossa	Red
2	Ferrari	Testarossa	Green
3	Ferrari	355	Blue
4	Ferrari	355	Black
5	Porsche	911	British Racing Green
6	Porsche	911	Blue
7	Porsche	911	Black
8	Porsche	924	British Racing Green
9	Porsche	924	Black
10	Porsche	944	Red

Figure 14.3: The independent query constituting a CTE

14.2 Calculating Averages across Multiple Values Using a CTE

One simple metric can tell many businesses if they are on the path to profitability. This is the average profit for each type of product. A CTE helps you produce this analysis for the CEO of Prestige Cars:

```
WITH Sales_CTE
AS
(
SELECT      MK.MakeName
            ,SalePrice - (
                          ST.Cost
                          + ST.RepairsCost
                          + ISNULL(ST.PartsCost, 0)
                          + ST.TransportInCost
                         ) AS Profit
FROM        Data.Make AS MK
INNER JOIN Data.Model AS MD ON MK.MakeID = MD.MakeID
INNER JOIN Data.Stock AS ST ON ST.ModelID = MD.ModelID
INNER JOIN Data.SalesDetails SD ON ST.StockCode = SD.StockID
)

SELECT      MakeName, AVG(Profit) AS AverageProfit
FROM        Sales_CTE
GROUP BY    MakeName
```

If you run this query, you see the results that are shown in *Figure 14.4*.

	MakeName	AverageProfit
1	Alfa Romeo	758.272727
2	Aston Martin	10433.064935
3	Austin	197.142857
4	Bentley	13831.400000
5	BMW	2500.000000
6	Bugatti	53890.500000
7	Citroen	1962.333333
8	Delahaye	3473.250000
9	Delorean	16910.000000
10	Ferrari	29664.107142
11	Jaguar	4997.360000
12	Lagonda	18175.000000
13	Lamborghini	27957.000000
14	McLaren	44650.000000
15	Mercedes	4572.214285

Figure 14.4: Calculating averages across multiple values using a CTE

How It Works

Calculating averages is fundamental to much data analysis, and this is something that SQL does well. The preceding piece of SQL uses multiple fields to calculate the profit for each car sold, and then it returns the average profit per make.

You may be wondering why you even need a CTE to carry out this calculation. After all, surely you could just average the sale price and the various cost elements and then perform the math?

Indeed, you can do this; however, adding and subtracting overall averages is not the same thing as calculating the average profit. To get this information, you really need to calculate the profit per car and then work out the average of this figure. This is a prime example of how a CTE can prove invaluable. It allows you

First:	To calculate the profit figure for each car in the Stock table. This metric is worked out at the most detailed level possible—that of each car in the Stock table. What is more, using CTEs lets you handle NULLs at the most granular level possible—as you can see from teh use of the ISNULL() function inside the CTE.
Finally:	To return the average of the profit figure, aggregated by Make in the main query.

14.3 Reusing CTEs in a Query

When you are trying to control costs, it can help to compare various metrics to a multiple of an average value in order to focus on higher-than-expected values. This is exactly what the finance director wants. In fact, he has asked for a report that finds all makes and models sold where the discount was more than twice the average discount for any vehicle sold in that year. The following piece of SQL is an example of this type of analysis.

```
;
WITH Discount2015_CTE (Make, Model, Color, SalePrice, LineItemDiscount)
AS
(
SELECT     MK.MakeName, MD.ModelName, ST.Color
           ,SD.SalePrice, SD.LineItemDiscount
FROM       Data.Make AS MK
INNER JOIN Data.Model AS MD ON MK.MakeID = MD.MakeID
INNER JOIN Data.Stock AS ST ON ST.ModelID = MD.ModelID
INNER JOIN Data.SalesDetails SD ON ST.StockCode = SD.StockID
INNER JOIN Data.Sales AS SA ON SA.SalesID = SD.SalesID
```

```
WHERE      YEAR(SaleDate) = 2015
)
SELECT     Make, Model, Color, LineItemDiscount, SalePrice
           ,(SELECT AVG(LineItemDiscount) * 2 FROM Discount2015_CTE)
           AS AverageDiscount
FROM       Discount2015_CTE
WHERE      LineItemDiscount > (SELECT AVG(LineItemDiscount) * 2
                                FROM Discount2015_CTE)
```

Running this query gives the results that you can see in *Figure 14.5*.

	Make	Model	Color	LineItemDiscount	SalePrice	AverageDiscount
1	Ferrari	355	Blue	60000.00	220000.00	9655.294116

Figure 14.5: Reusing a CTE in a query

How It Works

This piece of analytical SQL uses a CTE to produce a list of the makes and models of car sold in 2015. It also displays the color, sale price, and sales discount (a column named LineItemDiscount) for each model.

Once the CTE has defined the data subset that will be used by the main query, a few interesting things happen:

First:	The rest of the query selects the fields passed into it by the CTE.
Then:	A WHERE clause in the main query reuses the CTE to calculate the average sales discount for 2015. This is then doubled and used as a filter so that only sales where a discount greater than twice the average sales discount for the year has been applied appear in the final output.
Finally:	The average sales discount for 2015 is recalculated and added to the SELECT clause as a subquery.

The key point here is that a CTE can be reused `several times` in the main query. This approach is based on two fundamental ideas:

- You only have to write the SQL that defines a subset of data `once`, because you can reuse it over and over again. In this example, the main advantage of this approach is that the filter (the WHERE clause that limits the data to the sales for a specific year) is only applied once—in the CTE.

- Whenever the CTE is reused to calculate or to display the average value, the filter that it contains is applied `every time`.

CTE or Derived Table?

When you see how a CTE works, you may be struck by its similarity to the derived tables that you saw in a previous chapter.

Well, this similarity should come as no surprise, as they are largely identical. Both are independent of the query that they are used by, both must specify the fields that can be read by the outer query, and both must have an alias.

CTEs, however, can help when you are developing a SQL solution. This is because they help you isolate sections of a data challenge. Indeed, they can help considerably when you are conceptualizing a solution because they guide you toward separating out data subsets as CTEs. This approach can also make SQL queries less intimidating and easier to extend and maintain.

If you have a challenging query that lends itself to using a derived table or a CTE, simply choose the approach that suits you. There is probably no "best" way—only the way that you feel most at ease with to solve your analytical problem.

There are several clear advantages to this way of working:

Less complexity	Subqueries can sometimes be fairly complex, so having to rewrite the same piece of SQL (or adapt it without making any errors) to use in a subquery can become laborious and time-consuming. Reusing a CTE means that you only write the core query `once` to get a reusable dataset.
Avoid repetition	This means you are less likely to make a SQL syntax error or enter a wrong value in one of the multiple WHERE clauses that would otherwise be necessary when you reuse the data in the data subset.
Forgetting is harder	You do not have to remember to add or update a WHERE clause in multiple subqueries.
Modification is easier	If you want to filter the data on a different year, all you have to do is to change the WHERE clause in the CTE. This change cascades through to the main query everywhere the CTE is used, so you only have to change filter values in one place. Equally, any other modifications (such as calculations) that you make to a CTE are subsequently available wherever the CTE is used in the main query.

Tricks and Traps

A set of key points are worth noting here:

- The CTE used in this example begins with a semicolon (;). Although this mark is only really necessary if your code contains other elements before you add the CTE, I begin CTEs with a semicolon from now on because it is better practice, and because it avoids the error message that arises if we forget the semicolon and then add more code before the CTE.

- As was the case with derived tables, the SELECT clause of the CTE `must` include all the fields that you want to use in the main query. If you do not select a field in the CTE, then it is completely invisible downstream in the main query that returns the final recordset based on the CTE.

- Although you absolutely `must` use a CTE if you have added one to your code, you are not obligated to use `all` the fields that you have selected in the CTE elsewhere in your query. In practice, however, it is probably best `only` to select the fields that you `need` when creating a CTE.

- You can make sure a CTE makes clear the names of the fields that it returns—as the CTE in this example does—by placing a list of fields in parentheses after the CTE name. However, this is not compulsory. Doing so is really nothing more than a way of giving aliases to the fields that the CTE outputs. This can be useful when you are making the column names in underlying tables easier to understand for users.

14.4 Using a CTE in a Derived Table to Deliver Two Different Levels of Aggregation

The sales director for Prestige Cars wants a slightly subtler analysis of who the most valuable customers are. In this case, she wants a list of customers who bought the most expensive model of car for each make in 2015. The following piece of SQL lets you deliver this information.

```
;
WITH ExpensiveCar_CTE (
                MakeName, ModelName, SalePrice
                ,Color, TransportInCost, SaleDate
                ,InvoiceNumber, CustomerName
)
```

```
AS
(
SELECT      MK.MakeName, MD.ModelName, SD.SalePrice, ST.Color
            ,ST.TransportInCost, SA.SaleDate, SA.InvoiceNumber
            ,CU.CustomerName
FROM        Data.Make AS MK
INNER JOIN Data.Model AS MD ON MK.MakeID = MD.MakeID
INNER JOIN Data.Stock AS ST ON ST.ModelID = MD.ModelID
INNER JOIN Data.SalesDetails SD ON ST.StockCode = SD.StockID
INNER JOIN Data.Sales AS SA ON SA.SalesID = SD.SalesID
INNER JOIN Data.Customer CU ON SA.CustomerID = CU.CustomerID
WHERE       YEAR(SaleDate) = 2015
)
SELECT      SLS.MakeName, SLS.ModelName, SLS.Color, CustomerName
            ,SLS.TransportInCost, SLS.SaleDate, SLS.InvoiceNumber
FROM        ExpensiveCar_CTE SLS
            INNER JOIN (
                    SELECT      MakeName
                                ,MAX(SalePrice) AS MaxSalePrice
                    FROM        ExpensiveCar_CTE
                    GROUP BY MakeName
                    ) MX
            ON SLS.MakeName = MX.MakeName
            AND SLS.SalePrice = MX.MaxSalePrice
```

Running this query gives the results that you can see in *Figure 14.6.*

	MakeName	ModelName	Color	CustomerName	TransportInCost	SaleDate	InvoiceNumber
1	Ferrari	355	Blue	Snazzy Roadsters	1950.00	2015-01-25 00:00:00.000	GBPGB002
2	Porsche	911	Black	Convertible Dreams	150.00	2015-11-10 00:00:00.000	GBPGB025
3	Aston Martin	Virage	Black	Theo Kowalski	750.00	2015-10-30 00:00:00.000	USDUS024
4	Bentley	Flying Spur	British Racing Green	Wonderland Wheels	750.00	2015-04-30 00:00:00.000	GBPGB011
5	Mercedes	280SL	Red	La Bagnole de Luxe	150.00	2015-06-04 16:37:00.000	EURFR015
6	Alfa Romeo	Giulia	Red	Convertible Dreams	150.00	2015-07-12 00:00:00.000	GBPGB016
7	Jaguar	XK150	Night Blue	Alexei Tolstoi	150.00	2015-07-15 00:00:00.000	GBPGB017
8	Triumph	TR5	Green	Peter McLuckie	150.00	2015-09-05 00:00:00.000	GBPGB020

Figure 14.6: Using a CTE in a derived table to deliver two different levels of aggregation

How It Works

The challenge here is to isolate the highest-value car sold for each make as well as return all the important details for each sale. Fortunately, a CTE can really help here:

First:	You define a CTE that contains all the key sales information (customer, sale price, make, model, etc.).
Second:	You select all the important data from this CTE.
Third:	You use the CTE a second time in a derived table that groups and aggregates the data from the CTE by make and maximum sale price.
Finally:	You join the derived table to the main query on the MakeName and SalePrice fields (or, rather, you join the maximum sale price field from the derived table to the sale price field from the main query).

 This way the derived table filters out all cars from the main query where the sale price is not equal to the greatest sale price—in effect isolating the most expensive car sold for each make.

Once again you have reused a CTE. This time, rather than rewrite complex joins in a derived table, you used the CTE as the basis for a simple aggregation. This allowed you to concentrate on getting the initial query (the one used in the CTE) correct and then focus separately on how to use this data twice:

- Once to find the most expensive car for each make

- Once to list the details of that particular sale

To more easily understand this, take a look at *Figure 14.7*, which provides a visual breakdown of the query used in this example.

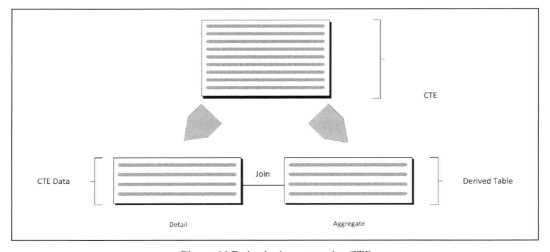

Figure 14.7: *Analyzing a complex CTE*

Tricks and Traps

When creating more complex CTEs, you need to remember

- If you have created a CTE that outputs many fields, then you need to pay attention to the list of column names that you add inside the parentheses that follow the name of the CTE. This involves doing the following:
  - o First, make sure that you have the same number of fields as those in the SELECT clause of the CTE.
  - o Second, ensure that all the fields are in the same order both in the SELECT clause and inside the parentheses. It is all too easy to mix up the order of the fields—and produce some really bizarre output as a result.

14.5 Using a CTE to Isolate Data from a Separate Dataset at a Different Level of Detail

The sales director has asked you to produce a regular report that ensures that the salespeople are meeting their targets. To do so, you need to compare sales figures to budget projections. The SQL that follows is one way of doing this.

```
;
WITH SalesBudget_CTE

AS

(

SELECT      BudgetValue, BudgetDetail, Year, Month

FROM        Reference.Budget

WHERE       BudgetElement = 'Country'

)


SELECT      CO.CountryName, YEAR(SA.SaleDate) AS YearOfSale

            ,MONTH(SA.SaleDate) AS MonthOfSale

            ,SUM(SD.SalePrice) AS SalePrice

            ,SUM(CTE.BudgetValue) AS BudgetValue

            ,SUM(CTE.BudgetValue)

            - SUM(SD.SalePrice) AS DifferenceBudgetToSales
```

```
FROM       Data.Make AS MK
INNER JOIN Data.Model AS MD ON MK.MakeID = MD.MakeID
INNER JOIN Data.Stock AS ST ON ST.ModelID = MD.ModelID
INNER JOIN Data.SalesDetails SD ON ST.StockCode = SD.StockID
INNER JOIN Data.Sales AS SA ON SA.SalesID = SD.SalesID
INNER JOIN Data.Customer CU ON SA.CustomerID = CU.CustomerID
INNER JOIN Data.Country CO ON CU.Country = CO.CountryISO2
INNER JOIN SalesBudget_CTE CTE
           ON CTE.BudgetDetail = CO.CountryName
           AND CTE.Year = YEAR(SA.SaleDate)
           AND CTE.Month = MONTH(SA.SaleDate)
GROUP BY   CO.CountryName, YEAR(SA.SaleDate), MONTH(SaleDate)
```

Running this query gives the results that you can see in *Figure 14.8*.

	CountryName	YearOfSale	MonthOfSale	SalePrice	BudgetValue	DifferenceBudgetToSales
1	Belgium	2016	8	125000.00	100000.00	-25000.00
2	Belgium	2017	2	12500.00	15500.00	3000.00
3	Belgium	2017	3	86500.00	100000.00	13500.00
4	Belgium	2017	7	45950.00	137850.00	91900.00
5	Belgium	2017	11	34000.00	68000.00	34000.00
6	Belgium	2018	1	950.00	950.00	0.00
7	Belgium	2018	6	6950.00	6950.00	0.00
8	France	2015	4	19600.00	19600.00	0.00
9	France	2015	5	8950.00	8950.00	0.00
10	France	2015	6	22950.00	22950.00	0.00
11	France	2015	7	75500.00	151000.00	75500.00
12	France	2016	1	2550.00	2550.00	0.00
13	France	2016	2	39500.00	39500.00	0.00
14	France	2016	5	49580.00	49580.00	0.00
15	France	2016	6	180150.00	720600.00	540450.00

Figure 14.8: Using a CTE to isolate data from a separate dataset at a different level of detail

How It Works

Once again you are probably thinking, "this is using a CTE like it is a derived table." You are right—this is exactly what we are doing.

More precisely, we are using the CTE to isolate the budget data from the Budget table so that it can be joined to a query in a way that allows us to compare actual and budget data. Now, the budget data does not really fit into the tightly structured "relational" model of the main tables of the Prestige Cars database. However, it is possible to produce budget data that returns a list of makes along with the predicted sales for each month and year. The SELECT query that makes up the CTE does exactly this. To get a clearer idea of how this works, take a look at *Figure 14.9*, which shows you the output from the CTE if you select the SQL and run it independently.

Figure 14.9: The records returned by a CTE that filters data

As you can see, this is nothing more than a "virtual table" of selected budget data. However, you can now join this data to sales data in the following three fields:

CountryName	Which maps to the BudgetDetail field in the Budget table (once the BudgetDetail table is filtered to show the makes)
Year of Sale	Which requires you to use the YEAR() function to extract the year from the SaleDate field
Month of Sale	Which requires you to use the MONTH() function to extract the month from the SaleDate field

The main query in this code snippet then joins the CTE to the other tables as if it is just another table—which it almost is. The main query can then select any necessary fields as well as carry out any required calculations.

Tricks and Traps

When using a CTE to join data from separate data areas at different levels of granularity, be sure to remember that

- In the main query, all the numeric values in the query have to be aggregated (using SUM() functions in this example) and the text fields have to appear in a GROUP BY clause. This is because you are comparing budget data that is pre-aggregated by country, year, and month with data that is at a more detailed level. So, to make the figures meaningful, the detailed sales data also has to be aggregated to country, year, and month, or it cannot be joined to the CTE.

14.6 Multiple Common Table Expressions

It may be near the end of the day, but the sales director has appeared at your desk with an urgent request. She wants to see how her budget predictions for sales by color stack up against actual sales for 2016. Fortunately, you can answer this request in a few minutes with the kind of SQL that you can see here:

```
WITH
ColorSales_CTE
AS
(
SELECT     ST.Color
           ,SUM(SD.SalePrice) AS TotalSalesValue
FROM       Data.Stock ST
INNER JOIN Data.SalesDetails SD
           ON ST.StockCode = SD.StockID
INNER JOIN Data.Sales SA
           ON SD.SalesID = SA.SalesID
WHERE      YEAR(SA.SaleDate) = 2016
GROUP BY   Color
)
,
ColorBudget_CTE
AS
(
SELECT  BudgetDetail AS Color, BudgetValue
FROM    Reference.Budget
WHERE   BudgetElement = 'Color'
        AND YEAR = 2016
)

SELECT     BDG.Color, SLS.TotalSalesValue, BDG.BudgetValue
           ,(SLS.TotalSalesValue - BDG.BudgetValue) AS BudgetDelta
FROM       ColorSales_CTE SLS
INNER JOIN ColorBudget_CTE BDG
           ON SLS.Color = BDG.Color
```

Running this code gives you the result that you can see in Figure *14.10*. In this figure, you can also see the output of the two separate CTEs.

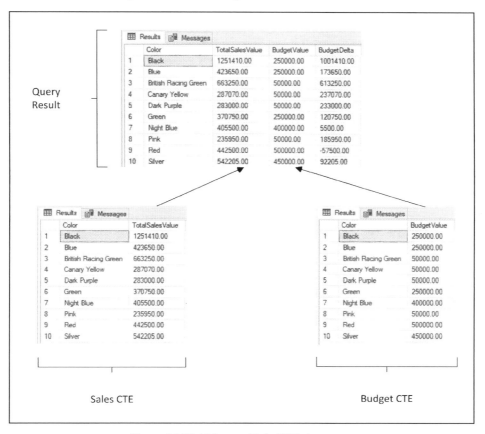

Figure 14.10: *Using multiple CTEs in a query*

How It Works

This query uses two separate CTEs to isolate two different datasets that are then joined in the final "output" query.

The first CTE	Joins the Sales, Stock, and SalesDetails tables to return all the required sales values per color of vehicle sold for 2016. This CTE is called ColorSales_CTE.
The second CTE	Isolates the budget data for colors for 2016 from the Budget table. If you remember, the budget table contains data for many budget elements, and so it needs to be filtered on both the budget element (color, in this example) and the year that you want to get data for. This CTE is called ColorBudget_CTE.

| The output query | Joins the two "source" CTEs on the shared color field and returns both the sales and budget values for all the available colors. As a final flourish, it uses the values to calculate any sales that are over—or under—budget values. |

This example illustrates how you can use CTEs to generate completely independent datasets that you can then use together to deliver insight. In the Prestige Cars database, budget data is held completely independently from sales data, and moreover, has its own unique structure. However, using CTEs to isolate the two datasets before you join them shows you that

| First: | You can isolate separate data elements from each other before attempting to combine them. |
| Second: | The two CTEs are totally separate—neither has any effect on the other. |

Indeed, using multiple separate CTEs like this can prove to be a valuable analytical technique. This is because you can concentrate on each dataset individually (and even test the output of each CTE in isolation). Often this can be a valuable way to break down your analysis into smaller, more digestible pieces that you then combine for a final result.

Tricks and Traps

If you decide to use multiple independent CTEs in your queries be aware that

- You can use multiple independent CTEs as a way of testing various approaches to solving data analysis challenges.

- You only need to introduce CTEs with a single WITH keyword. After that, you merely separate each CTE from the others with a comma.

14.7 Nested Common Table Expressions

As part of your analytical quest to deliver the insight that will lead to increased sales and profits, you want to take a look at the cars that sell more than a minimum quantity. More specifically, you want to display all the makes of car sold in a given year where more than two cars are sold per make. After all, perhaps these are the ones that the company should be pitching to potential buyers. The following SQL shows you how to do this:

```
;
WITH Outer2015Sales_CTE
AS
```

```
(
SELECT      MK.MakeName
FROM        Data.Make AS MK
INNER JOIN Data.Model AS MD ON MK.MakeID = MD.MakeID
INNER JOIN Data.Stock AS ST ON ST.ModelID = MD.ModelID
INNER JOIN Data.SalesDetails SD ON ST.StockCode = SD.StockID
INNER JOIN Data.Sales AS SA ON SA.SalesID = SD.SalesID
WHERE       YEAR(SA.SaleDate) = 2015
)
,
CoreSales_CTE (MakeName, NumberOfSales)
AS
(
SELECT      MakeName
            ,COUNT(*)
FROM        Outer2015Sales_CTE
GROUP BY    MakeName
HAVING      COUNT(*) >= 2
)

SELECT      CTE.MakeName, MK2.MakeCountry AS CountryCode
            ,CTE.NumberOfSales
FROM        CoreSales_CTE CTE
INNER JOIN Data.Make MK2
            ON CTE.MakeName = MK2.MakeName
```

Running this query gives the results that you can see in *Figure 14.11*.

	MakeName	CountryCode	NumberOfSales
1	Ferrari	ITA	4
2	Porsche	GER	8
3	Aston Martin	GBR	7
4	Jaguar	GBR	4
5	Triumph	GBR	2

Figure 14.11: Nested CTE output

How It Works

This query shows how you can create a short sequence of two CTEs where the second uses the output from the first as its source of data. This way, CTEs can be used as a way of breaking down the initial requirement into a series of successive steps that lead to the solution. What the query does is take a three-phased approach:

First:	The initial CTE joins all the tables that are required to produce a list of all makes of vehicle sold in 2015. Even though only two fields are actually used by this query (MakeName and SaleDate), these fields are in the Sales and Make tables, and so several "intermediate" tables must be part of the FROM clause to link the source data tables correctly.
Then:	The second CTE (CoreSales_CTE) is built using the first CTE (Outer2015Sales_CTE) as its data source. This query is an aggregate query that only returns makes of car where more than two have been sold. Because this CTE is based on the first CTE, only sales for 2015 are analyzed.
Finally:	A regular query lists the makes of vehicle returned by the second CTE. It joins this result to the Make table to add further columns to the output.

Once again, it might be easier to grasp this concept with the aid of a more visual representation. *Figure 14.12* explains nested CTEs graphically.

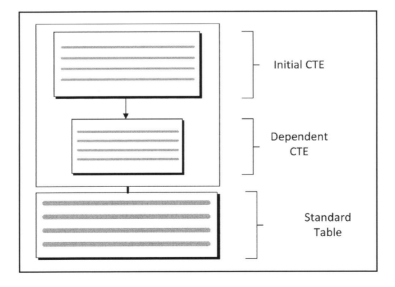

Figure 14.12: The data flow in nested CTEs

Although you could probably arrive at the same result using different approaches, this example shows you that CTEs can be "linked" in a way that lets you make your SQL reflect the analytical challenge that you are faced with. It has the advantage of being more sequential than some other approaches since it lets you see these steps, which are required to produce the final output, more clearly:

First:	Filter the data.
Second:	Aggregate the data.
Finally:	Extend the data selection.

Tricks and Traps

Here are a couple of points to take away:

- When you are writing SQL that uses multiple CTEs, the core principles to using any CTE still apply. Remember that you have to begin with a semicolon (;) if there is any other code before the CTE, and you **must** use all of the CTEs that you write. This means you still need a SQL query after the final CTE to output the data.

- When writing dependent CTEs like this, you only need to use a single WITH keyword. This serves to introduce any number of CTEs. The CTEs can be independent from one another or derived from one another—it makes no difference.

14.8 Using Multiple Common Table Expressions to Compare Disparate Datasets

When an existing customer contacts Prestige Cars, the sales director wants to know if they are profitable. Consequently, she wants to see how much each customer has spent in 2017, and how this relates to Prestige Cars' total annual sales. What is more, she wants to see sales per customer expressed as a percentage of total sales. The following SQL snippet gives you precisely this information:

```
;
WITH Initial2017Sales_CTE
AS
(
SELECT     SD.SalePrice, CU.CustomerName, SA.SaleDate
FROM       Data.Make AS MK
INNER JOIN Data.Model AS MD ON MK.MakeID = MD.MakeID
INNER JOIN Data.Stock AS ST ON ST.ModelID = MD.ModelID
```

```
INNER JOIN Data.SalesDetails SD ON ST.StockCode = SD.StockID
INNER JOIN Data.Sales AS SA ON SA.SalesID = SD.SalesID
INNER JOIN Data.Customer CU ON SA.CustomerID = CU.CustomerID
WHERE      YEAR(SA.SaleDate) = 2017
)
,
AggregateSales_CTE (CustomerName, SalesForCustomer)
AS
(
SELECT     CustomerName, SUM(SalePrice)
FROM       Initial2017Sales_CTE
GROUP BY   CustomerName
)
,
TotalSales_CTE (TotalSalePrice)
AS
(
SELECT     SUM(SalePrice)
FROM       Initial2017Sales_CTE
)

SELECT
 IT.CustomerName
,IT.SalePrice
, IT.SaleDate
,FORMAT(IT.SalePrice / AG.SalesForCustomer, '0.00%')
         AS SaleAsPercentageForCustomer
,FORMAT(IT.SalePrice / TT.TotalSalePrice, '0.00%') AS SalePercentOverall
FROM       Initial2017Sales_CTE IT
           INNER JOIN AggregateSales_CTE AG
           ON IT.CustomerName = AG.CustomerName
           CROSS APPLY TotalSales_CTE TT
 ORDER BY  IT.SaleDate, IT.CustomerName
```

Running this query gives the results that you can see in *Figure 14.13*.

	CustomerName	SalePrice	SaleDate	SaleAsPercentageForCustomer	SalePercentOverall
1	Eat My Exhaust Ltd	85000.00	2017-01-01 00:00:00.000	60.71%	1.08%
2	Peter Smith	125000.00	2017-01-01 00:00:00.000	43.48%	1.59%
3	Vive La Vitesse	22500.00	2017-01-01 00:00:00.000	2.47%	0.29%
4	La Bagnole de Luxe	1250.00	2017-01-10 00:00:00.000	100.00%	0.02%
5	Le Luxe en Motion	22500.00	2017-01-11 00:00:00.000	7.61%	0.29%
6	Magic Motors	125950.00	2017-01-12 00:00:00.000	28.01%	1.60%
7	Le Luxe en Motion	8850.00	2017-01-13 00:00:00.000	2.99%	0.11%
8	Posh Vehicles Ltd	9950.00	2017-01-14 00:00:00.000	18.11%	0.13%
9	Vive La Vitesse	56500.00	2017-01-30 00:00:00.000	6.21%	0.72%
10	Honest Pete Motors	56950.00	2017-01-31 00:00:00.000	10.79%	0.72%
11	Screamin' Wheels	55000.00	2017-01-31 00:00:00.000	32.63%	0.70%
12	Vive La Vitesse	365000.00	2017-02-07 00:00:00.000	40.13%	4.64%
13	Laurent Saint Yves	395000.00	2017-02-08 00:00:00.000	44.71%	5.02%
14	Screamin' Wheels	21500.00	2017-02-09 00:00:00.000	12.76%	0.27%
15	Screamin' Wheels	6500.00	2017-02-10 00:00:00.000	3.86%	0.08%

Figure 14.13: Using multiple CTEs to compare disparate datasets

How It Works

I imagine that when you first see this piece of SQL, you think, "Wow, this is complicated!" After all, this example uses no less than three CTEs to deliver the required analysis. What is more, the second CTE is based on the first CTE. However, before looking at the code, let's see exactly what we are trying to deliver. In essence, the request is for the following pieces of information:

Individual Customer Sales	We need the detail of each sale for each customer for the given period (2017).
Total Customer **Sales**	We want the total sales figure for each customer for the given period.
Total Sales	We also require the total overall sales for the sales period.

Each of the three CTEs used in this query corresponds to one of these analytical requirements.

Initial2017Sales_ CTE	Provides the sales data at a detail level. It joins all the necessary tables needed to output the date of each sale, the customer, and the amount of the sale. This CTE also filters the data to restrict it to a specified year.
AggregateSales_ CTE	Takes the data supplied by the initial CTE (Initial2017Sales_ CTE) and aggregates it by customer. This way you also can obtain the total sales per customer.

| TotalSales_CTE | Also takes the data supplied by Initial2017Sales_CTE and aggregates it, only this time, only the total figure for the dataset is returned, without any grouping. |

Once the CTEs have been defined (or "declared" as the techies say), the final query can then assemble the data from all of them. It does this in two ways:

| First: | Initial2017Sales_CTE (the detailed list of sales) is joined to AggregateSales_CTE (the total sales per customer). As both contain the CustomerName field, they are joined on this field. This join allows you to return the total sales per customer as well as the detail of each sale for every sale. Dividing the total sales per customer by the value of each sale gives you the percentage of total customer sales that each individual sale represents. |
| Second: | The total overall sales figure is added to the query. This is done using the CROSS APPLY operator. What this does is add the total sales figure to each row that is output. Once the total is there, it can be used to provide the percentage of total sales that each individual sale represents. |

This example shows you just how versatile CTEs can be. As you can see, the initial detailed CTE (Initial2017Sales_CTE) is used not only in the final query but also in the other two CTEs. This makes the code much simpler, as it means that you do not have to repeat a series of table joins several times. Instead, you define a source dataset once that you then reuse on multiple occasions to help deliver different levels of aggregation. Not only that, but if you need to change the filter that underlies the analysis (the year, in this case), you only need to alter it once in the top CTE for the filter to be cascaded down through the subsequent, dependent CTEs.

Tricks and Traps

Despite its apparent complexity, this CTE needs only one principal comment:
- In the SQL, we have formatted the percentage output using the FORMAT() function. This makes the output more readable. If you are feeding this data into another application, you may want to remove this function from the code because it can cause the percentages to be interpreted as text by some programs.

Conclusion

This chapter showed you how to harness the power of SQL to rise to the most daunting data analysis challenges. You did this using Common Table Expressions (CTEs)—a technique that lets you break down data analysis problems into smaller, more manageable parts that you can then join together to obtain the result that you want.

CTEs not only solve technical problems, they also help you handle data analysis one step at a time. This combination makes them one of the most useful SQL techniques available—and, almost certainly, a valuable tool in your armory.

Core Knowledge Learned in This Chapter

The concepts and keywords that you have seen in this chapter are

Concept	Description
Common Table Expressions (CTEs)	A CTE is a separate derived table that allows you to define a dataset outside the main query for use—and reuse—in the body of the query. Multiple CTEs can be used in the same query, CTEs can be chained so that one CTE depends on the output of another CTE and CTEs can be independent from each other.
WITH	This keyword introduces one or more CTEs in a query.

CHAPTER 15
Correlated Subqueries

I realize that the title of this chapter may seem a little hard to understand when you first read it. After all, the term correlated subqueries is more than a little technical—if not incomprehensible—at first sight. However, since it is the term that database people use, we have to use it, too. What this expression means is, quite simply, that certain kinds of subquery can be used to filter the data in the outer query in a particular way. This is done by applying a specific method to join the subquery to the outer query, which means that each query depends on the other. Using correlated subqueries can often enable you to deliver some uniquely powerful data analysis.

Why Use Correlated Subqueries?

As with so many database concepts, this is easier to understand if you see it in action. In this chapter, you see how to

- Calculate ratios and percentages of parts relative to a whole.

- Filter data in a table only if corresponding data exists in another table.

- Filter data based on a calculation that relates to a specific aspect of the data.

- Isolate data according to certain characteristics of another linked dataset.

Since an example is worth a thousand words, let's take a look at a few correlated subqueries that will extend your knowledge of SQL. This will help you push your analytical abilities to a higher level so that you can solve ever more challenging requests.

15.1 Simple Correlated Subqueries

Most of the clients of Prestige Cars only buy one vehicle at a time; however, some do buy two or more at once. To this end, the sales director wants a list of all invoice items as well as the total for the invoice so that she can do some further analysis. The following SQL provides this:

```
SELECT
SD.SalesDetailsID
,SalePrice
,(SELECT TotalSalePrice FROM Data.sales
WHERE      SalesId = SD.SalesId) AS TotalSales
FROM       Data.SalesDetails SD
ORDER BY   SalesDetailsID
```

Running this SQL returns the data that you can see in *Figure 15.1*. Although the sale price is equal to the total sales in most cases, on occasion—such as in lines 11 and 12—two lines make up a single invoice and the sale price is only part of the total sales.

	SalesDetailsID	SalePrice	TotalSales
1	1	65000.00	65000.00
2	2	220000.00	220000.10
3	3	19500.00	19500.00
4	4	11500.00	11500.00
5	5	19950.00	19900.00
6	6	29500.00	29500.00
7	7	49500.00	49500.20
8	8	76000.00	76000.90
9	9	19600.00	19600.00
10	10	36500.00	36500.00
11	11	8500.00	89000.00
12	12	80500.00	89000.00
13	13	169500.00	169500.00
14	14	8950.00	8950.00
15	15	195000.00	195000.00

Figure 15.1: A simple correlated subquery

How It Works

This query is created from an outer query and an inner query, just like many of the examples that you saw in the previous three chapters. Nonetheless, this example has one really important difference. The two queries are **not** independent of each other; they are linked. More specifically, they **both** contain the SalesID field, and this field is used in the WHERE clause of the subquery to connect the inner and outer queries.

Once the subquery is "connected" to the outer query (or once it becomes a correlated subquery, as it is called in the world of SQL), then the way that the whole query works alters radically. The `outer query now depends on the inner query`, and the inner query is run once for each record in the outer query.

Once again, I prefer to illustrate this concept graphically to help you to understand what exactly a correlated subquery is doing. You can see this in *Figure 15.2.*

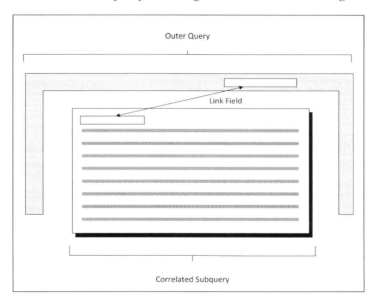

Figure 15.2: The concept of a correlated subquery

This graphic illustrates how the inner and outer queries relate one to the other.

The outer query	Returns the first record that it finds from the SalesDetails table (which is the list of line items in every invoice) and passes a "link" field (SalesID) to the correlated subquery (the inner query).
The inner query	Reads the Sales table (the invoice header table) and returns the total sales price *only* for records containing the SalesID passed in from the outer query.

This is, admittedly, a simple example where we are not doing very much with the data that is returned. In the real world you would probably use this information to calculate the percentage of line items per invoice. Just read on and see how to apply the concept of correlated subqueries to deliver precisely the kinds of analysis that are difficult or even impossilbe without correlated subqueries.

Tricks and Traps

There is one fundamental point to memorize when creating correlated subqueries:

- You cannot execute the correlated subquery independent of the outer query because the correlated subquery depends on the outer query in its WHERE clause. You can, however, remove the WHERE clause from the correlated subquery and then execute the SQL for the inner query.

15.2 Correlated Subqueries to Display Percentages of a Specific Total

When she is negotiating each sale, the sales director wants to see a history of all previous sales for every client as well as the percentage of the total value of vehicles sold to the client that each individual sale represents. She says that this will help her develop a discount strategy. The next piece of SQL uses a correlated subquery to deliver this insight:

```
SELECT
 CS.CustomerName
,SA.INVOICENUMBER
,SD.SalePrice
,SD.SalePrice
/
(
SELECT     SUM(SDC.SalePrice)
FROM       Data.SalesDetails SDC
INNER JOIN Data.Sales SAC
           ON SDC.SalesID = SAC.SalesID
INNER JOIN Data.Customer CSC
           ON SAC.CustomerID = CSC.CustomerID
WHERE      SAC.CustomerID = CS.CustomerID
) * 100 AS PercentSalesPerCustomer
FROM       Data.SalesDetails SD
```

```
INNER JOIN Data.Sales SA
        ON SD.SalesID = SA.SalesID
INNER JOIN Data.Customer CS
        ON SA.CustomerID = CS.CustomerID
ORDER BY   CS.CustomerName
```

Running this piece of SQL displays the percentage of each sale for each client relative to the total sales for the client, as you can see in *Figure 15.3*. If you add up the percentage sales records for each client, you will see that they equate to 100 percent per client.

	CustomerName	INVOICENUMBER	SalePrice	PercentSalesPerCustomer
1	Alex McWhirter	GBPGB308	17850.00	100.0000000000000000
2	Alexei Tolstoi	GBPGB055	205000.00	39.3104374005254176
3	Alexei Tolstoi	GBPGB063	102500.00	19.6552187002627088
4	Alexei Tolstoi	GBPGB046	9950.00	1.9079944006596483
5	Alexei Tolstoi	GBPGB046	39500.00	7.5744501332719707
6	Alexei Tolstoi	GBPGB026	69500.00	13.3271970699342269
7	Alexei Tolstoi	GBPGB023	22600.00	4.3337360256188997
8	Alexei Tolstoi	GBPGB017	22990.00	4.4085217357955090
9	Alexei Tolstoi	GBPGB081	3500.00	0.6711538092772632
10	Alexei Tolstoi	GBPGB092	45950.00	8.8112907246543558
11	Alicia Almodovar	EURES098	12500.00	3.2714805412337407
12	Alicia Almodovar	EURES109	39500.00	10.3378785102986207
13	Alicia Almodovar	EURES244	45950.00	12.0259624695752310
14	Alicia Almodovar	EURES237	15950.00	4.1744091706142532
15	Alicia Almodovar	EURES232	5690.00	1.4891779423695988

Figure 15.3: *Using a correlated subquery to calculate percentages of a subset*

How It Works

This query extends the correlated subquery principle that you saw in the previous example to more complex data sets. More specifically, the code consists of

An outer query	That joins the Sales, SalesDetails, and Customer tables to return the details—the customer name and sale amount—for every sale made by the company.
A correlated subquery	That calculates the *total sales* per customer. This uses the same tables as the outer query (Sales, SalesDetails, and Customer); however, it groups the data by customer to give the total sales for each customer. The correlated subquery is joined to the outer query by the CustomerID field, so the total returned is only for the customer from the outer list and *not* for the whole SalesDetails table.

The overall query essentially works as a whole. When each record of the outer query is returned, the correlated subquery calculates the individual sales only for the relevant customer. This figure is then used in the percentage calculation of the sales ratio for this particular sale.

Tricks and Traps

There is one point to note here:

- Since the correlated subquery is linked to the outer query, you cannot just select the SQL for the subquery and run it. Should you wish to test the subquery, I advise that you copy the correlated subquery into a new query window and replace the reference to the outer query (CS.CustomerID in this example) with a real customer ID. Indeed, you may find it helpful to develop and test a correlated subquery in this way before adding it to the outer query.

15.3 Comparing Datasets Using a Correlated Subquery

Once again, the finance director is determined to reduce the cost of repairs. This time he has asked you to produce a list of vehicle repair costs that are 50 percent higher than the average for each make. The following code lets you deliver this for him:

```
SELECT      MKX.MakeName, STX.RepairsCost, STX.StockCode

FROM        Data.Make AS MKX INNER JOIN Data.Model AS MDX

            ON MKX.MakeID = MDX.MakeID

INNER JOIN Data.Stock AS STX ON STX.ModelID = MDX.ModelID

INNER JOIN Data.SalesDetails SDX ON STX.StockCode = SDX.StockID

WHERE       STX.RepairsCost >

              (

                SELECT      AVG(ST.RepairsCost) AS AvgRepairCost

                FROM        Data.Make AS MK

                INNER JOIN Data.Model AS MD

                        ON MK.MakeID = MD.MakeID

                INNER JOIN Data.Stock AS ST

                        ON ST.ModelID = MD.ModelID

                WHERE       MK.MakeName = MKX.MakeName
```

```
) * 1.5
```

Running this query gives the results that you can see in *Figure 15.4*.

	MakeName	RepairsCost	StockCode
1	Porsche	1360.00	2189D556-D1C4-4BC1-B0C8-4053319E8E9D
2	Aston Martin	2500.00	E6E6270A-60B0-4817-AA57-17F26B2B8DAF
3	Aston Martin	3250.00	CEDFB8D2-BD98-4A08-BC46-406D23940527
4	Aston Martin	1950.00	D63C8CC9-DB19-4B9C-9C8E-6C6370812041
5	Aston Martin	2175.00	18E980AB-452D-42EF-8728-12822AD20C60
6	Porsche	1360.00	3F3BED8D-1203-4D3E-8AC0-3ACAC73BDE17
7	Lamborghini	5500.00	88AFBF67-13A6-4BC5-AE50-8C64F0F25453
8	Porsche	2000.00	B165CAEF-FF77-4E63-98C1-59D97F97E7C9
9	Alfa Romeo	1360.00	07F0D746-085B-4FB9-9F82-6CEAC851FBC3
10	Jaguar	2000.00	8F278478-CA0B-4CDB-8F02-1A054AAE88A9
11	Porsche	1360.00	518125AE-9A67-45A6-B3FD-557C785796FC
12	Ferrari	9250.00	66C9034C-23A3-44F1-B946-2DDA65E684D8
13	Porsche	1490.00	E00D10E9-7F7F-49A9-BDC0-4C2611580B4E
14	Porsche	1360.00	AAF61ECC-0BAC-4EAF-9E50-01749253329A
15	Triumph	970.00	0B0E0FC2-E72B-4BD4-9C46-1AF98F17BEC4

Figure 15.4: *A correlated query used for comparison*

How It Works

Finding exceptions—especially costly exceptions—is a core requirement in data analysis. Correlated subqueries are especially useful when you need to compare values to an aggregated value such as an average for a particular category of items. This query begins by calculating the average repair cost for all vehicles in stock and then multiplying this figure by 150 percent. However, since it is a correlated subquery where the inner and outer queries are linked using the MakeName field, this average is calculated for `every record in the outer query`. The result is that the repair cost is evaluated not for `all` vehicles in stock, but as the average for `each make` of vehicle in stock. This changes the calculation completely. Now, for each record in the outer query, the average repair cost is only calculated relative to that particular make of car. If the repair cost for a car is over 1.5 times the average repair cost for that make, then the query output shows the repair cost for the car.

Tricks and Traps

Exception reporting can prove tricky in practice. Be sure to take note of the following points if you want to get better results:

- The "filter" effect of a correlated subquery is not limited to finding records that are (or are not) in a dataset as was the case with the three previous examples. You can use a correlated subquery to compare values using all the traditional comparison operators—greater than (>), less than (<), greater than or equal to (>=), less than or equal to (<=), or not equal to (<>). This example only shows how to compare using less than, but all the others are available if your analysis requires them.

- You are also not limited to comparing results to an average. You can just as easily use the MAX() or MIN() functions to find records that are close to the upper and lower limits of a dataset for a specific element.

- In this example, the two queries—inner and outer—use very similar datasets. This is not always the case with correlated subqueries. It can, however, be a frequent occurrence.

- In a correlated subquery it is vital to create individual aliases for any tables that are used in both the inner and outer tables of the query. Because many of the same tables are used in both the outer query and the correlated subquery, we distinguished them by adding an "X" for each outer query table alias.

15.4 Duplicating the Output of a Correlated Subquery in the Query Results

The finance director was pleased with the data that you just sent him; however, he now wants the average repair cost per make to appear in the resulting data while keeping the filter on the average repair cost per make that you set up previously.

If you want to be absolutely certain that this query is working, the best way to find out is to display the average repair cost per make in the output. This means you need to duplicate the correlated subquery that you use in the WHERE clause in the actual SELECT clause of the query. If you do this, the code looks like the following:

```
SELECT     MKX.MakeName, STX.RepairsCost, STX.StockCode
,(
    SELECT     AVG(ST.RepairsCost) AS AvgRepairCost
    FROM       Data.Make AS MK
    INNER JOIN Data.Model AS MD
               ON MK.MakeID = MD.MakeID
    INNER JOIN Data.Stock AS ST
               ON ST.ModelID = MD.ModelID
    WHERE      MK.MakeName = MKX.MakeName
) AS MakeAvgRepairCost
```

```
FROM        Data.Make AS MKX
INNER JOIN Data.Model AS MDX
           ON MKX.MakeID = MDX.MakeID
INNER JOIN Data.Stock AS STX ON STX.ModelID = MDX.ModelID
INNER JOIN Data.SalesDetails SDX ON STX.StockCode = SDX.StockID
WHERE       STX.RepairsCost >
            (
            SELECT      AVG(ST.RepairsCost) AS AvgRepairCost
            FROM        Data.Make AS MK
            INNER JOIN Data.Model AS MD
                        ON MK.MakeID = MD.MakeID
            INNER JOIN Data.Stock AS ST
                        ON ST.ModelID = MD.ModelID
            WHERE       MK.MakeName = MKX.MakeName
            ) * 1.5
```

The output looks like that shown in *Figure 15.5*.

	MakeName	RepairsCost	StockCode	MakeAvgRepairCost
1	Porsche	1360.00	2189D556-D1C4-4BC1-B0C8-4053319E8E9D	848.0208
2	Aston Martin	2500.00	E6E6270A-60B0-4817-AA57-17F26B2B8DAF	1236.6666
3	Aston Martin	3250.00	CEDFB8D2-BD98-4A08-BC46-406D23940527	1236.6666
4	Aston Martin	1950.00	D63C8CC9-DB19-4B9C-9C8E-6C6370812041	1236.6666
5	Aston Martin	2175.00	18E980AB-452D-42EF-8728-12822AD20C60	1236.6666
6	Porsche	1360.00	3F3BED8D-1203-4D3E-8AC0-3ACAC73BDE17	848.0208
7	Lamborghini	5500.00	88AFBF67-13A6-4BC5-AE50-8C64F0F25453	3481.00
8	Porsche	2000.00	B165CAEF-FF77-4E63-98C1-59D97F97E7C9	848.0208
9	Alfa Romeo	1360.00	07F0D746-085B-4FB9-9F82-6CEAC851FBC3	673.0434
10	Jaguar	2000.00	8F278478-CA0B-4CDB-8F02-1A054AAE88A9	1002.9032
11	Porsche	1360.00	518125AE-9A67-45A6-B3FD-557C785796FC	848.0208
12	Ferrari	9250.00	66C9034C-23A3-44F1-B946-2DDA65E684D8	4645.00
13	Porsche	1490.00	E00D10E9-7F7F-49A9-BDC0-4C2611580B4E	848.0208
14	Porsche	1360.00	AAF61ECC-0BAC-4EAF-9E50-01749253329A	848.0208
15	Triumph	970.00	0B0E0FC2-E72B-4BD4-9C46-1AF98F17BEC4	628.1818

Figure 15.5: Using a correlated query in two parts of a query

How It Works

This query extends the SQL from the previous section by repeating the entire content of the subquery in the main query's SELECT clause. Both the identical correlated subqueries are linked to the outer query using the MakeName field.

15.5 Aggregated Correlated Subqueries

The sales director has appeared at your desk. She has a new challenge—a report that shows the top two customers per country by sales.

This kind of challenge proves that there are times when you need to look at multiple categories of data in order to get a better idea of the relative importance of certain data items. Isolating the top (or bottom) few records for a specific category is a case in point. The following SQL is an example of this—for each country, it isolates the top two customers:

```
SELECT      CUX.CustomerName
            ,CUX.Town
            ,COX.CountryName
FROM        Data.Customer CUX
INNER JOIN Data.Country COX ON CUX.Country = COX.CountryISO2
WHERE       CUX.CustomerID IN
                 (
                 SELECT      TOP (2) CU.CustomerID
                 FROM        Data.Make AS MK
                 INNER JOIN Data.Model AS MD
                            ON MK.MakeID = MD.MakeID
                 INNER JOIN Data.Stock AS ST
                            ON ST.ModelID = MD.ModelID
                 INNER JOIN Data.SalesDetails SD
                            ON ST.StockCode = SD.StockID
                 INNER JOIN Data.Sales AS SA
                            ON SA.SalesID = SD.SalesID
                 INNER JOIN Data.Customer CU
                            ON SA.CustomerID = CU.CustomerID
                 INNER JOIN Data.Country CO
                            ON CU.Country = CO.CountryISO2
```

```
        WHERE        CUX.Country = CU.Country

        GROUP BY     CU.CustomerID

        ORDER BY     SUM(SD.SalePrice) DESC

        )
ORDER BY     COX.CountryName, CUX.CustomerName
```

Running this query gives the results that you can see in *Figure 15.6.*

	CustomerName	Town	CountryName
1	Diplomatic Cars	Brussels	Belgium
2	Stefan Van Helsing	Brussels	Belgium
3	Laurent Saint Yves	Marseille	France
4	Vive La Vitesse	Marseille	France
5	Glitz	Stuttgart	Germany
6	WunderKar	Berlin	Germany
7	Smooth Rocking Chrome	Milan	Italy
8	Stefano DiLonghi	Rome	Italy
9	Antonio Maura	Madrid	Spain
10	Prestige Imports	Barcelona	Spain
11	Le Luxe en Motion	Geneva	Switzerland
12	Matterhorn Motors	Lausanne	Switzerland
13	Honest Pete Motors	Stoke	United Kingdom
14	Magic Motors	Birmingham	United Kingdom
15	Sondra Horowitz	Los Angeles	United States

Figure 15.6: *An aggregate correlated subquery*

How It Works

This example is an extension of the previous one, but if you look carefully, you see that the correlated subquery is an aggregate query—it uses the GROUP BY clause to find the top two customers by value per country. It does this by sorting the data in the subquery in descending order of sales.

Let's take a closer look at how this query works:

The outer query	Creates a list of customers by town and country. It does this by joining the Customer and Country tables.
The inner query	Then takes the country field for each customer and uses this as the filter for a query that joins the Make, Model, Stock, SalesDetails, Sales, Customer, and Country tables to obtain a complete dataset of sales information. This dataset groups the data using the CustomerID field to aggregate the total sales for each customer in the specific country that was passed in from the outer query. Because the correlated subquery orders the data by the sales amount, only the top two records are returned.
The outer query	Then detects whether the customer ID returned by the correlated subquery matches the customer for the record that is being analyzed. If it does, then the record from the outer query is displayed.

To resume, because the subquery is linked to the outer query on the Country field, it now finds the top two customers per country when the whole query is run. This is because, once again, the inner query runs once for each record in the outer query. Because the country field links the two queries, the inner query only aggregates customers per country.

Once the IDs of the top two customers by country have been identified by the subquery—and passed up to the outer query via its WHERE clause—the outer query can select all required fields and order the result just as you would for any standard query.

Note: It is important to remember that although the outer query is filtering on customer IDs, the *correlation* is on the country. This makes the point that the filter and the correlation can be completely separate.

Tricks and Traps

There are a few points that you may want to take note of when using aggregated correlated subqueries:

- A correlated subquery can be an aggregate query if your query logic requires it to be so. This is also the case for ordinary subqueries. In this respect, the outer and inner queries are structurally independent. Either can be a simple detail query or an aggregate query, no matter what type the other query is.

- Because the correlated subquery is passing two elements back to the outer query for each make of car, it is important to use the IN operator for the outer query WHERE clause, and not the equal (=) operator. Remember that you can only use the equal operator if a `single value` is used in a WHERE clause.

- This example shows that the inner and outer queries can be quite different query types. However, they do share a field that allows them to be linked as well as some way of using the result from the subquery to filter the outer query, and this is all that is really necessary to create a correlated subquery.

15.6 Using Correlated Subqueries to Filter Data on an Aggregate Value

No firm wants to spend too much when buying goods, so it follows that you have to be able to analyze purchases that exceed certain calculated thresholds. As the finance director is homing in on purchasing costs as part of his drive to control spending, he wants you to create a report that shows all models of car where the maximum purchase cost is more than one and a half times the average purchase price for that model. The following SQL is an example of how to do this:

```
SELECT     MKX.MakeName, MDX.ModelName
FROM       Data.Make AS MKX
           INNER JOIN Data.Model AS MDX ON MKX.MakeID = MDX.MakeID
           INNER JOIN Data.Stock AS STX ON STX.ModelID = MDX.ModelID
GROUP BY   MKX.MakeName, MDX.ModelName
HAVING     MAX(STX.Cost) >=
               (
                 SELECT     AVG(ST.Cost) * 1.5 AS AvgCostPerModel
                 FROM       Data.Make AS MK
                 INNER JOIN Data.Model AS MD
                            ON MK.MakeID = MD.MakeID
                 INNER JOIN Data.Stock AS ST
                            ON ST.ModelID = MD.ModelID
                 WHERE      MD.ModelName = MDX.ModelName
                            AND MK.MakeName = MKX. MakeName
               )
```

Running this query gives the results that you can see in *Figure 15.7.*

	MakeName	ModelName
1	Peugeot	205
2	Mercedes	280SL
3	Peugeot	404
4	Porsche	911
5	Porsche	924
6	Porsche	944
7	Lamborghini	Countach
8	Aston Martin	DB2
9	Aston Martin	DB6
10	Aston Martin	DB9
11	Alfa Romeo	Giulia
12	Alfa Romeo	Giulietta
13	Austin	Lichfield
14	Jaguar	Mark X
15	Rolls Royce	Phantom

Figure 15.7: Using a correlated subquery in the HAVING clause of the outer query

How It Works

For a change, let's begin by looking at the outer query in this example.

The outer query generates a list of vehicle makes and models based on the Make, Model, and Stock tables. It uses a GROUP BY to make this into an aggregate list where the make and model name only appear once.

Then the outer query gets interesting. Since it is an aggregate query, it can have a HAVING clause (if you remember, this clause filters data at the level of the aggregation, not at the level of individual records). It applies a HAVING clause to say, "only if the maximum cost for any make and model is greater than or equal to 150 percent of the average cost for this make and model."

It is the correlated subquery that calculates 150 percent of the average cost. Yet again, since this is a correlated subquery, it is filtered on data passed in from the outer query—in this case, the make and model. The subquery calculates the average cost for a specific make and model, then multiplies it by 1.5. This result is, in turn, passed back up to the outer query so it can be compared to the greatest vehicle cost for each make and model combination. Finally, the comparison operator (>=, or greater than or equal to) allows `only those records that meet the filter criterion` to pass through into the final output. That is, only makes and models are shown if any car of this type costs more than one and a half times the average for that particular car.

Tricks and Traps

There are only a few points to take away from this section:

- Correlated subqueries are, at their heart, a filtering mechanism, so you need to analyze what kind of filter you are looking for. If you are filtering data row by row, then you will probably use the correlated subquery in the WHERE clause. If, however, you are filtering records to compare a value with an aggregate result (such as the maximum cost for a vehicle model here), then you will almost inevitably want to apply the correlated subquery to the HAVING clause of the outer query.

- If the outer query is an aggregation query, then you can use any of the classic aggregation functions—SUM(), AVG(), MIN(), or MAX(), for instance—in the HAVING clause. This allows you to compare a result from the subquery to the total, the average, the highest, or the lowest aggregate value for a specific data group.

- Correlated queries can be joined to the outer query on several fields—as you can see in this example.

15.7 Using Correlated Subqueries to Detect If Records Exist

"Know your customer" is the mantra that resounds throughout businesses across every continent. For many firms, however, the refrain could just as well be "know who your customer is." The following SQL shows you how to create a list of all the active clients of Prestige Cars in 2017:

```
SELECT DISTINCT    CU.CustomerName
FROM               Data.Customer CU
WHERE              EXISTS
                   (
                    SELECT    *
                    FROM      Data.Sales SA
                    WHERE     SA.CustomerID = CU.CustomerID
```

```
                          AND YEAR(SA.SaleDate) = 2017

            )
ORDER BY        CU.CustomerName
```

The list that you can see in *Figure 15.8* shows only the customers that have bought a vehicle from Prestige Cars in a specific year—2017, in this example. Any potential customer in the Customer table who did not buy a car in 2017 is not displayed.

	CustomerName
1	Alicia Almodovar
2	Antonio Maura
3	Autos Sportivos
4	Birmingham Executive Prestige Vehicles
5	Capots Reluisants S.A.
6	Casseroles Chromes
7	Convertible Dreams
8	Diplomatic Cars
9	Eat My Exhaust Ltd
10	Glittering Prize Cars Ltd
11	Glitz
12	Honest Pete Motors
13	Kieran O'Harris
14	King Leer Cars
15	La Bagnole de Luxe

Figure 15.8: A simple correlated subquery using EXISTS

How It Works

Correlated subqueries are not just for calculations. They can also be very useful in determining whether data should be included in a result set. In practice, what this means is that you need to apply the EXISTS keyword to the query. When you use this new keyword, the outer query checks to see if any records exist for this specific customer ID. If one does, then the customer name is output. The flip side to this is that if no records exist then data for this customer is not displayed.

This means that if the correlated subquery contains any records for this particular CustomerID, then the customer name is returned by the outer query. This is because the filter in the outer query says, "Where a record exists in the inner query." If there is no corresponding record in the correlated subquery, then no customer name is output. This way the query as a whole only returns data from one dataset when a criterion applied to a second set of data is met.

Tricks and Traps

When using correlated subqueries, you need to be aware that

- Correlated subqueries depend on a link existing between the inner and outer queries, so, if you can use a JOIN to link tables in a query, then you can use the same tables in a correlated subquery.

- When you use the EXISTS keyword, you are looking simply for the existence of a record in the subquery. This means that you can make the SELECT clause of the correlated subquery really simple and not even specify any particular column names. After all, column names in the subquery will not be used in this type of correlated subquery since you are only looking to see if records exist.

- You have already seen queries in the previous two chapters that compare data in tables. However, the use of correlated subqueries is specifically tailored to tables that can be joined.

15.8 Using a Correlated Subquery to Exclude Data

No business wants to carry excess stock. Consequently, I am sure that you understand why the company finance director wants to know which vehicles have not yet been sold and are paralyzing valuable cash in the parking lot. The following SQL code shows you how to produce this list for him:

```
SELECT      MakeName + ', ' + ModelName AS VehicleInStock, ST.STOCKCODE

FROM        Data.Make AS MK

INNER JOIN Data.Model AS MD ON MK.MakeID = MD.MakeID

INNER JOIN Data.Stock AS ST ON ST.ModelID = MD.ModelID

WHERE       NOT EXISTS

                    (SELECT  *
                     FROM    Data.SalesDetails SD
                     WHERE   ST.StockCode = SD.StockID)
```

Running this query gives the results that you can see in *Figure 15.9*. You can see all the results if you scroll down this list.

	VehicleInStock	STOCKCODE
1	Ferrari, Testarossa	DE3096AD-76F9-4AAF-B2E1-49FA8E2C377F
2	Ferrari, Testarossa	8BD326B3-8DE8-4DC9-9F96-FD132C5E1BF2
3	Ferrari, 355	C82D133F-3442-464B-A16A-D5419A9E1CDF
4	Ferrari, 308	FBF39066-2C13-469D-B913-EBCF22CCFD63
5	Ferrari, Dino	F187F74F-3909-4291-A15B-F793AB88DE3B
6	Ferrari, 360	579AD98F-B7A5-456A-8F17-5B77A5479767
7	Porsche, 944	74F717DA-B4DA-44F2-857A-F062AC60052E
8	Porsche, 944	52F665EA-2D6D-4ECA-8A14-553522A45B04
9	Aston Martin, DB2	62611547-0F2D-41B1-BA32-E34AB67E10A3
10	Aston Martin, DB2	532B985F-94AC-45DF-AE17-431FBCC66D0C
11	Aston Martin, DB2	51451AC8-A35F-4597-B4BC-94E92C150C3D
12	Aston Martin, DB4	4831A9DA-09BD-4AC3-8984-947F284CD4A8
13	Aston Martin, DB5	2309FF52-564A-4A2C-B6EB-D94AA321D687
14	Aston Martin, DB6	26A3D067-DCEA-4FF1-9A97-E7AEE0D2BC14
15	Aston Martin, DB6	373B7D39-B5A3-4018-883C-AC81EF3B5D8F

Figure 15.9: A correlated subquery using NOT EXISTS

How It Works

Just as you may need to know when data exists (as was the case in the previous example), there could be cases when you need to find out when data is **not** present in related tables. In the Prestige Cars data model, the Stock table contains all the vehicles ever bought. The SalesDetails table contains all the vehicles ever sold. A correlated subquery can compare the data in one table with the data in the other.

When you want to run this kind of analysis, it is probably easier to use the table that contains the most data as the outer query and the table that contains a mode-limited set of data as the correlated (or inner) subquery. The code above does exactly this.

The outer query	Joins the Make, Model, and Stock tables so that the required fields can be output—as well as ensuring access to a field that can be shared with the subquery (the StockCode field in this example).
The inner query	Selects all the data from the SalesDetails table, but as this is a correlated subquery, it only finds records where the StockID matches the StockCode of the outer query.

Once again, the subquery is rerun for every record that the outer query finds. If there is a match on the StockCode/StockID fields, then the WHERE clause of the outer query comes into play. This filter says, "tell me if there is not a match," which is the colloquial way of saying WHERE NOT EXISTS. If the two tables do **not match** for a record in the outer query, this record is returned by the query.

Tricks and Traps

It takes a little practice to successfully use the NOT EXISTS function, so when you are applying this concept to your queries, be sure to remember the following key points:

- A correlated subquery that uses NOT EXISTS is also only looking for the existence of data in the subquery—the actual fields selected by the subquery are irrelevant.

- A correlated subquery like this can run much more slowly than a simpler query does. This should not worry you; it is precisely because the inner query has to run once for every record in the outer query. However, you need to be aware that a query like this can take quite a while to run for a large dataset.

15.9 Complex Joins in Correlated Subqueries

Diligent purchasing can require an in-depth knowledge of your products, so it follows that the buyers for Prestige Cars want to track any vehicles that seem unduly expensive compared to similar models. The following piece of SQL helps you keep tabs on your costs by listing all makes where the maximum purchase cost is over twice the average purchase cost for that make and model for the year:

```
SELECT     MKX.MakeName, YEAR(STX.DateBought) AS PurchaseYear
FROM       Data.Make AS MKX INNER JOIN Data.Model AS MDX
           ON MKX.MakeID = MDX.MakeID
           INNER JOIN Data.Stock AS STX ON STX.ModelID = MDX.ModelID
WHERE      YEAR(STX.DateBought) IN (2015, 2016)
GROUP BY   MKX.MakeName, YEAR(STX.DateBought)
HAVING     MAX(STX.Cost) >=
                   (
                   SELECT   AVG(ST.Cost) * 2 AS AvgCostPerModel
                   FROM     Data.Make AS MK
                            INNER JOIN Data.Model AS MD
```

```
                    ON MK.MakeID = MD.MakeID
                    INNER JOIN Data.Stock AS ST
                    ON ST.ModelID = MD.ModelID
            WHERE     MK.MakeName = MKX.MakeName
                      AND YEAR(ST.DateBought)
                          = YEAR(STX.DateBought)
        )
```

Running this query gives the results that you can see in *Figure 15.10*.

Results | Messages

	MakeName	PurchaseYear
1	Aston Martin	2015
2	Aston Martin	2016
3	Bentley	2016
4	Jaguar	2016
5	Lamborghini	2016
6	Porsche	2016

Figure 15.10: *A correlated subquery with a complex join*

How It Works

Some questions require you to be more restrictive in your analysis. You might want to add multiple elements to the calculated comparison, not just one, as was the case in the previous couple of examples. Correlated subqueries allow you to join the inner and outer queries on more than one field. Consequently, this query `also` calculates an average value for a subset of data. This time the value that is passed in to the correlated subquery from the outer query is a calculation—double the average cost for each make. This figure is then compared to the aggregate maximum cost per make in the HAVING clause of the outer query.

What makes this query a little subtler is the use of a more complex link between the outer and inner queries. This time there are two elements:

- The make of vehicle
- The year that the car was bought

A double connection like this has the effect of limiting the comparison even further. Now it is the `maximum cost per make per year` that is used as the comparison element. The net result is that certain makes of car can appear in the final result more than once, because at least one item in stock costs more than twice the average for that make in any of several years.

The outer query also adds a filter in the form of a WHERE clause. Since the field that is used in the WHERE clause is also used to join the outer query to the correlated subquery, the choice of years is applied in both queries, even though it is only added once—to the outer query.

Tricks and Traps

When applying complex joins you need to take away a fundamental point concerning correlated subqueries:

- Being able to join the inner and outer queries on several fields is, in fact, a powerful tool for simplifying certain types of analysis. In Chapter 12, you saw that if you filtered an ordinary query that contained a subquery, you also had to filter the subquery in certain cases to get the result that you wanted. If you are filtering the outer query on a field that is used to create the correlation between the two queries, then you are automatically applying the WHERE clause of the outer query to the inner query. This avoids repetition—and minimizes the risk of error.

15.10 Using a Correlated Subquery to Verify Values across Tables

No organization wants erroneous data. This is especially true where invoices are concerned. Fortunately SQL is a perfect tool when it comes to data validation. Specifically, let's suppose that you want to check that invoice header totals correspond to invoice line aggregation. The following short piece of SQL shows how to do this:

```
SELECT     SalesID
           ,TotalSalePrice
           ,CASE WHEN
                     (
                       SELECT SUM(SalePrice)
                         FROM   Data.SalesDetails
                        WHERE   SalesID = Data.Sales.SalesID
                     ) = TotalSalePrice
                          THEN 'OK'
                          ELSE 'Error in Invoice'
```

```
                    END AS LineItemCheck
FROM        Data.Sales
```

Running this query gives the results that you can see in *Figure 15.11*.

	SalesID	TotalSalePrice	LineItemCheck
1	1	65000.00	OK
2	2	220000.10	Error in Invoice
3	3	19500.00	OK
4	4	11500.00	OK
5	5	19900.00	Error in Invoice
6	6	29500.00	OK
7	7	49500.20	Error in Invoice
8	8	76000.90	Error in Invoice
9	9	19600.00	OK
10	10	36500.00	OK
11	11	89000.00	OK
12	12	169500.00	OK
13	13	8950.00	OK
14	14	195000.00	OK
15	15	22950.00	OK

Figure 15.11: *Using a correlated subquery to verify values across tables*

How It Works

Despite the best efforts of programmers and data entry staff everywhere, errors can creep into data. Fortunately, SQL can also carry out automated checks and balances on your data. This code works because the two tables that it uses—Sales and SalesDetails—are part of a relational structure. More specifically, the Sales table is in a one-to-many relationship with the SalesDetails table. That is, several sales details records can be linked to a single Sales record. What is more, the Sales table contains a field—SalePrice—that should contain the total sales value of all the corresponding detail records for that particular sale in the SalesDetails table.

This query begins with a subquery that returns the sum of the SalePrice for the SalesDetails table. However, to prevent the query from merely returning the total for every record, a correlation is set up between the subquery and an outer query that lists the SalePrice for every record in the Sales table. This forces the inner query to calculate only the total sales for the records that are linked to the Sales table.

The trick in this query is how the output from the correlated subquery is used. Rather than just returning the total sales for each sale from the SalesDetails table, this aggregate figure is compared—using a CASE statement—with the sales figure from the Sales table. If the two are identical, the query returns "OK." Should they not match, it returns "Error in Invoice."

This way the query can verify that the data is as it should be, and if not, bring any erroneous records to your attention for further investigation.

Conclusion

This short chapter introduced you to a new tool to extend your SQL skillset—correlated subqueries. Correlated subqueries let you link subqueries to main queries and filter the data in the outer query by checking every record that it contains against the result of a subquery.

Core Knowledge Learned in This Chapter

The keywords and concepts that you have seen in this chapter are

Concept	Description
Correlated subqueries	Correlated subqueries let you link subqueries to main queries and filter the data in the outer query by checking every record that it contains against the result of a subquery.
EXISTS	This keyword tests for the existence of a record in a subquery that is linked to the outer query.
NOT EXISTS	This keyword tests for the absence of a record in a subquery that is linked to the outer query.

CHAPTER 16
Dataset Manipulation

Sometimes the data that you use may not be in a single table (as you might expect it to be) but can be spread across a series of tables with identical structures. Moreover, since much data analysis is comparative, you may want to compare one specific set of data with another possibly separate, dataset and isolate any differences. You can accomplish this by seeing if two sets of data overlap, for instance. Yet another potential requirement can consist of isolating the data that exists in one dataset but not in another. These challenges involve handling entire datasets.

Using Datasets to Mix and Match Data

This short chapter takes you further into the domain of comparative analysis of data using SQL Server. It builds on the techniques that you saw in the previous chapters and teaches you how to mix and match datasets in order to delve deep into the information they contain.

More specifically, in this chapter you learn how to

- Read data from several identically structured tables simultaneously.

- Create separate subsets of data that you can use for comparison purposes.

- Compare the data in two tables and only display data that is common to both tables.

- Compare the data in two tables and only display data that is in one table but not the other.

16.1 Read Data from Multiple Identical Tables Using the UNION Operator

Data comes in a multitude of shapes and forms and is not always available as a relational set of tables that can be joined. Sometimes you may have to query data from two or more tables that have identical structures—meaning each table contains a slice of a total dataset. As an example of this, imagine that you have been asked to look at `three tables` of sales information, one for sales in each of the years 2015, 2016, and 2017. All three tables contain the `same columns of data in the same order`.

The SQL to query the three tables at once looks like this:

```
SELECT  MakeName, ModelName, CustomerName, CountryName
        ,Cost, RepairsCost, PartsCost, TransportInCost
        ,SalePrice, SaleDate
FROM    DataTransfer.Sales2015
UNION
SELECT  MakeName, ModelName, CustomerName, CountryName
        ,Cost, RepairsCost, PartsCost, TransportInCost
        ,SalePrice, SaleDate
FROM    DataTransfer.Sales2016
UNION
SELECT  MakeName, ModelName, CustomerName, CountryName
        ,Cost, RepairsCost, PartsCost, TransportInCost
        ,SalePrice, SaleDate
FROM    DataTransfer.Sales2017
```

Running this query gives the results in *Figure 16.1*. As you can see, the data is returned for any of the three years, whereas each table only contains data for a single year.

	MakeName	ModelName	CustomerName	CountryName	Cost	RepairsCost	PartsCost	TransportInCost	SalePrice	SaleDate
1	Alfa Romeo	Giulia	Convertible Dreams	United Kingdom	6956.00	400.00	750.00	150.00	8695.00	2015-07-12 00:00:00.000
2	Alfa Romeo	Giulia	Convertible Dreams	United Kingdom	20000.00	1360.00	750.00	150.00	25000.00	2017-11-01 00:00:00.000
3	Alfa Romeo	Giulia	Glitz	Germany	4800.00	500.00	750.00	150.00	6000.00	2016-02-17 00:00:00.000
4	Alfa Romeo	Giulia	Jason B. Wight	United States	10000.00	500.00	750.00	150.00	12500.00	2016-07-06 00:00:00.000
5	Alfa Romeo	Giulia	M. Pierre Dubois	France	2040.00	500.00	750.00	150.00	2550.00	2016-01-07 00:00:00.000
6	Alfa Romeo	Giulia	Silver HubCaps	United Kingdom	14000.00	1360.00	750.00	150.00	17500.00	2016-04-30 00:00:00.000
7	Alfa Romeo	Giulia	Stefan Van Helsing	Belgium	8400.00	500.00	750.00	150.00	10500.00	2017-11-06 00:00:00.000
8	Alfa Romeo	Giulietta	Prestissimo!	Italy	5200.00	500.00	750.00	150.00	6500.00	2017-05-16 00:00:00.000
9	Alfa Romeo	Giulietta	Screamin' Wheels	United States	17200.00	500.00	500.00	150.00	21500.00	2017-02-09 00:00:00.000
10	Alfa Romeo	Spider	King Leer Cars	United Kingdom	4520.00	500.00	750.00	150.00	5650.00	2017-06-22 00:00:00.000
11	Alfa Romeo	Spider	Mme Anne Duport	France	9200.00	500.00	750.00	150.00	11500.00	2017-11-12 00:00:00.000
12	Alfa Romeo	Spider	Stefan Van Helsing	Belgium	10000.00	500.00	750.00	150.00	12500.00	2017-07-01 00:00:00.000
13	Alfa Romeo	Spider	Wonderland Wheels	United Kingdom	10000.00	500.00	750.00	150.00	12500.00	2016-04-30 00:00:00.000
14	Aston Martin	DB2	Glitz	Germany	36000.00	500.00	750.00	550.00	45000.00	2017-05-24 00:00:00.000
15	Aston Martin	DB2	Ronaldo Bianco	Italy	49200.00	1360.00	750.00	550.00	61500.00	2017-05-10 00:00:00.000

Figure 16.1: *Joining data from multiple identically structured queries using the UNION operator*

How It Works

SQL lets you read data from multiple tables at once if—and only if—the structure of the queries is identical. You carry out this operation by writing a SELECT query for each table and then by amalgamating the queries using the UNION operator.

Clearly using UNION to merge the data from several tables is only useful if you have a database that contains identically structured tables. Because this is often the case for data analysis and reporting (where the original, relational data is kept separate) or when dealing with data sent from outside suppliers, you could find this technique useful in practice.

In this example, you joined the three tables sequentially (or "vertically") rather than "horizontally," as you have done in many queries so far in this book. Put another way, you have added the contents of one table to the contents of another. *Figure 16.2* illustrates conceptually what you have done.

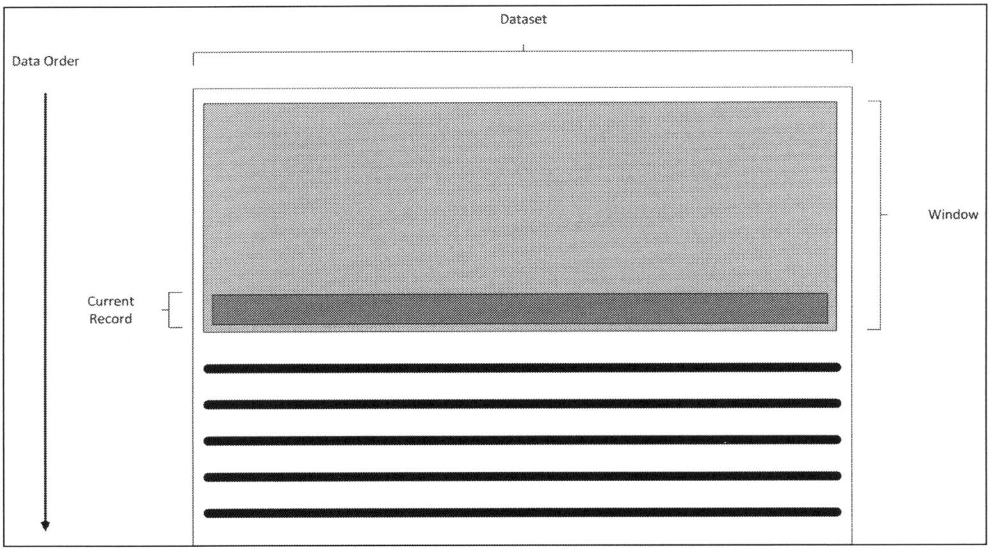

Figure 16.2: Compiling a dataset from multiple identical tables

Tricks and Traps

Although simple enough, the UNION operator does require you to remember that

- You can use aliases to rename the columns in a UNION query just as you can in an SQL query; however, you only need to add aliases to the **first query** in the series—that is, the query for 2015 sales in this example. The other queries use the aliases that you applied to the topmost query. After all, a column can only have one name, so the name is taken from the topmost query.

- In a UNION query, it is vital that you select the columns from each of the separate queries in the same order.

- If the underlying tables do not contain identical columns in the same order, you can replace the name of any columns that are missing from a table with NULL in the SELECT statement. For instance, if the table Sales2016 does not contain a TransportInCost field, you can write the following SQL so that the query over the three tables will still work:

```
SELECT  MakeName, ModelName, CustomerName, CountryName, Cost,
RepairsCost, Par'tsCost, NULL, SalePrice, SaleDate
```

16.2 Isolate Identical Data in Multiple Tables Using the INTERSECT Operator

The sales director needs to compare elements that are similar across separate time periods. Her exact requirement is to find all the makes bought this year that were also bought the previous year. The following query does exactly this, using the separate tables of yearly sales that you saw in the previous section:

```
SELECT      MK.MakeName

FROM        Data.Make AS MK

INNER JOIN Data.Model AS MD ON MK.MakeID = MD.MakeID

INNER JOIN Data.Stock AS ST ON ST.ModelID = MD.ModelID

WHERE       YEAR(ST.DateBought) = 2015

INTERSECT

SELECT      MK.MakeName

FROM        Data.Make AS MK

INNER JOIN Data.Model AS MD ON MK.MakeID = MD.MakeID

INNER JOIN Data.Stock AS ST ON ST.ModelID = MD.ModelID

WHERE       YEAR(ST.DateBought) = 2016
```

Running this query gives the results that you can see in *Figure 16.3*.

	MakeName
1	Alfa Romeo
2	Aston Martin
3	Bentley
4	Ferrari
5	Jaguar
6	Porsche
7	Triumph

Figure 16.3: Using the INTERSECT operator

How It Works

In this query you actually have two separate queries:

The first	Joins the Stock, Make, and Model tables and adds only the MakeName field to the SELECT clause. This query then filters the results so that `only vehicles bought in 2015` are returned.
The second	Duplicates the first query, but it sets the year to `2016`.

Combining these two queries with the INTERSECT operator runs both queries and then identifies which results are common to both. Only these shared results are finally output.

A Venn diagram (see *Figure 16.4*) can help you better understand how an INTERSECT query works.

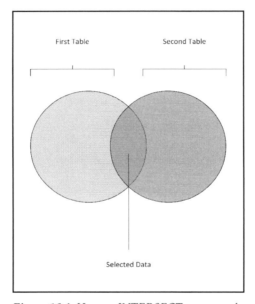

Figure 16.4: *How an INTERSECT query works*

Tricks and Traps

As you might imagine, there are several key points to note with an operator as powerful as INTERSECT:

- The two queries in this example are not, technically, subqueries, since they are both on the same "level." Consequently, they do not have to be placed inside parentheses. However, they are completely separate datasets—just like subqueries.

- You can see that an INTERSECT query automatically removes any duplicates in the final result. If you run each query separately, you see that many examples of each make are sold in either of the two years (this is shown in *Figure 16.5*); however, the final result removes all duplicates from the output.

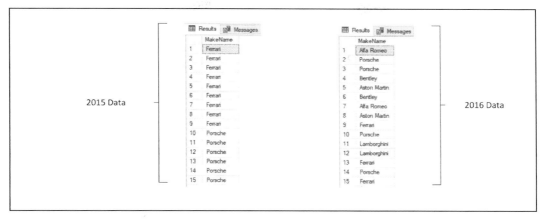

Figure 16.5: Duplicate data before it is removed using the INTERSECT operator

- An INTERSECT query `must have the same fields in the same order in the SELECT clause`. If this is not the case, it does not return the correct result—or, indeed (in most cases), any result at all. In all other respects queries can be completely different, as long as they return the datasets that you want to compare.

- You are not limited to just two queries in an INTERSECT query. You can add multiple queries—all linked with the INTERSECT keyword—if you need to.

- You do not have to select `all` the fields that are in each table to isolate data; however, any fields that you do select must be identical in all the source tables if the record is to be returned.

16.3 Isolating Nonidentical Records Using the EXCEPT Operator

Sometimes it is not overlap of data that interests you but the data that is not shared between two datasets. A practical example of this is when the CEO requests a list of all the vehicle models sold this year but not in the previous year. The following SQL shows you how to isolate this kind of result:

```
SELECT     MK.MakeName + ' ' + MD.ModelName AS MakeModel
FROM       Data.Make AS MK
INNER JOIN Data.Model AS MD ON MK.MakeID = MD.MakeID
INNER JOIN Data.Stock AS ST ON ST.ModelID = MD.ModelID
INNER JOIN Data.SalesDetails SD ON ST.StockCode = SD.StockID
INNER JOIN Data.Sales AS SA ON SA.SalesID = SD.SalesID
WHERE      YEAR(SA.SaleDate) = 2015
```

EXCEPT

```
SELECT     MK.MakeName + ' ' + MD.ModelName
FROM       Data.Make AS MK
INNER JOIN Data.Model AS MD ON MK.MakeID = MD.MakeID
INNER JOIN Data.Stock AS ST ON ST.ModelID = MD.ModelID
INNER JOIN Data.SalesDetails SD ON ST.StockCode = SD.StockID
INNER JOIN Data.Sales AS SA ON SA.SalesID = SD.SalesID
WHERE      YEAR(SA.SaleDate) = 2016
```

Running this query gives the results that you can see in *Figure 16.6.*

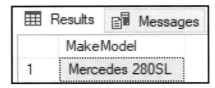

Figure 16.6: *Using the EXCEPT operator to isolate data*

How It Works

This query is similar in certain respects to the queries that you saw in the two previous examples. Once again, you have multiple queries that output identical field sets in the same order. This time, however, the EXCEPT operator is used to link the datasets returned by the individual queries.

This operator finds all the elements (the make and model of vehicles sold in a specific year) and then compares these rows with the make and model of vehicles sold the following year. Any models of car that are present in both datasets are left out of the final result. This way you can see which cars were sold in 2015 but not in 2016.

Figure 16.7 shows you, conceptually, how this approach works.

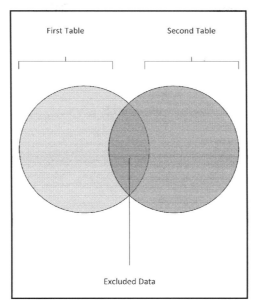

Figure 16.7: Excluding the shared items from two sets of data

Tricks and Traps

I have only one comment to make here:

- The two queries used in this example are, once again, completely separate. Indeed, they have to be different for the query to work properly. Consequently, each query has its own WHERE clause, and this is what allows you to specify completely different datasets, even if the two queries are otherwise identical.

16.4 Joining Multiple Identical Tables in a Subquery

The CEO has gone back to the sales data that you joined together in the first section of this chapter and is now requesting that you produce a simple list of makes and models from all three tables that were sold to German clients.

After a little thought, you adapt the query that you used previously to satisfy her request. The SQL looks like this:

```
SELECT  MakeName, ModelName
FROM
(
    SELECT  MakeName, ModelName, CustomerName, CountryName, Cost
```

```
        ,RepairsCost, PartsCost, TransportInCost, SalePrice, SaleDate
        FROM    DataTransfer.Sales2015
        UNION
        SELECT  MakeName, ModelName, CustomerName, CountryName, Cost
        ,RepairsCost, PartsCost, TransportInCost, SalePrice, SaleDate
        FROM    DataTransfer.Sales2016
        UNION
        SELECT  MakeName, ModelName, CustomerName, CountryName, Cost
        ,RepairsCost, PartsCost, TransportInCost, SalePrice, SaleDate
        FROM    DataTransfer.Sales2017
) SQ
WHERE   CountryName = 'Germany'
```

Running this code produces the output that you can see in *Figure 16.8*.

	MakeName	ModelName
1	Alfa Romeo	Giulia
2	Aston Martin	DB2
3	Aston Martin	DB9
4	Aston Martin	Rapide
5	Austin	Lichfield
6	Bentley	Flying Spur
7	Ferrari	360
8	Lamborghini	Diabolo
9	Lamborghini	Jarama
10	Porsche	924
11	Porsche	944

Figure 16.8: Using a derived query with tables joined using the UNION operator

How It Works

The ability of SQL to deliver the output from multiple identical tables is certainly useful in many occasions; however, you need a way to make the resulting data easy to filter. Moreover, undoubtedly you will have times when you want to select only some of the columns that each table contains.

This is a perfect opportunity for wrapping the UNION query inside an outer query and treating the UNION query as a derived table. This simple technique allows you to select only the fields that you require, then filter the data using a single WHERE clause, and even group the data if you so choose.

Tricks and Traps

I have only a couple of comments to make here:

- It is perfectly possible to apply the same SELECT and WHERE clauses to each query that is used in a UNION query. However, this can be both more laborious and more error-prone than making the UNION query into a derived table and filtering on the combined data.

- Extending a query to include a derived table is a great example of code reuse, where just a small tweak can make SQL that you created previously even more applicable, so remember to save your code snippets in case they turn out to be important at a later date.

Conclusion

Despite being brief, this chapter helped you to extend your knowledge of the way that data analysis in SQL Server depends on using datasets correctly. You saw how to filter separate datasets individually in order to effect comparisons over time as well as combine multiple tables to create a single result set.

Finally, you saw how to extract overlapping data from two tables. Then you discovered how to do the opposite and return data that is present in one table but not in another.

Core Knowledge Learned in This Chapter

The concepts that you have seen in this chapter are

Concept	Description
UNION	This operator lets you pull data from multiple tables or views that are identical in structure and removes duplicates.
UNION ALL	This operator lets you pull data from multiple tables or views that are identical in structure and preserves duplicates.
INTERSECT	This operator returns a subset of data that is common to two tables or views.
EXCEPT	This operator returns a subset of data that is present in one table or view, but not in another.

CHAPTER 17
Using SQL for More Advanced Calculations

In the first part of this book you saw how to perform elementary math on the data in a SQL Server database. Although SQL is not a language that is designed to carry out advanced mathematical calculations, it can go much further than the simple addition, subtraction, division, and multiplication that you have seen previously. However, these more advanced calculations also require you to understand more completely how SQL handles numbers.

Additional Calculation Techniques

The aim of this chapter is to extend your skills when it comes to performing essential math with SQL Server. This does not mean that you will be following a math course in SQL. Instead we take a more real-world approach and show you how SQL Server deals with numbers internally. Initially this means showing you how to ensure that SQL accepts data as being numeric. This may be necessary because what appears to be a number to us humans may not be interpreted as a numeric value by SQL. Making sure that numbers are correctly handled will help you to write robust SQL that can handle potentially unpleasant surprises and deliver the results that you expect to see. After you learn this, you begin learning to use SQL to write more complex formulas to analyze your data.

In this chapter you will learn how to

- Ensure that you are using the appropriate data types in certain types of calculation.

- Understand numeric data types.

- Remove currency symbols from source data so that you can calculate columns that are not "pure" numbers.

- Handle divide-by-zero errors.

- Use calculated columns several times in a SQL snippet—without having to copy the calculation.

- Test for errors in SQL calculations—and deal with them—so that your queries do not fail, but perform the appropriate calculation where this is feasible.

This chapter is for you, then, if you want to extend the results of your analysis with some more complex calculation techniques. It gives you the confidence to deliver sound and accurate metrics to enhance your analysis with SQL.

17.1 Calculating the Percentage Represented by Each Record in a Dataset

All businesses like repeat customers, so it is perfectly understandable that the CEO of Prestige Cars wants to know what percentage of individual sales can be attributed to each client. The following SQL does this for you:

```
SELECT      CU.CustomerName

            ,FORMAT(

                    CAST(COUNT(CU.CustomerName) AS NUMERIC)

                    / (SELECT CAST(COUNT(*) AS NUMERIC)

                      FROM Data.Sales)

                    , '0.00 %')

            AS PercentageSalesPerCustomer

FROM        Data.Sales SA

INNER JOIN  Data.Customer CU

            ON CU.CustomerID = SA.CustomerID

GROUP BY    CU.CustomerName

ORDER BY    CU.CustomerName
```

Running this query gives the results that you can see in *Figure 17.1*. If you scroll down the list, you will see all the customers and the percentage of individual sales for each one. Moreover, if you add up all the percentage sales per customer, you will find that the total is 100 percent.

	CustomerName	PercentageSalesPerCustomer
1	Alex McWhirter	0.31 %
2	Alexei Tolstoi	2.47 %
3	Alicia Almodovar	2.16 %
4	Andrea Tarbuck	0.62 %
5	Andy Cheshire	0.62 %
6	Antonio Maura	1.85 %
7	Autos Sportivos	0.31 %
8	Beltway Prestige Driving	0.62 %
9	Birmingham Executive Prestige Vehicles	1.85 %
10	Bling Bling S.A.	0.31 %
11	Bling Motors	0.93 %
12	Boris Spry	0.62 %
13	Bravissima!	0.62 %
14	Capots Reluisants S.A.	1.85 %
15	Casseroles Chromes	1.23 %

Figure 17.1: Converting integers to the numeric data type with the CAST() function

How It Works

Given the SQL experience that you have acquired by now, I imagine that this query is not too hard to understand. Indeed, you might even be wondering exactly what is so "advanced" about it. Take a closer look; this query should draw your attention to an apparently minor point that we first looked at briefly previously.

After joining the Sales and Customer tables, you group on the CustomerName field to see a record for each customer. Then you select

First:	The customer name.
Second:	The number of records for each customer. This is done using the COUNT()function.
Then:	You create a subquery to calculate the total number of records in the joined table set.
Finally:	You divide the number of sales (or records representing an individual sale) by the total number of sales to give the percentage of individual sales per customer. To make the result more instantly comprehensible, this is formatted as a percentage.

So far, so good, you are probably thinking. Yet this query performs one extra step over and above the basic counts and math. It also forces the results of each calculation to be output as a NUMERIC data type. This is done using the CAST()function, which specifies that the data is converted to a NUMERIC data type.

Here is the reason for this: when SQL uses the COUNT() function, it returns the figures for both the sales per customer and the overall sales as `integers`—or whole numbers if you prefer. This is logical in that a total number of records is never anything other than a whole number (fractions of records simply do not exist). However, this means that when SQL Server divides the sales per customer by the overall sales, it `also returns an integer`. This is because using an integer data type in a calculation forces all other numeric data to be treated as integers—no matter what the precise data type is that has been defined in the database. Given that the result of this calculation is always less than 1, the output simply cannot be displayed accurately, even if the calculation is performed correctly. In this case, as the resulting percentage is less than 1, a 0 is returned. So if you do not use the CAST() function, and instead use a query like this,

```
COUNT(CustomerName) / (SELECT COUNT(*) FROM Data.Sales)
```

SQL Server gives the results that you can see in *Figure 17.2.*

	CustomerName	PercentageSalesPerCustomer
1	Alex McWhirter	0.00 %
2	Alexei Tolstoi	0.00 %
3	Alicia Almodovar	0.00 %
4	Andrea Tarbuck	0.00 %
5	Andy Cheshire	0.00 %

Figure 17.2: *Dividing by integers*

I am sure that you will agree that this result is extremely disconcerting. The upshot is that, when calculating ratios, you **must** cast any field or function that uses integers to a data type that accepts decimals. By far the easiest way to do this is to cast the result as NUMERIC. This automatically applies up to 19 decimals, which should suffice for most ratios.

Tricks and Traps

Here are a couple of points to remember when calculating percentages:

- You can, of course, be more precise in the choice of data type and the number of decimals that you want to use. To specify 4 decimals and a maximum of 6 figures before the decimal point, you would write

```
CAST(COUNT(*) AS NUMERIC(10,4))
```

- This conversion says, "Allow 10 characters in all. Because there are 4 decimals, deduce that I want 6 in the mantissa."

- You can multiply the result of the division in the calculation by 100 if you wish; however, this does not alter the fact that the figures are integers. Consequently, the result still does not display any decimals.

17.2 Replacing Multiple Subqueries

The sales director wants to see a list of all vehicles sold in 2017, with the percentage of sales each sale represents for the year as well as the variation to the average sales figure. You know that this will require adding a couple of subqueries—and then you remember that SQL allows you to use a single subquery in cases like these! After a few minutes, you produce the code that follows:

```
SELECT      MakeName, ModelName, SalePrice
            ,(SalePrice / CRX.TotalSales) * 100 AS PercentOfSales
            ,SalePrice - CRX.AverageSales AS DifferenceToAverage
FROM        Data.SalesByCountry
CROSS JOIN  (SELECT SUM(SalePrice) AS TotalSales
                    ,AVG(SalePrice) AS AverageSales
             FROM    Data.SalesByCountry
             WHERE   YEAR(SaleDate) = 2017) AS CRX
WHERE       YEAR(SaleDate) = 2017
```

Running this code produces the output that is shown in *Figure 17.3.*

	MakeName	ModelName	SalePrice	PercentOfSales	DifferenceToAverage
1	Aston Martin	DB6	45000.00	0.5719315080245168	-34475.505050
2	Porsche	911	49500.00	0.6291246588269685	-29975.505050
3	Aston Martin	DB6	225000.00	2.8596575401225840	145524.494950
4	Triumph	TR6	12500.00	0.1588698633401436	-66975.505050
5	Porsche	Boxster	22500.00	0.2859657540122584	-56975.505050
6	Aston Martin	Virage	125000.00	1.5886986334014355	45524.494950
7	Rolls Royce	Silver Shadow	85000.00	1.0803150707129762	5524.494950
8	Peugeot	203	1250.00	0.0158869863340144	-78225.505050
9	Mercedes	280SL	22500.00	0.2859657540122584	-56975.505050
10	Ferrari	355	125950.00	1.6007727430152865	46474.494950
11	Triumph	TR7	8850.00	0.1124798632448216	-70625.505050
12	Triumph	TR5	9950.00	0.1264604112187543	-69525.505050
13	Aston Martin	Vanquish	56500.00	0.7180917822974489	-22975.505050
14	Aston Martin	Rapide	55000.00	0.6990273986966316	-24475.505050
15	Aston Martin	Vanquish	56950.00	0.7238110973776940	-22525.505050

Figure 17.3: Replacing multiple subqueries by a CROSS JOIN

How It Works

Some calculations require multiple subqueries. This, potentially, means writing very similar subqueries several times. You might need one subquery to return a total, another to get an average, yet another to find a standard deviation, and so on. Fortunately, you can apply a workaround to make the SQL both more comprehensible and easier to maintain.

The trick is to write a subquery that calculates all the aggregate values that you need in a single query and then uses the CROSS JOIN operator to apply the output from the subquery for every single record returned from the main query.

The overall query works like this:

First:	It begins with a subquery (once again it is the subquery that contains the heart of the solution). The subquery quite simply calculates the total sales and average sales for 2017. It uses the SalesByCountry view as the source of this data.
Then:	The main query extracts the make name, model name, and sale price from the same data source (the SalesByCountry view) for the same year (2017). The next step: Is to join the main query to the subquery using the CROSS JOIN function. This ensures that every record can use the output from the subquery in the main query and that the join does not filter the data in any way.
Finally:	The SELECT clause of the main query is extended to use the output from the cross-joined subquery. In this example, we are dividing the sale price of each vehicle sold by the total sales for the year to calculate the percentage of total sales that this figure represents. As a final flourish, we subtract the average selling price from the sale price of each car to find out how much each sale differs from the average sale price for the year.

If you want to verify that the calculations are accurate, you can always select the SQL for the subquery and run it. You will see the output that is shown in *Figure 17.4.*

Figure 17.4. The output from the subquery

Tricks and Traps

Using CROSS JOIN can simplify certain calculations. Nonetheless, you need to be aware that

- The subquery is a perfectly standard subquery. This means that it is completely independent of the main query, so any filters that you apply to restrict the output from the subquery may have to be applied to the main query as well—assuming that you want to use them both to examine similar ranges of data.

- CROSS JOIN does not require an ON clause because it is not attempting to link the tables or queries in any way. Indeed, it specifically wants to use all the fields from both tables and/or queries together.

- Since the subquery is aliased, you need to use the subquery alias when referring to the fields that are output from the subquery in the calculations in the main query's SELECT clause.

17.3 Reusing Calculated Values in Queries

If you are analyzing profit margins, then you need to control your costs. That, at least, is the mantra of the finance director. He wants to see cars with indirect costs (that is, the total of the repair, parts, and transport costs) over a certain threshold—£10,000.00 in this case. This you can do using the following SQL:

```
SELECT      MakeName
            ,Cost AS PurchaseCost
            ,TotalOtherCosts
            ,Cost + TotalOtherCosts AS VehicleCost
FROM        Data.SalesByCountry
CROSS APPLY
    (
      SELECT RepairsCost + ISNULL(PartsCost, 0) + TransportInCost
        AS TotalOtherCosts
    ) SQ
WHERE       TotalOtherCosts > 10000
```

Running this query gives the results that you can see in *Figure 17.5*.

	MakeName	PurchaseCost	TotalOtherCosts	VehicleCost
1	Lamborghini	176400.00	10600.00	187000.00
2	Ferrari	164000.00	11950.00	175950.00
3	Lamborghini	135600.00	12700.00	148300.00
4	Ferrari	100760.00	13400.00	114160.00
5	Ferrari	316000.00	13400.00	329400.00
6	Aston Martin	180000.00	10600.00	190600.00
7	Rolls Royce	111600.00	13400.00	125000.00
8	Bugatti	176400.00	13400.00	189800.00
9	Ferrari	204000.00	12700.00	216700.00
10	McLaren	236000.00	14350.00	250350.00
11	Rolls Royce	132000.00	14350.00	146350.00
12	Ferrari	124000.00	11950.00	135950.00
13	Bugatti	284000.00	18700.00	302700.00
14	Bugatti	284000.00	13400.00	297400.00
15	Lamborghini	116000.00	12700.00	128700.00

Figure 17.5. *Using CROSS APPLY to reuse a calculated element*

How It Works

This query uses the data in the SalesByCountry view to save you from having to join multiple tables again. Then it displays several metrics for each car purchased.

However, it is the way that the query is designed that really interests us. This is because it reuses a calculated metric several times, while only defining it once. The metric is the total for the repair cost, the parts cost, and the transport cost. Instead of having to add the three fields three times in three separate locations (twice in the SELECT clause and once in the WHERE clause), you define a calculated metric only once but reuse it as many times as you want.

You do this by using the CROSS APPLY clause in SQL. The clause works like this:

First:	After the FROM clause in the query, you use a CROSS APPLY similar to the way you use a JOIN.
Then:	You create a subquery—in parentheses, of course—that defines the calculated field TotalOtherCosts. In this example, it is the sum of the repair cost, the parts cost, and the transport cost.
Finally:	You use this calculated field in the query just like a "normal" field.

The outcome is that the query uses the result of the CROSS APPLY in every record that is produced. This saves you from having to duplicate the SQL that defines the calculated field several times.

Tricks and Traps

CROSS APPLY is an extremely powerful operator; however, if you use it, you should be mindful of the following points:

- Using CROSS APPLY like this is particularly useful when the calculated field is used in the WHERE clause. This is because you only have to make any changes once—in the CROSS APPLY clause—for them to affect the filter and the data that is displayed. This means you have less risk of making mistakes and forgetting to change the code in several places.

- The CROSS APPLY clause is pretty much an extension of the main query rather than a completely independent subquery. Consequently, it does not have its own FROM clause but uses the table(s) in the core query. Nonetheless, it must have an alias for the code to work.

- Queries that use CROSS APPLY can sometimes run fairly slowly. Be careful when using CROSS APPLY to handle large datasets.

17.4 Remove Decimals in Calculations

If you are trading high-value products, you might not need to show pennies (or cents or centimes) in your results. Indeed, the financial director wants a list of vehicles sold that shows core costs without pennies to avoid rounding errors. An easy way to deliver on this requirement is shown in the following SQL:

```
SELECT      MakeName
            ,ModelName
            ,CAST(Cost AS INT) AS Cost
            ,CAST(RepairsCost AS INT) AS RepairsCost
            ,CAST(PartsCost AS INT) AS PartsCost
            ,CAST(SalePrice AS INT) AS SalePrice
FROM        Data.SalesByCountry
```

Running this query gives the results that you can see in *Figure 17.6*.

	MakeName	ModelName	Cost	RepairsCost	PartsCost	SalePrice
1	Ferrari	Testarossa	52000	2175	1500	65000
2	Ferrari	355	176000	5500	2200	220000
3	Porsche	911	15600	660	0	19500
4	Porsche	924	9200	500	750	11500
5	Porsche	944	15960	1360	500	19950
6	Aston Martin	DB4	23600	500	750	29500
7	Aston Martin	DB5	39600	2500	1500	49500
8	Aston Martin	DB6	60800	3250	750	76000
9	Porsche	911	15680	890	500	19600
10	Aston Martin	DB5	29200	1950	500	36500
11	Porsche	944	6800	250	225	8500
12	Aston Martin	DB6	36000	1250	750	45000
13	Bentley	Flying Spur	64400	500	750	80500
14	Ferrari	355	135600	5500	2200	169500
15	Porsche	944	7160	500	750	8950

Figure 17.6: Using the CAST() function for a specific numeric data type conversion

How It Works

You have seen the CAST() function a few times in previous chapters, but I have never really explained how useful it can be when dealing with numbers. In this example, you take the SalesByCountry view (to avoid having to join seven tables) and selected five key fields. However, in this view, the fields that contain numeric values are all either in the Money or the Numeric data types. Since both of these data types allow decimals, the fastest way to remove any decimals and present only whole number is to convert these fields to integers.

This is done by applying the CAST() function to the numeric fields and specifying that each is converted as an INT. The result is that the values are now integers—and the decimals have disappeared.

In this exercise, you have effectively done something similar to what you did in Section 2 when you calculated percentages. Previously you wrote SQL to include decimals. This time, you removed any decimals from the calculation. Both techniques use the same function—CAST().

17.5 Numeric Data Types

In Chapter 10 you saw how to find out the data type of a field. In the last couple of sections, you have seen how to convert numeric data types to other numeric data types as and when required.

As a result, now is probably a good moment to explain all the various ways that SQL Server can store and manipulate numbers. In other words, it is time to look at all the numeric data types that SQL Server offers. Each has its uses and limitations, and they are given in *Table 17.1.*

Data Type	Range	Comments
Bit	0 or 1	Essentially used for true or false (also called Boolean) values
Tinyint	0 to 255	An integer value without any decimals
SmallInt	−32,768 to +32,767	An integer value without any decimals
Int	−2,147,483,648 to +2,147,483,647	An integer value without any decimals
Bigint	−9,223,372,036,854,775,808 to +9,223,372,036,854,775,807	An integer value without any decimals
SmallMoney	−214,748.3648 to +214,748.3647	Four decimals are set
Money	−922,337,203,685,477.5808 to +922,337,203,685,477.5807	Four decimals are set
Numeric	−10^38 (then subtract one) to +10^38 (then subtract one)	You must specify the precision and scale (total allowable numbers and numbers after the decimal)
Decimal	−10^38(then subtract one) to +10^38 (then subtract one)	You must specify the precision and scale (total allowable numbers and numbers after the decimal)

Data Type	Range	Comments
Float	–1.79E+308 to –2.23E–308, 0 and 2.23E–308 to 1.79E+308	Potentially huge numbers—but not stored precisely
Real	–3.40E +38 to –1.18E – 38, 0 and 1.18E –38 to 3.40E +38	Potentially huge numbers— but not stored precisely

Table 17.1: Numeric Data Types

'You may be wondering why there are so many numeric data types—especially for integers. The reasons are largely a question of the space that data can take up on disk and in memory. Put simply, if a field uses a data type that can contain the maximum value that will ever be stored in that field, it will take up less space. It will also make fetching data from disk into memory faster.

This means that database designers nearly always try and use appropriate numeric data types so that databases run faster and cost less to maintain. It is as simple as that.

Originally this was because disk storage and main memory were extremely expensive. Now, despite ever-lower hardware costs, the exponential growth of data means that it is still important to choose appropriate numeric data types when designing and building databases.

Tricks and Traps

Handling numeric data types can require a little practice. So here are a few essential points to help you:

- When casting numeric data to an integer data type, you must `always` use an integer type that can hold the largest value that you are converting to an integer. So, for example, if the field that you want to cast contains values in the millions, you cannot use the SmallInt data type since it only goes up to 32,767. This data type physically cannot store a larger value. Indeed, if you try a data type conversion on a field that contains values that are simply too large for the destination data type to hold, then SQL Server refuses to display any output and only shows an error message.

- When casting numbers (or texts that can be converted to numbers, as you discover in the following section) to the Numeric or Decimal data types, you should specify the total allowable numbers (including decimals) as well as the number of decimal places.

So, for instance, the following code

```
CAST(COST AS NUMERIC(10,2))
```

- converts the contents of the Cost field to the numeric data type. It allows a maximum value of 99999999.99—ten figures in all, and two decimal places.

- You should only convert to the Float or Real data type if your calculations do not require total accuracy. These data types can handle extremely large values, but they do not necessarily restitute the number that they contain completely accurately, so I do not advise you to use them for business or financial calculations. Remember that these data types were specifically designed for scientific data analysis where precision is less important.

- The CAST() function is very powerful, but it can be rather picky about the data that it converts. If a field that you are trying to convert using CAST() contains a text or a number that cannot be converted (whatever the reason) then the `whole query fails to work`.

17.6 Handling Source Data Where Figures Are Stored as Text

The sales director has been using a spreadsheet to juggle some data and has then had it loaded into SQL Server by the Prestige Cars IT department. You now have to query that data. However, all the figures have been saved as strings of text—and not always cleanly. This can make handling the data trickier than it needs to be. The following SQL helps you work around this kind of issue by converting texts to numbers wherever possible:

```
SELECT      CountryName
            ,MakeName
            ,TRY_CAST(Cost AS NUMERIC(20,4)) AS Cost
            ,TRY_CAST(SalePrice AS NUMERIC(20,4)) AS SalePrice
FROM        SourceData.SalesText
```

Running this query gives the results that you can see in *Figure 17.7*.

	CountryName	MakeName	Cost	SalePrice
1	France	Ferrari	NULL	255950.0000
2	France	Ferrari	NULL	310000.0000
3	France	Ferrari	NULL	269500.0000
4	France	Ferrari	NULL	395000.0000
5	France	Ferrari	NULL	155000.0000
6	France	Ferrari	NULL	365000.0000
7	United Kingdom	Ferrari	132000.0000	165000.0000
8	United Kingdom	Ferrari	176000.0000	220000.0000
9	United States	Ferrari	127600.0000	159500.0000
10	United States	Ferrari	200000.0000	250000.0000
11	United States	Ferrari	156000.0000	195000.0000
12	United Kingdom	Ferrari	125200.0000	156500.0000
13	United Kingdom	Ferrari	82360.0000	102950.0000
14	United Kingdom	Ferrari	124000.0000	155000.0000
15	United Kingdom	Ferrari	164000.0000	205000.0000

Figure 17.7: Using the TRY_CAST() function to convert text to numeric values

How It Works

This example uses a table of data that is new to you. This is the SalesText table that I am introducing to make the point that not all the data that you will have to deal with will be perfect. In this example, the original data in the table SalesText really looks like the output shown in *Figure 17.8*.

	CountryName	MakeName	Cost	SalePrice
1	France	Ferrari	2 000,00 USD	255950.00
2	France	Ferrari	2 000,00 USD	310000.00
3	France	Ferrari	2 000,00 USD	269500.00
4	France	Ferrari	2 000,00 USD	395000.00
5	France	Ferrari	2 000,00 USD	155000.00

Figure 17.8: Invalid numeric data that cannot be converted "as is" to a numeric value

As you can see, the Cost field contains spaces as well as currency units. These make it impossible for SQL Server to convert the underlying values to numbers.

Nonetheless, SQL Server can help you deal with situations like this. In these cases, you can use the TRY_CAST() function to convert strings that are composed of numbers into numeric values where this is technically possible. Unlike the CAST()

function, the TRY_CAST() function does not cause the entire query to fail if a string cannot be successfully converted to a number. Instead it returns a **NULL** in the place of the unusable source data.

To prove this point, try executing the following code snippet where TRY_CAST() has been replaced by CAST():

```
SELECT      CountryName

            ,MakeName

            ,CAST(Cost AS NUMERIC(20,4)) AS Cost

            ,CAST(SalePrice AS NUMERIC(20,4)) AS SalePrice

FROM        SourceData.SalesText
```

All that happens is that you see an error message saying

```
Msg 8114, Level 16, State 5, Line 1
Error converting data type varchar to numeric.
```

As you can see, using TRY_CAST() is an extremely practical way of dealing with imperfect data.

Tricks and Traps

I have only one comment to make here:

- Converting invalid source data is a vast subject and one that is outside the scope of a book such as this one. TRY_CAST() merely helps your query to function; it does not solve the underlying bad data problem. When faced with complex data that causes SQL to choke, you are probably best advised to have the data converted by IT professionals.

17.7 Converting Formatted Source Data into Useable Numbers

After you complained that the data that you were given was not usable, the sales director had the IT department process his spreadsheet so that SQL Server can read it. Unfortunately, it left the currency symbols in the numeric fields. If you want to glance back at Figure 17.7, you will see the original data. The good news is that SQL Server can handle this without any real difficulty, as you can see from the following code snippet:

```
SELECT      MakeName

            ,ModelName

            ,PARSE(VehicleCost AS money USING 'EN-GB') AS VehicleCost
```

```
FROM        SourceData.SalesInPounds
```

Running this query gives the results that you can see in *Figure 17.9*.

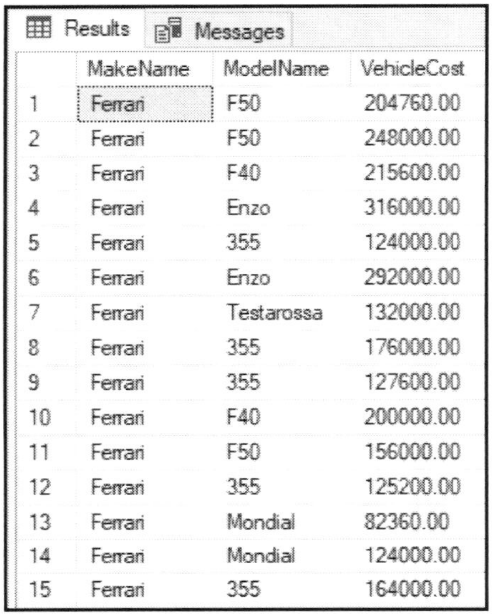

	MakeName	ModelName	VehicleCost
1	Ferrari	F50	204760.00
2	Ferrari	F50	248000.00
3	Ferrari	F40	215600.00
4	Ferrari	Enzo	316000.00
5	Ferrari	355	124000.00
6	Ferrari	Enzo	292000.00
7	Ferrari	Testarossa	132000.00
8	Ferrari	355	176000.00
9	Ferrari	355	127600.00
10	Ferrari	F40	200000.00
11	Ferrari	F50	156000.00
12	Ferrari	355	125200.00
13	Ferrari	Mondial	82360.00
14	Ferrari	Mondial	124000.00
15	Ferrari	355	164000.00

Figure 17.9: Using the PARSE() function

How It Works

Although not strictly a calculation, making numeric data usable by SQL Server is often a prerequisite to performing math on the data. This is where the PARSE() function can prove invaluable. It can remove formatting from numbers and convert them to valid numeric values.

The PARSE() function requires you to enter (or `pass in`, as the geeks say) three elements:

First:	The field that you want to strip the formatting from.
Second:	The AS keyword followed by the numeric data type that you want to convert the values to.
Third:	The USING keyword and the cultural specification that lets the PARSE() function accurately guess how to handle the formatting elements. In this example, the culture specification is 'EN-GB'. This means that the formatting is in the British English numeric style. Consequently, the decimal point is a period, the thousands separator is a comma, and the currency symbol is the UK pounds sign "£."

To give you a better idea of what this function has done, take a look at the source data in *Figure 17.10*.

Figure 17.10: *Formatted data that can be converted by the PARSE() function*

As you can see, the result of using the PARSE() function is that the currency symbol is stripped out and any decimal or thousands separator is recognized. Finally, only the number is left.

Tricks and Traps

PARSE() is a powerful function, but it does require you to be aware of the following points:

- The PARSE() function only works if the field that you want to convert is text (or a string, if you prefer).

- Sometimes the source data cannot be converted to a number despite SQL Server's best efforts. If this happens, you can rewrite the PARSE() function like this:

```
TRY_PARSE(VehicleCost AS money USING 'EN-GB')
```

This prevents the entire query from failing with an annoying error message. Instead, any source values that cannot be parsed appear as NULLs in the output. Source values that can be converted will be output in the required numeric data type.

- There are many, many culture specifications that PARSE() recognizes as defining the type of numeric formatting. These are simply too voluminous to list here. I suggest that you search online for the reference that matches the data format that you have to use.

17.8 Avoiding Divide-by-Zero Errors

The people in the Finance department really love their ratios. This time they want to see what the multiple of the cost of parts is when compared to the cost of each vehicle in stock. Happy to oblige, as ever, you use the following SQL:

```
SELECT      MD.ModelName
            ,ST.Cost
            ,CASE
                WHEN ST.PartsCost != 0 THEN ST.Cost / ST.PartsCost
                ELSE 0
            END AS PartsCostMultiple
FROM        Data.Stock ST
            INNER JOIN Data.Model MD
            ON ST.ModelID = MD.ModelID
```

Running this query gives the results that you can see in *Figure 17.11*.

	ModelName	Cost	PartsCost Multiple
1	Testarossa	52000.00	34.6666
2	355	176000.00	80.00
3	911	15600.00	0.00
4	924	9200.00	12.2666
5	944	15960.00	31.92
6	Testarossa	176000.00	55.873
7	DB4	23600.00	31.4666
8	DB5	39600.00	26.40
9	DB6	60800.00	81.0666
10	Testarossa	172000.00	1146.6666
11	911	15680.00	31.36
12	DB5	29200.00	58.40
13	944	6800.00	30.2222
14	DB6	36000.00	48.00
15	Flying Spur	64400.00	85.8666

Figure 17.11: Using CASE statements to handle divide-by-zero errors

How It Works

At its heart, this query is straightforward. It joins the Stock and Make tables so that you can access the Make name and vehicle cost elements. Then it divides the Cost field by the PartsCost field.

However, at least one record has a zero as the parts cost. This, unfortunately, is a problem for SQL Server, as it prevents any data from being returned and instead causes the following error message to appear:

```
Divide by zero error encountered
```

This is, to put it mildly, a pain. However, it can be handled using a CASE statement. What this does is

First:	Test the contents of the PartsCost field. If the field contains anything other than a zero, it divides the Cost field by the PartsCost field.
Otherwise:	It returns a zero and does not calculate anything, because this would be a division by zero, which is what we are trying to avoid.

Take a look at the third record in Figure 17.10; this shows zero for the parts cost multiple. This is the record that has a zero in the PartsCost field—or it is one of them, at least. In any case, the calculation now works perfectly, and you can hand your results to the people in Finance.

Tricks and Traps

You can apply many techniques to avoid divide-by-zero errors. You may also want to note that

- You can also use the IIF() function to handle divide-by-zero errors. For this particular example, the code is

```
IIF(PartsCost != 0,  ST.Cost / ST.PartsCost, 0 ) AS
PartsCostMultiple
```

17.9 Finding the Remainder in a Division Using the Modulo Function

The marketing director's latest idea has left you speechless. She wants you to generate a list of clients who will receive a letter saying that they have won a special customer discount on their next purchase of a classic sports car. She insists that this process must produce a list of around one third of the client base.

Once you have recovered from your bemusement at all things concerning marketing wizardry, you write the following code:

```
SELECT    CustomerID
FROM
    (
    SELECT    CustomerID
              ,CustomerID % 3 AS ModuloOutput
              ,CASE
                  WHEN CustomerID % 3 = 1 THEN 'Winner'
```

```
                    ELSE NULL

              END AS LuckyWinner

   FROM         Data.Customer

   ) Rnd

WHERE         LuckyWinner IS NOT NULL
```

Running this query gives the results that you can see in *Figure 17.12.*

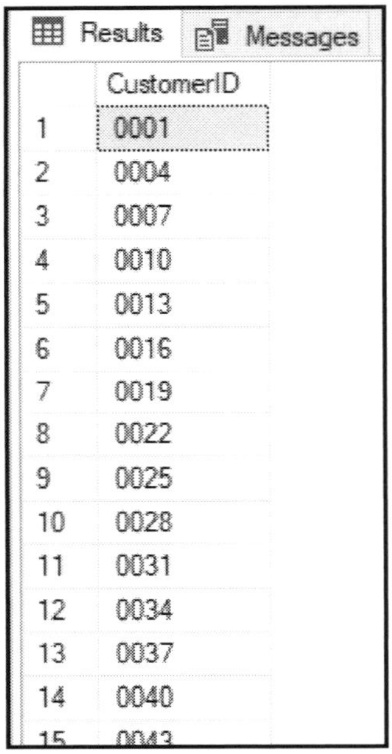

Figure 17.12: Using the modulo function to return the remainder in a calculation

How It Works

As befits a language that can carry out basic math, SQL can calculate the remainder after dividing one number by another. This is called a `modulo` operation, and SQL Server calls the function that carries out this calculation the modulo operator.

What happens is

First:	A field is defined that contains a numeric value. In this example, it is the CustomerID field.
Then:	The modulo operator (%) is added after the field name.
Finally:	The value that you are dividing the field by is added.

So, the key part of this code is

```
CustomerID % 3
```

However, as merely finding the remainder is of little practical interest, a small amount of logic is added to the calculation. What this logic does is to say, "if the remainder is 1, then flag the record." The logical selection is then used as a subquery so that only winning records are returned in the final output.

To make this clearer, take a look at *Figure 17.13* where you can see the output from the subquery. This illustrates how the modulo function displays the remainder of a calculation and also shows the output from the CASE statement for every record.

Results | Messages

	CustomerID	ModuloOutput	LuckyWinner
1	0001	1	Winner
2	0002	2	NULL
3	0003	0	NULL
4	0004	1	Winner
5	0005	2	NULL
6	0006	0	NULL
7	0007	1	Winner
8	0008	2	NULL
9	0009	0	NULL
10	0010	1	Winner

Figure 17.13: *The modulo function applied to all records*

Tricks and Traps

A couple of interesting aspects to this example are

- The figure that is used by a modulo operator does not have to be a number, provided that the text value can be converted internally by SQL Server to a number.
- You do not have to display the modulo output in a calculation. We did it here to make the use of this operator clearer.

17.10 Creating Financial Calculations

"Money is expensive" is one of the finance director's recurring mantras. It would appear that he has devoted countless hours to developing spreadsheets that count the cost of unsold stock in the showroom. Now, unfortunately, he wants you to adapt his basic compound interest calculation to SQL so that your reports can show how much "dead metal" (to use the term he uses to describe unsold stock) actually costs the company.

To help you in your work he has added that

- You are to use a standard compound interest calculation.

- The interest is to be compounded monthly.

- The rate that he wants to apply is 0.75 percent per month.

- You are only to calculate interest when a vehicle was in stock for over two months.

- You only need to analyse vehicles that have been sold.

As a further hint, he has kindly emailed you the exact calculation that he wants you to apply. This is the one in *Figure 17.14*.

$$CI = K * \left(1 + \frac{P}{100} \right)^{t}$$

Figure 17.14: A compound interest calculation

In this formula

- CI is the compound interest (including the original capital value)

- K is the initial value

- P is the interest rate

- t is the number of periods

After some thought, you come up with the following SQL that shows not only the interest charge, but also the number of months in stock as well as the cost price and the total cost including interest for all cars sold.

```
SELECT
 InitialCost
,MonthsSincePurchase
,(InitialCost * POWER(1 + (0.75 / 100), MonthsSincePurchase))
- InitialCost AS InterestCharge
```

```
,InitialCost * POWER(1 + (0.75 / 100), MonthsSincePurchase)
 AS TotalWithInterest
FROM
(
   SELECT
   DATEDIFF(mm, SK.DateBought, SL.SaleDate) AS MonthsSincePurchase
   ,(SK.Cost + ISNULL(SK.PartsCost, 0) + SK.RepairsCost)
                  AS InitialCost
      FROM        Data.Stock SK
      INNER JOIN  Data.SalesDetails SD
                  ON SK.StockCode = SD.StockID
      INNER JOIN  Data.Sales SL
                  ON SL.SalesID = SD.SalesID
      WHERE       DATEDIFF(mm, SK.DateBought, SL.SaleDate) > 2
) SRC
```

Running this code snippet gives the result that you can see in *Figure 17.15*.

	InitialCost	Months Since Purchase	InterestCharge	Total With Interest
1	38000.00	23	7125.266000	45125.266000
2	7930.00	9	551.618730	8481.618730
3	130550.00	12	12246.503850	142796.503850
4	45075.00	29	10906.211775	55981.211775
5	40600.00	16	5155.875200	45755.875200
6	188650.00	8	11620.651350	200270.651350
7	11250.00	4	341.313750	11591.313750
8	153600.00	16	19505.971200	173105.971200
9	1725.00	11	147.770400	1872.770400
10	6522.00	11	558.700608	7080.700608
11	9210.00	5	350.597070	9560.597070

Figure 17.15: Calculating compound interest

How It Works

Creating complex calculations in SQL is a vast subject. Indeed, entire books and papers have been written on this subject. So, although I want to show you the basics of using SQL to handle intricate financial mathematics, I am not delving too profoundly into this subject.

Given that this challenge could be complex, I have started by breaking it down into two parts:

An inner query	That calculates the total cost of a vehicle by adding up the purchase cost, cost of spares, and any repair costs. This query then also determines the number of months between the purchase date and the sale date.
	This query uses the Stock, SalesDetails, and Sales tables to source the required information. Once the joins are in place, it adds a WHERE clause to restrict the output to vehicles where the time between purchase and sale is more than two months. The inner join between the Stock and SalesDetails tables ensures that only vehicles that have been sold are taken into consideration.
An outer query	That displays the two fields isolated by the inner query (InitialCost and MonthsSincePurchase). The outer query then uses these two fields as core elements in calculating the compound interest.

What is both interesting and new in this query is the compound interest calculation, so now you need to look at this in more detail.

Essentially you have applied a two-step process to calculating compound interest:

First:	Take the arithmetical formula and adapt it so that it can be read on a single line.
Second:	Convert the single-line formula to SQL.

Converting the formula from Figure 17.14 to a single line gives you the following:

$$CI = K * (1 + P/100)t$$

The SQL that delivers the compound interest (CI) takes the initial value (K) to be the purchase cost, cost of spares, and any repair costs. It then "hard-codes" the interest rate as 0.75 and divides by 100 to express it as a percentage. Finally it uses the POWER() function to apply the number of periods (t) as the exponent for the formula. The number of periods is, in fact, the number of months between purchase and sale.

The POWER() function takes two parameters:

First:	The base value you wish to raise to the power of the exponent (one plus the percentage interest rate in this example)
Second:	The exponent to apply (the number of months in this example)

As a final tweak, this calculation is applied a second time. Only on this occasion, the initial cost is subtracted from the compound interest to leave the actual interest amount. This way you can see the total cost as well as the interest.

This is, of course, only a simple example. Financial calculations can get much more complicated than this one. However, it is a starting point on which you can build to develop much more complex analyses if you need to.

Tricks and Traps

There is one idea that you can take away from this example:

- It is possible to write a query like this one without actually using a subquery; however, I feel that the improved simplification and increased clarity that a subquery brings to both the analysis and the coding make a subquery worth any extra effort.

17.11 Using a Tally Table to Produce a Sequential List of Numbers

The CFO has come with a request for you. He wants to be able to calculate the straight-line depreciation for any vehicle in stock. After a few minutes' thought, you come up with the following code:

```
SELECT                  RowNo AS PeriodNumber
                        ,Cost
                        ,Cost / 5 AS StraightLineDepreciation
                        ,Cost - ((Cost / 5) * RowNo) AS RemainingValue

FROM                    Data.Stock
CROSS APPLY
(
SELECT 1 AS RowNo
UNION ALL
SELECT 2
UNION ALL
SELECT 3
UNION ALL
SELECT 4
UNION ALL
SELECT 5
) Tally
WHERE                   StockCode =
                            'A2C3B95E-3005.4840.8CE3.A7BC5F9CFB5F'
```

Running this piece of code gives the result that you can see in *Figure 17.16.*

	PeriodNumber	Cost	StraightLineDepreciation	RemainingValue
1	1	176000.00	35200.00	140800.00
2	2	176000.00	35200.00	105600.00
3	3	176000.00	35200.00	70400.00
4	4	176000.00	35200.00	35200.00
5	5	176000.00	35200.00	0.00

Figure 17.16: Using a tally table to calculate straight-line depreciation

How It Works

Producing a depreciation table requires a sequence of time periods against which the series of amortization amounts can be calculated. However, SQL Server is not a spreadsheet where you can just enter a series of numbers to represent the time periods. You need another solution. The answer is a concept called a `tally table`. This is a recordset (it can be a table but does not have to be) that contains a series of numbers, generally starting from 1, that increment regularly and have no gaps in the series. This suite of numbers can then be used to create sets of records.

In the case of a depreciation table, the first thing that you need is a recordset that contains the number of records corresponding to the number of years over which the vehicle will be amortized. In this example, I presume that this is a five-year period, so a recordset containing five rows is created using a set of UNION queries. You can see this in the CROSS APPLY clause of the SQL. Running the code inside the CROSS APPLY clause produces the result that you can see in *Figure 17.17.*

	RowNo
1	1
2	2
3	3
4	4
5	5

Figure 17.17: The output from a tally table

Once you have the tally table, you can calculate the depreciation and the residual value of a specific car. Calculating the depreciation each year is as simple as dividing the cost of the vehicle by the number of years. Calculating the residual value means subtracting the accumulated depreciation each year from the cost. So, to work out the accumulated amortization amount, you multiply the depreciation amount by the number of years. This number is provided by the tally table; in effect, it takes the single record for the car cost and makes it into a table of five records by using a CROSS APPLY clause to multiply the number of records in the SELECT clause (one) by the number of records in the CROSS APPLY clause (all five of them). As a final, and necessary, flourish, the row number of the tally table is used as the multiplier to calculate the accumulated depreciation.

Tricks and Traps

I have only a few comments here:

- If you need to include a salvage cost in the calculation for the depreciation, you can subtract the salvage cost from the cost of the vehicle every time the Cost field is used.

- You will discover other ways to create a tally table in a later chapter.

- You can use tally tables in many situations to resolve otherwise seemingly impossible SQL issues. Although they may not be something that you use daily, they can be a valuable resource in certain circumstances.

17.12 Generating Completely Random Sample Output from a Dataset

The CEO wants to call up a handful of clients at random and ask them about the service that they have received from Prestige Cars. She asks you to produce a totally random list of sales with the relevant customers. It takes you just a few seconds to produce the following piece of SQL to satisfy her request.

```
SELECT      TOP 5 PERCENT *
FROM        Data.SalesByCountry
ORDER BY    NEWID()
```

Running this code delivers the results that you can see in *Figure 17.18.*

	CountryName	MakeName	ModelName	Cost	RepairsCost	PartsCost	TransportInCost	Color	SalePrice	LineItemDiscount	InvoiceNumber	SaleDate	CustomerName	SalesDetailsID
1	Germany	Porsche	924	9200.00	500.00	750.00	150.00	British Racing Green	11500.00	NULL	EURDE004	2015-02-16 08:00:00.000	WunderKar	4
2	United Kingdom	Porsche	924	13200.00	500.00	750.00	150.00	British Racing Green	16500.00	NULL	GBPGB068	2016-08-13 00:00:00.000	Peter McLuckie	74
3	United States	Porsche	911	14000.00	2000.00	500.00	150.00	British Racing Green	17500.00	NULL	USDUS041	2016-04-30 00:00:00.000	Jason B. Wight	44
4	France	Rolls Royce	Silver Seraph	79960.00	1490.00	750.00	750.00	Blue	99950.00	NULL	EURFR172	2017-07-01 18:26:00.000	Mme Anne Duport	198
5	United States	Aston Martin	DB6	90872.00	500.00	225.00	750.00	Night Blue	113590.00	NULL	USDUS284	2018-08-01 00:00:00.000	Jayden Jones	307
6	Germany	Ferrari	360	79600.00	500.00	750.00	750.00	Black	99500.00	500.00	EURDE043	2016-04-30 00:00:00.000	Glitz	46
7	France	Jaguar	XK120	47200.00	2000.00	750.00	550.00	Blue	59000.00	4500.00	EURFR311	2018-10-31 00:00:00.000	Casseroles Chromes	337
8	France	Ferrari	F50	248000.00	9250.00	7900.00	1950.00	Silver	310000.00	NULL	EURFR235	2018-03-15 00:00:00.000	Capots Reluisants S.A.	257
9	United Kingdom	Delorean	DMC 12	79600.00	1490.00	750.00	750.00	Night Blue	99500.00	NULL	GBPGB157	2017-05-22 11:18:00.000	Pierre Blanc	170
10	United Kingdom	Aston Martin	Vanquish	44000.00	500.00	150.00	550.00	Silver	55000.00	NULL	GBPGB088	2016-09-11 00:00:00.000	Magic Motors	95
11	United Kingdom	Jaguar	XK150	18392.00	390.00	150.00	150.00	Night Blue	22990.00	NULL	GBPGB017	2015-07-15 00:00:00.000	Alexei Tolstoi	18
12	United Kingdom	Aston Martin	DB2	50000.00	500.00	750.00	550.00	British Racing Green	62500.00	1250.00	GBPGB207	2018-01-02 00:00:00.000	Silver HubCaps	226
13	France	Delahaye	135	20400.00	1360.00	750.00	150.00	Dark Purple	25500.00	NULL	EURFR300	2018-09-15 00:00:00.000	Khader El Ghannam	324
14	United Kingdom	Aston Martin	DB4	45560.00	500.00	1500.00	550.00	Pink	56950.00	NULL	GBPGB210	2018-01-02 00:00:00.000	Clubbing Cars	229
15	France	Jaguar	XK120	15680.00	1360.00	150.00	150.00	Night Blue	19600.00	1250.00	EURFR091	2016-09-16 00:00:00.000	La Bagnole de Luxe	98
16	United Kingdom	Porsche	924	7160.00	360.00	750.00	150.00	Black	8950.00	950.00	GBPGB021	2015-09-15 10:00:00.000	Posh Vehicles Ltd	23
17	United Kingdom	Austin	Cambridge	18000.00	1360.00	750.00	150.00	Black	22500.00	NULL	GBPGB225	2018-02-13 00:00:00.000	Impress The Neighbours.Com	245
18	United States	Mercedes	250SL	18080.00	1360.00	500.00	150.00	Black	22600.00	500.00	USDUS179	2017-08-04 11:29:00.000	Screamin' Wheels	195

Figure 17.18: *Generating random output from a table using NEWID()*

How It Works

T-SQL has a function—NEWID()—that adds a 32.character unique alphanumeric identifier to a record. This string is guaranteed to be unique by SQL Server. Not only that, but its structure is completely random; that is, there is no sequence or order to the way that it is generated.

This query uses NEWID() to randomize data selection like this:

First:	You write a simple SELECT query to return data from the SalesByCountry view.
Then:	You add a NEWID() field to the output from a query to produce a completely random identifier. The NEWID() field does not have to be in the SELECT clause to be added to the dataset. Adding it to the ORDER BY clause still adds the field, but without it being visible; so by sorting the data using this field, you have a recordset in a random sort order.
Finally:	You add a TOP n PERCENT clause to the SELECT clause to output only the first few percent (5 percent in this example) of the recordset.

The final result is a random subset of data from a database.

Tricks and Traps

I have one comment to make about this technique:

- If you want to see what one of these unique identifier fields looks like, you can run code like the following snippet:

```
SELECT      NEWID()
FROM        Data.SalesByCountry
```

This gives the kind of result that you can see in *Figure 17.19*.

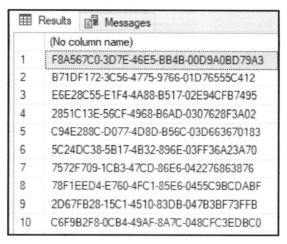

Figure 17.19: Generating unique identifiers using NEWID()

Conclusion

This chapter explained some of the techniques that you may need to use when carrying out more advanced calculations in SQL. These include handling data type conversions, managing divide-by-zero errors, and avoiding other circumstances where SQL can, potentially, prevent some calculations from working properly. You also learned more about numeric data types and how to convert numbers to numeric values when they are stored as text. Finally, you saw a few examples of how you can use SQL to carry out more complex calculations.

Core Knowledge Learned in This Chapter

The keywords that you have seen in this chapter are

Concept	Description
CAST()	The CAST() function is used to convert data types—where this is possible. It can convert a numeric data type to a different numeric data type or convert a string that is, in effect, a number, to a numeric data type.
TRY_CAST()	The TRY_CAST() function is also used to convert data types; however, it is less likely to cause an entire query to fail if a single value cannot be converted. Instead, it outputs a NULL in place of a value that cannot be converted.
PARSE()	The PARSE() function converts text (strings) that contains formatted numbers to numeric values without the formatting.
TRY_PARSE()	The TRY_PARSE() function also converts text (strings) that contains formatted numbers to numeric values without the formatting; however, it is less likely to cause an entire query to fail if a single value cannot be converted. Instead it outputs a NULL in place of a value that cannot be converted.
CROSS JOIN	Applies all the records returned by one query to another query without filtering the data.
CROSS APPLY	The CROSS APPLY operator carries out an operation on each row of the query using the elements defined in the CROSS APPLY subquery.
% (modulo)	The % function—called the modulo function—returns the remainder after dividing one value by another.
POWER()	POWER() is a math function used to raise one value to the power of another.
NEWID()	This function adds a 32.character unique alphanumeric identifier to a record.

Please note that you can also use the CAST(), TRY_CAST(), PARSE(), and TRY_PARSE() functions to convert (or attempt to convert) values to dates. Please see Chapter 20 for examples of using them with dates.

CHAPTER 18

Segmenting and Classifying Data

Selecting and filtering information can certainly help you reach a deep insight into your data, yet there are times when you really need to prioritize and classify lists of data in order to analyze the elements that really matter. In this chapter, you see how applying a few analytical functions can help you deliver real insight from your data. Indeed, this chapter will teach you a range of analytical techniques that can help you isolate the valuable information hidden inside your data. This can help both you and your organization stay one step ahead of the competition.

Ranking and Segmenting Data

SQL Server offers a useful set of functions that can help you when it comes to segmenting datasets. Specifically, it can

- Rank data according to a given criterion

- Break down recordsets into multiple segments

- Isolate the top or bottom elements in multiple data segments

- Return the top percentage of a recordset

- Determine median values

412 Querying SQL Server

Analyzing data in this way is a first step on the path to in-depth statistical analysis. We do not—rest assured—expect you to be an expert in statistics in order to use the SQL functions that you meet in this chapter. However, we hope that, as you learn how to slice and dice data in this chapter, you come to appreciate the power of SQL in data analysis.

18.1 Organizing Data by Rank

Turning data into information is what analysis is all about. In order to tailor your offering for your clients you need to see how individual sales compare. In fact, the sales director wants a list that shows sales per for 2018 with an indicator of their relative value. The following SQL can help you deliver this:

```
SELECT          CustomerName
                ,MakeName + ', ' + ModelName AS MakeAndModel
                ,SalePrice
                ,RANK() OVER (ORDER BY SalePrice DESC)
                        AS SalesImportance
FROM            Data.SalesByCountry
WHERE           YEAR(SaleDate) = 2018
ORDER BY        SalesImportance
```

Running this query gives the results that you can see in *Figure 18.1*. A figure that indicates the relative position of each sale shows the rank for each record.

	CustomerName	MakeAndModel	SalePrice	SalesImportance
1	La Bagnole de Luxe	Bugatti, 57C	365000.00	1
2	Andrea Tarbuck	Bugatti, 57C	355000.00	2
3	Bling Bling S.A.	Bugatti, 57C	345000.00	3
4	Capots Reluisants S.A.	Ferrari, F50	310000.00	4
5	Laurent Saint Yves	Ferrari, F40	269500.00	5
6	Kieran O'Harris	Lamborghini, Diabolo	255000.00	6
7	Smooth Rocking Chrome	Ferrari, Dino	195000.00	7
8	Stephany Rousso	Ferrari, F50	195000.00	7
9	Capots Reluisants S.A.	Bentley, Brooklands	189500.00	9
10	Sondra Horowitz	Rolls Royce, Phantom	182500.00	10
11	King Leer Cars	Ferrari, Mondial	155000.00	11
12	Antonio Maura	Lamborghini, 400GT	145000.00	12
13	Andy Cheshire	Ferrari, Daytona	145000.00	12
14	Smooth Rocking Chrome	Ferrari, 360	135000.00	14
15	El Sport	Ferrari, 360	128500.00	15

Figure 18.1. The RANK() function

How It Works

This query starts by joining all the tables that are required to let you display the CustomerName, Make, Model, and SalePrice fields, only it does this using the SalesByCountry view to save you from having to join all the tables. Then, once a WHERE clause has been added to filter on a specific year for sales, these fields are added to the SELECT clause. Then, as a final touch, the customers are clearly ranked by order of importance using a new function—RANK().

As its name implies, RANK() indicates where a row stands in a list of elements. We also used the RANK() function to sort the records so that you can see clearly what the relative importance of each row is. In this example we used the alias applied to the RANK() function in the ORDER BY clause to sort the data by rank without repeating the complete calculation.

However, the RANK() function needs to know how to classify the data that it will convert into an ordered hierarchy, so to set up a ranked dataset, you need the following elements at a minimum:

RANK()	This function tells SQL Server that you want to classify a dataset.
OVER	This keyword is compulsory and follows the RANK() keyword.
ORDER BY	This statement is added inside parentheses after the OVER keyword and you then add the field that will be used to "grade" the results.

In this example, the vehicle sale price is used as the basis for ranking the output. The final result is a list of sales ordered and ranked by value.

Tricks and Traps

The RANK() function can be a really powerful addition to your SQL toolkit; however, you need to be aware of the following points when using it:

- The RANK() function is one of a group of SQL functions that are known as the `windowing functions`. You will see many of these in both this chapter and the next.

- The ORDER BY clause in a windowing function works just like a standard SQL ORDER BY clause. You can use multiple fields separated by a comma, or add the ASC (for ascending) or DESC (for descending) keywords to tell SQL Server how to sort your data.

- It is not strictly necessary to add an alias for the column that displays the result of the RANK() function, but it helps make the output clearer. An added benefit of this approach is that it avoids you repeating teh entire RANK() function code inside the ORDER BY clause.

- Adding a RANK() function sorts the output data automatically.

18.2 Creating Multiple Groups of Rankings

Classifying product sales can be essential for an accurate understanding of which products sell best. At least that is what the CEO said when she requested a report showing sales for 2017 ranked in order of importance by make. The following short piece of SQL shows you how to look at the relative sales value of each model for each make of car:

```
SELECT       MK.MakeName + ', ' + MD.ModelName AS MakeAndModel
             ,SD.SalePrice
             ,RANK() OVER (PARTITION BY MakeName
                           ORDER BY SD.SalePrice DESC) AS
SalesImportance
FROM         Data.Make AS MK
INNER JOIN   Data.Model AS MD ON MK.MakeID = MD.MakeID
INNER JOIN   Data.Stock AS ST ON ST.ModelID = MD.ModelID
INNER JOIN   Data.SalesDetails SD ON ST.StockCode = SD.StockID
INNER JOIN   Data.Sales AS SA ON SA.SalesID = SD.SalesID
WHERE        YEAR(SA.SaleDate) = 2017
ORDER BY     MK.MakeName
```

Running this query gives the results that you can see in *Figure 18.2.*

	MakeAndModel	SalePrice	SalesImportance
1	Alfa Romeo, Giulia	25000.00	1
2	Alfa Romeo, Giulietta	21500.00	2
3	Alfa Romeo, Spider	12500.00	3
4	Alfa Romeo, Spider	11500.00	4
5	Alfa Romeo, Giulia	10500.00	5
6	Alfa Romeo, Giulietta	6500.00	6
7	Alfa Romeo, Spider	5650.00	7
8	Aston Martin, DB6	225000.00	1
9	Aston Martin, Virage	125000.00	2
10	Aston Martin, DB9	99500.00	3
11	Aston Martin, Rapide	99500.00	3
12	Aston Martin, Rapide	86500.00	5
13	Aston Martin, DB9	77500.00	6
14	Aston Martin, Vantage	66500.00	7
15	Aston Martin, DB2	61500.00	8

Figure 18.2: *Applying the PARTITION BY clause to a RANK() function*

How It Works

The core of this code snippet is the set of tables that allows you to access the MakeName, ModelName, SalePrice, and SaleDate fields. Once you have created the required dataset, you can then assemble a query that lists the fields that you need.

With the core elements of the query in place, you can add a RANK() function. As was the case in the previous example, you need the RANK() keyword, the OVER clause, and an ORDER BY statement with the field that you are using to prioritize the data.

This time you want to classify the output in a subtler way. Specifically, you want to grade each model of car, not compared to all the sales for the year, but relative to all models of the same make rather than relative to all sales for the year.

This is done—quite simply—by adding the PARTITION BY clause and a field name inside the parentheses that follow the OVER keyword. In this way, you are, in effect, telling SQL that you want to break the data down into subgroups by make of car. The PARTITION BY clause is, in effect, creating subgroups by make of vehicle. The ORDER BY clause then grades the records for each subgroup on the SalePrice field.

Tricks and Traps

When partitioning—or grouping datasets, if you prefer to think of it like that—you need to remain aware of a couple of key points:

- SQL Server can handle situations where there is a tie that occurs when data is ranked. What it does is give any tied rows the same ranking, and then it makes the next-lowest record two or more places lower. *Figure 18.3* shows you an example of this from further down the list.

	MakeAndModel	SalePrice	SalesImportance
13	Aston Martin, DB9	77500.00	6
14	Aston Martin, Vantage	66500.00	7
15	Aston Martin, DB2	61500.00	8
16	Aston Martin, Vanquish	56950.00	9
17	Aston Martin, Vanquish	56500.00	10
18	Aston Martin, DB9	56500.00	10
19	Aston Martin, DB9	56500.00	10
20	Aston Martin, Rapide	55000.00	13
21	Aston Martin, DB2	49500.00	14

Figure 18.3: *The effect of tied records when using the RANK() function*

- Most, if not all, of the time, you are likely to find yourself ranking data on a numeric field. You will nearly always partition data using a text field. This is not, however, inevitable, merely likely. You can just as easily partition on a numeric field and order on an alphabetical field.

18.3 Creating Multiple Ranked Groups and Subgroups

The finance director has realized that he does not yet know how to grade customers on a scale of profitability per sale, so he has requested an immediate report that shows the profit per vehicle sold ranked in order of importance by make per customer. After a little thought, you come to the conclusion that what he wants is a list of customers in which you can see which makes of vehicle each client bought and where the data is ranked by customer, make and profit. The following SQL query uses a windowing function and a CTE (Common Table Expression) to deliver this essential piece of analysis:

```
;
WITH
AllSalesProfit_CTE (CustomerName, MakeName, ModelName, SalePrice,
ProfitPerModel)
AS
(
SELECT      CustomerName, MakeName, ModelName
            ,SalePrice
            ,((SalePrice -
                (Cost + ISNULL(RepairsCost,0)
                + PartsCost + TransportInCost))
            / SalePrice) * 100
FROM        Data.SalesByCountry
)


SELECT      CustomerName, MakeName, ModelName, ProfitPerModel, SalePrice
            ,RANK() OVER
                    (PARTITION BY CustomerName, MakeName
                    ORDER BY ProfitPerModel DESC) AS SalesImportance
FROM        AllSalesProfit_CTE
ORDER BY    CustomerName, MakeName, SalesImportance
```

Running this query gives the results that you can see in *Figure 18.4.*

	CustomerName	MakeName	ModelName	ProfitPerModel	SalePrice	SalesImportance
1	Alex McWhirter	Jaguar	XJ12	9.523809523809524	17850.00	1
2	Alexei Tolstoi	Aston Martin	Virage	15.682926829268293	102500.00	1
3	Alexei Tolstoi	Aston Martin	DB6	14.618705035971223	69500.00	2
4	Alexei Tolstoi	Ferrari	355	14.170731707317073	205000.00	1
5	Alexei Tolstoi	Jaguar	XK150	16.998695084819487	22990.00	1
6	Alexei Tolstoi	Jaguar	XJS	13.097345132743363	22600.00	2
7	Alexei Tolstoi	Jaguar	E-Type	11.645569620253165	39500.00	3
8	Alexei Tolstoi	Jaguar	XJS	5.929648241206030	9950.00	4
9	Alexei Tolstoi	Porsche	911	15.059847660500544	45950.00	1
10	Alexei Tolstoi	Triumph	GT6	-20.000000000000000	3500.00	1
11	Alicia Almodovar	Alfa Romeo	Giulietta	-4.604569420035149	5690.00	1
12	Alicia Almodovar	Aston Martin	DB6	16.082698585418934	45950.00	1
13	Alicia Almodovar	Ferrari	Testarossa	18.140000000000000	250000.00	1
14	Alicia Almodovar	Porsche	959	16.075949367088608	39500.00	1
15	Alicia Almodovar	Porsche	928	12.789968652037618	15950.00	2

Figure 18.4: *Combining a CTE with a RANK() function to create multiple ranked groups and subgroups*

How It Works

This piece of code is in two parts:

First:	A CTE that calculates the net profit for every car sold.
Finally:	A query that uses the data from the CTE to classify the output.

A CTE can help you define the key data that is required by the overall query. Although not absolutely necessary, it can help isolate the core data that you then use to categorize and hierarchize data. This example uses a CTE to define the essential data that is required. Once the essential data has been isolated using the SalesByCountry view as the data source, the relevant fields (Customer, Make, Model, and Profit) are output and a RANK() function is added to the final query that delivers the categorized output based on the recordset defined by the CTE.

If you think back to Chapter 14, you will remember that a CTE can be executed separately from the rest of the query. So if you select the SQL that is contained inside the CTE and execute it, you obtain the output that you can see in *Figure 18.5* (remember that the final column is aliased in the CTE header).

	CustomerName	MakeName	ModelName	SalePrice	(No column name)
1	Magic Motors	Ferrari	Testarossa	65000.00	13.192307692307692
2	Snazzy Roadsters	Ferrari	355	220000.00	15.613636363636364
3	Birmingham Executive Prestige Vehicles	Porsche	911	19500.00	15.846153846153846
4	WunderKar	Porsche	924	11500.00	7.826086956521739
5	Casseroles Chromes	Porsche	944	19950.00	9.924812030075188
6	Magic Motors	Aston Martin	DB4	29500.00	15.254237288135593
7	Birmingham Executive Prestige Vehicles	Aston Martin	DB5	49500.00	10.808080808080808
8	Eat My Exhaust Ltd	Aston Martin	DB6	76000.00	13.750000000000000
9	M. Pierre Dubois	Porsche	911	19600.00	12.142857142857143
10	Sondra Horowitz	Aston Martin	DB5	36500.00	11.780821917808219

Figure 18.5: CTE output to be used in a ranking query

This dataset calculates sales figures and profit per sale, so it can be used in the final query to group and rank the records by customer and make.

A couple of aspects of this query make it a little subtler than the previous two that you have seen.

First:	The output is ranked by customer and make. As you can see, the PARTITION BY clause (rather like an ORDER BY clause) can specify multiple fields. All the fields that you use in the PARTITION BY clause must be commA.separated.
Second:	You can override the sort order that is provided by the RANK() function by adding a standard ORDER BY clause in the final query. In this example, the ORDER BY clause is applied to guarantee that the final output is both clear and comprehensible.

Tricks and Traps

We have a couple of remarks to make about using CTEs when ranking datasets:

- You could just as easily use a derived table instead of a CTE. The two techniques are essentially interchangeable, and the approach that you choose is largely a matter of personal preference.

- If the query inside the CTE does not have column names, then you must add names to the output fields inside parentheses at the top of the CTE after the CTE name.

18.4 Filtering Data by Ranked Items

Buyer psychology is a peculiar thing. To better understand Prestige Cars' clients, the sales director has decided that she wants to find the bestselling make for each color of vehicle sold. The following short SQL snippet gives you this information:

```
SELECT      Color, MakeName
FROM
            (
            SELECT       DISTINCT MK.MakeName, Color
                         ,RANK() OVER (PARTITION BY MakeName
                                        ORDER BY SD.SalePrice DESC)
                                        AS ColorRank
            FROM        Data.Make AS MK
            INNER JOIN  Data.Model AS MD
                        ON MK.MakeID = MD.MakeID
            INNER JOIN  Data.Stock AS ST
                        ON ST.ModelID = MD.ModelID
            INNER JOIN  Data.SalesDetails SD
                        ON ST.StockCode = SD.StockID
            ) SQ
WHERE       ColorRank = 1
ORDER BY MakeName
```

Running this query gives the results that you can see in *Figure 18.6*.

	Color	MakeName
1	Black	Alfa Romeo
2	Black	Aston Martin
3	Night Blue	Austin
4	Blue	Bentley
5	Black	BMW
6	Red	Bugatti
7	Blue	Citroen
8	Night Blue	Delahaye
9	Night Blue	Delorean
10	British Racing Green	Ferrari
11	Canary Yellow	Jaguar
12	Blue	Lagonda
13	Green	Lamborghini
14	Silver	McLaren
15	Canary Yellow	Mercedes

Figure 18.6: *Filtering on the results of a RANK() function in a subquery*

How It Works

This query works by breaking down the problem into its two constituent parts, the better to answer the question that is asked.

First:	A derived table joins all the required tables to produce a list of sales that displays only the make, color, sale price, and the hierarchy of each color sold per make using the RANK() function. The OVER clause specifies that the data is partitioned (grouped, if you prefer) by make of car and the value used to rank the data is the selling price.
Finally:	The outer query returns the make, color, and sale price of each car if —and only if—it is ranked first for each make. The outer query does this by applying a WHERE clause to the output from the derived table so that only records where the rank equals 1 are allowed through to the final data set.

To make this clearer, *Figure 18.7* shows a few of the records from the data that is returned by the derived table to the outer query.

	MakeName	Color	ColorRank
16	Alfa Romeo	Green	5
17	Alfa Romeo	Night Blue	4
18	Alfa Romeo	Night Blue	9
19	Alfa Romeo	Night Blue	19
20	Alfa Romeo	Red	14
21	Aston Martin	Black	1
22	Aston Martin	Black	5
23	Aston Martin	Black	6
24	Aston Martin	Black	9
25	Aston Martin	Black	24
26	Aston Martin	Black	26
27	Aston Martin	Black	28

Figure 18.7: Grouping and classifying data using the RANK() function

This output shows you that the derived table has, effectively, classified sales by color for each make. Then the outer query simply discards most of the data that the derived table has returned so that only the top-ranked records for each make are displayed.

Tricks and Traps

There are a couple of points worth noting at this juncture:

- Remember that you `have to add an alias` to all columns that are used in a derived table. This is required by SQL itself and not just because you are using the output of the RANK() function to filter data. If you forget to add an alias to a column, you get an error message.

- You could have just as easily used a CTE instead of a derived table to perform the initial ranking of the data. It is entirely up to you which you prefer to use.

18.5 Classifying Data by Strict Order of Rank

Segmenting data in order to deliver real insight is what SQL is all about. Management now wants you to push the envelope and perform a more complex analysis of the Prestige Cars' sales data by finding the ten highest-selling sales values but only when these cars belong to the category of the five bestselling colors by quantity sold. The SQL that does this is slightly longer than some of the code snippets that you have seen so far; however, it is definitely worth a closer look:

```
SELECT      Color, MakeAndModel, SalesImportance
FROM
(
SELECT      ST.Color, MK.MakeName + ', ' + MD.ModelName AS MakeAndModel
            ,SD.SalePrice
            ,DENSE_RANK() OVER (ORDER BY SD.SalePrice DESC)
                    AS SalesImportance
FROM        Data.Make AS MK
INNER JOIN  Data.Model AS MD ON MK.MakeID = MD.MakeID
INNER JOIN  Data.Stock AS ST ON ST.ModelID = MD.ModelID
INNER JOIN  Data.SalesDetails SD ON ST.StockCode = SD.StockID
INNER JOIN
            (
            SELECT TOP (5)  ST.Color, COUNT(*) AS NumberOfSales
            FROM            Data.Stock AS ST
            INNER JOIN      Data.SalesDetails SD
                            ON ST.StockCode = SD.StockID
            GROUP BY        ST.Color
```

```
ORDER BY        NumberOfSales
) CL
ON CL.Color = ST.Color
) RK
WHERE       SalesImportance <= 10
ORDER BY    SalesImportance
```

Running this query gives the results that you can see in *Figure 18.8.*

	Color	MakeAndModel	SalesImportance
1	Green	Lamborghini, Jarama	1
2	Dark Purple	Ferrari, F40	2
3	Green	Ferrari, F50	3
4	Green	Ferrari, Testarossa	3
5	Green	Rolls Royce, Phantom	4
6	Dark Purple	Rolls Royce, Wraith	5
7	Night Blue	Ferrari, Testarossa	5
8	Green	Aston Martin, Vantage	6
9	Green	Aston Martin, Virage	6
10	Dark Purple	Ferrari, Dino	7
11	Green	Rolls Royce, Phantom	8
12	Night Blue	Aston Martin, DB6	9
13	Pink	Aston Martin, Virage	10

Figure 18.8: *Using the DENSE_RANK() function to classify items*

How It Works

Sometimes an analytical request can seem more complicated than it really is. However, if you break the problem down into its component parts, then it can prove to be easier than you think. This query is case in point. Let's look more closely at what is required and then see how SQL can provide the information that you want to extract from the data.

Top five by color	First you need to isolate the five bestselling colors by quantity. This has to be done first, as it restricts the data only to those vehicles whose color is one of the five bestselling colors.
Top ten bestselling	Then you need to find the bestselling cars that make up the ten best sales by value if the vehicle color is one of the five bestselling colors.

Getting this query right requires a nested derived table inside a derived table. Let's begin at the lowest level of the query—the inner derived table that deduces the five bestselling colors by quantity.

The inner derived table finds the five bestselling colors by joining the Stock and SalesDetails tables and then by counting the number of sales per color. Then it selects only the top five records, giving you the list of the five bestselling colors. If you select the query that makes up the inner derived table (the one that is aliased as CL), you see something like the data in *Figure 18.9*.

Figure 18.9: Using a derived table to filter a subset of elements that are passed up to an outer query

Once you have the list of colors that make up the five bestselling colors, you can build the "core" query that returns the make and model of car sold along with its color, the sale price, and the ranking of the sale relative to the selling prices of all vehicles sold. The inner derived table is used in the outer derived table's JOIN clause to filter the colors so that only the five returned by the inner query are used in the outer query. If you select this query (which includes the inner derived table, aliased as RK), you see something like the data in *Figure 18.10*.

Figure 18.10: A derived table that filters data based on an inner derived table

Once you have a list of all the sales of cars in a ranked dataset, it is easy to add the final step. This consists of using this derived table as the data source for the outermost query where you select only those cars whose rank is 10 or less. This is done in the WHERE clause that says, "WHERE SalesImportance <= 10". An ORDER BY clause is added as a final tweak to present that data in an order that visually enhances the result by sorting the output in ascending sequence of sales importance.

Notice that this SQL uses the DENSE_RANK() function rather than the RANK() function. The two are virtually identical but have one vital difference. You saw in previous examples that the RANK() function skips numbers if there is a tie. The DENSE_RANK() function does not do this and continues the numbering sequentially. This way, you are sure to get the top ten sales values—even if there are duplicate values for some sales. This is why the final output shows thirteen records when you only asked for the top ten. This is because there are only ten distinct top-selling prices, but these represent thirteen different sales since there can always be more than one sale at the same price.

Tricks and Traps

A query as complex as this one inevitably means that there will be a few key points to take away:

- This query could also be solved by nesting the inner derived table inside a CTE and then using the output from the CTE for the final query. Once again, how you solve it is simply a question of personal preference.

- The inner derived table can be used by the outer derived table either in a JOIN with the outer query (as is the case here) or in a WHERE clause. Either of these approaches gives the same result.

- You might be tempted to use a TOP 10 clause in the outer derived table to get the top ten sales. However, this might not give you exactly the top ten values. This is because TOP n merely returns a specified number of rows. In the case of this query, it is perfectly possible that the top ten values could represent eleven or more sales. Only showing the TOP 10 would not exactly answer the question since it might not display a full ten `values`, just ten `records`.

18.6 Segment Data into Deciles

While we are still exploring the area of data classification, suppose that the sales director wants to group sales by sale price into `deciles`— that is "`buckets`" of equal size where each group of data contains one tenth of the records in the total dataset. The top decile will contain the most expensive cars, the second decile the next most expensive cars and so on. The following SQL does this for you:

```
SELECT      ST.Color, MK.MakeName + ', ' + MD.ModelName AS MakeAndModel
            ,SD.SalePrice
            ,NTILE(10) OVER (ORDER BY SD.SalePrice DESC) AS
SalesDecile
FROM        Data.Make AS MK
INNER JOIN  Data.Model AS MD ON MK.MakeID = MD.MakeID
INNER JOIN  Data.Stock AS ST ON ST.ModelID = MD.ModelID
INNER JOIN  Data.SalesDetails SD ON ST.StockCode = SD.StockID
ORDER BY    SalesDecile, ST.Color, MakeAndModel
```

Running this query gives the results that you can see in *Figure 18.11.* You have to scroll down the result to see how the SalesDecile field changes every 35 records or so.

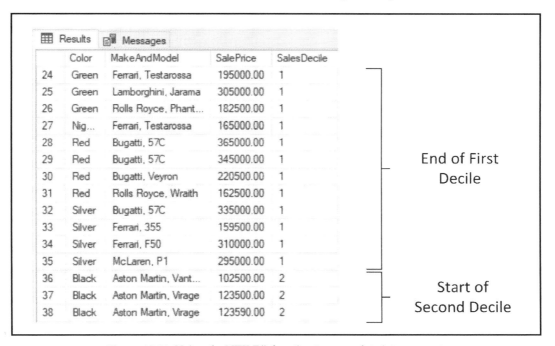

Figure 18.11: Using the NTILE() function to group data into segments

How It Works

You can see from the output that this query has added a field that indicates the decile (or segment, or bucket, if you prefer) that each record belongs to. You can then use this segmentation to pursue your analysis.

This query delivers an easy solution to a potentially complex question—all thanks to the NTILE() function. What this windowing function does is segment the dataset into as many separate subgroups as you have specified when you apply the function. Quite simply, the figure that you place inside the function defines the number of data "buckets" that you want to create. Whatever the number of records in the dataset, the NTILE() function subdivides them into the number of groups that you specify as a parameter of the function.

This query is, at its heart, a simple SELECT query where you joined the necessary tables and selected the required fields. Then you added a final field using the NTILE() function.

Just like the RANK() and DENSE_RANK() functions, the NTILE() function requires you to add the OVER keyword and an ORDER BY clause inside parentheses— in addition to a value that is used for classifying the data. The NTILE() function requires one further element—the number of "buckets" that you want to appear in the output. This is defined by adding a number inside the parentheses just after the NTILE() function. The number that you add is the number of groups into which the dataset will be divided.

Tricks and Traps

We have only one comment to make here:

- NTILE() can also contain a PARTITION BY clause to add a further level of segmentation should you need it. It works exactly as it does for the RANK() function as you saw in previous sections.

18.7 Plot Values for a Percentile

SQL can be particularly useful when it comes to teasing out meaning from statistics. At least, that is what the sales director seems to believe, since she has come to you with this request: provide her with a dataset that contains the total cost for vehicles for each cost percentile and the corresponding repair cost. She wants to use this to create a chart that displays any potential correlation between the cost of a car and its repair cost.

```
;
WITH PercentileList_CTE
AS
(
SELECT     RepairsCost
           ,Cost
           ,NTILE(100) OVER (ORDER BY Cost DESC) AS Percentile
```

```
FROM        Data.Stock
)
SELECT      Percentile
            ,SUM(Cost) AS TotalCostPerPercentile
            ,SUM(RepairsCost) AS RepairsCostPerPercentile
               ,SUM(RepairsCost) / SUM(Cost) AS RepairCostRatio
FROM        PercentileList_CTE
GROUP BY    Percentile
ORDER BY    RepairCostRatio DESC
```

Execute this code snippet and you obtain the results that you can see in *Figure 18.12*.

	Percentile	TotalCostPerPercentile	RepairsCostPerPercentile	RepairCostRatio
1	100	1520.00	1000.00	0.6578
2	99	2312.00	1500.00	0.6487
3	98	2840.00	1500.00	0.5281
4	97	3080.00	1500.00	0.487
5	96	3748.00	1500.00	0.4002
6	95	6720.00	2000.00	0.2976
7	94	7480.00	2000.00	0.2673
8	93	8036.00	2000.00	0.2488
9	92	11320.00	2000.00	0.1766
10	91	13640.00	2000.00	0.1466
11	90	17600.00	2000.00	0.1136
12	89	18160.00	2000.00	0.1101
13	88	19560.00	2000.00	0.1022
14	72	42592.00	4190.00	0.0983
15	87	20912.00	2000.00	0.0956

Figure 18.12: Purchase cost versus repairs cost per percentile

How It Works

This piece of SQL is essentially in two stages:

A CTE	That attributes each sale to a percentile of sales. It also gives the repair cost for each sale. This CTE uses the NTILE() function and specifies that the function is to distribute the results over 100 groups, in effect segmenting the sales into percentiles.

A query	That aggregates the output from the CTE to obtain the total for each percentile.

The CTE produces the output that you can see in *Figure 18.13*.

Results | Messages

	RepairsCost	Cost	Percentile
1	2000.00	340000.00	1
2	9250.00	316000.00	1
3	3950.00	292000.00	1
4	9250.00	284000.00	1
5	9250.00	284000.00	2
6	5500.00	276000.00	2
7	2000.00	268000.00	2
8	9250.00	248000.00	2
9	3950.00	244000.00	3
10	5500.00	236000.00	3

Figure 18.13: *Attributing each sale to a percentile*

Once you have the percentile that each sale belongs to, it is simple to aggregate the output so that you are grouping the result on each percentile and using the SUM() function to return the total for sales and repair costs per percentile.

Tricks and Traps

It is well worth noting that

- Although SQL Server cannot generate charts, it can isolate the data that you can then copy and paste into a spreadsheet. Alternatively, you can connect many applications directly to a SQL Server database. Indeed, you can use SQL Server Management Studio (SSMS) to hone your queries and then copy the query into the application that you are using to display and/or analyze the data.
- If all you want is the output from a query for a spreadsheet, then simply click inside the output in SSMS and right-click. Select Copy with Headers from the context menu. You can then paste the entire table into a spreadsheet.
- Be careful when copying large result sets from SSMS into other applications. It is easy to forget that they can run to millions of records and prove too much for either the destination workstation or the capacity of the spreadsheet.

18.8 Extract Data from a Specific Quintile

Prestige Cars caters to a wide range of clients, and the sales director does not want to forget about the 80 percent that are outside the top 20 percent of customers. She wants you to take a closer look at the second quintile of customers—those making up the second 20 percent of sales. Her exact request is this: "Find the sales details for the top three selling makes in the second 20 percent of sales." Here is the SQL to do this:

```
;
WITH Top20PercentSales_CTE
AS
(
SELECT     SalesDetailsID, MK.MakeName, MD.ModelName, SD.SalePrice
           ,NTILE(5) OVER (ORDER BY SD.SalePrice DESC)
               AS SalesQuintile
FROM       Data.Make AS MK
INNER JOIN Data.Model AS MD ON MK.MakeID = MD.MakeID
INNER JOIN Data.Stock AS ST ON ST.ModelID = MD.ModelID
INNER JOIN Data.SalesDetails SD ON ST.StockCode = SD.StockID
)


SELECT     MakeName, ModelName, SalePrice
FROM       Top20PercentSales_CTE CTE
WHERE      MakeName IN (
                      SELECT   TOP 3 MakeName
                        FROM   Top20PercentSales_CTE
                      WHERE    SalesQuintile = 2
                      GROUP BY MakeName
                      ORDER BY SUM(SalePrice) DESC
                      )
ORDER BY   SalePrice DESC
```

Running this query gives the results that you can see in *Figure 18.14.*

	MakeName	ModelName	SalePrice
1	Aston Martin	DB6	225000.00
2	Bentley	Brooklands	189500.00
3	Rolls Royce	Phantom	182500.00
4	Rolls Royce	Wraith	165000.00
5	Rolls Royce	Wraith	162500.00
6	Rolls Royce	Silver Seraph	139500.00
7	Rolls Royce	Silver Shadow	135000.00
8	Aston Martin	Virage	125500.00
9	Aston Martin	Virage	125000.00
10	Aston Martin	Vantage	125000.00
11	Aston Martin	Virage	123590.00
12	Aston Martin	Virage	123500.00
13	Rolls Royce	Silver Seraph	120000.00
14	Rolls Royce	Phantom	119600.00
15	Aston Martin	DB6	113590.00

Figure 18.14. Using the NTILE() function to isolate a segment of data

How It Works

The ability to segment and classify your customers can make or break a business. This query shows you how to isolate a segment of sales data to produce exactly this kind of really useful information. The SQL in this example uses a CTE as the core of the query. The CTE uses the NTILE() function to list makes, models, and sale prices for all cars sold. Then it calculates the quintile for each sale.

Once the quintile has been defined, the subsequent query carries out two operations:

First:	It uses a subquery to isolate the top three makes belonging to the second quintile.
Then:	Once these makes have been found, the outer query outputs all sales for these makes from the CTE.

Tricks and Traps

Segmenting data can be a challenge—but an interesting one. Be sure to remember the following essential points when you have to deal with this kind of query:

- What is interesting here is that the CTE is used twice. The key technique is first to define the quintile, and then to select a specific quintile from the dataset. However, because the CTE also joins the tables required to list the make, model, and sale price, it can be `reused in the main query` so you don't have to rewrite all the SQL that is needed to produce this specific output.

• You can, of course, isolate deciles, percentiles—indeed any segment of data. All you have to do is enter the appropriate figure inside the parentheses that are part of the NTILE() function. For a `decile`, you would have entered the following SQL in the preceding example:

```
NTILE(10) OVER (ORDER BY SalePrice DESC) AS SalesDecile
```

18.9 Display Median Values

The CEO has a solid background in statistics and has just asked for a report that shows the difference between the median discount and the actual discount for all sales per customer. SQL can also isolate a median value from a dataset—as this piece of SQL shows:

```
SELECT      DISTINCT  CU.CustomerName
            ,SA.TotalSalePrice
            ,SA.TotalSalePrice - PERCENTILE_CONT(0.5)
            WITHIN GROUP(ORDER BY SA.TotalSalePrice)
                    OVER(PARTITION BY CU.CustomerName)
            AS SaleToMedianDelta
FROM        Data.Sales AS SA
INNER JOIN Data.Customer CU ON SA.CustomerID = CU.CustomerID
```

Running this query gives the results that you can see in *Figure 18.15*.

	CustomerName	TotalSalePrice	SaleToMedianDelta
1	Alex McWhirter	17850.00	0
2	Alexei Tolstoi	3500.00	-44200
3	Alexei Tolstoi	22600.00	-25100
4	Alexei Tolstoi	22990.00	-24710
5	Alexei Tolstoi	45950.00	-1750
6	Alexei Tolstoi	49450.00	1750
7	Alexei Tolstoi	69500.00	21800
8	Alexei Tolstoi	102500.00	54800
9	Alexei Tolstoi	205000.00	157300
10	Alicia Almodovar	5690.00	-10260
11	Alicia Almodovar	12500.00	-3450
12	Alicia Almodovar	15950.00	0
13	Alicia Almodovar	39500.00	23550
14	Alicia Almodovar	45950.00	30000
15	Alicia Almodovar	250000.00	234050

Figure 18.15: Displaying median values with the PERCENTILE_CONT() function

How It Works

There are times when you need to get a purely statistical answer from your data. Finding a median (rather than an average) value and comparing this to sales prices is one example of this. However, SQL does not have a median function in the same way that it has an AVG() function. Nonetheless, you can calculate a median using the built-in PERCENTILE_CONT() function. Finding a median value requires you to use the following SQL elements:

PERCENTILE_CONT(0.5)	The PERCENTILE_CONT() function finds a percentile in a dataset. Because you are looking for the median value, you need to indicate this by entering 0.5 inside the parentheses.
WITHIN GROUP	This lets you specify the numeric field that you want to extract the median value from. You also have to include the ORDER BY clause.
OVER (PARTITION BY)	As with the other windowing functions that you have seen in this chapter, PERCENTILE_CONT() allows you to segment the dataset into subgroups so that you can find the median value for each of the fields (or combinations of fields) that you specify after the PARTITION BY clause.

In this example, the query joins the Sales and Customer tables since they contain the fields that you need. Once the CustomerName and SalePrice fields have been selected, you add the clause required to extract the median value per customer and then subtract this from the sale price for each vehicle sold. In this case, this means specifying the SalePrice field for the WITHIN GROUP argument and partitioning by the CustomerName in the OVER clause.

Tricks and Traps

We have one important comment to make here:

- The result of the PERCENTILE_CONT() function is a calculated value and not an actual piece of data from the database.

Conclusion

This chapter introduced you to some of the ways that you can use SQL to segment and classify data. You saw how to deliver hierarchies of data that can also segment the output according to the criteria that you specify. You also saw how to subset data into deciles and quintiles that you can extract for further analysis.

Core Knowledge Learned in This Chapter

The keywords that you have seen in this chapter are

Concept	Description
RANK()	The RANK() function hierarchizes data according to the criterion that you define.
OVER	The OVER keyword is used by the RANK() function to introduce the ranking criteria
PARTITION BY	The PARTITION BY keyword is used by the RANK() function to separate the data into multiple hierarchies.
DENSE_RANK()	The DENSE_RANK() function hierarchizes data without any gaps in the ranking.
NTILE()	The NTILE() function distributes the rows in an ordered partition into a specified number of groups.
PERCENTILE_CONT()	The PERCENTILE_CONT() function is used (among other things) to calculate a median value.
WITHIN GROUP	The WITHIN GROUP keyword is used by the PERCENTILE_CONT() function to return a median value.

CHAPTER 19

Rolling Analysis

Few metrics exist in isolation. Most of the time, you not only want to compare these metrics with other figures, but you also want to see how they evolve over time. This lets you discern trends, track growth, and establish a solid factual base that you can use to make predictions.

Running Totals, Running Averages, Running Counts, and Comparative Values

SQL Server provides a range of functions that can help you show how data evolves over time—or, indeed, over any sequence or progression. These functions are both simple and easy to use. They help you deliver a range of running calculations, including

- Running totals
- Running averages
- Running counts

Fortunately, SQL Server does not require you to learn any new functions in order to deliver this kind of rolling analysis. It simply extends the use of a handful of functions that you know already, such as SUM(), AVG(), and COUNT(). Once you have mastered these extensions, you are also able to use this new approach with a few new functions to isolate

- Comparative values across a range of records
- The first or last element in a series
- The relative standing of a record in a recordset
- The most recent element in a series for comparison

Indeed, the great thing about these calculations is that they all work in a very similar way. The upshot is that once you have mastered the basics of how these functions work, you can apply them to your queries to give your analysis a new power and depth.

This set of functions goes under the name of `windowing functions`, because they group datasets into "windows" of data behind the scenes. They also allow you to specify what elements are calculated and exactly how they are grouped. This means that you can ask SQL Server to restart the running total at specific breakpoints. Consequently, you can restart a running calculation with every new year, month, or day if you want—and, in so doing, you can track how metrics evolve over time.

19.1 Adding a Running Total

The sales director does not always want complex analyses; sometimes she wants fairly simple lists as well. This time he has requested a list of sales for 2017 that includes running totals of both sales to date and average sales. Fortunately, windowing functions make this not too difficult, as the following code snippet displays:

```
SELECT        InvoiceNumber
              ,FORMAT(SA.SaleDate, 'd', 'en-gb') AS DateOfSale
              ,SD.SalePrice
              ,SUM(SD.SalePrice)
              OVER (ORDER BY SaleDate ASC) AS AccumulatedSales
              ,AVG(SD.SalePrice)
              OVER (ORDER BY SA.SaleDate ASC)
                  AS AverageSalesValueToDate
FROM          Data.SalesDetails SD
INNER JOIN    Data.Sales AS SA ON SA.SalesID = SD.SalesID
WHERE         YEAR(SA.SaleDate) = 2017
ORDER BY      SA.SaleDate
```

Running this query gives the results that you can see in *Figure 19.1.*

	InvoiceNumber	DateOfSale	SalePrice	AccumulatedSales	AverageSalesValueToDate
1	EURFR110	01/01/2017	22500.00	22500.00	22500.000000
2	GBPGB111	05/01/2017	125000.00	147500.00	73750.000000
3	GBPGB112	10/01/2017	85000.00	232500.00	77500.000000
4	GBPCH114	11/01/2017	22500.00	255000.00	63750.000000
5	GBPGB115	12/01/2017	125950.00	380950.00	76190.000000
6	GBPCH116	13/01/2017	8850.00	389800.00	64966.666666
7	GBPGB117	14/01/2017	9950.00	399750.00	57107.142857
8	EURFR113	21/01/2017	1250.00	401000.00	50125.000000
9	EURFR118	30/01/2017	56500.00	457500.00	50833.333333
10	GBPGB119	31/01/2017	55000.00	569450.00	51768.181818
11	GBPGB120	31/01/2017	56950.00	569450.00	51768.181818
12	EURFR121	07/02/2017	365000.00	934450.00	77870.833333
13	EURFR122	08/02/2017	395000.00	1329450.00	102265.384615
14	USDUS123	09/02/2017	21500.00	1350950.00	96496.428571
15	GBPGB124	10/02/2017	6500.00	1357450.00	90496.666666

Figure 19.1: *Generating running totals with the OVER clause*

How It Works

A classic analytical requirement is to see how values change over time. This short piece of SQL shows not only how to list sales values, but also how the running total and average sale price change with each new sale.

The core of this query is a list of sales dates and values taken from the Sales and SalesDetails tables. The data is filtered to limit the result to sales for a given year. Finally, to give this initial list some coherence, it is sorted by sales date.

Then two windowing functions are added to enhance the output and to turbocharge the level of information that the query delivers. They do this by extending the use of two functions that you have come to know well: SUM() and AVG().

Each of these functions is extended with an OVER clause that causes the function to be applied to the field that you are calculating from the beginning of the dataset up to and including the current record. This way, both the SUM() function and the AVG() function perform their tasks (adding up the total sales and averaging the sale price, respectively) for each record, up to and including the current record, while the AVG() function also calculates the average sale price for each record up to and including the current record. The final result is a mixture of the detailed sales information for each sale and the overall data up to that date. Essentially, the OVER clause ensures that the functions are only applied to a part of the dataset, and not to the entire set, as has been the case up until now.

As you analyze how data evolves over time, it is important to ensure that the OVER function orders the data using a field, or fields, that sequence the records over time. In this example, we are using the SaleDate field so that the OVER function essentially says, "from the start of the filtered dataset up to the current record where the dataset is ordered by sale date."

Since this is a new use of the SUM() and AVG() functions, you may find that looking at an image makes it easier for you to grasp the concepts that are being applied. *Figure 19.2* shows how windowing functions work more graphically.

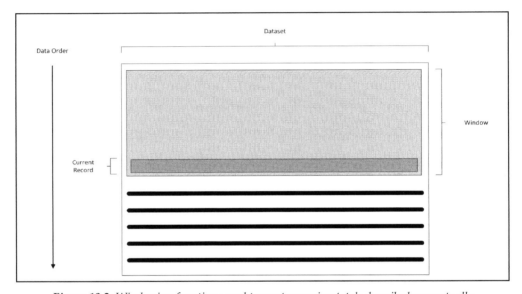

Figure 19.2: Windowing functions used to create running totals described conceptually

Tricks and Traps

Windowing functions are extremely powerful; however, they do require you to remain aware of a few key points if you are to use them correctly:

- Because you are listing the individual records for each sale, it helps if you display some piece of information (such as the invoice number in this example) that lets the reader see what makes each record unique.

- In this example, we formatted the date purely for presentation purposes. You can, of course, leave the date data in its raw state when you output the query results.

- When using several running totals in a single query, it is important to make sure that they use the same ORDER BY clause in the OVER operator or you could get results that are not what you are looking for.

- A running total, just like any other aggregation, needs an alias if you want a column title to be displayed in the output.

19.2 Using Windowing Functions in an Aggregated Query

Because Prestige Cars is perfectly capable of buying several cars on the same day, the CFO wants a report that displays the purchase cost per day with the cumulative cost for the year 2016. This is exactly what the following SQL code achieves:

```
SELECT      DateBought
            ,SUM(Cost) AS PurchaseCost
            ,SUM(SUM(Cost))
                OVER (ORDER BY DateBought ASC) AS CostForTheYear
FROM        Data.Stock
WHERE       YEAR(DateBought) = 2016
GROUP BY    DateBought
ORDER BY    DateBought
```

Running this query gives the results that you can see in *Figure 19.3*.

	DateBought	PurchaseCost	CostForTheYear
1	2016-01-02	35760.00	35760.00
2	2016-01-10	45560.00	81320.00
3	2016-01-31	44800.00	126120.00
4	2016-02-01	52712.00	178832.00
5	2016-02-10	4800.00	183632.00
6	2016-02-11	38280.00	221912.00
7	2016-02-27	125560.00	347472.00
8	2016-03-15	31600.00	379072.00
9	2016-03-19	2920.00	381992.00
10	2016-04-17	176400.00	558392.00
11	2016-04-26	82360.00	640752.00
12	2016-04-29	14000.00	654752.00
13	2016-05-02	93600.00	748352.00
14	2016-05-11	10000.00	758352.00
15	2016-05-25	7960.00	766312.00

Figure 19.3: Using windowing functions in an aggregated query

How It Works

Sometimes you might need to see an aggregated value, such as the cost of goods bought per day, alongside the running total over time of these same costs. You do this by grouping data from the Stock table on the DateBought field and by displaying this field alongside the SUM() of the Cost field. To avoid getting drowned in data, make sure the output is restricted to only purchases for 2016.

After this, ask SQL Server to provide a running total using a SUM()...OVER windowing function. However, because this function is a grouped query (or an `aggregated query`, if you prefer), it needs to be aggregated as well. You have to make the SUM(Cost) function into an aggregate function by writing it as SUM(SUM(Cost)).

Tricks and Traps

We have only one point that really needs your attention here, but it is a very important one. This example is based on a simple technique that you must bear in mind when aggregating data using windowing functions:

- It may seem peculiar, and even counterintuitive, to wrap a SUM() function inside another SUM() function. But if you write this query as

```
SUM(Cost)) OVER (ORDER BY DateBought ASC)
```

then the query fails. This is because you are grouping data in a query and consequently you must `also` group data used in running totals.

19.3 Grouping Running Totals

You can use running totals to get an idea of how your key metrics evolve. Sometimes, however, you want to reset a grouping element so that you can start over when some key piece of data changes—like beginning a new year, for instance. So, when the sales director requests a list that shows all sales to date with a running count of sales per year, you are relieved that you can use a windowing function to answer her query. The following SQL snippet shows you how to reset a counter or a running total:

```
SELECT      FORMAT(SA.SaleDate, 'd', 'en-gb') AS DateOfSale
            ,CU.CustomerName, CU.Town
            ,SD.SalePrice
            ,COUNT(SD.SalesDetailsID)
            OVER (PARTITION BY YEAR(SA.SaleDate)
```

```
                ORDER BY SA.SaleDate ASC)

              AS AnnualNumberOfSalesToDate
FROM        Data.SalesDetails SD
INNER JOIN  Data.Sales AS SA ON SA.SalesID = SD.SalesID
INNER JOIN  Data.Customer CU ON SA.CustomerID = CU.CustomerID
ORDER BY    SA.SaleDate
```

Running this query gives the results that you can see in *Figure 19.4*.

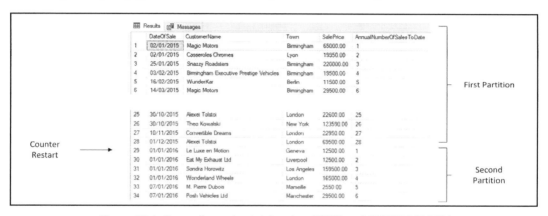

Figure 19.4: *Grouped running totals using OVER and PARTITION BY*

How It Works

This query begins by joining the Customer, Sales, and SalesDetails tables so that you can return sales and customer information—such as the date of sale, customer name, and sale price—for each sale. No filter is applied because you want to see all sales since Prestige Cars began trading. The query is sorted by date to ensure that the data appear in a clear and comprehensible way.

You can now add the running counter of sales over time. You build it like this:

First:	Work out the number of sales by adding a COUNT() function.
Second:	Extended this function to make it a windowing function by adding an OVER clause.
Third:	Order the resulting counter by a unique field combination—the SaleDate field and the SalesDetailsID field—so there is no aggregation of the data and each individual record displays.

Finally:	Add a PARTITION BY clause so that the counter `restarts` when the field specified after the PARTITION BY clause (the year) `changes`.

The end result is a list of all sales over time where you can see not only the accumulated sales as the year progresses, but also the total sales for the year at year end.

Once again, a visual representation may help you understand this better. *Figure 19.5* shows you how a PARTITION BY clause works with a windowing function.

Figure 19.5: *A PARTITION BY clause with a windowing function*

Tricks and Traps

When you add a PARTITION BY clause to a windowing function, you need to remember the following key points:

- It is important to use the appropriate fields in the ORDER BY clause of the OVER function to achieve your desired output. If you use the wrong fields, it probably will not return the result that you expect. In practice, this means you need to select a field that contains the finest level of granularity of the data that is meaningful. In this example, each individual sale is what matters, so you use the SalesDetailsID field in both the COUNT() function and the ORDER BY clause because it contains a unique value for each record. This ensures that all records are output individually and not aggregated in any way.

- If you use the SaleDate field instead of the SalesDetailsID field in this query, SQL Server counts the days with sales throughout the year. Since there may well be days with multiple sales—or no sales at all—the resulting recordset will not give the same results.

- Generally, you want to make sure that you are repeating the field(s) that you are using to sort the data in the query (that is, the field or fields that you are using in the main ORDER BY clause) in the OVER clause. This ensures that the output is visually coherent with the actual data analysis.

19.4 Applying Windowing Functions to a Subquery

The CEO has become obsessed with analyzing key metrics over time. Her latest request is that you obtain the total sales to date and then display the running total of sales by value for each year. The following code snippet shows how to do this:

```
SELECT      FORMAT(SaleDate, 'd', 'en-us') AS DateOfSale

            ,DailyCount AS NumberOfSales

            ,SUM(DailyCount) OVER

                    (PARTITION BY YEAR(SaleDate) ORDER BY SaleDate ASC)

                    AS AnnualNumberOfSalesToDate

            ,SUM(DailySalePrice) OVER

                    (PARTITION BY YEAR(SaleDate) ORDER BY SaleDate ASC)

                    AS AnnualSalePriceToDate

FROM        (

            SELECT      SA.SaleDate

                        ,COUNT(SD.SalesDetailsID) AS DailyCount

                        ,SUM(SD.SalePrice) AS DailySalePrice

            FROM        Data.SalesDetails SD

            INNER JOIN  Data.Sales AS SA

                        ON SA.SalesID = SD.SalesID

            GROUP BY    SA.SaleDate

            ) DT

ORDER BY    SaleDate
```

Running this query gives the results that you can see in *Figure 19.6*.

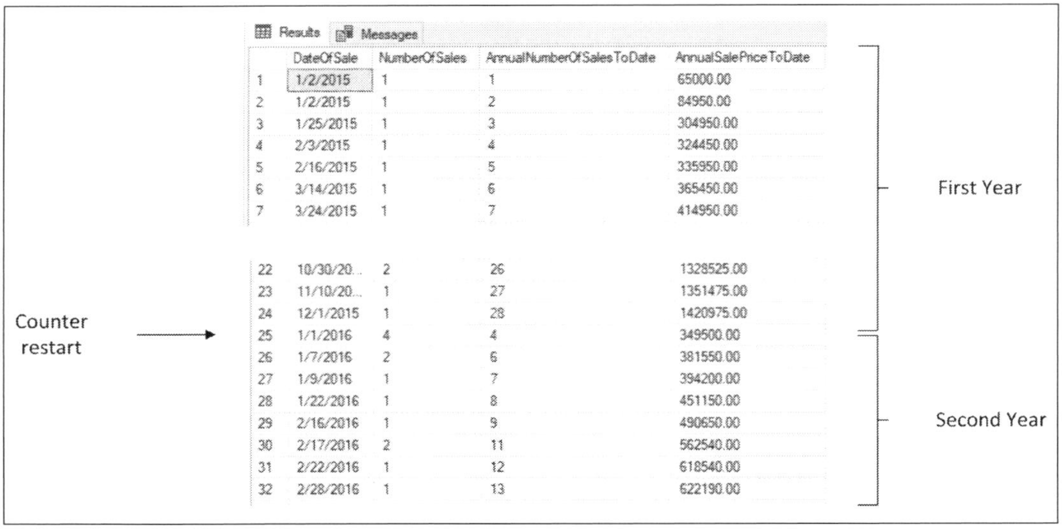

	DateOfSale	NumberOfSales	AnnualNumberOfSalesToDate	AnnualSalePriceToDate
1	1/2/2015	1	1	65000.00
2	1/2/2015	1	2	84950.00
3	1/25/2015	1	3	304950.00
4	2/3/2015	1	4	324450.00
5	2/16/2015	1	5	335950.00
6	3/14/2015	1	6	365450.00
7	3/24/2015	1	7	414950.00
22	10/30/20...	2	26	1328525.00
23	11/10/20...	1	27	1351475.00
24	12/1/2015	1	28	1420975.00
25	1/1/2016	4	4	349500.00
26	1/7/2016	2	6	381550.00
27	1/9/2016	1	7	394200.00
28	1/22/2016	1	8	451150.00
29	2/16/2016	1	9	490650.00
30	2/17/2016	2	11	562540.00
31	2/22/2016	1	12	618540.00
32	2/28/2016	1	13	622190.00

Figure 19.6: *Using windowing functions and a subquery*

How It Works

Possibly the easiest way to achieve the objectives that you have set yourself in this query is to break the task into two parts:

First:	Create a derived table that counts the number and value of sales per day for each individual date.
Second:	Create an outer query that returns the cumulative sales ver the year in addition to the running total of sales revenue from the derived table.

In this example, the subquery is an aggregate query that groups the result by date and provides a COUNT() of sales and a SUM() of sales value. We did not apply any filters so that all sales from the start of trading are included. To get a clearer idea of what is included, take a look at *Figure 19.7*, which shows the output from the subquery.

	SaleDate	DailyCount	DailySalePrice
1	2015-01-02 00:00:00.000	1	65000.00
2	2015-01-02 10:33:00.000	1	19950.00
3	2015-01-25 00:00:00.000	1	220000.00
4	2015-02-03 00:00:00.000	1	19500.00
5	2015-02-16 00:00:00.000	1	11500.00
6	2015-03-14 00:00:00.000	1	29500.00
7	2015-03-24 00:00:00.000	1	49500.00
8	2015-03-30 00:00:00.000	1	76000.00
9	2015-04-04 00:00:00.000	1	36500.00
10	2015-04-06 00:00:00.000	1	19600.00

Figure 19.7: *Subquery output*

The outer query can then take the three elements that are generated by the inner query (sale date, daily sales count, and daily sales value) and use them as follows:

SaleDate	Is displayed in the output "as is" and is also used to sort the query results.
DailyCount	Is also output "as is" to display the number of sales for each day that there are sales.
DailyCount	Is reused in a windowing function to provide the running total of sales to date. We achieve the running total by applying the COUNT() function over the sale date. In this example, this aggregate value is also partitioned by year using the PARTITION BY clause so that the count restarts with each new year.
DailySalePrice	Is reused (and output as AnnualNumberOf SalesToDate) in a separate windowing function that is also ordered by sale date and partitioned by the year. This allows you to show the cumulative sales to date for each year.

Using a derived table to perform the initial aggregation is an effective way of preparing the initial data that you then use to provide the running totals. It also allows you to test the initial data simply by selecting and executing the query that underlies the derived table; this way you can check each part of the process as you build the query.

19.5 Adding Unique IDs on the Fly Using ROW_NUMBER()

None of the sales staff like using the complex identifiers that appear in the billing system. They have asked you to create your own numbering system to identify sales sequentially. The following SQL shows how to add this kind of distinguishing feature without changing the source data:

```
SELECT          FORMAT(SA.SaleDate, 'd', 'en-gb') AS DateOfSale
                ,SD.SalePrice, CU.CustomerName, CU.Town, MK.MakeName
                ,COUNT(SD.SalesDetailsID)
                  OVER (PARTITION BY YEAR(SaleDate)
                  ORDER BY SA.SaleDate ASC)
                    AS AnnualNumberOfSalesToDate
                ,ROW_NUMBER() OVER (ORDER BY SA.SaleDate ASC)
                    AS SalesCounter
FROM            Data.Make AS MK
INNER JOIN      Data.Model AS MD ON MK.MakeID = MD.MakeID
INNER JOIN      Data.Stock AS ST ON ST.ModelID = MD.ModelID
INNER JOIN      Data.SalesDetails SD ON ST.StockCode = SD.StockID
INNER JOIN      Data.Sales AS SA ON SA.SalesID = SD.SalesID
INNER JOIN      Data.Customer CU ON SA.CustomerID = CU.CustomerID
ORDER BY        SA.SaleDate
```

Running this query gives the results that you can see in *Figure 19.8.*

	DateOfSale	SalePrice	CustomerName	Town	MakeName	AnnualNumberOfSalesToDate	SalesCounter
1	02/01/2015	65000.00	Magic Motors	Birmingham	Ferrari	1	1
2	02/01/2015	19950.00	Casseroles Chromes	Lyon	Porsche	2	2
3	25/01/2015	220000.00	Snazzy Roadsters	Birmingham	Ferrari	3	3
4	03/02/2015	19500.00	Birmingham Executive Prestige Vehicles	Birmingham	Porsche	4	4
5	16/02/2015	11500.00	WunderKar	Berlin	Porsche	5	5
6	14/03/2015	29500.00	Magic Motors	Birmingham	Aston Martin	6	6
7	24/03/2015	49500.00	Birmingham Executive Prestige Vehicles	Birmingham	Aston Martin	7	7
8	30/03/2015	76000.00	Eat My Exhaust Ltd	Liverpool	Aston Martin	8	8
339	05/12/2018	59500.00	Jason B. Wight	Washington	Aston Martin	119	339
340	05/12/2018	123500.00	Ronaldo Bianco	Milan	Aston Martin	119	340
341	08/12/2018	99500.00	Andrea Tarbuck	Birmingham	Aston Martin	122	341
342	08/12/2018	54500.00	Boris Spry	Birmingham	Aston Martin	122	342
343	08/12/2018	1590.00	Boris Spry	Birmingham	Trabant	122	343
344	16/12/2018	11500.00	Antonio Maura	Madrid	Triumph	123	344
345	17/12/2018	17950.00	Screamin' Wheels	Los Angeles	Alfa Romeo	124	345
346	31/12/2018	5500.00	Laurent Saint Yves	Marseille	Citroen	127	346
347	31/12/2018	950.00	Mrs. Ivana Telford	Liverpool	Reliant	127	347
348	31/12/2018	145000.00	Andy Cheshire	Stoke	Ferrari	127	348

Figure 19.8: *Using the ROW_NUMBER() windowing function to add unique IDs to a recordset*

How It Works

Source data does not always come with all the elements that you need. At times, you may require a way of numbering records to identify each row individually. The ROW_NUMBER() function lets you do just this, and it has no effect on the underlying data.

This query starts by joining all the tables that are necessary, which allows you to display the fields that you want to output (SaleDate, SalePrice, CustomerName, Town, and MakeName). Then it adds these fields—with any necessary formatting and aliases—to the SELECT clause.

Then two windowing functions are added:

COUNT()	To display the number of sales per day per year. This function is partitioned by year (so that the counter restarts each time the year changes) and ordered by date.
ROW_NUMBER()	To show an individual and progressively incrementing number to identify each record that is output.

The special feature in this query is the use of the ROW_NUMBER() windowing function. This function lets you add a series of numbers to an output dataset. The series starts at 1 and increases by one for each record in the windowed dataset.

The ROW_NUMBER() also requires you to add an OVER clause containing an ORDER BY statement. To ensure that these virtual IDs are numbered sequentially in a comprehensible manner, the ROW_NUMBER() function is ordered by the sale date. Since we want a continuous range of numbers defined for all the source data, we choose not to add a PARTITION BY clause to the windowing function. The result is a series of numbers that are consecutively incremented in the query output, even if there is no numbering in the source data.

Tricks and Traps

There is one important point to remember when you are applying the ROW_NUMBER() function:

- ROW_NUMBER() is not the same as COUNT()—despite the superficial similarities. If you look at the output for this query for April 30, 2015, you see two records for this date. The COUNT() windowing function shows a total of 12 sales to date for this day—and this is the same for either of the day's sales (as it should be). The ROW_NUMBER() function attributes a different number to each record, even if the ORDER BY clause for the function is the SaleDate field.

So the ROW_NUMBER() function `always` differentiates the records that are returned. This can mean applying the numbering sequence arbitrarily to certain rows. You can see this in the two sales for April 30, 2015.

Of course, if you really want to specify a completely comprehensive numbering system, you can extend the sort order that is applied by the ROW_NUMBER() function. So, you could, for instance, tweak the SQL to read

```
ROW_NUMBER() OVER (ORDER BY SaleDate, Make, Model ASC) AS SalesCounter
```

19.6 Displaying Records for Missing Data

The CEO has just had another idea; you can tell by the smile on her face as she walks over to your desk. Hiding your trepidation, you listen as she tells you that she needs a weekly calendar of sales for 2016. She makes it clear that she wants to see a list of all the weeks in the year, whether there were any sales in that week or not.

After a little effort, you produce the following SQL to deliver the sales report that she was hoping for:

```
;
WITH Tally_CTE
AS
(
SELECT      TOP 52 ROW_NUMBER() OVER (ORDER BY StockCode) AS Num
FROM        Data.Stock
)


SELECT          CTE.Num, SLS.SalesForTheWeek
FROM            Tally_CTE CTE
LEFT OUTER JOIN
                (
                SELECT      SUM(TotalSalePrice) AS SalesForTheWeek
                            ,DatePart(wk, SaleDate) AS WeekNo
                FROM        Data.Sales
                WHERE       YEAR(SaleDate) = 2016
                GROUP BY    DatePart(wk, SaleDate)
                ) SLS
                ON CTE.Num = SLS.WeekNo
```

Running this SQL produces output like that shown in *Figure 19.9*.

	Num	SalesForTheWeek
1	1	349500.00
2	2	44700.00
3	3	NULL
4	4	56950.00
5	5	NULL
6	6	NULL
7	7	NULL
8	8	111390.00
9	9	56000.00
10	10	3650.00
11	11	NULL
12	12	NULL
13	13	220500.00
14	14	NULL
15	15	102950.00

Figure 19.9: *Displaying missing data using a sequence list*

How It Works

Delivering output when the data exists is rarely an issue; however, you may need to apply slightly different querying techniques if you need to show "missing" data. By this, we mean that SQL does not naturally create complete lists of dates, or date elements such as weeks, where there is no corresponding data in a database.

To understand this problem more clearly, run the SQL from the preceding snippet that returns the total sales per week for 2016, which is contained in the derived table with the alias SLS. The output from the derived table looks like that shown in *Figure 19.10*.

	SalesForTheWeek	WeekNo
1	349500.00	1
2	44700.00	2
3	56950.00	4
4	111390.00	8
5	56000.00	9
6	3650.00	10
7	220500.00	13
8	102950.00	15
9	155800.00	18
10	99030.00	23

Figure 19.10: *The source data with missing values*

Although the figures are accurate, the data contains holes since there are no sales for certain weeks. Since these holes could be precisely the data that you want to focus on, it is important to return a full list of weeks—whether they contain data or not.

Forcing SQL Server to return a complete sequence (whether it is dates, weeks, or any other series of information) requires you to extend the SQL with a list that contains an unbroken and consecutive list of all the elements that you need to view. You can then use this list as the basis for a query that adds the aggregated output that you require.

A sequence like this is often called a `tally table` or a `numbers list`. What you have done in this SQL is

First:	Created a CTE (Common Table Expression) that contains a numbers list.
Second:	Joined the CTE to a query (the derived subquery in this example) that calculates the sales per week.

Let's begin by looking at the numbers table. Although we call this a table, it is really a dataset generated by a CTE. If you run the code inside the CTE named Tally_CTE, you see the output in *Figure 19.11*.

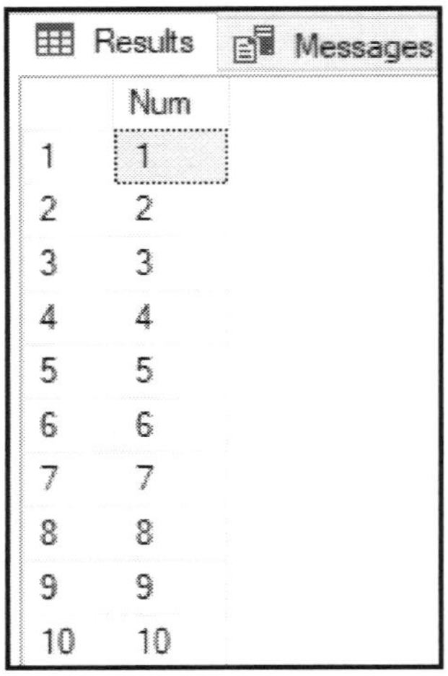

Figure 19.11: A sequence list or tally table

As you can see, this CTE simply returns a sequence of numbers. You obtain this sequence by

First:	Choosing a table that contains more records than you need in the numbers table (the CTE output). This can be any table in the database.

Then:	Selecting the first n records from this table that correspond to the number of items in the sequence that you require. In this example, there are 52 weeks in the year, so you use TOP 52 to limit the number of elements in the tally table.
Finally:	Since you are not interested in the actual data that the source table (Stock) contains, but only in the number of records, you define a ROW_NUMBER() function (ordered by any field in the table) to provide a sequence of numbers.

The CTE at the start of the SQL serves only to provide a sequential list that provides a row for each week in the year.

Once you have the tally table set up, join this to the derived table that returns the actual data for each week of sales. Because you have extracted the week number from the SaleDate field using the DATEPART() function, you can join the week number for each week of sales to the corresponding record in the tally table. Defining the join as a LEFT OUTER join from the tally table (the CTE) to the derived query ensures that every record from the CTE is displayed, whether or not any corresponding data is in the derived query.

The result is the output from *Figure 19.9*, shown previously, that shows all the weeks in 2016 with the sales figures, even if there are no sales for a specific week.

Note: If you use a single table as the basis for the tally table, it must contain at least as many records as you need for the sequential list. The next section explains a technique you can use to guarantee enough rows if you are worried that a single source table will not contain enough records.

19.7 Displaying a Complete Range of Dates and Relevant Data

You really impressed the CEO with your calendar of weekly sales. The only downside is that she clearly told the sales director to look at increasing sales and avoiding days with no sales, because the sales director has just requested a list of daily sales for a six-month period (from January 1 to June 30, 2017, to be precise).

After a little head-scratching, you come up with the following piece of SQL:

```
;
WITH Tally_CTE
AS
(
SELECT     TOP 10000 ROW_NUMBER() OVER (ORDER BY ST1.StockCode) -1 AS
Num
```

```
FROM        Data.Stock ST1
CROSS JOIN Data.Stock ST2
)
,DateRange_CTE
AS
(
SELECT      DATEADD(DD, Num,'20170101') AS DateList FROM Tally_CTE
WHERE       Num <= DATEDIFF(DD, '20170101', '20170630')
)

SELECT           CAST(DateList AS DATE) AS SaleDate, SalesPerDay
FROM             DateRange_CTE CTE
LEFT OUTER JOIN
                 (
                 SELECT      CAST(SaleDate AS DATE) AS DateOfSale
                             ,SUM(TotalSalePrice) AS SalesPerDay
                 FROM        Data.Sales
                 GROUP BY    CAST(SaleDate AS DATE)
                 ) SLS
                 ON CTE.DateList = SLS.DateOfSale
```

Running this code delivers the output that you can see in *Figure 19.12*.

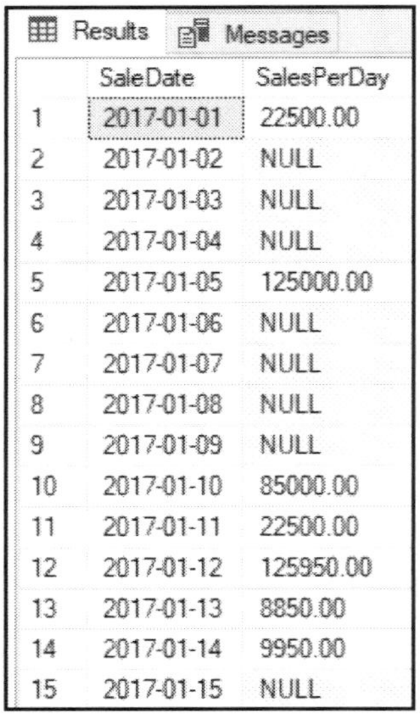

	SaleDate	SalesPerDay
1	2017-01-01	22500.00
2	2017-01-02	NULL
3	2017-01-03	NULL
4	2017-01-04	NULL
5	2017-01-05	125000.00
6	2017-01-06	NULL
7	2017-01-07	NULL
8	2017-01-08	NULL
9	2017-01-09	NULL
10	2017-01-10	85000.00
11	2017-01-11	22500.00
12	2017-01-12	125950.00
13	2017-01-13	8850.00
14	2017-01-14	9950.00
15	2017-01-15	NULL

Figure 19.12: A complete range of dates including dates without any corresponding data

How It Works

Once again, the source data used in this example does not necessarily contain records for empty values—that is, there is not necessarily a sale every day during the relevant period. Once again, you need to ensure that you have a sequence of a range of dates where there are no missing values.

You accomplish this using two CTEs:

The first CTE	Is a tally table (or a numbers list if you prefer) that ensures a large sequence of numbers. This guarantees that you can request a range of dates over several years if necessary.
The second CTE	Uses the tally table to create a sequence of dates between a start date and an end date.

As each of these CTEs carries out a specific task, it is probably easier to look at each of them in turn.

The tally table CTE works like this:

First:	It specifies a large incremented list of a range of numbers (10,000 in this case—enough for nearly 30 years of individual days) using the ROW_NUMBER() function. Because the tally table begins at 1 by default, in this example, we tweaked it to start at 0 by subtracting 1 from the output of the function. This way, the DATEADD() and DATEDIFF() functions begin and end with the actual start and end dates the SQL snippet uses (DATEADD() starts the list of dates by adding 0 days to the start date—effectively beginning at the date used in the code).
Second:	It uses two tables (or the same table twice with two different aliases) that are joined using the CROSS APPLY operator. This approach multiplies the number of records in the first table by the number of records in the second table producing a large set of records that become the basis for the number sequence.

The DateRange CTE works like this:

First:	The DATEADD() function is used to increment a start date (January 1, 2017) with a sequence of days. This CTE is based on the value in the first CTE, which it, in effect, converts to a date by adding the value in the first CTE to the start date.
Second:	A WHERE clause filters the upper limit of the date range to June 30, 2017. It does this by using the DATEDIFF() function to calculate the number of days between the start and end dates, which are also specified in the DATEDIFF() function. The number of days becomes the upper threshold for the largest record number from the tally dataset.

If you run the following code snippet just after the two CTEs (in line 15 of the code, on the blank line before the final SELECT clause), you can see the range of continuous calendar dates shown in *Figure 19.13*.

```
SELECT * FROM DateRange_CTE
```

	DateList
1	2017-01-01 00:00:00.000
2	2017-01-02 00:00:00.000
3	2017-01-03 00:00:00.000
4	2017-01-04 00:00:00.000
5	2017-01-05 00:00:00.000
6	2017-01-06 00:00:00.000
7	2017-01-07 00:00:00.000
8	2017-01-08 00:00:00.000
9	2017-01-09 00:00:00.000
10	2017-01-10 00:00:00.000

Figure 19.13: A complete range of dates based on a tally table

Finally, the second CTE—DateRange_CTE—is joined to the derived query that aggregates daily sales. As was the case in the previous example, it is the range of dates that is the "core" table in the query so that an unbroken range of dates is output. A LEFT OUTER join to the derived table ensures that a complete range of dates is output. Joining the derived table and the second CTE join on their respective date fields allows the query to return sales data where there is a sale date.

Tricks and Traps

We have a couple of comments worthy of note at this point:

- The cross join to get a large number of records from two tables is called, technically, a `Cartesian join`. This kind of join shows each record from one table joined to each record from the other table. Although this can be dangerous when you are carrying out precise queries, this approach is useful when you need to create a tally table.

- Unless you are sure that the date fields that you are using to join the derived table and the tally dataset are of the DATE data type, it is worth converting the date fields to DATEs. This ensures that the join is successful.

19.8 Comparing Data with the Data from a Previous Record

Prestige Car's sales director is keen to track customer spend. She wants you to track sales over time and highlight the difference between previous and current sale values per customer for each sale. The following piece of SQL lets you satisfy her demand:

```
SELECT      CU.CustomerName

            ,SA.SaleDate

            ,SA.TotalSalePrice

            ,SA.TotalSalePrice - LAG(SA.TotalSalePrice,1)

                        OVER (PARTITION BY CU.CustomerName

                        ORDER BY SA.SaleDate)

                            AS DifferenceToPreviousSalePrice

FROM        Data.Sales SA
INNER JOIN  Data.Customer CU

            ON SA.CustomerID = CU.CustomerID

ORDER BY    SaleDate
```

Running this query gives the results that you can see in *Figure 19.14*.

	CustomerName	SaleDate	TotalSalePrice	DifferenceToPreviousSalePrice
1	Magic Motors	2015-01-02 00:00:00.000	65000.00	NULL
2	Casseroles Chromes	2015-01-02 10:33:00.000	19900.00	NULL
3	Snazzy Roadsters	2015-01-25 00:00:00.000	220000.10	NULL
4	Birmingham Executive Prestige Vehicles	2015-02-03 00:00:00.000	19500.00	NULL
5	WunderKar	2015-02-16 00:00:00.000	11500.00	NULL
6	Magic Motors	2015-03-14 00:00:00.000	29500.00	-35500.00
7	Birmingham Executive Prestige Vehicles	2015-03-24 00:00:00.000	49500.20	30000.20
8	Eat My Exhaust Ltd	2015-03-30 00:00:00.000	76000.90	NULL
9	Sondra Horowitz	2015-04-04 00:00:00.000	36500.00	NULL
10	M. Pierre Dubois	2015-04-06 00:00:00.000	19600.00	NULL
11	Wonderland Wheels	2015-04-30 00:00:00.000	89000.00	NULL
12	London Executive Prestige Vehicles	2015-05-10 00:00:00.000	169500.00	NULL
13	M. Pierre Dubois	2015-05-20 00:00:00.000	8950.00	-10650.00
14	Glittering Prize Cars Ltd	2015-05-28 00:00:00.000	195000.00	NULL
15	La Bagnole de Luxe	2015-06-04 16:37:00.000	22950.00	NULL

Figure 19.14: Comparing data between records using the LAG() function

How It Works

Although we have seen how to compare individual pieces of data with groups of data, so far in this book, we have not compared individual records to other records. As a first example of how to look at how a sequence of records varies from record to record, this piece of SQL shows how each sale compares to the previous one for the same customer.

In this piece of code you meet the LAG() function for the first time. This function allows you to look back over a subset of records and return data from a previous record, or records.

The query works like this:

First:	A perfectly normal query is constructed that returns a list of individual sales with the sale price and the customer who bought the car using the Sales and Customer tables.
Then:	A LAG() function is added that goes back through the recordset until it finds the previous sale for the same customer as the one in the current record. It returns the previous sale price and, for this customer, subtracts this figure from the current record's sale price to give the difference between the two sale prices for the vehicles.

Just like the other windowing functions that you have seen, the LAG() function requires a few parameters to work properly. In this example they are

OVER	This operator introduces a windowing function.
PARTITION BY	This operator tells SQL Server how to group the data when searching for a previous record. Since this example has PARTITION BY CustomerName inside the OVER clause, SQL only jumps back to records that have the same customer name as the current record.
ORDER BY	This clause sorts the subset of data (that is grouped by customer) in chronological order, since it is the SaleDate field that provides the sort order.
Field	This indicates the `data to return from the preceding record`. In this example, it is the SalePrice field.
Offset Value	This is the number of records to jump back for this customer. The value is set to 1 in this example because we want the `previous` record for the same customer.

Once all these elements are in place, the LAG() function can "subset" the data into an invisible group based on the customer field. Since this data subset is a list of records over time relative to the current record, the function steps back into the preceding record for the customer and returns the previous sale price. As you can see in the output, there is, by definition, no previous sale for the first sale for each customer. This is why the LAG() function returns a NULL value.

If you can visualize what is happening, it may help you d eal with previous records. Take a look at *Figure 19.15*; in it, you can see a high-level overview of how the LAG() value works.

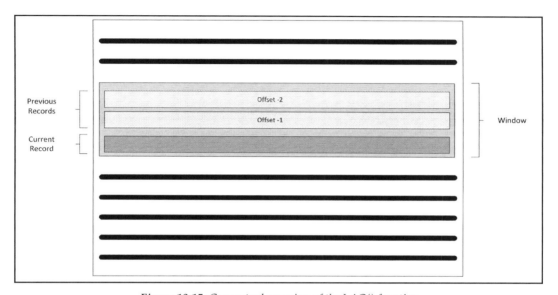

Figure 19.15: *Conceptual overview of the LAG() function*

Tricks and Traps

The LAG() function is extremely powerful. This inevitably means that you have to master a few subtleties if you want to apply it constructively:

- The field that you place inside the LAG() function does **not** have to appear in the SELECT clause; however, it must be in one of the tables contained in the FROM clause of the query.

- If you do not want to see records where there is no difference with any previous sale (because this was the first sale), you can use nearly all of this query as a derived table and wrap it in an outer query. This query then selects the columns from the derived table and adds a WHERE clause to eliminate the PreviousSalePriceDifference records that contain NULLs. The code looks like this:

```
SELECT *
FROM
    (
```

```
SELECT      CU.CustomerName
            ,SA.SaleDate
            ,SA.TotalSalePrice
            ,SA.TotalSalePrice - LAG(SA.TotalSalePrice,1)
                        OVER (PARTITION BY CU.CustomerName
                            ORDER BY SA.SaleDate)
                                AS
PreviousSalePriceDifference
FROM        Data.Sales SA
            INNER JOIN Data.Customer CU
            ON SA.CustomerID = CU.CustomerID
) SQ
WHERE PreviousSalePriceDifference IS NOT NULL
ORDER BY    SaleDate
```

Running this query gives the output that you can see in *Figure 19.16.*

	CustomerName	SaleDate	TotalSalePrice	PreviousSalePriceDifference
1	Magic Motors	2015-03-14 00:00:00.000	29500.00	-35500.00
2	Birmingham Executive Prestige Vehicles	2015-03-24 00:00:00.000	49500.20	30000.20
3	M. Pierre Dubois	2015-05-20 00:00:00.000	8950.00	-10650.00
4	Peter McLuckie	2015-09-15 00:00:00.000	15600.00	2950.00
5	Alexei Tolstoi	2015-10-30 00:00:00.000	22600.00	-390.00
6	Theo Kowalski	2015-10-30 00:00:00.000	123590.00	118090.00
7	Convertible Dreams	2015-11-10 00:00:00.000	22950.00	14255.00
8	Alexei Tolstoi	2015-12-01 00:00:00.000	69500.00	46900.00
9	Eat My Exhaust Ltd	2016-01-01 00:00:00.000	12500.00	-63500.90
10	Wonderland Wheels	2016-01-01 00:00:00.000	165000.00	76000.00
11	Sondra Horowitz	2016-01-01 00:00:00.000	159500.00	123000.00
12	Posh Vehicles Ltd	2016-01-07 00:00:00.000	29500.00	20550.00
13	M. Pierre Dubois	2016-01-07 00:00:00.000	2550.00	-6400.00
14	SuperSport S.A.R.L.	2016-02-16 00:00:00.000	39500.00	-36000.00
15	Magic Motors	2016-02-28 00:00:00.000	3650.00	-25850.00

Figure 19.16: Using a subquery with a LAG() function in a derived table

You cannot simply apply the WHERE clause inside the original query to filter the recordset and remove any records with NULL values for the sale price. This is because windowing functions can `only be used in SELECT or ORDER BY clauses`. Consequently, you have to move the ORDER BY clause from the derived table to the outer query.

- A PARTITION BY function is not required when using the LAG() function. However, without one, the LAG() function returns data from a record that precedes the current record in the overall dataset without attempting to group the comparative dataset by a specific element—such as the customer.

19.9 Comparing Data over Time Using the FIRST_VALUE() and LAST_VALUE() Functions

Prestige Cars is continuing its drive to maximize revenue per customer. This time, the sales director wants to find the initial and final sale prices for each car sold to each customer and then compare these prices with the current selling price. You create the following piece of SQL to do this for her:

```
SELECT      CU.CustomerName

            ,SA.SaleDate

            ,SA.TotalSalePrice AS CurrentSale

            ,FIRST_VALUE(SA.TotalSalePrice)

            OVER (PARTITION BY CU.CustomerName

                  ORDER BY SA.SaleDate, SalesID)

                    AS InitialOrder

            ,LAST_VALUE(TotalSalePrice)

            OVER (PARTITION BY CU.CustomerName

                  ORDER BY SaleDate, SA.SalesID

                  ROWS BETWEEN CURRENT ROW AND UNBOUNDED FOLLOWING)

                    AS FinalOrder

FROM        Data.Sales SA

INNER JOIN  Data.Customer CU

            ON SA.CustomerID = CU.CustomerID
```

Running this query gives the results that you can see in *Figure 19.17*.

	CustomerName	SaleDate	CurrentSale	InitialOrder	FinalOrder
1	Alex McWhirter	2018-10-31 00:00:00.000	17850.00	17850.00	17850.00
2	Alexei Tolstoi	2016-09-16 00:00:00.000	45950.00	22990.00	45950.00
3	Alexei Tolstoi	2016-09-04 00:00:00.000	3500.00	22990.00	45950.00
4	Alexei Tolstoi	2016-08-02 00:00:00.000	102500.00	22990.00	45950.00
5	Alexei Tolstoi	2016-07-25 00:00:00.000	205000.00	22990.00	45950.00
6	Alexei Tolstoi	2016-05-30 00:00:00.000	49450.00	22990.00	45950.00
7	Alexei Tolstoi	2015-12-01 00:00:00.000	69500.00	22990.00	45950.00
8	Alexei Tolstoi	2015-10-30 00:00:00.000	22600.00	22990.00	45950.00
9	Alexei Tolstoi	2015-07-15 00:00:00.000	22990.00	22990.00	45950.00
10	Alicia Almodovar	2018-04-15 00:00:00.000	45950.00	12500.00	45950.00
11	Alicia Almodovar	2018-04-02 00:00:00.000	15950.00	12500.00	45950.00
12	Alicia Almodovar	2018-03-05 00:00:00.000	5690.00	12500.00	45950.00
13	Alicia Almodovar	2017-09-20 00:00:00.000	250000.00	12500.00	45950.00
14	Alicia Almodovar	2017-05-10 00:00:00.000	12500.00	12500.00	45950.00
15	Alicia Almodovar	2016-12-31 00:00:00.000	39500.00	12500.00	45950.00

Figure 19.17: Using the FIRST_VALUE() and LAST_VALUE() functions to compare sale prices

How It Works

A useful way to analyze how data evolves over time is to see how a record compares to the first or last record for a common element. This query starts by joining the Customer and Sales tables so that it can access customer and sale data. Then it outputs the CustomerName, SaleDate, and TotalSalePrice fields.

Then a new twist is added. Two output fields are added that are based, respectively, on the FIRST_VALUE() and LAST_VALUE() functions. These act like the LAG() function that you saw in the previous example in that for each record, they create an invisible dataset that is grouped on a shared field (CustomerName in this example). However, in this case, it is not a selected preceding record that is selected, but the very first (or very last) record in this virtual subgroup.

FIRST_VALUE() and LAST_VALUE() require the following elements to work correctly:

OVER	This clause starts the windowing function.
PARTITION BY	This function tells SQL Server how to subset the data when searching for the first record; in this example, this means the first value for the customer of the current record.

The PARTITION BY function is not strictly necessary, but it is used to compare data that share a common element rather than merely returning the first or last value from the entire dataset.

ORDER BY	This clause sorts the data subset.
Field	This indicates the data to return from the preceding record. In this example, it is the SalePrice field.

The FIRST_VALUE(), LAST_VALUE(), and LAG() functions can be particularly useful because by using them, you avoid having to create multiple, complex subqueries or derived tables to isolate values from the data. These functions traverse the data for each element that is specified in the PARTITION BY clause (the client in this example) and return the record that you are looking for.

Figure 19.18 illustrates how these functions work.

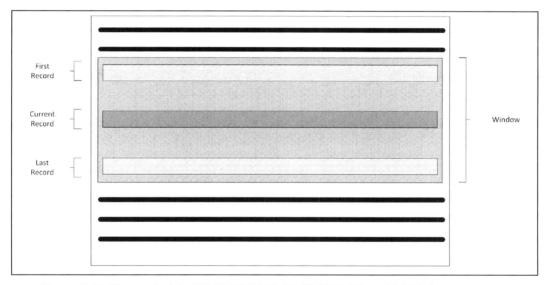

Figure 19.18: *The way that the FIRST_VALUE(), LAST_VALUE(), and LAG() functions operate*

19.10 Displaying Rolling Averages over a Specified Number of Records

This time the sales director thinks he has a real challenge for you. She wants to see how average sale prices evolve over time for each customer in a report that shows the rolling average sale value for the last three sales per customer. Fortunately, SQL makes such reports easy as the following code shows:

```
SELECT      CU.CustomerName
           ,SA.SaleDate
           ,SA.TotalSalePrice
           ,AVG(SA.TotalSalePrice)
            OVER (PARTITION BY CU.CustomerName ORDER BY SA.SaleDate
            ROWS BETWEEN 3 PRECEDING AND CURRENT ROW)
               AS AverageSalePrice
FROM        Data.Sales AS SA
INNER JOIN Data.Customer CU ON SA.CustomerID = CU.CustomerID
ORDER BY    CU.CustomerName, SA.SaleDate
```

Running this query gives the results that you can see in *Figure 19.19*.

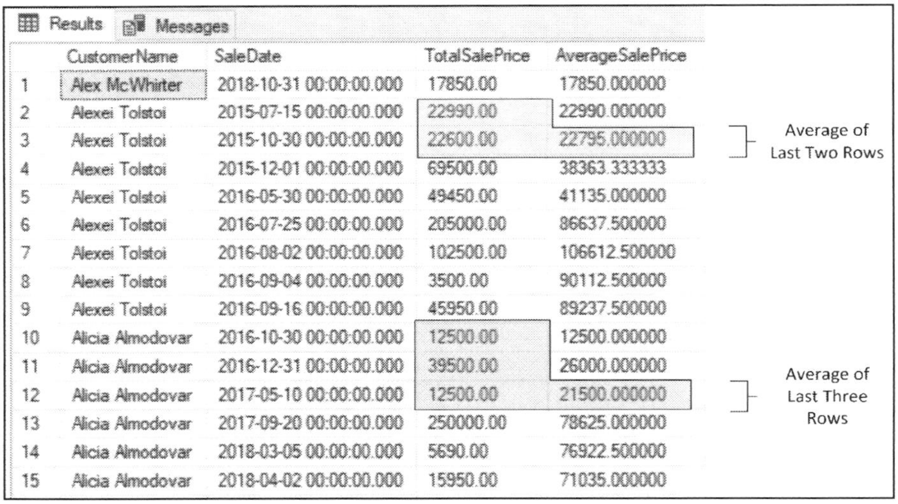

	CustomerName	SaleDate	TotalSalePrice	AverageSalePrice
1	Alex McWhirter	2018-10-31 00:00:00.000	17850.00	17850.000000
2	Alexei Tolstoi	2015-07-15 00:00:00.000	22990.00	22990.000000
3	Alexei Tolstoi	2015-10-30 00:00:00.000	22600.00	22795.000000
4	Alexei Tolstoi	2015-12-01 00:00:00.000	69500.00	38363.333333
5	Alexei Tolstoi	2016-05-30 00:00:00.000	49450.00	41135.000000
6	Alexei Tolstoi	2016-07-25 00:00:00.000	205000.00	86637.500000
7	Alexei Tolstoi	2016-08-02 00:00:00.000	102500.00	106612.500000
8	Alexei Tolstoi	2016-09-04 00:00:00.000	3500.00	90112.500000
9	Alexei Tolstoi	2016-09-16 00:00:00.000	45950.00	89237.500000
10	Alicia Almodovar	2016-10-30 00:00:00.000	12500.00	12500.000000
11	Alicia Almodovar	2016-12-31 00:00:00.000	39500.00	26000.000000
12	Alicia Almodovar	2017-05-10 00:00:00.000	12500.00	21500.000000
13	Alicia Almodovar	2017-09-20 00:00:00.000	250000.00	78625.000000
14	Alicia Almodovar	2018-03-05 00:00:00.000	5690.00	76922.500000
15	Alicia Almodovar	2018-04-02 00:00:00.000	15950.00	71035.000000

Figure 19.19: *Using the ROWS() windowing function to display a rolling average*

How It Works

A classic analytical metric is the `rolling average`. A rolling average requires you to isolate a certain number of records up to and including a current record and then calculate the average of a value in all the specified records. The ROWS windowing function lets you do exactly this. This approach requires you to specify no fewer than seven different elements as part of the windowing function in order for it to work correctly:

AVG()	Is defined as the aggregation function to apply in the query.
OVER	Indicates that this is a windowing function that is being applied to a set of records.
PARTITION BY	Specifies how records are assembled into a subgroup inside the overall recordset. In this example, the CustomerName field is used so that a rolling average per customer can be calculated.
ORDER BY	Is used inside the OVER operator to define how the records for the subset are sorted. This is essential to define the sequencing for the range of records used for the rolling average.
ROWS BETWEEN	Indicates that this operator applies to a set of records relative to the current record.
PRECEDING	Says how many rows back the function must go to find the starting row for the running average.
AND CURRENT ROW	Tells the windowing function to stop at the current record and include it in the total.

In effect, using all these elements to create the rolling average says, "create virtual groups of records for each customer, order them by date, then calculate the average from three rows before the current row up to and including the current row."

So, in this example, you begin by creating the basic query to show the customer name, sales date, and the selling price for each vehicle sold by Prestige Cars. You then add a final column to the query that calculates the running average using the ROWS function.

Tricks and Traps

A few points are worth remembering when you use the ROWS() windowing function:

- A rolling total can be created in exactly the same way as a rolling average. Just use the SUM() function instead of the AVG() function and you have a rolling total.

- Once again, we prefer to add an ORDER BY clause at the end of the query to guarantee that the output is sorted exactly as we want. This is because the ORDER BY clause inside the OVER function is not guaranteed to sort the final output correctly.

- You may prefer to apply a totally different sort order to the final output. Doing so has no effect on the way the running average is calculated. To make this clearer, try tweaking the sort order code to read

```
ORDER BY  SaleDate, CustomerName
```

This returns a list rather like the one in *Figure 19.20.*

	CustomerName	SaleDate	TotalSalePrice	AverageSalePrice
1	Magic Motors	2015-01-02 00:00:00.000	65000.00	65000.000000
2	Casseroles Chromes	2015-01-02 10:33:00.000	19900.00	19900.000000
3	Snazzy Roadsters	2015-01-25 00:00:00.000	220000.10	220000.100000
4	Birmingham Executive Prestige Vehicles	2015-02-03 00:00:00.000	19500.00	19500.000000
5	WunderKar	2015-02-16 00:00:00.000	11500.00	11500.000000
6	Magic Motors	2015-03-14 00:00:00.000	29500.00	47250.000000
7	Birmingham Executive Prestige Vehicles	2015-03-24 00:00:00.000	49500.20	34500.100000
8	Eat My Exhaust Ltd	2015-03-30 00:00:00.000	76000.90	76000.900000
9	Sondra Horowitz	2015-04-04 00:00:00.000	36500.00	36500.000000
10	M. Pierre Dubois	2015-04-06 00:00:00.000	19600.00	19600.000000
11	Wonderland Wheels	2015-04-30 00:00:00.000	89000.00	89000.000000

Figure 19.20: Using a different sort order in the window function and the overall query

As you can see, the output is based on the sale date, not on the customer name. However, the calculation for the running average has not changed. It still calculates the average from last three records per customer, up to and including the current record for that customer; however, the output is less intuitively comprehensible and shows no clear pattern, even if it is arithmetically accurate.

- If you want to show a running average or a running total that does not include the current row, you can replace CURRENT ROW with 1 PRECEDING in the SQL. This carries out the calculation up to but not including the current row.

- You can specify any row range relative to the current row for a running total—you can even cover rows that are further down the display list (or at a later date than the current record if you prefer). You do this by replacing CURRENT ROW with 3 FOLLOWING in the SQL. You can specify any number for the range of records that you want to use as a basis for your calculation.

19.11 Show the First Sale and Last Four Sales per Client

Sales at the company are increasing and senior management is convinced that effective analytics is a key factor of corporate success. The latest request to arrive in your inbox is for a report that shows both the first order and the last four sales for each customer. One way of doing this is shown using the following SQL:

```
SELECT
 CU.CustomerName
,SA.SaleDate
,SA.TotalSalePrice
,FIRST_VALUE(SA.TotalSalePrice) OVER (PARTITION BY CU.CustomerName
                                    ORDER BY SA.SaleDate) AS FirstOrder
,LAG(TotalSalePrice, 3) OVER (PARTITION BY CU.CustomerName
                            ORDER BY SA.SaleDate) AS LastButThreeOrder
,LAG(TotalSalePrice, 2) OVER (PARTITION BY CU.CustomerName
                            ORDER BY SA.SaleDate) AS LastButTwoOrder
,LAG(TotalSalePrice, 1) OVER (PARTITION BY CU.CustomerName
                            ORDER BY SA.SaleDate) AS LastButOneOrder
,LAST_VALUE(TotalSalePrice) OVER (PARTITION BY CU.CustomerName
                                ORDER BY SA.SaleDate) AS LatestOrder
FROM     Data.Sales AS SA
         INNER JOIN Data.Customer CU ON SA.CustomerID = CU.CustomerID
```

Running this query gives the results that you can see in *Figure 19.21*.

	CustomerName	SaleDate	TotalSalePrice	FirstOrder	LastButThreeOrder	LastButTwoOrder	LastButOneOrder	LatestOrder
1	Alex McWhirter	2018-10-31 00:00:00.000	17850.00	17850.00	NULL	NULL	NULL	17850.00
2	Alexei Tolstoi	2015-07-15 00:00:00.000	22990.00	22990.00	NULL	NULL	NULL	22990.00
3	Alexei Tolstoi	2015-10-30 00:00:00.000	22600.00	22990.00	NULL	NULL	22990.00	22600.00
4	Alexei Tolstoi	2015-12-01 00:00:00.000	69500.00	22990.00	NULL	22990.00	22600.00	69500.00
5	Alexei Tolstoi	2016-05-30 00:00:00.000	49450.00	22990.00	22990.00	22600.00	69500.00	49450.00
6	Alexei Tolstoi	2016-07-25 00:00:00.000	205000.00	22990.00	22600.00	69500.00	49450.00	205000.00
7	Alexei Tolstoi	2016-08-02 00:00:00.000	102500.00	22990.00	69500.00	49450.00	205000.00	102500.00
8	Alexei Tolstoi	2016-09-04 00:00:00.000	3500.00	22990.00	49450.00	205000.00	102500.00	3500.00
9	Alexei Tolstoi	2016-09-16 00:00:00.000	45950.00	22990.00	205000.00	102500.00	3500.00	45950.00
10	Alicia Almodovar	2016-10-30 00:00:00.000	12500.00	12500.00	NULL	NULL	NULL	12500.00
11	Alicia Almodovar	2016-12-31 00:00:00.000	39500.00	12500.00	NULL	NULL	12500.00	39500.00
12	Alicia Almodovar	2017-05-10 00:00:00.000	12500.00	12500.00	NULL	12500.00	39500.00	12500.00
13	Alicia Almodovar	2017-09-20 00:00:00.000	250000.00	12500.00	12500.00	39500.00	12500.00	250000.00
14	Alicia Almodovar	2018-03-05 00:00:00.000	5690.00	12500.00	39500.00	12500.00	250000.00	5690.00
15	Alicia Almodovar	2018-04-02 00:00:00.000	15950.00	12500.00	12500.00	250000.00	5690.00	15950.00

Figure 19.21. *Using the FIRST_VALUE(), LAST_VALUE(), and LAG() functions over time*

How It Works

In order to compare sales (or other metrics) you need to extract elements from several records and place them on the same row. The idea behind this query is to give the recipient an idea of how much each client is spending and see how sales are evolving over time. The output displays

- The first sale made by a customer
- The most recent sale
- The three sales before the most recent sale

Each sale is a separate record in a SQL database. The SQL used here uses three more windowing functions to extract data from a subset of data. In this case, it is the successive sales per customer. The query selects the customer name and the date for each sale using the Sales and Customer tables. It then uses the following functions to compare the current sale with other sales for the same customer:

FIRST_VALUE	Shows the sale price for the first-ever purchase made by this customer.
LAST_VALUE	Shows the sale price for the latest purchase made by this customer.
LAG	Shows a previous specific sale—it can be the preceding sale or any previous sale.

Because you are once again dealing with windowing functions to output data from multiple records in the same row, these functions also need you to apply the following keywords:

OVER	To indicate to SQL Server that you are using a windowing function.
ORDER BY	To specify how the records are being sorted in a subset.
PARTITION BY	To group records by a criterion so that you can compare values meaningfully.

In this example, you are partitioning by the client name so that you can see the sales per client. The ORDER BY clause in the OVER function uses the SaleDate field so that you can compare sales over time.

The FIRST_VALUE and LAST_VALUE functions do what their names imply. They look at all the sales for a common element (defined in the PARTITION BY clause—in this case the customer) and find the oldest and most recent purchases, respectively. The LAG() function lets you go back in time over a set of sales for a customer and return the item in the list that matches the figure that you used in the LAG() function. This way, if you say LAG(SalePrice,1), you display the previous sale to a customer.

19.12 Calculating Cumulative Distribution

This time a sales person wants to know the relative standing of each sale by make. In other words, she expects to see a list with a column that shows what percentage of sales were made for less than the current record for each make of car. The following piece of SQL does exactly this:

```
SELECT       MK.MakeName, MD.ModelName, SA.InvoiceNumber, SD.SalePrice
             ,ROUND(CUME_DIST()
             OVER (PARTITION BY MK.MakeName ORDER BY SD.SalePrice),2)
             AS RelativeStanding
FROM         Data.Make AS MK
INNER JOIN   Data.Model AS MD ON MK.MakeID = MD.MakeID
INNER JOIN   Data.Stock AS ST ON ST.ModelID = MD.ModelID
INNER JOIN   Data.SalesDetails SD ON ST.StockCode = SD.StockID
INNER JOIN   Data.Sales AS SA ON SA.SalesID = SD.SalesID
ORDER BY     MK.MakeName, SD.SalePrice, RelativeStanding
```

Running this query gives the results that you can see in *Figure 19.22*. We have scrolled down the data that is returned to give you a better idea of what the output looks like for a couple of makes of car.

	MakeName	ModelName	InvoiceNumber	SalePrice	RelativeStanding
127	BMW	Isetta	GBPGB182	5500.00	0.33
128	BMW	Alpina	EURFR226	21500.00	0.67
129	BMW	E30	EURFR158	33500.00	1
130	Bugatti	Veyron	EURFR143	220500...	0.17
131	Bugatti	57C	GBPGB142	295000...	0.33
132	Bugatti	57C	GBPGB173	335000...	0.5
133	Bugatti	57C	EURFR282	345000...	0.67
134	Bugatti	57C	GBPGB230	355000...	0.83
135	Bugatti	57C	EURFR221	365000...	1
136	Citroen	Rosalie	GBPGB139	990.00	0.17
137	Citroen	Rosalie	GBPGB252	1350.00	0.33
138	Citroen	Rosalie	GBPCH161	2350.00	0.5
139	Citroen	Rosalie	EURFR322	5500.00	0.67
140	Citroen	Traaction ...	EURFR300	25000.00	0.83

Figure 19.22: Displaying cumulative distribution with the CUME_DIST() function

How It Works

Putting things into perspective is what data analysis can be all about, so it can help if you are able to see the relative position of a value compared to other values. In this windowing function, you used the CUME_DIST() function to see how each sale is situated relative to all other sales for the same make of car. Only this time you do not see a strict ranking, but the percentage of cars sold for a lower price. This means that the bestselling car for a specific make will display 1 (100 percent) with all other cars showing a smaller percentage figure.

This query initially requires that you join all the tables that you need to select the required fields. In this case, the tables are Make, Model, Sales, SalesDetails, and Stock.

Then you can add the CUME_DIST() function to the SELECT clause. As is the case with the other windowing functions that you have seen so far in this chapter, you need to specify an ORDER BY element (the sale price in this example). Then you extend the windowing function with a PARTITION BY clause that uses the make of vehicle to group the records into multiple subsets. This lets you isolate the sale price for each record relative to cars of the same make.

The end result is that for each make of car, you can see which is the most expensive sale and what percentage of cars sells for each sale per make.

Tricks and Traps

Creating a cumulative distribution with the CUME_DIST() function does require some attention to detail. The key points to take away are

- The PARTITION BY clause is `optional` with this function. If you want, you can remove it and instead display the percentage of vehicles that sell for less than the current car for `all sales`, irrespective of make.

- The field that you use in the ORDER BY function of the OVER clause to establish the relative standing must be numeric.

- We have added the ROUND() function to the CUME_DIST() function to prevent the display of the 15 decimal places that otherwise appear by default. You can, of course, leave this function out of the query if you prefer.

- You may prefer to sort a dataset such as this by the sale price in descending order so that you can see the most expensive sale per make first. In any case, the sort order that is applied to the overall query is independent of the ORDER BY clause that is applied to the CUME_DIST() function.

19.13 Classifying Data Using the PERCENT_RANK() Function

To conclude her analyses of vehicle sales, the sales director not only wants to see vehicle sales for each country by value but also wants to get an idea of the percentile in the sale hierarchy for each vehicle sold. The next piece of SQL delivers exactly what she is looking for:

```
SELECT      CO.CountryName, SA.SaleDate, SA.InvoiceNumber
            ,FORMAT(PERCENT_RANK()
```

```
            OVER (PARTITION BY CO.CountryName
            ORDER BY SA.TotalSalePrice), '0.00 %') AS PercentageRanking
FROM        Data.Sales AS SA
INNER JOIN Data.Customer CU ON SA.CustomerID = CU.CustomerID
INNER JOIN Data.Country CO ON CU.Country = CO.CountryISO2
ORDER BY    CO.CountryName, SA.TotalSalePrice DESC
```

Running this query gives the results that you can see in *Figure 19.23*.

	CountryName	SaleDate	InvoiceNumber	PercentageRanking
1	Belgium	2016-08-23 00:00:00.000	EURBE074	100.00 %
2	Belgium	2017-03-12 00:00:00.000	EURBE132	83.33 %
3	Belgium	2017-07-01 00:00:00.000	EURBE171	66.67 %
4	Belgium	2017-11-06 00:00:00.000	EURBE193	50.00 %
5	Belgium	2017-02-12 00:00:00.000	EURBE125	33.33 %
6	Belgium	2018-06-03 00:00:00.000	EURBE264	16.67 %
7	Belgium	2018-01-10 00:00:00.000	EURBE218	0.00 %
8	France	2017-02-08 00:00:00.000	EURFR122	100.00 %
9	France	2017-02-07 00:00:00.000	EURFR121	98.36 %
10	France	2018-01-15 00:00:00.000	EURFR221	96.72 %
11	France	2018-07-31 00:00:00.000	EURFR282	95.08 %
12	France	2018-03-15 00:00:00.000	EURFR235	93.44 %
13	France	2017-05-21 00:00:00.000	EURFR156	91.80 %
14	France	2018-05-15 00:00:00.000	EURFR254	90.16 %
15	France	2017-05-12 00:00:00.000	EURFR151	88.52 %

Figure 19.23: Using the PERCENT_RANK()function to classify groups of data

How It Works

One useful analytical technique is to indicate the relative rank of a row inside a group of rows. This query starts when you select the necessary tables (Sales, Customer, and Country). Then you add any fields that you want to display and use the ORDER BY clause so that the data that is returned is more comprehensible.

Finally, you add the PERCENT_RANK() function to the SELECT clause. It requires the OVER clause and an ORDER BY function that takes a numeric value as the field to sort on (SalePrice). In this example (although this is optional), you added a PARTITION BY clause to the windowing function to subset the relative sale position by country.

The end result is an ordered list of sales per country. Starting with the highest-value sale, the list displays each vehicle sale in descending order by value and where each record stands in relation to all the other sales for the country. This "ranking" is expressed as a percentage of the number of records that appear below the current record. This means that the top record shows 100 percent, and the bottom record shows 0 percent.

Tricks and Traps

When using PERCENT_RANK() be sure to note that

- The field that you use in the ORDER BY function of the OVER clause to establish the relative standing must be numeric.

- You do not need to add the field used as the basis for the PERCENT_RANK() function to the SELECT clause; however, adding it can make the output easier to understand.

- You do not need to format the output for the PERCENT_RANK() function as a percentage; however, we feel that it makes the output easier to comprehend.

19.14 Using the LAG() Function with Alphabetical Data

The marketing director wants a list of all the company's customers in alphabetical order. However, here is the twist—she also wants a phone-book-style presentation with all customers grouped by the first letter of their name.

After a little thought, you come up with the following code.

```
SELECT      CASE
                WHEN LEFT(CustomerName, 1) =
                    LAG (LEFT(CustomerName, 1))
                    OVER (ORDER BY CustomerName) THEN NULL
                ELSE LEFT(CustomerName, 1)
            END AS IndexLetter
            ,CustomerName
FROM        Data.SalesByCountry
GROUP BY    CustomerName
ORDER BY    CustomerName
```

Running this code gives the output that you can see in *Figure 19.24*.

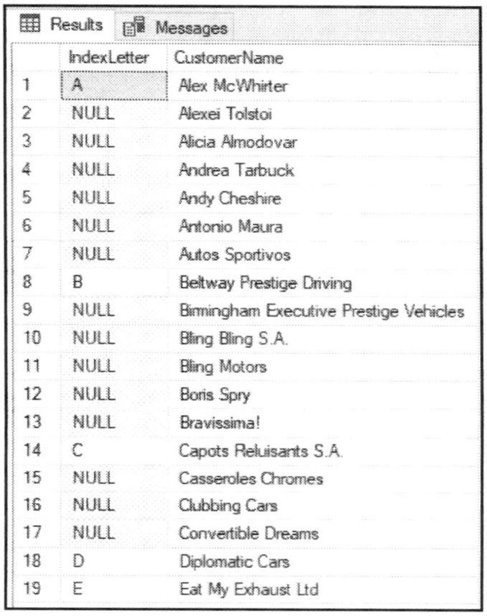

	IndexLetter	CustomerName
1	A	Alex McWhirter
2	NULL	Alexei Tolstoi
3	NULL	Alicia Almodovar
4	NULL	Andrea Tarbuck
5	NULL	Andy Cheshire
6	NULL	Antonio Maura
7	NULL	Autos Sportivos
8	B	Beltway Prestige Driving
9	NULL	Birmingham Executive Prestige Vehicles
10	NULL	Bling Bling S.A.
11	NULL	Bling Motors
12	NULL	Boris Spry
13	NULL	Bravissima!
14	C	Capots Reluisants S.A.
15	NULL	Casseroles Chromes
16	NULL	Clubbing Cars
17	NULL	Convertible Dreams
18	D	Diplomatic Cars
19	E	Eat My Exhaust Ltd

Figure 19.24: *Using the LAG() function to produce an alphabetical index*

How It Works

It is really quite easy to isolate the first letter of the name of every client. Applying the LEFT() function (and specifying 1 as the number of characters to extract) to the CustomerName field in the SalesByCountry View does this. However, tweaking this function so that it only shows the index letter when a new letter of the alphabet occurs requires a little more effort.

The answer is to use the LAG() function. As you have seen, this function shows the contents of a field in the previous record in the output. What this code snippet does is

First:	Apply the LAG() function to the LEFT() function that is applied to the customer name, and specify 1 as the number of rows to go backward. In effect this selects the first letter of the customer name in the previous record. The LAG() function is ordered by the CustomerName field to ensure that the customer records are handled in alphabetical order when it is comparing records.
Then:	A CASE statement compares the first letter of the customer name for the current record with the first letter of the customer name for the previous record. If the two are the same, then nothing (or rather NULL) is output. However, if the two are different (which means that the customer name of the current record begins with a different letter than the customer name of the previous record), then the first letter is output.

The end result is a list of customers with a structure rather like the index of a book.

Conclusion

This chapter allowed you to focus on running totals and relative weighting when analyzing your data. You saw how to create running totals, running averages, and running counts using SQL. You then learned how to segment the output so that the "rolling" result restarted when a specified element changed.

Finally, you saw how to extend these techniques to show the first or last element in a series, how to display the first or last element in a series, and ways to illustrate the relative weighting of a value in a list.

Core Knowledge Learned in This Chapter

The functions that you have seen in this chapter are

Concept	Description
ROW_NUMBER()	This function adds a system-generated sequential number to each record in the dataset.
LAG()	This function lets you reach back over the previous records in a recordset or subgroup of records to calculate metrics over a defined series of rows relative to the current record.
FIRST_VALUE()	This function returns the starting value in a field in a recordset or subgroup of records.
LAST_VALUE()	This function returns the final value in a field in a recordset or subgroup of records.
ROWS BETWEEN	Used with a windowing function, this operator lets you define the range of records used in a running calculation.
PRECEDING	Used with a windowing function, this operator also lets you define the range of records used in a running calculation.
CURRENT ROW	Used with a windowing function, this operator helps you specify a range of records including the current row.
CUME_DIST()	This function returns a cumulative distribution—the relative position of a value compared to other values.
PERCENT_RANK()	This function returns a figure indicating what percentage of a subgroup of records can be found with smaller values than a defined column in a recordset or subgroup of records.

CHAPTER 20

Analyzing Data Over Time

This chapter is all about enhancing your analytical abilities so that you can compare and contrast data over time. Here, we build on the core techniques that you saw previously and extend your knowledge to make you completely at ease when slicing and dicing data that contains a time element. Of course, when we talk about dealing with time, we mean looking at both date and time elements in SQL Server. Mastering these techniques helps you track the evolution of sales, profits, or any metric over any time period—from years to days to hours and seconds.

Time Analysis

Analyzing data over time has the potential to be a vast subject. This is because no two people's requirements are ever going to be identical. So, to give you an idea of what to expect, the kinds of time analysis that you learn in this chapter include

- Month-to-date, quarter-to-date, and year-to-date calculations

- Comparing metrics with those from previous time periods

- Parallel period calculations—comparing figures for the same month in the previous year

- Comparing values for a current month to date with the same month to date from the previous year

- Displaying timespans as years, months, and days

- Calculating weekdays and weekends

- Displaying time differences in hours and minutes

- Grouping data by time slots

Once you have mastered the essentials of adding a time factor to your SQL queries, you will probably be pleasantly surprised at the new analytical horizons that are available for you to apply in your queries. Admittedly, you need to pay close attention to some of the techniques that are used; however, we are sure that you will find that the investment is well worth the sheer power of the analysis that is now possible when you use SQL to slice and dice data over time.

20.1 Aggregating Values for the Year to Date

The sales director keeps one eye firmly on the accumulated sales for the year so that she can quickly take any corrective actions that may prove necessary. SQL makes giving her the data that she wants really easy, as the following code shows (for sales in 2017):

```
SELECT      MK.MakeName, SUM(SD.SalePrice) AS CumulativeSalesYTD

FROM        Data.Make AS MK INNER JOIN Data.Model AS MD

            ON MK.MakeID = MD.MakeID

INNER JOIN Data.Stock AS ST ON ST.ModelID = MD.ModelID

INNER JOIN Data.SalesDetails SD ON ST.StockCode = SD.StockID

INNER JOIN Data.Sales AS SA ON SA.SalesID = SD.SalesID

WHERE       SA.SaleDate BETWEEN DATEFROMPARTS(YEAR(GETDATE()),1,1)

            AND CONVERT(CHAR(8), GETDATE(), 112)

GROUP BY    MK.MakeName

ORDER BY    MK.MakeName ASC
```

Figure 20.1 shows the results returned by this query (for a query run in late 2017).

	MakeName	CumulativeSalesYTD
1	Alfa Romeo	71150.00
2	Aston Martin	1341400.00
3	Austin	8750.00
4	BMW	39000.00
5	Bugatti	850500.00
6	Citroen	69230.00
7	Delahaye	29500.00
8	Delorean	99500.00
9	Ferrari	2051900.00
10	Jaguar	109000.00
11	Lagonda	156500.00
12	Lamborghini	785000.00
13	McLaren	295000.00
14	Mercedes	155275.00
15	Noble	129500.00

Figure 20.1: *Calculating aggregate values for the year to date*

How It Works

Collating the sales for the year to date is a fairly regular requirement in many organizations. In this sort of query, all the effort goes (once again) into the WHERE clause. This is because what you do in this clause is set a range of dates in a BETWEEN…AND operator in order to specify a precise date range. The timespan is defined by

A lower boundary	The first of January for the current year that you passed into the query as DATEFROMPARTS(YEAR(GETDATE()),1,1). This is another way of saying "January 1, 2017" (assuming you run the query anytime in 2017).
An upper boundary	The time that the query was run, defined by the GETDATE() function. Since the GETDATE() function returns both date and time values, you ensure that `only the year, month, and day part of the current date` are used by wrapping GETDATE() in the CONVERT() function that you saw in Chapter 8.

The trick that you are using here is finding the `current year`, since the query needs to be dynamic (that is, you want to be able to run it in any year to get the sales for the year to date). It follows that you do not want to enter a fixed year, so you are using the YEAR function to extract the current year from the GETDATE() function. The

GETDATE() function, after all, returns the current date and time for the computer hosting the SQL Server database.

Tricks and Traps

Working with dates can involve using several different SQL functions all at the same time. Be sure to remember that

- The actual results vary depending on the date that you run the query. This example was run in November 2017.

- If you are using a version of SQL Server prior to the 2012 version, you cannot use the DATEFROMPARTS() function. Instead, you can write the following code to return January 1 for the current year:

```
CAST(YEAR(GETDATE()) AS CHAR(4)) + '0101'
```

- This code snippet extracts the year part from the current date and converts it to a string of four characters. It then adds 0101 (to represent the month and day, which is January 1) to the year to give the date in the format YYYYMMDD for the current year.

- It is worth noting that this technique requires one final tweak to work properly. The potential problem lies in the fact that the YEAR() function returns a number, but you need to tell SQL that the date for January 1 needs to be read as a string (a series of letters if you prefer to think of it like this). The CAST() function simply converts the four numbers for the year to four letters. Once this is done, SQL can join this string (2015 here) to the day and month for January 1 (0101)—giving 20150101 as one of the boundaries for the date range to filter on.

- If you are using the BETWEEN … AND keywords to set a range, you must always place the lower boundary after BETWEEN and the upper boundary after AND. This query would not have worked if you typed it as

```
WHERE     SA.SaleDate BETWEEN CONVERT(CHAR(8), GETDATE(), 112)
          AND DATEFROMPARTS(YEAR(GETDATE()),1,1)
```

- Isolating parts of dates is an essential technique for defining date ranges in SQL. We admit that it can get a little laborious at times separating out the year from the month from the day elements that make up a date—and sometimes even having to convert them, individually, to strings. The upside, however, is that this approach does give you unprecedented control and precision when it comes to setting date ranges.

20.2 Aggregating Values for the Month to Date

Since the sales staff has monthly targets to meet, you have been asked to write a query that can show sales for the month to date. SQL can do this, of course, as the following piece of code shows:

```
SELECT      MK.MakeName, SUM(SD.SalePrice) AS CumulativeSalesMTD
FROM        Data.Make AS MK INNER JOIN Data.Model AS MD
            ON MK.MakeID = MD.MakeID
INNER JOIN Data.Stock AS ST ON ST.ModelID = MD.ModelID
INNER JOIN Data.SalesDetails SD ON ST.StockCode = SD.StockID
INNER JOIN Data.Sales AS SA ON SA.SalesID = SD.SalesID
WHERE       SA.SaleDate
            BETWEEN
            DATEADD(MONTH, DATEDIFF(MONTH, 0, GETDATE()), 0)
            AND GETDATE()
GROUP BY    MK.MakeName
ORDER BY    MK.MakeName ASC
```

This SQL gives the following result for November 2017 as you can see in *Figure 20.2*. You might see something completely different if you are running this query on a different date.

	MakeName	CumulativeSalesMTD
1	Alfa Romeo	25000.00
2	Lamborghini	245000.00
3	Porsche	49500.00
4	Triumph	39500.00

Figure 20.2: *Aggregate metrics for the month to date*

How It Works

If you (or other staff) have monthly targets to meet, then you are likely to want to track metrics for the month to date. This type of query, like its predecessor, sets a date range. This time the range is from the start of the current month to the current date.

First:	You need to find the date that corresponds to the first day of the current month and set this as the lower date threshold for the range of dates. The technique that we are using here is, we admit, a bit of an SQL insider's trick, but it works beautifully and, consequently, is well worth learning. You start by applying the DATEDIFF() function to the current date and specifying "month" and "0" as the two other parameters. Then you wrap this function in the DATEADD() function and specify "month" and "0" as the two other parameters. The result is that SQL Server returns the first day of the current month from this combination of functions.
Second:	You define the upper date threshold using the GETDATE() function.

You can run this query at any time without having to adjust date parameters because it always adjusts the WHERE clause to look at the sales for the current month.

Tricks and Traps

There are a couple of key points to take away when aggregating values over time:

- You can also write the beginning of month in other ways if you prefer. One classic way is to use code like the following SQL snippet:

```
CAST(YEAR(GETDATE()) AS CHAR(4))
+ RIGHT('0' + CAST(MONTH(GETDATE()) AS VARCHAR(2)),2) + '01'
```

- This approach re-creates a date by isolating the year, month, and day from the current date. The YEAR() function is easy to understand, since it defines the first of the month as a hard-coded figure. The month, however, is slightly more problematic because it has to be entered as two digits for the converted date string to be usable by SQL Server. The months of October, November, and December are not a problem, as they are the months 10, 11, and 12, respectively, and are composed of two digits. The problem arises with the first nine months of the year because these are each only a single digit (1 through 9). In the case of the first nine months, you have to add a leading zero—which you do manually, adding a zero (as a string in single quotes to keep SQL from complaining). This means that the last three months will look like 010, 011, and 012, so you then wrap the month figure (with the leading zero) in the RIGHT() function to force SQL to chop off the leftmost character— **if** there is one. This may seem a little clunky, but it is wonderfully effective, since it leaves the leading zero when it is needed and removes it when it is superfluous. The net result is that you get the month as two digits—from 01 to 12.

- When converting the month from a number to a letter, you use the VARCHAR() function instead of the CHAR() function as you did for the year. This is because the month can be one digit or two, and VARCHAR()

accepts a variable number of characters—up to the maximum (two in this example) that you specified.

20.3 Returning Aggregate Values for the Quarter to Date

Not content with a one-click solution that displays monthly sales, the sales team has now requested a report showing quarterly sales to date as well. The SQL that follows lets you keep them happy:

```
SELECT      MK.MakeName, SUM(SD.SalePrice) AS CumulativeSalesQTD
FROM        Data.Make AS MK INNER JOIN Data.Model AS MD
            ON MK.MakeID = MD.MakeID
INNER JOIN Data.Stock AS ST ON ST.ModelID = MD.ModelID
INNER JOIN Data.SalesDetails SD ON ST.StockCode = SD.StockID
INNER JOIN Data.Sales AS SA ON SA.SalesID = SD.SalesID
WHERE       SA.SaleDate BETWEEN DATEADD(q, DATEDIFF(q, 0, GETDATE()), 0)
            AND CONVERT(CHAR(8), GETDATE(), 112)
GROUP BY    MK.MakeName
ORDER BY    MK.MakeName ASC
```

Figure 20.3 shows what happens when you run this code snippet on November 3, 2017.

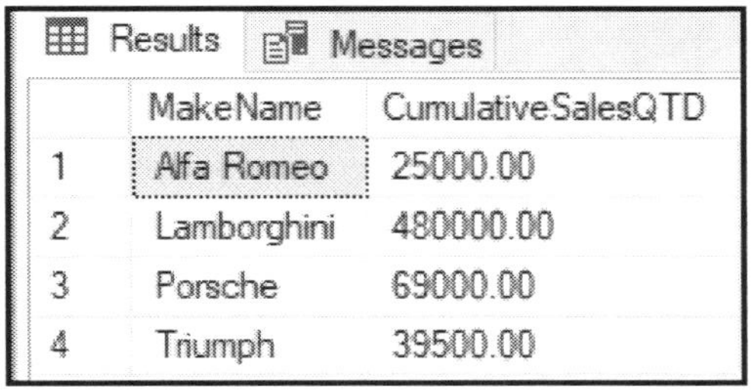

	MakeName	CumulativeSalesQTD
1	Alfa Romeo	25000.00
2	Lamborghini	480000.00
3	Porsche	69000.00
4	Triumph	39500.00

Figure 20.3: *Aggregating a metric for the quarter to date*

How It Works

To end this short period-to-date trilogy of solutions, this example shows how to calculate the sales for the quarter to date.

First, as is the case with just about any query, you join the required tables to ensure that you can access the fields that you need. Then you add the GROUP BY and

ORDER BY clauses to make this an aggregated query that displays the output in the correct sort order.

Finally, you need to concentrate on getting the WHERE clause right, since this is the key to achieving the desired result.

First:	Deduce the start of the current quarter using the DATEDIFF() and DATEADD() technique that you applied in the previous section. The only difference is that as you are intent on finding the date for the `first day in the quarter`; you use the q parameter for both these functions to indicate to SQL Server that you are looking at `quarterly` data (and not daily or monthly dates).
Finally:	You set the upper threshold using the GETDATE() function to set the current date and time as the upper limit of the date range.

In this example, we use the CONVERT()function to strip out the time element from the GETDATE() function. This, in effect, sets the upper date threshold to midnight at the `start of the current day.` Consequently, it `excludes all sales on the current day` and only includes sales up until the end of the previous day. When writing queries like this, you need to confirm with the business exactly what they mean by "current day" before you write the query.

Tricks and Traps

There are only a couple of short points to remember at this stage:

- Remember that when you use the BETWEEN ... AND operator, you must place the `lower` threshold after the BETWEEN keyword and the `upper` threshold after the AND keyword.

- You can also use the DATEADD() and DATEDIFF() technique that we explained in the previous section to get the start of the current year if you want. One way to do this is to use the following SQL:

```
SELECT DATEADD(YY, DATEDIFF(YY, 0, GETDATE()), 0)
```

20.4 Isolating Data for the Previous Month

In his push for increased profits, the CFO always wants to know how this month's purchases compare to last month's figures. As a result, he wants to see purchases by make for the previous calendar month. SQL can help you produce data like this really easily as the following code shows:

```
SELECT    MK.MakeName, SUM(ST.Cost) AS TotalCost

FROM      Data.Make AS MK INNER JOIN Data.Model AS MD
```

```
            ON MK.MakeID = MD.MakeID
INNER JOIN Data.Stock AS ST ON ST.ModelID = MD.ModelID
WHERE       DateBought BETWEEN
            CAST(YEAR(DATEADD(m, -1, GETDATE())) AS CHAR(4))
            + RIGHT('0' + CAST(MONTH(DATEADD(m, -1, GETDATE()))
            AS VARCHAR(2)),2) + '01'
            AND EOMONTH(DATEADD(m, -1, GETDATE()))
GROUP BY    MK.MakeName
```

Running this code displays the data that you can see in *Figure 20.4* (for November 2017—it will, of course, be different if run on another date).

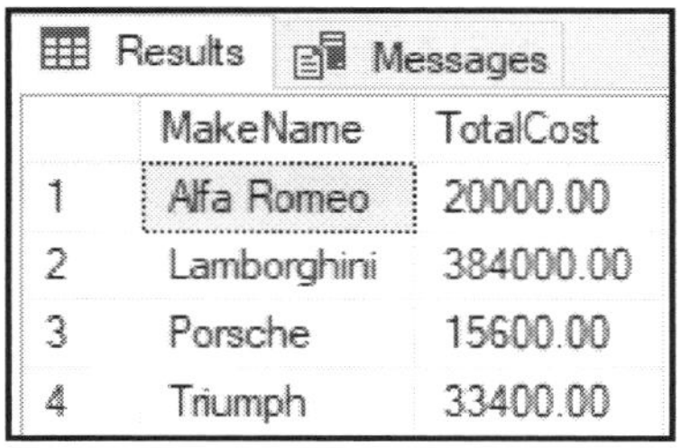

	MakeName	TotalCost
1	Alfa Romeo	20000.00
2	Lamborghini	384000.00
3	Porsche	15600.00
4	Triumph	33400.00

Figure 20.4: *Filtering on data for the previous month using the DATEADD() and EOMONTH() functions*

How It Works

You might be called on at any time to calculate metrics for the preceding month—such as, for instance, when you compile the month end figures at the start of the following month. Once again, in this kind of time-based query you are defining a date range. On this occasion, however, the WHERE clause uses the DATEADD() function to set both the start and end dates for the period to the `first day` and the `last day` of the previous month.

The `first day of the preceding month` is set by assembling the required date as a YYYYMMDD; however, this requires you to assemble the three parts of the date (year, month, and day) separately.

The Year	Is calculated by finding the previous month (which could be December of the previous year) using the DATEADD() function. In this case, you use the m date part type and a –1 to indicate that you want to go back one month. Then you extract the year, using the YEAR() function, and finally, you convert this to a string, as you have done previously.

The Month	Is defined by (once again) finding the previous month using the DATEADD() function with the m date part type and a –1 as the number of months to go back. Then you extract the month, using the MONTH() function, and finally, you convert this to a string, too. Defining the start of the current month requires you to find the current year and then convert this to a string, just as you did in the previous section. Then you have to find the current month.
The Day	Is the easy part. Because it is always the first of the month, all you have to do is to hardcode the value '01'.

The `last day of the preceding month` is easier to calculate, because SQL has a specific function for doing this. The function is EOMONTH(), and it returns the last day of the month for a date. In this example, you want the last day of the previous month, so you use the DATEADD() function with the m date part type and a –1 as the number of months to go back to ask SQL to give you the final day of the previous month.

By using these two date calculations in the BETWEEN…AND clause, you set the entire previous month as the date range. This works no matter how many days are in the month as well going back to previous years.

Tricks and Traps

Isolating dates can seem a little verbose in SQL, but it is not really difficult. Just remember that

- Calculating the first day of the month in this way can seem a little disconcerting at first. However, it is typical of the way that SQL works—nesting functions in functions to break data down into the smallest constituent parts, only to reassemble them in a way that allows you to achieve the desired result.

- You can, of course use either of the other techniques that you saw in previous examples to calculate the first day of the month.

- Another way to specify the beginning of the month is to use the following SQL:

```
SELECT DATEADD(d, 1, EOMONTH(DATEADD(m, -2, GETDATE())))
```

20.5 Using a Derived Table to Compare Data with Values from a Previous Year

Seasonal variations can often be very revealing, or at least this is what the CFO thinks. He has asked you to provide some analysis of like-for-like sales so he can see the average sales by color for the same month in both the previous year and the current year. The following code lets you keep him happy:

```
SELECT      ST.Color, AVG(SA.TotalSalePrice) AS AverageMonthSales
            ,MAX(AveragePreviousMonthSales)
                AS AveragePreviousYearMonthSales
FROM        Data.Make AS MK
INNER JOIN Data.Model AS MD ON MK.MakeID = MD.MakeID
INNER JOIN Data.Stock AS ST ON ST.ModelID = MD.ModelID
INNER JOIN Data.SalesDetails SD ON ST.StockCode = SD.StockID
INNER JOIN Data.Sales AS SA ON SA.SalesID = SD.SalesID
            LEFT OUTER JOIN
                (
                    SELECT      Color, AVG(SA.TotalSalePrice)
                                AS AveragePreviousMonthSales
                    FROM        Data.Make AS MK
                    INNER JOIN Data.Model AS MD
                                ON MK.MakeID = MD.MakeID
                    INNER JOIN Data.Stock AS ST
                                ON ST.ModelID = MD.ModelID
                    INNER JOIN Data.SalesDetails SD
                                ON ST.StockCode = SD.StockID
                    INNER JOIN Data.Sales AS SA
                                ON SA.SalesID = SD.SalesID
                    WHERE       YEAR(SA.SaleDate)
                                = YEAR(GETDATE())- 1
                                AND MONTH(SA.SaleDate)
                                = MONTH(GETDATE())
                    GROUP BY    Color
                ) SQ
            ON SQ.Color = ST.Color
WHERE       YEAR(SA.SaleDate) = YEAR(GETDATE())
            AND MONTH(SA.SaleDate) = MONTH(GETDATE())
GROUP BY    St.Color
```

Running this query gives the results that you can see in *Figure 20.5*—if you run the code in August 2018. For other dates, you get different results.

	Color	AverageMonthSales	AveragePreviousYearMonthSales
1	Black	69683.333333	38800.000000
2	Blue	47250.000000	5500.000000
3	Night Blue	85595.000000	45000.000000
4	Silver	78150.000000	NULL

Figure 20.5: Displaying figures for a parallel time period using a derived table

How It Works

This query is in two main parts:

A derived table	That calculates the sales by color for the same month in the previous year.
An outer query	That calculates the sales by color for the current month and year.

Each of these elements uses the same core query. First the Make, Model, Stock, SalesDetails, and Sales tables are joined. Then the Color field is added to the SELECT and GROUP BY clauses to aggregate data by color. Finally, the average sale price is calculated. The only real difference is that the derived table (the inner query) looks at last year's data. This is done by adjusting the GETDATE() function for the year so that it reads

```
YEAR(GETDATE()) - 1
```

Then the two parts of the query are joined. We do this using a LEFT OUTER JOIN to ensure that all the colors for sales this year will be shown. If you use an INNER JOIN instead, then you will not see any colors that sold this year but not last year. Remember that the LEFT OUTER JOIN means "all records from the first dataset, including any that match from the second dataset."

Finally, you added the average sale price for last year's sales to the outer query. However, as this, too, is an aggregate query, you cannot just add the AveragePreviousMonthSales field from the derive table, or SQL Server complains that it is not "contained in either an aggregate function or the GROUP BY clause." To allow the result to be used, you have to wrap it in the MAX() function. Once the result is handled like this, it can appear in the query output. The MAX() function does not alter the result of the AveragePreviousMonthSales field in any way since it is already aggregated and correct. The function merely allows the result to be used in the outer aggregate query.

Using derived tables in subqueries is a standard technique for comparing data over time in SQL. *Figure 20.6* explains this concept more visually.

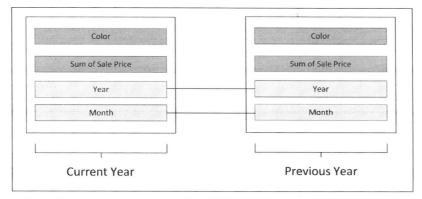

Figure 20.6: *Comparing data over time using a derived table*

Tricks and Traps

To extend your SQL knowledge, you might like to note this technique:

- As an alternative way to having the derived table return only the data for the previous year, you can use the DATEADD() function, like this:

```
WHERE       YEAR(SA.SaleDate) = YEAR(DATEADD(yy, GETDATE(), - 1))
```

20.6 Finding the Total Amount for Each Weekday

The sales director is on a mission to find out if certain weekdays are better for sales than others. You have prepared the following query for her so she can analyze sales for each day of the week in 2017.

```
;
WITH TallyTable_CTE
AS
(
SELECT      ROW_NUMBER() OVER (ORDER BY StockCode) - 1 AS ID
FROM        Data.Stock
)
,DateList_CTE
AS
```

```
(
SELECT          DATEADD(DD, ID, DATEFROMPARTS(2017, 1, 1))
                AS WeekdayDate
                ,DATENAME(DW, DATEADD(DD, ID, DATEFROMPARTS(2017, 1, 1)))
                AS WeekdayName
FROM            TallyTable_CTE
WHERE            DATEPART(dw, DATEADD(DD, ID, DATEFROMPARTS(2017, 1, 1)))
                BETWEEN 2 AND 6
                AND
                CAST(DATEADD(DD, ID, DATEFROMPARTS(2017, 1, 1)) AS DATE)
                <= '20171231'
)
SELECT          CTE.WeekdayDate
                ,CTE.WeekdayName
                ,SUM(SLS.SalePrice) AS TotalDailySales
FROM            Data.SalesByCountry SLS
INNER JOIN      DateList_CTE CTE
                ON CTE.WeekdayDate = CAST(SLS.SaleDate AS DATE)
GROUP BY        CTE.WeekdayDate
                ,CTE.WeekdayName
ORDER BY        CTE.WeekdayDate
```

If you run this query you see the result shown in *Figure 20.7*.

	WeekdayDate	WeekdayName	TotalDailySales
1	2017-01-05	Thursday	125000.00
2	2017-01-10	Tuesday	85000.00
3	2017-01-11	Wednesday	22500.00
4	2017-01-12	Thursday	125950.00
5	2017-01-13	Friday	8850.00
6	2017-01-30	Monday	56500.00
7	2017-01-31	Tuesday	111950.00
8	2017-02-07	Tuesday	365000.00
9	2017-02-08	Wednesday	395000.00
10	2017-02-09	Thursday	21500.00
11	2017-02-10	Friday	6500.00
12	2017-02-14	Tuesday	2250.00
13	2017-03-10	Friday	213000.00
14	2017-03-30	Thursday	305000.00
15	2017-03-31	Friday	313940.00

Figure 20.7: The total sales for weekdays

How It Works

This query is built in three stages. For the moment, let's take a closer look at the first two parts of the code.

First:	A tally table is created to provide a list from 0 to nearly 400. The exact number is irrelevant as long as it is at least 365—the number of days in the year (or 366 if you are dealing with a leap year). In this example, we are creating a `tally` CTE by creating an initial CTE (Common Table Expression) that uses the Stock table to create a sequential list using the ROW_NUMBER() function. You can base the tally list on any table that contains enough records (or even more than one table if you need a lot of records in the list). If you select the code for the first CTE (named TallyTable_CTE) and run it, you see a list like the one shown in *Figure 20.8*.

Figure 20.8: The output from a tally table CTE

Second:	A second CTE that uses the tally CTE to generate a sequential list of every date in the year. This is done by using the DATEADD() function, which is applied to every record in the tally table.

What the DATEADD() function does is take January 1, 2017—defined using the DATEFROMPARTS() function—and add to this the number in the ID column of the tally table. This gives a sequence of dates. Indeed, the tally table is deliberately set to start at zero so that the first DATEADD() function in the list of dates returns January 1 (as the function adds zero days to the start date).

This technique is then used a total of four times:

First:	To give the date resulting from the DATEADD() sequence.
Second:	Inside a DATENAME function to return the name of the day of the week.
Third:	Inside the WHERE clause of the second CTE. Specifically the DATEADD() sequence is enclosed in a DATEPART() function to return the number of the day in the week. Because day 0 and day 7 (Sunday and Saturday, respectively) are not weekdays, the WHERE clause excludes these. One way of doing this is to filter so that only day numbers between 2 and 6 (Monday to Friday) pass the conditions set by the WHERE clause.
Finally:	The WHERE clause adds an upper limit to the list that is generated by the two CTEs by setting the date of the last day of 2017.

To get an idea of how these two CTEs work, you can replace the entire final query with a SELECT statement to show the output of the second CTE using the following code.

```
SELECT * FROM DateList_CTE
```

If you run the two CTEs followed by the SELECT statement, you see the output from the second CTE (which uses the date from the first CTE) as shown in *Figure 20.9*.

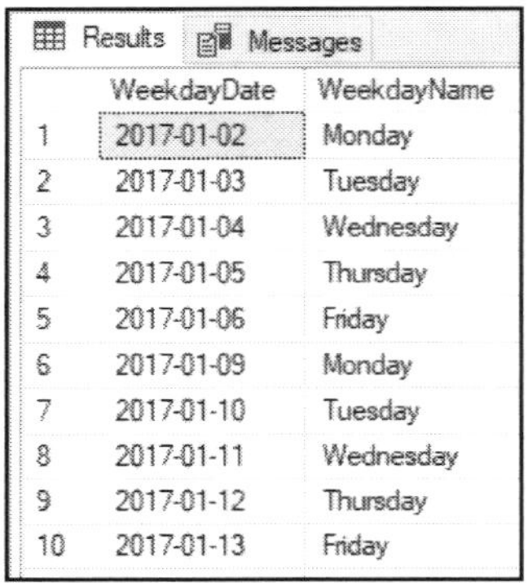

	WeekdayDate	WeekdayName
1	2017-01-02	Monday
2	2017-01-03	Tuesday
3	2017-01-04	Wednesday
4	2017-01-05	Thursday
5	2017-01-06	Friday
6	2017-01-09	Monday
7	2017-01-10	Tuesday
8	2017-01-11	Wednesday
9	2017-01-12	Thursday
10	2017-01-13	Friday

Figure 20.9: *Using a CTE to isolate the weekdays*

The output from the second CTE then becomes the basis for the final query, since it displays the dates and weekday names for all the days in the year 2017. The final query joins the CTE output to the SalesByCountry view using the SaleDate field. As a precaution, the SQL applies a CAST() function to the SaleDate field so that any `time` element is removed that would otherwise prevent the tables from joining on the date. Because there could be several sales on a single day—and we want the aggregate value for the sales for each weekday—the final query uses a GROUP BY clause on the date and weekday fields and wraps the sales value in a SUM() function.

Tricks and Traps

Given that this is a fairly complex sequence of SQL, we have a few points to make here:

- If you are looking at a list of weekdays for several years, be sure to create a tally table that contains at least as many records as there are consecutive days in the total number of years.

- You can choose to limit the initial tally table to the exact number of days in the year (or between the two dates if you are using a date range); however, this means calculating the exact number of days and adding this to a WHERE clause in the first CTE.

- This piece of SQL only displays the weekdays where there is a sale. If you want a complete list of dates, including any days where there were no sales, you can change the INNER JOIN to a RIGHT OUTER JOIN in the final query. You can see this in the following SQL snippet (since the two CTEs remain the same, we are not showing them again).

```
SELECT            CTE.WeekdayDate
                  ,CTE.WeekdayName
                  ,SUM(SLS.SalePrice) AS TotalDailySales
FROM              Data.SalesByCountry SLS
RIGHT OUTER JOIN  DateList_CTE CTE
                  ON CTE.WeekdayDate = CAST(SLS.SaleDate AS
DATE)
GROUP BY          CTE.WeekdayDate
                  ,CTE.WeekdayName
ORDER BY          CTE.WeekdayDate
```

Running this altered query gives the output that you can see in *Figure 20.10*, where the weekdays without sales are also displayed.

	WeekdayDate	WeekdayName	TotalDailySales
1	2017-01-02	Monday	NULL
2	2017-01-03	Tuesday	NULL
3	2017-01-04	Wednesday	NULL
4	2017-01-05	Thursday	125000.00
5	2017-01-06	Friday	NULL
6	2017-01-09	Monday	NULL
7	2017-01-10	Tuesday	85000.00
8	2017-01-11	Wednesday	22500.00
9	2017-01-12	Thursday	125950.00
10	2017-01-13	Friday	8850.00

Figure 20.10: *Using an OUTER JOIN with a tally table to display NULL date records*

- Because i described the full range of DATEPART() and DATENAME() elements in previous chapters, i will not repeat them here.

20.7 Find the Weekend Dates Inside a Date Range

Human resources needs to plan for extra support staff on certain weekends, so they want a simple list of Saturdays and Sundays for the first two weeks of December 2017. The following short piece of SQL delivers this.

```
;
WITH TallyTable_CTE
AS
(
SELECT     ROW_NUMBER() OVER (ORDER BY StockCode) - 1 AS ID
FROM       Data.Stock
)
SELECT       CAST(DATEADD(DD, ID, '20171201') AS DATE) AS WeekdayDate
FROM         TallyTable_CTE
WHERE        ID <= DATEDIFF(DD, '20171201', '20171213')
             AND DATEPART(dw, DATEADD(DD, ID, '20171201')) IN (1,7)
```

Running this piece of code gives the result that you can see in *Figure 20.11*.

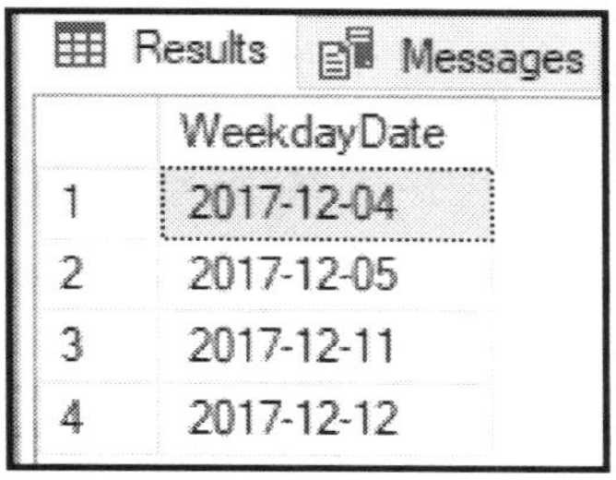

Results | Messages

	WeekdayDate
1	2017-12-04
2	2017-12-05
3	2017-12-11
4	2017-12-12

Figure 20.11: *Displaying weekend dates*

How It Works

Once again, in this example, you use a CTE to produce a sequence of numbers beginning with 0. Then a query uses this list to produce a sequence of dates using the DATEADD() function, as you saw in the previous section. Because the requirement was to start the list on December 1, 2017, this specific date is used as the starting date in the DATEADD() function.

The interesting part of this query resides in the WHERE clause, which does two things:

First:	The WHERE clause sets a date range. It does this by ensuring that the number (the ID column from the tally CTE) is less than or equal to the end date for the required range of dates (December 13, 2017). Since the tally table started on December 1, the DATEDIFF() function is used to calculate the number of days between the start date and the end date of the required period.
Second:	A DATEPART() function is applied to the DATEADD() function that delivers a range of dates. This function extracts the weekday number from each date. Because we only want to display Saturdays and Sundays, only days numbered 1 and 7 are required. The simplest way to achieve this is to use an IN clause.

Tricks and Traps

We have a couple of points to make here:

- It is perfectly normal that certain dates are repeated at several places in the SQL. This is because the dates are used in several independent functions.
- It is possible to use a DATENAME() function rather than a DATEPART() function in the WHERE clause to filter on Saturday and Sunday to extract only weekends from the list of dates.

20.8 Count the Number of Weekend Days between Two Dates

As a prelude to delivering some more complex analysis of staff deployment, the HR department wants to know how many weekend days there are in March and April 2018. This requires some clever SQL, as you can see in the following code snippet.

```
;
WITH TallyTable_CTE
AS
(
SELECT     ROW_NUMBER() OVER (ORDER BY StockCode) - 1 AS ID
FROM       Data.Stock
)
,WeekendList_CTE
AS
(
SELECT      CAST(DATEADD(DD, ID, '20180301') AS DATE) AS WeekdayDate
FROM        TallyTable_CTE
WHERE       DATEPART(dw, DATEADD(DD, ID, '20180301')) IN (1,7)
            AND ID <= DATEDIFF(DD, '20180301', '20180430')
)
SELECT    COUNT(*) AS WeekendDays FROM WeekendList_CTE
```

When you run this query, you should see the output that is shown in *Figure 20.12*.

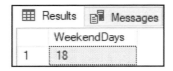

Figure 20.12: *Counting the number of non-weekdays for a date range*

How It Works

What this query does is create a table of all the days between two dates (March 1 and April 30, 2017, in this example). It then deduces the number of the day for each date and excludes Saturdays and Sundays. Finally, it counts the remaining number of records in the list.

The code works like this:

First:	A tally CTE is created to provide a sequential list of numbers starting with 0 (zero).
Then:	A second CTE uses the tally list as part of a DATEADD() function to create a list of dates. This list begins with 0 to give the starting date —by adding zero days to the lower date threshold that is the third parameter of the DATEADD() function—and then continues adding one day for each record in the tally list. The WHERE clause of the second CTE filters out any weekdays by • Reusing the same DATEADD() expression and enclosing this in a DATEPART() function that returns the number of the weekday. The filter only allows days 1 and 7 (Saturdays and Sundays) to appear in the second CTE output. • Limiting the number of records from the tally list that are used. It does this by creating a DATEDIFF() function that returns the number of days between the lower and upper threshold dates. This number of days is the number of records that the subquery should return. Consequently, the maximum number of records in the tally list is set by filtering on the maximum ID value for the second CTE output.
Finally:	A simple SELECT clause using the data from the second CTE counts the number of weekend days between the two dates.

Tricks and Traps

We have a couple of points to make here:

- Once again, you may have to repeat the date thresholds several times in queries like this one. The essential thing is to be careful and consider whether you should be using the lower or upper date thresholds in each case.

- Date tally lists are often fairly short; however, remember that you can make quite large tally lists if you need them by using the same table name two or even three times. This approach gives you code like this:

```
SELECT     ROW_NUMBER() OVER (ORDER BY Y.StockCode) - 1 AS ID
FROM       Data.Stock Y
CROSS JOIN Data.Stock Z
```

20.9 Aggregate Data for the Last Day of the Month

The sales director is still convinced that some days deliver better sales than others, so now she wants to see the sales for the last day of each month in 2016. SQL can handle this fairly easily, as the following piece of SQL shows:

```
;
WITH TallyTable_CTE
AS
(
SELECT      ROW_NUMBER() OVER (ORDER BY StockCode) AS ID
FROM        Data.Stock
)
,LastDayOfMonth_CTE
AS
(
SELECT      EOMONTH(DATEFROMPARTS(2016, ID, 1)) AS LastDayDate
FROM        TallyTable_CTE
WHERE       ID <= 12
)
SELECT       CTE.LastDayDate
            ,SUM(SLS.SalePrice) AS TotalDailySales
FROM        Data.SalesByCountry SLS
INNER JOIN  LastDayOfMonth_CTE CTE
            ON CTE.LastDayDate = CAST(SLS.SaleDate AS DATE)
GROUP BY    CTE.LastDayDate
ORDER BY    CTE.LastDayDate
```

If you run this query, you see the output that is shown in *Figure 20.13*.

	LastDayDate	TotalDailySales
1	2016-04-30	155800.00
2	2016-12-31	39500.00

Figure 20.13: Showing aggregate data for the last day of the month

How It Works

This query is composed of three fundamental elements.

A tally CTE	That delivers a list of incremental numbers. This CTE uses the ROW_NUMBER() function to create the list of numbers, starting with 1. The row number field is aliased as ID. The table that the set of numbers is based on is completely irrelevant, as it only serves as a basis for the records that are created, and none of the actual data in the underlying table is required.
A second CTE	That uses the tally CTE as the source for its data. This second CTE extracts 12 records from the tally CTE (because there are 12 months in the year). It does this by applying a WHERE clause to the ID field of the tally CTE that sets the maximum ID to 12. Then the second CTE creates a list of the 12 months of a year (2016 in this case) by applying the DATEFROMPARTS() function to the tally list. Since the tally list ID field is defined as being the second parameter of the DATEFROMPARTS() function (the month in other words), the second CTE generates a list of the 12 months in the year. The last day of each month is then extracted from the month date using the EOMONTH() function.
A query	That uses the second CTE as its data source. This query joins to the SalesByCountry view on the SaleDate field so that any sales that occurred on the last day of any month are returned. Once again a CAST() function is applied to ensure that the fields used to join the two tables are only using date elements for the join and that any time elements of the data are not used.

This sequence of datasets is probably easier to understand if you display the output from the second CTE. You can do this by placing the following piece of code under the second CTE and deleting the final query.

```
SELECT * FROM LastDayOfMonth_CTE
```

Figure 20.14 shows you the output from the second of two CTEs.

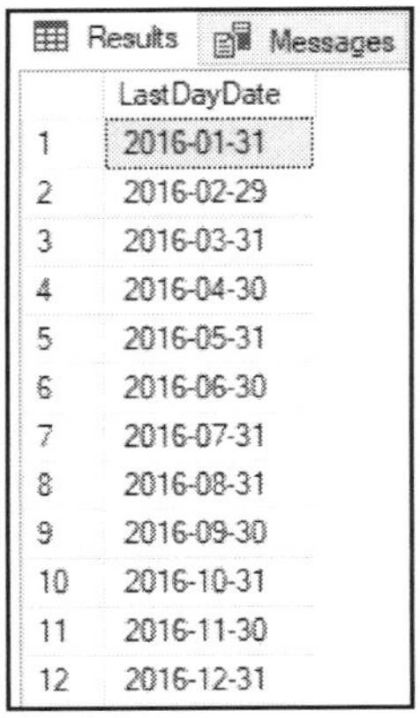

Figure 20.14: *Displaying the last day of the month*

20.10 Aggregate Data for the Last Friday of the Month

The HR director has indicated that she is going to want you to calculate sales commissions for payment on the last Friday of every month. However, before you actually carry out the math, she wants a list of the last Friday for every month of 2017. You can deliver this using the following piece of SQL:

```
;
WITH TallyTable_CTE
AS
(
SELECT      ROW_NUMBER() OVER (ORDER BY StockCode) AS ID
FROM        Data.Stock
)
,LastDayOfMonth_CTE
AS
(
SELECT       EOMONTH(DATEFROMPARTS(2017, ID, 1)) AS MonthEndDate
             ,DATEPART(DW, EOMONTH(DATEFROMPARTS(2017, ID, 1)))
             AS MonthEndDay
FROM         TallyTable_CTE
```

```
WHERE        ID <= 12
)
SELECT       MonthEndDate
                ,DATEADD(dd
                    ,CASE
                        WHEN MonthEndDay >= 6 THEN 6
                                        - MonthEndDay
                        ELSE (6 - MonthEndDay) - 7
                    END
                    ,MonthEndDate) AS LastFridayOfMonth
FROM         LastDayOfMonth_CTE
```

Running this code snippet produces the output that is shown in *Figure 20.15*.

	MonthEndDate	LastFridayOfMonth
1	2017-01-31	2017-01-27
2	2017-02-28	2017-02-24
3	2017-03-31	2017-03-31
4	2017-04-30	2017-04-28
5	2017-05-31	2017-05-26
6	2017-06-30	2017-06-30
7	2017-07-31	2017-07-28
8	2017-08-31	2017-08-25
9	2017-09-30	2017-09-29
10	2017-10-31	2017-10-27
11	2017-11-30	2017-11-24
12	2017-12-31	2017-12-29

Figure 20.15: Displaying the last Fridays of 2017

How It Works

This query (much like the last one) is based on

- A tally CTE to provide a sequence of numbers

- A second CTE that uses the tally list to produce a series of dates composed of the last day of the month

- A final query that takes the data from the second CTE and delivers the required result

Because the first two elements (the tally list and the CTE of month-end dates) are the same as those used in the previous section, we do not explain them again here.

The output query is a little different, however. It takes the date for the last day of the month and subtracts the required number of days necessary to discover the previous Friday (which is day 6) using a DATEADD() function. This function subtracts a specified number of days from the month-end date.

This requires first testing whether the last day is a Friday or Saturday. If it is (and this is the first part of the CASE statement), then the number of days to subtract is calculated to go back one or two days. If the last day is Sunday through Thursday, then a slightly different calculation is used.

This sequence of datasets is also probably easier to understand if you display the output from the second CTE. You can do this by placing the following piece of code under the second CTE and deleting the final query.

```
SELECT * FROM LastDayOfMonth_CTE
```

Adding this line of code after the second CTE and then running the SQL gives the result that you can see in *Figure 20.16.*

	MonthEndDate	MonthEndDay
1	2017-01-31	3
2	2017-02-28	3
3	2017-03-31	6
4	2017-04-30	1
5	2017-05-31	4
6	2017-06-30	6
7	2017-07-31	2
8	2017-08-31	5
9	2017-09-30	7
10	2017-10-31	3
11	2017-11-30	5
12	2017-12-31	1

Figure 20.16: Displaying the day number of the Friday of the month

20.11 Analyzing Timespans as Years, Months, and Days

The CEO of Prestige Cars is adamant. "Idle stock is a waste of resources," she maintains. To make sure no vehicles are waiting too long between being bought and sold, she has asked you to produce a report that shows the exact number of years, months, and days each car remains in stock. This has required some clever SQL, as you can see:

```
SELECT          ST.StockCode
                ,DATEDIFF(dd, ST.DateBought, SA.SaleDate) / 365 AS Years
                ,(DATEDIFF(dd, ST.DateBought, SA.SaleDate) % 365) / 30
                        AS Months
                ,(DATEDIFF(dd, ST.DateBought, SA.SaleDate)  % 365) % 30
                        AS Days
                ,DATEDIFF(dd, ST.DateBought, SA.SaleDate) / 30
                        AS TotalMonths
                ,DATEDIFF(dd, ST.DateBought, SA.SaleDate) % 365
                        AS DaysInYear
FROM            Data.Stock ST
INNER JOIN      Data.SalesDetails SD
                ON ST.StockCode = SD.StockID
INNER JOIN      Data.Sales SA
                ON SD.SalesID = SA.SalesID
ORDER BY         DATEDIFF(dd, ST.DateBought, SA.SaleDate) / 365 DESC
                ,DATEDIFF(dd, ST.DateBought, SA.SaleDate) % 365 DESC
```

Running this query gives the results that you can see in *Figure 20.17*.

	StockCode	Years	Months	Days	TotalMonths	DaysInYear
1	A6FCB276-6311-4B3E-9C99-23F197952F1C	2	4	21	29	141
2	EDCCE461-5DA8-4E2E-8F08-798431841575	1	11	6	23	336
3	2319EA77-F4D9-4E34-9771-C42DCA3E210C	1	4	17	16	137
4	1A210C04-C981-4EA4-83B9-A6E76B5B9BDB	1	4	1	16	121
5	C001858B-0B5D-4648-8F0D-80269964C921	1	0	9	12	9
6	A0098927-0C7D-4CC8-8022-57A24433EF61	0	11	28	11	358
7	9743A284-D059-4EEB-98AB-ACDE88C1E9F5	0	11	21	11	351
8	CE0A56A6-8218-4F4C-A0E2-63F3DC9E4AE6	0	9	10	9	280
9	7F08368D-B6EA-4DFC-A1EC-B1A1B0221F04	0	8	9	8	249
10	43195E1A-46B2-4554-B1A9-C849B1C0B53B	0	5	5	5	155
11	6943ADF3-01A4-4281-B0CE-93384FE60418	0	4	14	4	134
12	266404D4-FBC5-4DC6-BB7C-A2ED7246D6D7	0	0	28	0	28
13	27C180A1-7C39-4E88-B5DE-ACD0C9594F3C	0	0	24	0	24
14	BEC34DF7-3E37-4322-A406-04BB5DF2A0FE	0	0	24	0	24
15	F075AC9E-1124-4194-A05F-683F9D553335	0	0	24	0	24

Figure 20.17: *Using DATEDIFF() and arithmetic operators to calculate time in years, months, and days*

How It Works

What this query does is take advantage of the possibilities the modulo function offers to take a timespan that is represented in years and calculate the following metrics:

- The number of elapsed `years`
- The number of elapsed `months` over and above the elapsed years
- The number of elapsed `days` over and above the elapsed years and months
- The total number of elapsed months
- The number of days over and above any elapsed years

Since this query is based on the judicious use of the modulo function—which SQL Server presents as the percent sign (%)—you need to remember that this function divides one number by another and leaves only the remainder. Also, in these calculations, we are making the simplistic assumptions that there are 365 days in the year and 30 days in a month.

To begin with, this query joins the tables that are required to access the purchase and sales dates. That means joining the Stock and Sales tables using the SalesDetails table as a connecting "bridge" table.

At this point, you can create the five calculations that deliver the information that interests you:

Years elapsed	This calculation takes the number of days between the purchase and sale dates and divides by 365 to give the number of whole years elapsed between the two dates.
Months in excess of years	This calculation takes the number of days between the purchase and sale dates and returns the remainder. This figure is then divided by 30 to give the number of complete months that have passed.
Days in excess of months	This calculation takes the number of days between the purchase and sale dates and returns the remainder to produce the number of days over and above any complete years. It then applies a modulo of 30 to this figure and takes the remainder. This is the number of days over and above any complete years and months.
Total months elapsed	This calculation takes the number of days between the purchase and sale dates and divides by 30 to give the total number of months between the two dates.
Total days in excess of years	This calculation takes the number of days between the purchase and sale dates and returns the remainder.

You may not necessarily need all of these individual calculations when you are analyzing your time-related data; however, having them at hand might prove useful one day!

20.12 Isolate Time Periods from Date and Time Data

The sales team has been vying to sell cars faster and faster, so they want to know which cars have spent the shortest time in stock in 2017. This can sometimes prove to be only a matter of minutes or even seconds, as the following SQL illustrates:

```
SELECT      ST.DateBought
            ,SA.SaleDate
            ,MK.MakeName + '-' + MD.ModelName AS MakeAndModel
            ,(DATEDIFF(second, ST.DateBought, SA.SaleDate) % (24*60*60))
              / 3600    AS Hours
            ,((DATEDIFF(second, ST.DateBought, SA.SaleDate)
               % (24*60*60)) % 3600) / 60    AS Minutes
            ,(((DATEDIFF(second, ST.DateBought, SA.SaleDate)  % 365)
               % (24*60*60)) % 3600) % 60    AS Seconds
FROM        Data.Stock ST
            INNER JOIN Data.Model MD
            ON ST.ModelID = MD.ModelID
INNER JOIN  Data.Make MK
            ON MD.MakeID = MK.MakeID
INNER JOIN  Data.SalesDetails SD
            ON ST.StockCode = SD.StockID
INNER JOIN  Data.Sales SA
            ON SD.SalesID = SA.SalesID
WHERE       (DATEDIFF(dd, ST.DateBought, SA.SaleDate) % 365) = 1
            AND YEAR(SA.SaleDate) = 2017
```

Running this query gives the results that you can see in *Figure 20.18*.

	DateBought	SaleDate	MakeAndModel	Hours	Minutes	Seconds
1	2016-12-31	2017-01-01 11:12:00.000	Porsche-Boxster	11	12	5
2	2017-03-30	2017-03-31 14:09:00.000	Citroen-Rosalie	14	9	40
3	2017-04-30	2017-05-01 17:12:00.000	Rolls Royce-Phantom	17	12	10
4	2017-04-30	2017-05-01 10:12:00.000	Rolls Royce-Wraith	10	12	55
5	2017-05-11	2017-05-12 13:15:00.000	Ferrari-F50	13	15	25
6	2017-05-12	2017-05-13 20:16:00.000	Ferrari-F40	20	16	40
7	2017-05-15	2017-05-16 16:16:00.000	Alfa Romeo-Giulietta	16	16	55
8	2017-05-18	2017-05-19 21:17:00.000	Triumph-GT6	21	17	50
9	2017-05-19	2017-05-20 14:17:00.000	Reliant-Robin	14	17	35
10	2017-05-20	2017-05-21 16:18:00.000	McLaren-P1	16	18	55
11	2017-05-21	2017-05-22 11:18:00.000	Delorean-DMC 12	11	18	0
12	2017-05-22	2017-05-23 09:19:00.000	BMW-E30	9	19	40
13	2017-05-23	2017-05-24 17:19:00.000	Aston Martin-DB2	17	19	5
14	2017-05-25	2017-05-26 10:20:00.000	Aston Martin-DB9	10	20	50
15	2017-05-26	2017-05-27 21:20:00.000	Citroen-Rosalie	21	20	45

Figure 20.18: Using DATEDIFF() and arithmetic operators to calculate time in hours, minutes, and seconds

How It Works

This query begins by joining the tables that are needed to source the Make, Model, DateBought, and SaleDate fields. Then a WHERE clause is added that filters the records so that only vehicles that are sold within one day of being bought are displayed. This is done by using a DATEDIFF() function to calculate a number of days, and then only the remainder is returned once the number of days is divided by 365 using the modulo function. If this value equals 1, then the car was in stock for less than 24 hours.

Three formulas are added to the SELECT clause to return:

- The hours in stock

- The minutes in stock after any hours are subtracted from the total time in stock

- The seconds in stock after any hours and minutes are subtracted from the total time in stock

These three formulas work like this:

Hours	The DATEDIFF() function calculates the number of seconds between the purchase date and the sale date (which is, in fact, midnight since the DateBought field does not contain hours, minutes, or seconds). Then the modulo (%) function is applied to divide this figure by the number of seconds in the day (60 × 60 × 24 or 86,400). This is necessary in case you are calculating the difference over more than one day. The remainder is the number of seconds in the day that are left once any complete days are removed from the timespan. This is then divided by 3,600 (the number of seconds in an hour) to give the number of complete hours difference.
Minutes	Here the DATEDIFF() function also calculates the number of seconds between the purchase date and the sale date. Then the modulo (%) function is applied to divide this figure by the number of seconds in the day (in case you are calculating the difference over more than one day). The remainder is then calculated using % 3600 to return the number of seconds once any full hours are past. Finally, this figure is divided by 60 to give the number of minutes.
Seconds	The DATEDIFF() function also calculates the number of seconds between the purchase date and the sale date. Then the modulo (%) function is applied to divide this figure by the number of seconds in the day in case you are calculating the difference over more than one day. The remainder is then calculated (using % 3600) to return the number of seconds remaining once any complete hours are past. Finally, the remaining number of seconds is calculated by returning the remainder of the final figure using % 60.

Tricks and Traps

We have one additional point to make here:

- You can wrap the whole query in a CTE or a subquery and then order by the time in seconds between the purchase and sale dates (in descending order) if you want to view the fastest sales first.

20.13 Listing Data by Time of Day

Now the sales director wants to look at exactly when cars are sold to see if there are certain times of the day that are better for sales. You produced a list of vehicles sold in 2017 that includes the exact time the sale was made. The code for this is shown here:

```
SELECT      MakeName, ModelName, SalePrice

            ,FORMAT(SaleDate, 't') AS TimeOfDaySold
```

```
FROM        Data.SalesByCountry
WHERE       YEAR(SaleDate) = 2017
ORDER BY    CONVERT(TIME, SaleDate)
```

If you run this code you see the output displayed in *Figure 20.19.*

	MakeName	ModelName	SalePrice	TimeOfDaySold
1	BMW	E30	33500.00	9:19 AM
2	Jaguar	XK150	29500.00	9:25 AM
3	Triumph	TR5	9950.00	9:58 AM
4	Aston Martin	Rapide	55000.00	9:59 AM
5	Porsche	959	55600.00	10:07 AM
6	Rolls Royce	Wraith	162500.00	10:12 AM
7	Aston Martin	DB4	36500.00	10:20 AM
8	Aston Martin	DB9	77500.00	10:20 AM
9	Peugeot	205	3950.00	10:25 AM
10	Noble	M600	29500.00	10:25 AM
11	Alfa Romeo	Spider	12500.00	10:25 AM
12	Porsche	944	15750.00	10:33 AM
13	Bentley	Arnage	99950.00	10:39 AM
14	Aston Martin	Vanquish	56500.00	10:59 AM
15	Austin	Lichfield	6500.00	11:02 AM

Figure 20.19: Displaying records by time

How It Works

As long as the source data contains a time element, you can display the time of an event (such as a sale) when querying data. Fortunately, the Sales table (which is used in the SalesByCountry view) contains the SaleDate field that contains both a date and a time element. This query simply selects core information—including the SaleDate—from the SalesByCountry view.

Isolating the time part of a field like this (in fact, it is a DATETIME field) is as simple as selecting the SaleDate field and formatting the output from this field. The trick is to use the FORMAT() function. As you saw in Chapter 10, the FORMAT() function requires two parameters:

First:	The field to format
Second:	The format code to apply

In this example, we used the 't' format code. This code displays the output in a shortened time format with the hour, minutes, and AM/PM indicator.

The FORMAT() function lets you apply a series of built-in time formats. These are shown in *Table 20.1*.

Description	Format Code	Sample Output
Full date/time short time	f	*Tuesday, May 23, 2017 9:19 AM*
Full Date/Time Long Time	F	*Tuesday, May 23, 2017 9:19:00 AM*
General date/time short time	g	*5/23/2017 9:19 AM*
General date/time long time	G	*5/23/2017 9:19:00 AM*
Round-trip date/time	O	*2017.05.23T09:19:00.0000000*
RFC 1123	R	*Tue, 23 May 2017 09:19:00 GMT*
Short time	t	*9:19 AM*
Long time	T	*9:19:00 AM*
Universal sortable date/time	u	*2017.05.23 09:19:00Z*
Universal full date/time	U	*Tuesday, May 23, 2017 8:19:00 AM*

Table 20.1: Time Format Codes

Tricks and Traps

Inevitably, we have a few points to make here:

- You can extract the time element from DATETIME, DATETIME2, and TIME fields.

- The formatted output is converted to text. This means that you should not use it to sort the data or in-time calculations. Use the underlying data field to carry out these operations.

- If you want to extract the time element from a DATETIME or DATETIME2 field, you can use code like this, which removes the date element from the field:

```
CAST(SaleDate AS TIME)
```

Once a DATETIME or DATETIME2 field has been converted to a TIME field in this way, you can use it to sort the data.

20.14 Aggregating Data by Hourly Bandings

The CEO has been looking at some of the output that you have prepared for the sales director and is convinced that sales staff need to be aware that certain times of the day produce better sales, so she has asked for a list of 2017 sales aggregated by hour bands. The following SQL delivers this.

```
SELECT        CAST(HourOfDay AS VARCHAR(2)) + '-' + CAST(HourOfDay + 1
              AS VARCHAR(2)) AS HourBand
              ,SUM(SalePrice) AS SalesByHourBand

FROM
    (
    SELECT      SalePrice
                ,DATEPART(hh, SaleDate) AS HourOfDay
    FROM        Data.SalesByCountry
    WHERE       YEAR(SaleDate) = 2017
    ) A
GROUP BY    HourOfDay
ORDER BY    HourOfDay
```

Running this piece of code produces the output that you can see in *Figure 20.20*.

	HourBand	SalesByHourBand
1	9-10	127950.00
2	10-11	550250.00
3	11-12	617400.00
4	12-13	1193390.00
5	13-14	1052700.00
6	14-15	106905.00
7	15-16	85000.00
8	16-17	829400.00
9	17-18	672900.00
10	18-19	605450.00
11	19-20	668530.00
12	20-21	1117500.00
13	21-22	240700.00

Figure 20.20: Displaying data grouped and aggregated for hour bands

How It Works

The heart of this piece of SQL is a subquery that isolates the hour when a sale was made. It does this by applying the DATEPART() function to the SaleDate field of the SalesByCountry view. This function can extract date elements from a DATE or DATETIME field (as you have seen previously). However, it can also extract time elements from a DATETIME or TIME field. In this specific example, the first parameter of the DATETIME() function is hh, which indicates to SQL Server that it is the hour element that you wish to isolate from the time part of the field.

To make this clearer, take a look at *Figure 20.21* where you can see the output from the subquery (aliased as A in the SQL code).

	SalePrice	HourOfDay
1	45000.00	13
2	49500.00	17
3	225000.00	16
4	12500.00	16
5	22500.00	11
6	125000.00	11
7	85000.00	15
8	1250.00	13
9	22500.00	17
10	125950.00	18

Figure 20.21: *Extracting the hour part of a DATETIME field using the DATEPART() function*

Once the subquery has delivered the sale price and the hour of the sale, the outer query can take this information and use it as the basis for the final result.

The outer query simply aggregates the sale price by hour. As a final flourish, it displays the hour band as a range by displaying the hour twice—by simply adding 1 to the hour figure. Since the hour is a number, it has to be converted to text using the CAST() function so that another text element—the hyphen—can be used in the output.

The DATEPART() function can extract more than just hours from a TIME or DATETIME field. The various time elements that it can isolate are shown in **Table 20.2.**

Description	Format Code
Hour	hh
Minute	mi

Description	Format Code
Second	ss
Millisecond	ms

Table 20.2: Time Format Codes

Tricks and Traps

We have one idea to add:

- You can wrap the whole query in a CTE or a subquery and then order by the aggregate amount to see most profitable hours of the day if you want to extract even more analysis from the data.

20.15 Aggregate Data by Quarter of Hour

As a final part of the sales focus, the CEO wants to know which part of the hour is best for sales. You prepare the following piece of code to show sales for 2017 in quarter-hourly tranches.

```
SELECT       QuarterOfHour
            ,SUM(SalePrice) AS SalesByQuarterHourBand
FROM
    (
    SELECT      SalePrice
               ,(DATEPART(mi, SaleDate) / 15) + 1 AS QuarterOfHour
    FROM        Data.SalesByCountry
    WHERE       YEAR(SaleDate) = 2017
    ) A
GROUP BY    QuarterOfHour
ORDER BY    QuarterOfHour
```

Running this code snippet produces the output that you can see in *Figure 20.22*.

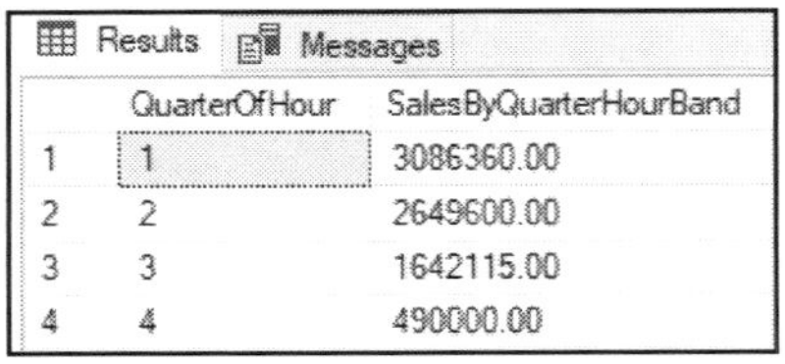

	QuarterOfHour	SalesByQuarterHourBand
1	1	3086360.00
2	2	2649600.00
3	3	1642115.00
4	4	490000.00

Figure 20.22: Data grouped in quarter-hour bands

How It Works

This piece of SQL consists of two queries:

An inner query	That looks at every sale date and time for 2017 (using the SalesByCountry view as the source of the data). This subquery extracts the minute at which each sale took place using the DATEPART() function and the mi parameter. Then the number of minutes is divided by 15 to give each quarter of an hour. The 15.minute slot is then incremented by 1, since otherwise it would begin with 0.
An outer query	That aggregates the sales amount from the inner query (aliased as A) and groups the amounts by each quarter of an hour.

Conclusion

This chapter showed you a more advanced set of techniques that you can use to analyze data over time. You have learned how to compare data across different time periods, to analyze how metrics accumulate over time, and to break down timespans into their constituent parts. Using these kinds of advanced time analysis can really help you discover trends in your source data.

Core Knowledge Learned in This Chapter

The keywords that you have seen in this chapter are listed here. We have included those that you may already have seen.

Concept	Description
EOMONTH()	This function returns the date for the last day of the month.
DATEDIFF()	This function finds the number of days, months, years, and so on between two given dates.
CAST()	This function converts a datetime data type to a date.
YEAR()	This function isolates the year part of a date.
MONTH()	This function isolates the month part of a date.
DAY()	This function isolates the day part of a date.
DATEPART()	This function returns the quarter, weekday, and so on for a date.
DATEADD()	This function adds or subtracts a number of days, months, years, and so on to or from a given data and finds the date in the future or the past.
DATENAME()	This function displays the name of part of the date—such as the month or weekday.

CHAPTER 21
Complex Data Output

Often the way data is presented is perceived as more important than the data itself. So you need to know not only how to analyze the data and deliver accurate results, but also how to shape the output so that the essence of your analysis is immediately comprehensible. The techniques covered in this chapter help you present your analysis in various ways that can make the results easier to read and understand.

Presenting Complex Output with SQL

The techniques that you discover in this chapter include

- Pivoting data to create crosstab tables
- Adding multiple separate subtotals and a grand total to an aggregate query
- Create indented output
- Displaying data from multiple records in separate columns in a single query
- Carrying out search and replace operations on the final output
- Assembling concatenated lists of results

These ways of enhancing the output from a query are as practical as they are useful. They can make your results as alluring as they are revelatory. In the real world, you may not use all of these techniques on a daily basis; nonetheless, it is probably best to know that they are available so that you can apply them when the need arises. What is more, these presentation techniques can only enhance your SQL skills. Indeed, you can apply several of the approaches that you see in this chapter to solve many other presentational challenges.

21.1 Creating a Pivot Table

The finance director has given you a new challenge—deliver a simple, compact table of sales by color for all the years that Prestige Cars has been trading. He is adamant that this must be presented as a "crosstab" or pivot table. T-SQL can pivot data in this way, as the following code snippet shows:

```
SELECT      Color, [2015], [2016], [2017], [2018]
FROM
            (
            SELECT      ST.Color, SD.SalePrice, YEAR(SA.SaleDate)
                                                AS YearOfSale
            FROM        Data.Stock ST
            INNER JOIN  Data.SalesDetails SD
                        ON ST.StockCode = SD.StockID
            INNER JOIN  Data.Sales SA
                        ON SA.SalesID = SD.SalesID
            ) SQ
PIVOT       (
            SUM(SalePrice) FOR YearOfSale
                        IN ([2015], [2016], [2017], [2018])
            ) AS PVT
```

Running this query gives the results that you can see in *Figure 21.1.*

	Color	2015	2016	2017	2018
1	Black	374490.00	1251410.00	3112550.00	1983695.00
2	Blue	284600.00	423650.00	708420.00	1186400.00
3	British Racing Green	111500.00	663250.00	872340.00	566385.00
4	Canary Yellow	132000.00	287070.00	104750.00	134045.00
5	Dark Purple	NULL	283000.00	219175.00	662640.00
6	Green	216600.00	370750.00	655090.00	599540.00
7	Night Blue	57990.00	405500.00	457500.00	600830.00
8	Pink	NULL	235950.00	54700.00	191600.00
9	Red	154795.00	442500.00	659150.00	932450.00
10	Silver	89000.00	542205.00	1093900.00	926030.00

***Figure 21.1:** Creating a pivot table using the PIVOT operator*

How It Works

Sometimes a simple list of data is not what you want. Comparing data in a list can be much harder than when it is presented as a table of intersecting rows and columns, as is the case with a pivot table. This table style of data presentation is also called a `crosstab`.

What matters when using the PIVOT operator is realizing that it is there to display `three` pieces of data in different ways. It needs

Row headers	These are the data elements that appear in the left-hand column of the output table.
Column headers	These are the data elements that appear at the top of each column. It is important to understand that these are `not field names`, but data from the database.
Table data	These are the aggregated numeric values that appear inside the final pivoted output table.

Therefore, the art of making a pivot table involves assembling these three pieces of data so that they can be used correctly to give you the result you are looking for. Here is what is actually done in this example:

Initially:	The inner query (which is technically a subquery) is defined to output the data elements that you want to see in the final pivot table. These are color, year of sale, and sale price. This is the core data that is used in the pivot table and it contains fields from the Stock, Sales, and SalesDetails tables.

If you select the SQL for the subquery and execute it, you see something like the output displayed in *Figure 21.2*. This is a simple list query and it contains hundreds of rows.

Figure 21.2: *The subquery that prepares data for the PIVOT operator*

Then:	You apply the PIVOT operator to the subquery. This is, in effect, another subquery. What it does is isolate two of the fields in the subquery for some special treatment—data to aggregate and column specification.
Finally:	A SELECT clause is applied that provides the `row data` for the output table. In this case, it is the `Color` field. Then you add the column headers that were defined as part of the PIVOT operator.

The PIVOT operator needs the following two elements:

Aggregated element:	A numeric field is aggregated so that it can be displayed in the `body` of the final output table. In this example, it is the SalePrice field.
Column definition:	The content—in whole or in part—of another field is individually listed inside parentheses after the FOR clause to provide the `column headers` of the final output table.

A pivot table has to use an aggregation function to handle the values that are displayed in the table. This is because each intersection of a row and a column (several black cars sold in 2015, for instance) can have more than one value. You can use any of the SQL aggregation functions in a pivot table; consequently, you can just as easily use AVG() or COUNT() here to return the average sale price or the number of vehicles. If you are using SUM() or AVG(), then the field that you are aggregating has to be numeric. COUNT() can also be applied to text fields to return the number of values rather than the sum of the values.

Writing pivot table SQL is easier once you understand the process that the code represents. To help conceptualize this technique, take a look at *Figure 21.3*.

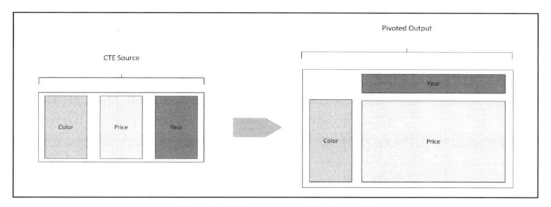

Figure 21.3: *The concept of the pivot table*

Tricks and Traps

Pivot tables require you to pay careful attention to the SQL that you are writing, so be sure to remember the following points when you create your own pivot tables:

* The only tricky part of writing the SQL that creates a pivot table is selecting the data that will constitute the column headers. It helps if you start by isolating this list of individual data elements before you start writing the rest of the code. In this example, you can return the list of years used in the PIVOT operator and the SELECT clause with the following SQL snippet:

```
SELECT DISTINCT YEAR(SaleDate) FROM Data.Sales
```

This returns the years (as you can see in *Figure 21.4*) that you can then copy and paste to create the list of column headers.

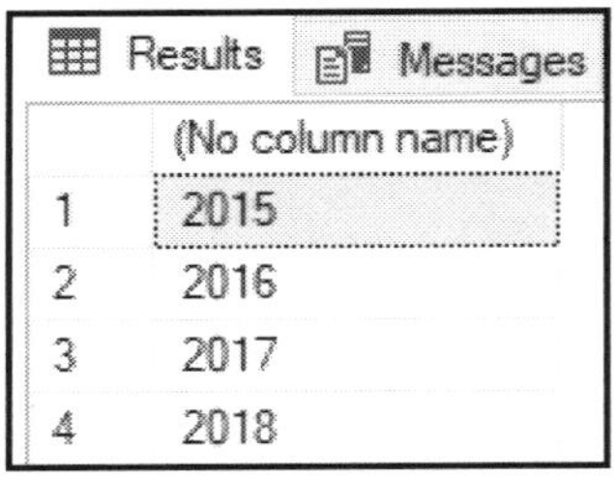

Figure 21.4: Preparing the data for the column titles of the PIVOT operator

- The list of data elements to be used as the column headers does not have to be enclosed in square brackets as they are in this example, however, it is good practice to use square brackets—otherwise any spaces or nonalphanumeric data from the dataset stops the pivot query from working.

21.2 Creating a Pivot Table Displaying Multiple Row Groupings

Fortunately, the finance director was delighted with your first pivot table. Unfortunately, this has created further demands from him for yet more analysis from you. What he would like now is another pivot table, only this time he wants to see the number of colors sold by make and model. The following code shows how this can be done:

```
WITH MakeAndModelCostByYear_CTE (MakeName, ModelName, Color, CostPrice)
AS
(
SELECT      MK.MakeName, MD.ModelName, ST.Color, ST.Cost
FROM        Data.Make MK
INNER JOIN  Data.Model MD ON MK.MakeID = MD.MakeID
INNER JOIN  Data.Stock ST ON ST.ModelID = MD.ModelID
)

SELECT      MakeName, ModelName, [Black], [Blue], [British Racing Green]
            ,[Canary Yellow], [Dark Purple], [Green], [Night Blue]
            ,[Pink], [Red], [Silver]
FROM        MakeAndModelCostByYear_CTE
PIVOT       (
```

```
COUNT(CostPrice) FOR Color IN
            (
            [Black], [Blue], [British Racing Green],
            [Canary Yellow], [Dark Purple], [Green],
            [Night Blue], [Pink], [Red], [Silver]
            )
    ) PVT
ORDER BY    MakeName, ModelName
```

Running this query gives the results that you can see in *Figure 21.5*.

	MakeName	ModelName	Black	Blue	British Racing Green	Canary Yellow	Dark Purple	Green	Night Blue	Pink	Red	Silver
1	Alfa Romeo	1750	1	1	0	0	0	0	0	0	0	0
2	Alfa Romeo	Giulia	3	0	3	0	0	1	0	0	1	0
3	Alfa Romeo	Giulietta	1	2	0	0	1	0	3	0	0	0
4	Alfa Romeo	Spider	4	1	0	0	0	1	0	0	0	0
5	Aston Martin	DB2	2	1	1	1	0	2	1	0	1	2
6	Aston Martin	DB4	3	0	0	1	0	1	1	1	0	1
7	Aston Martin	DB5	2	2	0	0	0	0	1	0	1	1
8	Aston Martin	DB6	4	0	3	2	0	1	2	0	2	2
9	Aston Martin	DB9	4	1	1	1	1	2	1	0	1	5
10	Aston Martin	Rapide	1	0	0	0	0	0	1	0	1	1
11	Aston Martin	Vanquish	2	0	0	0	1	1	2	0	1	1
12	Aston Martin	Vantage	2	0	1	0	0	1	0	0	0	0
13	Aston Martin	Virage	3	2	0	0	1	1	1	2	2	0
14	Austin	Cambridge	1	0	0	0	0	0	0	0	0	0
15	Austin	Lichfield	0	0	0	0	0	0	1	1	0	0

Figure 21.5: *A complex pivot operation based on a CTE*

How It Works

Pivot tables can be more complex than the simple table that you saw in the previous example. For more detailed output where more than one column of aggregated data is required, a CTE (Common Table Expression) can help you simplify both the SQL and the way that you approach the problem. This query follows the same pivot function principles that you saw previously:

- Identify and select the columns to display.
- Identify the data to pivot as column headers.
- Identify the value to aggregate and display in the table.

This query also begins by defining the source data for the pivot operation. This time, however, a CTE is used to do this. The CTE is based on the Make, Model, and Stock tables. If you select the query used in the CTE, you see a result like that shown in *Figure 21.6*.

	MakeName	ModelName	Color	Cost
1	Ferrari	Testarossa	Red	52000.00
2	Ferrari	355	Blue	176000.00
3	Porsche	911	British Racing Green	15600.00
4	Porsche	924	British Racing Green	9200.00
5	Porsche	944	Red	15960.00
6	Ferrari	Testarossa	Black	176000.00
7	Aston Martin	DB4	Night Blue	23600.00
8	Aston Martin	DB5	Black	39600.00
9	Aston Martin	DB6	Canary Yellow	60800.00
10	Ferrari	Testarossa	Red	172000.00

Figure 21.6: *Using a CTE to return the data used in a pivot*

This CTE isolates the two fields that appear as row headers (MakeName and ModelName) as well as the field that contains the data elements that are to be pivoted as column headers (Color).

The query is then built in four sections:

SELECT	This clause is where the output fields are defined: first the two fields that make up the row headers are specified followed by all the unique data fields from the Color column that become the column headers.
FROM	This clause uses the CTE as the data source.
PIVOT	This clause first specifies the aggregation that is used—COUNT() in this example. Then it states the field that is aggregated—CostPrice. Finally, a FOR expression is used to indicate which field contains the column headers (Color) and to list unique data elements from this field (the list of colors).
ORDER BY	Although optional, this clause guarantees comprehensible results by sorting the output.

All these elements together create the pivot SQL that you saw in boldface at the start of this section.

Tricks and Traps

We have only one point that you really need to remember when pivoting data like this:

- You only need to add square brackets for each field name in the pivot list if the data contains spaces or nonalphanumeric characters. That said, we consider it good practice always to add square brackets.

21.3 Unpivoting Data

Data is not always perfectly organized. Suppose that someone in the company comes to you with an already pivoted dataset. Let's imagine that it looks exactly like the pivot table that you can see in Figure 10.1. The challenge this time is to unpivot the data and display multiple records in fewer columns. The code to do this is as follows:

```
SELECT     Color, UPT.SaleValue, UPT.SaleYear
FROM       Data.PivotTable
UNPIVOT    (SaleValue FOR SaleYear IN ([2015], [2016], [2017],[2018]))
           AS UPT
```

Running this short piece of code gives the output that you can see in *Figure 21.7.*

	Color	SaleValue	SaleYear
1	Black	374490.00	2015
2	Black	1251410.00	2016
3	Black	3112550.00	2017
4	Black	1983695.00	2018
5	Blue	284600.00	2015
6	Blue	423650.00	2016
7	Blue	708420.00	2017
8	Blue	1186400.00	2018
9	British Racing Green	111500.00	2015
10	British Racing Green	663250.00	2016
11	British Racing Green	872340.00	2017
12	British Racing Green	566385.00	2018
13	Canary Yellow	132000.00	2015
14	Canary Yellow	287070.00	2016
15	Canary Yellow	104750.00	2017
16	Canary Yellow	134045.00	2018

Figure 21.7: Unpivoting data using the UNPIVOT operator

How It Works

This piece of SQL takes a source table that contains the following three kinds of element:

First	Color information in the left column.
Then	`Years in the other column headers.`
Finally	`Values from the intersection of these rows and columns across all the remaining rows and columns.`

The SQL uses a new operator—the UNPIVOT operator—to "unpick" this structure and deliver output where there are only three columns of data. These are Color, Year and the value for each combination of he first two elements.

To help you understand teh challenge more clearly, take a look at *Figure 21.8*. Here you can see, schematically, how the UNPIVOT operator works.

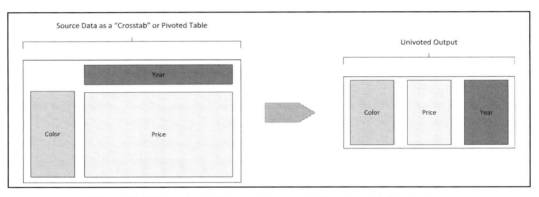

Figure 21.8: *How pivoted data can be converted to a classis table structure*

The UNPIVOT operator carries out the following operations:

- Identify the columns to unpivot and display as a single column.
- Identify the value to aggregate and display in the output.

As the core transformation is handled by the UNPIVOT operator itself, let's look at this first.

First	After the FROM clause that identifies the data source, you enter the UNPIVOT keyword, and a left parenthesis.
Next	You specify a column name that will be used for the values that will be unpivoted from the data in a set of columns that you will enumerate.

Then	You add the FOR keyword, followed by an alias (or column name if you prefer) where the column headers from all unpivoted columns will appear.
Next	You enter the IN operator.
Then	You enter a commA.separated list of all the column names in the source data containing data that you want to unpivot. This must be wrapped inside parentheses.
Finally	You end the unpivot operation with a final right parenthesis, the AS keyword and an alias—UPT in this example.

Adding an alias to the unpivoted data allows you to reference, independently, columns from the data source and column that result from the application of the UNPIVOT operator.

Finally you can add the SELECT clause of the SQL. Here, the Color field has `no alias` as it is pulled directly from the initial source table whereas the SaleValue and SaleYear fields are derived from the fields created by the UNPIVOT operator. So these two fields (SaleValue and SaleYear) `must use the alias that was set for the UNPIVOT operator` (UPT in this example).

Tricks and Traps

Unpivoting data also requires you to pay careful attention to the SQL that you are writing, so be sure to remember the following points when you npivot data:

- The square brackets that enclose the column headers that will be unpivoted—years in this example—are not strictly necessary. However it can be good practive to add them. This means that column names containing spaces or that could be misunderstood by SQL will be handled gracefully.

- If you are unpivoting a table that is, otself, the result of a pivot operation you need to be aware that you will not be outputting the data as it was originally. This is because the values have already been aggregated by the PIVOT operator. Consequently you will only be siing aggregated data when you unpivot the result of a pivot operation.

21.4 Adding Totals to Aggregate Queries

Although pleased with the lists of data that you can now deliver at the drop of a hat, the finance director wants one more thing. He prefers a more spreadsheet-like output that includes the subtotals in some cases; this will save him extra work in a spreadsheet. The following SQL snippet delivers exactly what he is looking for—a list of sales by color and make including the grand total:

```
SELECT      MK.MakeName, ST.Color, SUM(ST.Cost) AS Cost
```

```
FROM        Data.Make MK
INNER JOIN  Data.Model MD ON MK.MakeID = MD.MakeID
INNER JOIN  Data.Stock ST ON ST.ModelID = MD.ModelID
GROUP BY    GROUPING SETS ((MK.MakeName, ST.Color), ())
ORDER BY    MK.MakeName, ST.Color
```

Running this query gives the results that you can see in *Figure 21.9*.

	MakeName	Color	Cost
1	NULL	NULL	19703564.00
2	Alfa Romeo	Black	74500.00
3	Alfa Romeo	Blue	37160.00
4	Alfa Romeo	British Racing Green	16840.00
5	Alfa Romeo	Dark Purple	17200.00
6	Alfa Romeo	Green	26440.00
7	Alfa Romeo	Night Blue	28152.00
8	Alfa Romeo	Red	6956.00
9	Aston Martin	Black	1212008.00
10	Aston Martin	Blue	284400.00
11	Aston Martin	British Racing Green	250508.00
12	Aston Martin	Canary Yellow	239880.00
13	Aston Martin	Dark Purple	91680.00
14	Aston Martin	Green	560064.00
15	Aston Martin	Night Blue	529672.00

Figure 21.9: Creating totals with grouping sets

How It Works

Producing aggregations is something that you are now used to with SQL Server. So far, you have only seen how to deliver levels of aggregation or totals in separate queries; however, sometimes you need to see not just the subtotals, but also the grand total in a single query. This query extends the GROUP BY clause with an extension that is the GROUPING SETS clause. This new function allows you to specify exactly which totals and subtotals are returned in the final output.

First:	You begin with a perfectly normal aggregation query. In this example, the Make, Model, and Stock tables are joined and the make name and color fields are output along with the total for the cost of vehicles purchased. Since this is an aggregation query, any fields that are not aggregated must be added to a GROUP BY clause. In this example, these are the Make, Name, and Color fields.

Then:	The GROUPING SETS clause is added to the GROUP BY clause. This requires that you add parentheses that contain the fields that are to be aggregated. Each set of fields is inside its own parentheses. In this example, the make name and color fields are added so that the total for each combination of make and color will be calculated. Then, and separated with a comma, an empty pair of parentheses is added inside the outer grouping sets parentheses. This tells SQL Server to return the grand total for the dataset as well.

Reading the final result set is not completely intuitive, so we prefer to explain it. The total for each aggregated set of make and color is probably self-evident. However, the initial record without either a make or a color is probably less easy to understand. This is, in fact, the grand total. It is the record that is produced by the empty parentheses inside the GROUPING SETS clause. Since no fields are provided for the grand total in the GROUPING SETS clause, the grand total is represented by NULLs in the make name and color fields of the output.

Tricks and Traps

There is one fundamental point to remember when creating grouping sets:

*   When adding a grouping sets clause, you have to be careful to respect the sets of parentheses in the clause. There is always an outer pair of parentheses and then an inner pair for each aggregation that you add.

21.5 Creating Subtotals and Totals in Aggregated Queries

This time it is the CEO herself who wants a quick report to see sales by make and color including subtotals for all possible combinations of makes and sales. Fortunately, it only takes only a few minutes to write the code that can deliver this list for her:

```
SELECT      MK.MakeName, ST.Color, SUM(ST.Cost) AS Cost

FROM        Data.Make MK

INNER JOIN  Data.Model MD ON MK.MakeID = MD.MakeID

INNER JOIN  Data.Stock ST ON ST.ModelID = MD.ModelID

GROUP BY    GROUPING SETS ((MK.MakeName, ST.Color)
               , (MK.MakeName), (ST.Color), ())

ORDER BY    MK.MakeName, ST.Color
```

Running this query gives the results that you can see in *Figure 21.10.* You might want to scroll down this list to see the subtotals for other makes.

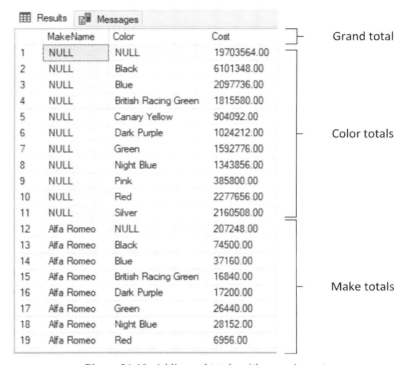

Figure 21.10: Adding subtotals with grouping sets

How It Works

SQL does not limit you to displaying the grand total and the totals for each aggregation. It can also show any intermediate totals. In this way, SQL can help you see both the big picture and the interesting nuggets of detail.

The code that can deliver this mix of high-level aggregation and low-level details is, at its heart, a fairly simple aggregation query. It takes the Make, Model, and Stock tables and joins them before outputting the total cost for each make and color.

However, the GROUP BY clause is extended with a more complex GROUPING SETS clause that requests

| A grand total | This is done by adding the empty parentheses inside the GROUPING SETS clause. |
| | Total for make   This is done by adding (MakeName)—in its own parentheses—inside the GROUPING SETS clause. |

Total for color	This is done by adding (Color)—in its own parentheses—inside the GROUPING SETS clause.
Aggregate totals	For make and color. These are requested just as you would request them in a standard GROUP BY clause—by adding the Make and Color fields separated by a comma. However, because this aggregation is a GROUPING SETS clause, these field names must be inside their own set of parentheses.

It can take a little practice to appreciate exactly what the GROUPING SETS query has delivered. More specifically, you have to look closely at the NULLs in the various columns to see how the subtotals are created when applying grouping sets to an aggregate query. Put simply

- If all columns except the value are NULL, then the row is the grand total.

- If a column contains a NULL alongside other elements, you are looking at the total for those elements. For instance, if the MakeName column is NULL and the Color column contains "British Racing Green," then the figure for that row is the total for the color "British Racing Green." Equally, if the MakeName column contains "Alfa Romeo" and the Color column contains NULL, then the figure shown in the record is the total for the make "Alfa Romeo."

Conceptually, the GROUPING SETS operator behaves in the way that is described in *Figure 21.11*.

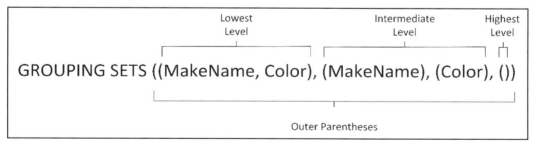

Figure 21.11: *Anatomy of a GROUPING SETS operator*

Tricks and Traps

We have two comments at this point:

- You do not have to add an ORDER BY clause when using grouping sets; however, it does often make the final output easier to understand.

- You do not have to add the lowest level of aggregation to a GROUPING SETS clause if you do not want to see the subtotals for each combination of make and color. For instance, if you alter the GROUP BY clause in this example so that it reads

```
GROUP BY    GROUPING SETS ((MakeName), (Color), ())
```

You only see the totals for Make, Color, and the grand total, as you can see in *Figure 21.12.*

	MakeName	Color	Cost
1	NULL	NULL	19703564.00
2	NULL	Black	6101348.00
3	NULL	Blue	2097736.00
4	NULL	British Racing Green	1815580.00
5	NULL	Canary Yellow	904092.00
6	NULL	Dark Purple	1024212.00
7	NULL	Green	1592776.00
8	NULL	Night Blue	1343856.00
9	NULL	Pink	385800.00
10	NULL	Red	2277656.00
11	NULL	Silver	2160508.00
12	Alfa Romeo	NULL	207248.00
13	Aston Martin	NULL	4470956.00
14	Austin	NULL	51600.00
15	Bentley	NULL	1413392.00
16	BMW	NULL	48400.00
17	Bugatti	NULL	1524400.00
18	Citroen	NULL	80864.00
19	Delahaye	NULL	103720.00
20	Delorean	NULL	79600.00
21	Ferrari	NULL	5343440.00
22	Jaguar	NULL	887756.00
23	Lagonda	NULL	174400.00
24	Lamborghini	NULL	1381720.00
25	Maybach	NULL	340000.00
26	McLaren	NULL	236000.00
27	Mercedes	NULL	414452.00
28	Morgan	NULL	14800.00
29	Noble	NULL	197600.00
30	Peugeot	NULL	18636.00
31	Porsche	NULL	963752.00
32	Reliant	NULL	2720.00
33	Rolls Royce	NULL	1355192.00
34	Trabant	NULL	8028.00
35	Triumph	NULL	384888.00

Figure 21.12: Displaying the higher aggregation levels using a GROUPING SETS clause

21.6 Creating Clear Tables That Include Totals and Subtotals

The good news is that the speed with which you delivered the previous subquery impressed the CEO. The bad news is that she now wants the same information in a more comprehensible format so that the board of directors will understand it. She is worried that the top executives will not understand NULLs in columns and wants something more explicit.

After shaking your head in disbelief at the intellectual limitations of senior executives, you come up with the following code:

```
;
WITH GroupedSource_CTE
AS
(
SELECT
MK.MakeName
,ST.Color
,Count(*) AS NumberOfCarsBought

FROM        Data.Make MK
            INNER JOIN Data.Model MD ON MK.MakeID = MD.MakeID
            INNER JOIN Data.Stock ST ON ST.ModelID = MD.ModelID
WHERE       MK.MakeName IS NOT NULL OR ST.Color IS NOT NULL
GROUP BY    GROUPING SETS ((MakeName), (Color), ())
)

SELECT AggregationType
,Category
,NumberOfCarsBought

FROM
(
SELECT    'GrandTotal' AS AggregationType, NULL AS Category
          ,NumberOfCarsBought, 1 AS SortOrder
FROM      GroupedSource_CTE
WHERE     MakeName IS NULL and Color IS NULL
```

```
UNION
SELECT    'Make Subtotals', MakeName, NumberOfCarsBought , 2
FROM      GroupedSource_CTE
WHERE     MakeName IS NOT NULL and Color IS NULL
UNION
SELECT    'Color Subtotals', Color, NumberOfCarsBought , 3
FROM      GroupedSource_CTE
WHERE     MakeName IS NULL and Color IS NOT NULL
) SQ
ORDER BY SortOrder, NumberOfCarsBought DESC
```

Running this query gives the results that you can see in *Figure 21.13*.

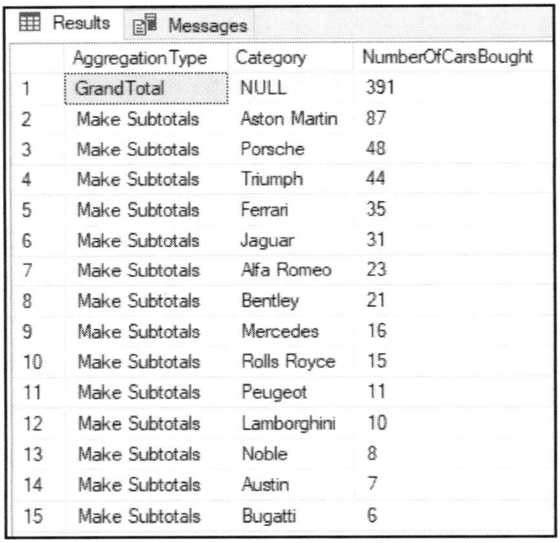

	Aggregation Type	Category	NumberOfCarsBought
1	GrandTotal	NULL	391
2	Make Subtotals	Aston Martin	87
3	Make Subtotals	Porsche	48
4	Make Subtotals	Triumph	44
5	Make Subtotals	Ferrari	35
6	Make Subtotals	Jaguar	31
7	Make Subtotals	Alfa Romeo	23
8	Make Subtotals	Bentley	21
9	Make Subtotals	Mercedes	16
10	Make Subtotals	Rolls Royce	15
11	Make Subtotals	Peugeot	11
12	Make Subtotals	Lamborghini	10
13	Make Subtotals	Noble	8
14	Make Subtotals	Austin	7
15	Make Subtotals	Bugatti	6

Figure 21.13: Displaying subtotals and grand total only with GROUPING SETS

How It Works

Whatever the data that you are producing, it is essential that you and your audience are able to understand what you are looking at. Consequently, the next piece of SQL harnesses the power of grouping sets and adds some extra presentation tweaks to make the data easier to understand at first sight.

This query is essentially in three parts:

A CTE	That aggregates the number of cars sold for each make, each color, and a grand total for all cars sold. This CTE uses the Make, Model, and Stock tables to isolate the cars that have been bought by Prestige Cars.
A subquery	This is a derived table in the FROM clause of the main query. It isolates each type of aggregation (color, make, grand total) by filtering on the NULLs in the MakeName and Color columns. Each type of total is a separate query that also adds a column specifying the aggregation type as text. The three queries are then joined in a UNION query so that they all appear in the same table structure. This table has three columns: the aggregation type, the make or color, and finally, the metric.
An outer query	That selects the three columns from the derived table and adds a CASE clause to add some text (a string of equals signs in this case) to replace any NULLs in the output. This is purely decorative and has no value other than to highlight the grand total.

This query shows, then, how you can use CTEs, derived tables, and UNION queries all together in a practical and useful way. It also shows how you can create your own table output on the fly and combine different data elements (colors and makes of car in this example) in a single column using UNION queries.

21.7 Handling Hierarchical Data

The CEO wants a list of staff and their managers that also displays each person's level in the company structure (with her at the top, obviously). A long time ago, you came across the Staff table, so you decide to use this data to display staff details along with their manager and the level of each manager and staff member in the corporate hierarchy. You use the following code to do this:

```
;
WITH HierarchyList_CTE
AS
(
SELECT      StaffID, StaffName, Department, ManagerID, 1 AS StaffLevel
FROM        Reference.Staff
WHERE       ManagerID IS NULL
UNION ALL
SELECT       ST.StaffID, ST.StaffName
            ,ST.Department, ST.ManagerID, StaffLevel + 1
FROM        Reference.Staff ST
INNER JOIN  HierarchyList_CTE CTE
```

```
                       ON ST.ManagerID = CTE.StaffID
)
SELECT           STF.Department
                 ,STF.StaffName
                 ,CTE.StaffName AS ManagerName
                 ,CTE.StaffLevel
FROM             HierarchyList_CTE CTE
INNER JOIN       Reference.Staff STF
                 ON STF.ManagerID = CTE.StaffID
```

Running this code produces the output that you can see in *Figure 21.14.*

	Department	StaffName	ManagerName	StaffLevel
1	Finance	Gerard	Amelia	1
2	Marketing	Chloe	Amelia	1
3	Sales	Susan	Amelia	1
4	Finance	Jenny	Gerard	2
5	Finance	Chris	Gerard	2
6	Marketing	Megan	Chloe	2
7	Sales	Andy	Susan	2
8	Sales	Steve	Susan	2
9	Sales	Stan	Susan	2
10	Sales	Nathan	Susan	2
11	Sales	Maggie	Susan	2
12	Finance	Sandy	Chris	3

Figure 21.14: Hierarchical output

How It Works

This query shows the levels of the staff hierarchy, despite the fact that these levels are not given in the source data. It does this by using a technique known as recursion. This means that at some point, a process repeats itself and references itself in a loop that is repeated.

In the case of this particular query, the core is a piece of code called a recursive CTE. This means that the CTE runs repeatedly, starting at the highest level of the staff hierarchy and progressing down through the personnel pyramid until it stops when it reaches the bottom.

What the code does is this:

Define a root query	This is the starting point for the CTE. This is the first query inside the actual CTE. It defines the starting point for the hierarchy of numbers that define the level of each staff member. You can see the output from this query in *Figure 21.15*.

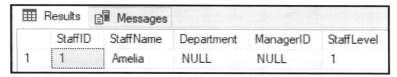

Figure 21.15: *The output from the root query in a recursive CTE*

Add a recursive query	This query is independent of the root query. It joins two datasets: the Staff table and the CTE itself. These are joined on the StaffID and the ManagerID so that the reference to each staff member's manager creates the hierarchy. It then increments the counter each time a new level is found in the Staff table, thus returning the depth of the staff hierarchy as a number. When a manager has no further lower levels of staff, the recursion stops.

To see this more clearly, take a look at *Figure 21.16* where the recursive CTE is explained graphically. Specifically, you can see that the second query in the CTE refers to the name of the CTE. This means that the second query is repeated each time a match exists between the join fields. In other words, for every match between a manager ID and a staff member ID, the query runs again.

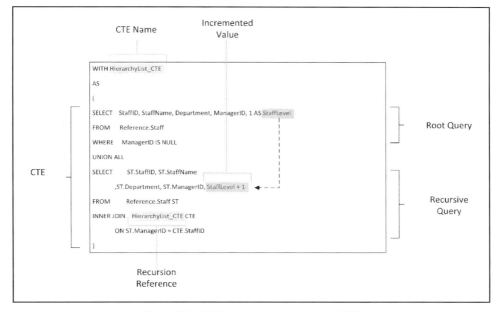

Figure 21.16: *The concept of a recursive CTE*

Finally, the output query takes the result from the CTE and joins it yet again to the staff table to obtain the manager of each staff member—just like you did in *Chapter 14*.

Tricks and Traps

There is one useful point to remember here:

- One cool use of this query is that you can easily extend it to show only the staff in a particular department if you add a final couple of lines of code like these:

```
WHERE          STF.Department = 'Finance'
ORDER BY       CTE.StaffLevel
```

Running the whole query now gives the result for the Finance department that you can see in *Figure 21.17*.

	Department	StaffName	ManagerName	ManagerLevel	StaffLevel
1	Finance	Gerard	Amelia	0	1
2	Finance	Jenny	Gerard	1	2
3	Finance	Chris	Gerard	1	2
4	Finance	Sandy	Chris	2	3

Figure 21.17: Filtering hierarchical output

21.8 Producing Indented Hierarchies

The CTO likes the staff hierarchy that you produced. Nonetheless, he wants you to add a fresh tweak. He wants the names of the staff to be indented so that the level in the hierarchy is more intuitively apparent. You can deliver this using the following piece of SQL.

```
;
WITH HierarchyList_CTE
AS
(
SELECT    StaffID, StaffName, Department, ManagerID, 1 AS StaffLevel
FROM      Reference.Staff
WHERE     ManagerID IS NULL
UNION ALL
SELECT        ST.StaffID, ST.StaffName
```

```
                 ,ST.Department, ST.ManagerID, StaffLevel + 1
FROM             Reference.Staff ST
INNER JOIN       HierarchyList_CTE CTE
                 ON ST.ManagerID = CTE.StaffID
)
SELECT            STF.Department
                 ,REPLICATE(' ', StaffLevel * 2) + STF.StaffName
                     AS StaffMember
                 ,CTE.StaffName AS ManagerName
                 ,CTE.StaffLevel
FROM             HierarchyList_CTE CTE
INNER JOIN       Reference.Staff STF
                 ON STF.ManagerID = CTE.StaffID
ORDER BY         Department, StaffLevel, CTE.StaffName
```

Running the modified code gives the output that you can see in *Figure 21.18.*

	Department	StaffMember	ManagerName	StaffLevel
1	Finance	Gerard	Amelia	1
2	Finance	Jenny	Gerard	2
3	Finance	Chris	Gerard	2
4	Finance	Sandy	Chris	3
5	Marketing	Chloe	Amelia	1
6	Marketing	Megan	Chloe	2
7	Sales	Susan	Amelia	1
8	Sales	Andy	Susan	2
9	Sales	Steve	Susan	2
10	Sales	Stan	Susan	2
11	Sales	Nathan	Susan	2
12	Sales	Maggie	Susan	2

Figure 21.18: Indenting output

How It Works

As you have probably noticed by now, SQL is not very interested in the way that lists are presented. Delivering accurate output is what good SQL is all about. However, if you are concerned with the visual presentation of the output as we are in this example, you can trick SQL into producing indents in a column by forcing the code to add extra spaces before the data.

This is done using a new function—REPLICATE(). This function allows you to repeat one or more characters a specified number of times. When you use spaces as the characters to be repeated, this effectively indents the following text. REPLICATE() requires two parameters:

| First: | The character (or sequence of characters) that you want to duplicate a number of times. In this example, we are using spaces. |
| Second: | A figure that tells the REPLICATE() function exactly how many times you want to reproduce the repeated text element. |

The trick in this specific example is to make the indentation depend on the level in the hierarchy of each staff member. Here, we are using the StaffLevel field as the second parameter in the REPLICATE() function. This way, staff at level 1 are indented by one space, staff at level 2 are indented by two spaces, and so on. The end result is a series of indentations that correspond to each person's level in the corporate hierarchy.

Tricks and Traps

If you want to avoid annoying error messages, ne point is worth remembering when you are using the REPLICATE() function:

- The REPLICATE() function assumes that you are replicating text, and so it delivers its output as text. This means that if you are using REPLICATE() with data from a numeric column, you have to use, say, the CAST() function on the numeric column to convert its data to text.

21.9 Ordering a Hierarchy Using HierearchID

The HR director is very proud of her new personnel database, but, although she knows that it is in SQL Server, she does not know how to query it efficiently. She asks you to produce a list of staff that has all staff appear with their managers organized by department and that also respects the corporate structure. You can do this with a few lines of SQL.

```
SELECT      CAST(STF.HierarchyReference AS VARCHAR(50))
                AS StaffHierarchy
            ,CAST(MGR.HierarchyReference AS VARCHAR(50))
                AS ManagerHierarchy
            ,STF.StaffName AS ManagerName
            ,MGR.StaffName
FROM        Reference.StaffHierarchy STF
```

```
INNER JOIN    Reference.StaffHierarchy MGR
              ON STF.ManagerID = MGR.StaffID
ORDER BY      MGR.HierarchyReference
```

Running this short query produces the output that you can see in *Figure 21.19*.

	StaffHierarchy	ManagerHierarchy	ManagerName	StaffName
1	/1/1/	/1/	Gerard	Amelia
2	/1/2/	/1/	Chloe	Amelia
3	/1/3/	/1/	Susan	Amelia
4	/1/1/1/	/1/1/	Jenny	Gerard
5	/1/1/2/	/1/1/	Chris	Gerard
6	/1/1/2/1/	/1/1/2/	Sandy	Chris
7	/1/2/1/	/1/2/	Megan	Chloe
8	/1/3/1/	/1/3/	Andy	Susan
9	/1/3/2/	/1/3/	Steve	Susan
10	/1/3/3/	/1/3/	Stan	Susan
11	/1/3/4/	/1/3/	Nathan	Susan
12	/1/3/5/	/1/3/	Maggie	Susan

Figure 21.19: *Using a HierarchyID to order hierarchical output*

How It Works

Organizing hierarchical data is not easy in databases because it can get complex tracking all the relationships between elements at the different levels. To help with the kinds of issues that hierarchy management has to face, SQL Server databases use a specific data type called HierarchyID. This data type indicates the level of a hierarchy for each record as well as the lineage of the record up to the top of the hierarchy.

Of course, if you are going to take advantage of a HierarchyID data type, then it must form part of the data that you are querying. Fortunately, the Prestige Cars database contains the table Reference.StaffHierarchy, which contains a field named HierarchyReference that is a HierarchyID data type. What is more, the contents of this field have been set up correctly to track the hierarchical position and relationships of each record in the table.

In this example, Amelia is the "root" of the hierarchy (the person at the top), so her HierarchyID is /1/. Her direct reports are Gerard, Cloe, and Susan. Their HierarchyIDs are, respectively, /1/1/, /1/2/, and /1/3/. As you can see, each person's HierarchyID—read from left to right—first indicates who they report to (the first figure) and then identifies them with a hierarchical reference. This reference is then used to indicate any staff who report to them further down the hierarchy. For example, Chris, who reports to Gerard, has a HierarchyID of /1/1/3/. This logic is then applied to every record in the table.

To better imagine the hierarchy as it is managed by a HierarchyID, take a look at *Figure 21.20.*

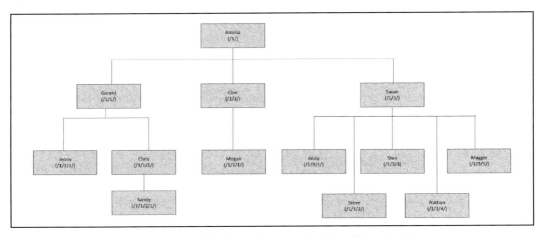

Figure 21.20: *The hierarchy maintained by a HierarchyID*

Once a correctly maintained HierarchyID field is in place, then querying the table and reflecting the hierarchy is not too hard. The join uses the Reference.StaffHierarchy table to itself so that it can output both the individual staff members and their supervisors. It does this by joining on the StaffManagerID and StaffID fields. Then it selects the HierarchyReference fields for both the staff member and the supervisor and converts these to text to make them readable. The really useful addition is sorting on the HierarchyID field (named HierarchyReference in this example). The result of the sort operation is a perfect hierarchical plan.

You need to be aware that you can only display the contents of the HierarchyReference field if you convert its contents to a VARCHAR (that is, a text) data type. This is necessary because the actual content of the HierarchyReference field is stored as binary (that is to say machine-readable) data. Indeed, if you add the HierarchyReference field to the SELECT clause without using CAST or CONVERT to transform it to text, you see something like *Figure 21.21.*

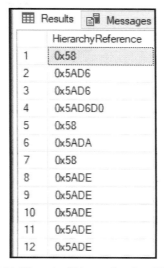

Figure 21.21: The actual binary data in a HierarchyID

We are sure that you agree that this is completely incomprehensible and that seeing the content converted to text is easier to understand.

Tricks and Traps

We have a few comments that are worth making here:

- In this query, we are assuming that a HierarchyID was not present in the previous two queries and so it could not be used in them.

- It is not necessary to add a HierarchyID field to a SELECT clause—doing so may even cause confusion. We only used it to show you the content of the field.

- There are many more ways to use HierarchyID fields to manage hierarchies; however, they are somewhat of a specialist area of SQL Server. Consequently, we advise you to check out the Microsoft documentation if you need more advice on this topic.

21.10 Replace Acronyms with Full Text in the Final Output

The sales manager needs a quick report of all the company's clients. However, she wants you to make the list more presentable by standardizing some of the output to compensate for some shortcomings in the source data. SQL makes this really easy, as the following code snippet shows:

```
SELECT      REPLACE(CustomerName, 'Ltd', 'Limited') AS NoAcronymName
FROM        Data.Customer
WHERE       LOWER(CustomerName) LIKE '%ltd%'
```

Running this query gives the results that you can see in *Figure 21.22*.

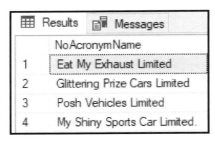

Figure 21.22: Using the REPLACE() function when outputting results

How It Works

Corporate data policies may prevent you from altering the data in a table; however, you may need to clean it up for presentation in some way. This is where the REPLACE() function becomes useful. It replaces specified text anywhere in a field with other text. All in all, it is a little like the search-and-replace function in a word processor. You can add some data cleansing at the query output stage without affecting the source data. This SQL snippet uses the Customer table and then applies the REPLACE() function to the data in the CustomerName field.

REPLACE() is another SQL function that needs you to specify three elements for it to work. Geeks call this `taking three arguments`. The arguments are

First:	The field whose data you want to modify
Second:	The text that you are looking for (Ltd in this example)
Third:	The text that you want to replace the search text with (Limited in this example)

As you can see from the code sample, these three arguments are separated by commas in the function.`

You may have times when you want to replace multiple words with another word (or even with several words). In these cases, you need to nest several REPLACE() functions inside one another. The following example replaces Ltd with Limited, S.A. with Société Anonyme, and Corp with Corporation:

```
SELECT      REPLACE(
                REPLACE(
```

```
         REPLACE(CustomerName, 'Ltd', 'Limited')
              ,'S.A.', 'Société Anonyme')
       ,'Corp', 'Corporation')
FROM      Data.Customer
```

Although not difficult, this nesting of functions does require you to be attentive to the structure and to ensure that each opening parenthesis has a corresponding closing parenthesis.

Tricks and Traps

The REPLACE() function is really quite simple. Nonetheless, be aware of the following when you apply it:

- Since this technique only applies to a SELECT clause here, it has absolutely no effect on the underlying data, which is not altered in any way.

21.11 Replacing a Specified Number of Characters with Other Text

Sales personnel at Prestige Cars are having difficulty using the complicated stock codes that the system uses. You want to make the codes easier to use in practice. The following piece of SQL shows you how to display a revamped stock code when outputting vehicles:

```
SELECT
 STUFF(StockCode,1,23,'PrestigeCars-') AS NewStockCode
,Cost
,RepairsCost
,PartsCost
,TransportInCost
FROM Data.Stock
```

Running this query gives the results that you can see in *Figure 21.23*.

	NewStockCode	Cost	RepairsCost	PartsCost	TransportInCost
1	PrestigeCars--A7BC5F9CFB3F	52000.00	2175.00	1500.00	750.00
2	PrestigeCars--A7BC5F9CFB5F	176000.00	5500.00	2200.00	1950.00
3	PrestigeCars--A83FA9559C41	15600.00	660.00	0.00	150.00
4	PrestigeCars--0C47361DDE2D	9200.00	500.00	750.00	150.00
5	PrestigeCars--4053319E8E9D	15960.00	1360.00	500.00	150.00
6	PrestigeCars--49FA8E2C377F	176000.00	1000.00	3150.00	1950.00
7	PrestigeCars--38079BB4049B	23600.00	500.00	750.00	150.00
8	PrestigeCars--17F26B2B8DAF	39600.00	2500.00	1500.00	550.00
9	PrestigeCars--406D23940527	60800.00	3250.00	750.00	750.00
10	PrestigeCars--FD132C5E1BF2	172000.00	750.00	150.00	1950.00
11	PrestigeCars--61D919E64979	15680.00	890.00	500.00	150.00
12	PrestigeCars--6C6370812041	29200.00	1950.00	500.00	550.00
13	PrestigeCars--8A4CA195248D	6800.00	250.00	225.00	150.00
14	PrestigeCars--798431841575	36000.00	1250.00	750.00	550.00
15	PrestigeCars--A219D4C691C6	64400.00	500.00	750.00	750.00

Figure 21.23: Using the STUFF()function to replace a specified number of characters with other text

How It Works

Occasionally you may need to tweak the output that a query returns so that the output is more comprehensible. In this example, you have decided that the first sets of letters and numbers that uniquely identify each vehicle in stock are superfluous (for the moment, anyway). You want to remove them from the invoices and lists that you produce and show something else instead.

This is where the STUFF() function can come in useful. It replaces a certain number of characters with another string of characters beginning at a specified position. So, unlike with the REPLACE() function, SQL is not looking for a specific character, but for any character at a specific place in a field.

In this example, the function is saying, "Take the Stock table then, starting at the first character in the StockCode field, replace the initial 23 characters with the text PrestigeCars."

Tricks and Traps

You need to be aware of a couple of points when applying a STUFF() function to your SQL:

- You may be wondering why you need to use the STUFF() function when you also have the REPLACE() function. The two are, in fact, different. The STUFF() function does not look for a specific character or series of characters; it only looks at `where a character is inside a string`. It always replaces a character or characters at the `same position` inside a text field, no matter what the actual characters are. The REPLACE() function looks for a text to replace anywhere inside a string.

- The STUFF() function can replace one or more characters with any number of other characters. The replacement string can contain fewer or more characters than the initial string of characters that you are replacing.

21.12 Creating a CommA.Separated List from Multiple Records

As your final task for the day, you have been asked to produce a list of cars sold by color. However—and this is the potential problem—you need to show the colors for each make and model combination as a commA.separated list, and not as a list of elements over multiple rows. The following code snippet shows how you can do this:

```
;
WITH ConcatenateSource_CTE (MakeModel, Color)
AS
(
SELECT DISTINCT  MK.MakeName + ' ' + MD.ModelName, Color
FROM             Data.Make MK
                 INNER JOIN Data.Model MD ON MK.MakeID = MD.MakeID
                 INNER JOIN Data.Stock ST ON ST.ModelID = MD.ModelID
)


SELECT   MakeModel, STRING_AGG(Color, ',') AS ColorList
FROM     ConcatenateSource_CTE
GROUP BY MakeModel
```

Running this query gives the results that you can see in *Figure 21.24*.

	MakeModel	ColorList
1	Alfa Romeo 1750	Black,Blue
2	Alfa Romeo Giulia	Black,British Racing Green,Green,Red
3	Alfa Romeo Giulietta	Black,Blue,Dark Purple,Night Blue
4	Alfa Romeo Spider	Black,Blue,Green
5	Aston Martin DB2	Black,Blue,British Racing Green,Canary Yellow,Green,Night Blue,Red,Silver
6	Aston Martin DB4	Black,Canary Yellow,Green,Night Blue,Pink,Silver
7	Aston Martin DB5	Black,Blue,Night Blue,Red,Silver
8	Aston Martin DB6	Black,British Racing Green,Canary Yellow,Green,Night Blue,Red,Silver
9	Aston Martin DB9	Black,Blue,British Racing Green,Canary Yellow,Dark Purple,Green,Night Blue,Red,Silver
10	Aston Martin Rapide	Black,Night Blue,Red,Silver
11	Aston Martin Vanquish	Black,Dark Purple,Green,Night Blue,Red,Silver
12	Aston Martin Vantage	Black,British Racing Green,Green
13	Aston Martin Virage	Black,Blue,Dark Purple,Green,Night Blue,Pink,Red
14	Austin Cambridge	Black
15	Austin Lichfield	Night Blue,Pink

Figure 21.24: Concatenating text using the STRING_AGG() function

How It Works

Tables are not the only way that SQL Server can deliver its output. It can also join together a series of elements as a list separated by commas (or, indeed, any other character or characters). SQL "thinks" in terms of tables, and naturally it delivers its results in tabular form. Nonetheless, at times you may not want to see a long table of output, or even a pivot table, but instead a simpler list that shows all the data that interests you in a single column. This is what has been done with this particular query. It has output a single record for each individual model of vehicle and then added a second column that lists every color of car sold for the model in question. On this occasion, however, the colors are shown as a simple commA.separated list. This technique—joining together a string of values—is called `concatenating` a series of elements.

This code snippet is in two parts:

A CTE	That delivers a unique list of makes and models of car ever held in stock along with each individual color bought for each model.
A query	That takes the output from the CTE and tweaks it to return a commA.separated list of the colors of vehicle bought by make and model using the STRING_AGG() function.

The CTE is really quite simple. It is a standard SELECT query that returns the Make and Model amalgamated as a single field and then adds a second column containing the color of each vehicle bought. Since the query contains the DISTINCT keyword, only one record is output for each combination of make, model, and color.

Running the CTE gives the results that you can see in *Figure 21.25*.

	(No column name)	Color
1	Alfa Romeo 1750	Black
2	Alfa Romeo 1750	Blue
3	Alfa Romeo Giulia	Black
4	Alfa Romeo Giulia	British Racing Green
5	Alfa Romeo Giulia	Green
6	Alfa Romeo Giulia	Red
7	Alfa Romeo Giulietta	Black
8	Alfa Romeo Giulietta	Blue
9	Alfa Romeo Giulietta	Dark Purple
10	Alfa Romeo Giulietta	Night Blue

Figure 21.25: The output from a CTE used to generate a commA.separated list

The main query (shown in bold in the code) is simply a SELECT query that uses the CTE as its source. The query does the following:

Groups data	On the make and model and selects the field containing the make and model.
Creates a list	Of colors for each make and model. It does this using the STRING_AGG() function.

The STRING_AGG() function only needs two parameters:

First:	The field that you will use as the source for all the data that will be amalgamated into a list.
Second:	The separator character that will isolate each element in the list.

Just remember that you will need

An identification field	Which is similar to the list of makes and models of car that we are using here.
A list field	That will be used as the basis for the concatenated list of elements, which is similar to the color field that we are using here.
A list separator	Like the comma that is used in this example.

Tricks and Traps

The ability to create concatenated lists is extremely useful in practice. Just be sure to remember the following points:

- This technique can be slow when applied to large datasets; however, it is extremely useful and can be a valuable way of delivering the information that you need.

- You can use any character to separate the elements in the concatenated list, even spaces. Some character is necessary, though, or the list will be unreadable.

- If the source data is simple, you may not need a CTE to prepare the data, but you can query the source table(s) directly.

21.13 Creating Multiple Records from a List

The marketing director has, once again, found some external data that she wants you to handle for her. This data is a list of vehicle classifications, and it looks like the table in *Figure 21.26*.

Figure 21.26: Source data containing a commA.separated list

What you need to do is break down this list into a complete set of rows in which each element in the MarketingType column is on a separate row, even if this means each make of car appears on multiple rows.

After a few minutes, you come up with the following code to do this:

```
SELECT        MakeName, Value AS VehicleType

FROM          Reference.MarketingCategories

CROSS APPLY   STRING_SPLIT(MarketingType, ',')
```

Executing this code gives the result that you can see in *Figure 21.27*.

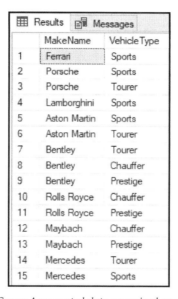

Figure 21.27: CommA.separated data organized as separate records

How It Works

SQL Server (since version 2016) enables you to separate out delimited lists into multiple records simply and easily. You can do this using the STRING_SPLIT() function. This is how you use it:

First:	Select the column that will contain the repeated elements in the output (MakeName in this example).
Second:	Add a comma and the word Value—which is the required field name for the split output from the column containing a separated list (MarketingType in this example).
Third:	Add an alias for the Value column (if you want to).

Fourth:	Define the source table in the FROM clause and add a CROSS APPLY function (this ensures that every record in the source data is processed).
Finally:	Enter the STRING_SPLIT() function. This takes two parameters: the column that contains the list of delimited elements to split and the `delimiter` (the character that separates each element in the list).

Once you have created a recordset of output like this, you can use it in other SQL queries, as required.

Tricks and Traps

We have a few points to make here:

- The delimiter character used in the STRING_SPLIT() function must be enclosed in single quotes.

- The delimiter character can be any character.

- The STRING_SPLIT() function does not exist in SQL Server versions prior to 2016.

21.14 Outputting Simple XML

The marketing director is in a bit of a panic. An external agency wants some data delivered in XML format, and naturally you are her first port of call to provide a solution. Fortunately, SQL Server can output query results as XML with incredible ease, so after a few minutes, you produce the following piece of code:

```
SELECT      MD.ModelName, ST.Color, ST.Cost
FROM        Data.Stock ST
INNER JOIN  Data.Model MD
            ON ST.ModelID = MD.ModelID
FOR XML PATH ('Stock'), ROOT ('PrestigeCars')
```

Running this code produces the result that you can see in *Figure 21.28*.

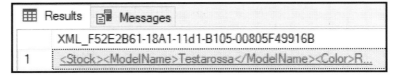

***Figure 21.28:** XML output from a FOR XML query*

This output is, to say the least, a little cryptic. However, if you click on the XML itself, a new window opens displaying the entire result. You can see some sample output in *Figure 21.29*; however, you need to be aware that we have cut much of the data to show only the start and end of the XML that is produced.

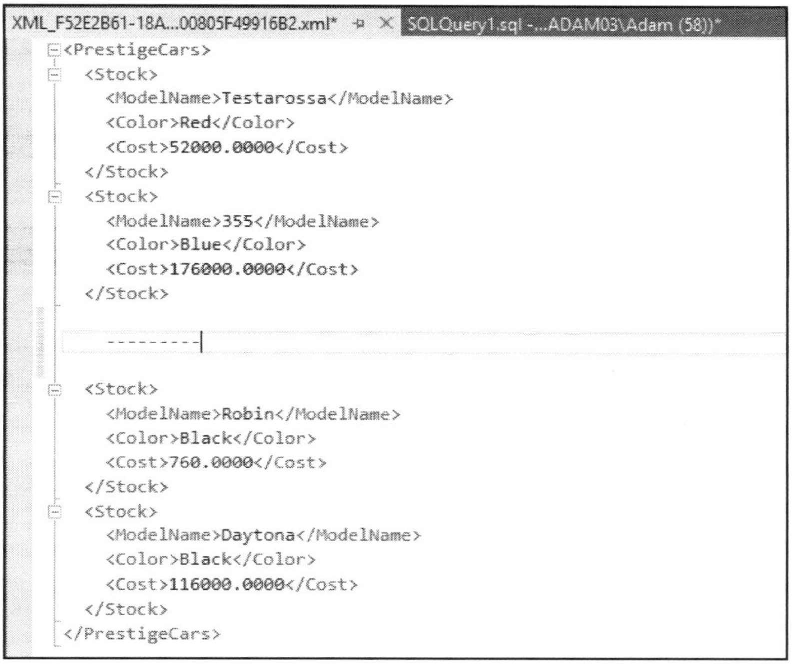

Figure 21.29: *Full XML output from a FOR XML query*

How It Works

XML (the acronym XML stands for e**X**tended **M**arkup **L**anguage) is, among other things, a standardized way of structuring data so that it can be transferred between different systems. It is particularly good for ensuring that data structures are respected when information is copied between databases. As you can see from *Figure 21.28*, it is also easy to read by humans (and most machines also find it easy to understand).

Producing XML from a SQL Server database can be as simple as adding the FOR XML PATH keywords at the end of an SQL query. This immediately transforms the output into XML rather than the standard list output that you have been using so far in this book.

In this example, the Stock and Model tables are joined so that you can select the model and color as well as various cost elements from the Stock table.

As an extra tweak, we have added two extra elements to the FOR XML PATH keywords:

('Element')	This is a row element that encloses each record in the output.
ROOT ('Element')	This adds a root element at the top and bottom of the entire output.

Unfortunately, it would take another small book to explain why, exactly, you might need a root element or when it is best to add row elements, which are both part of a more in-depth discussion of XML. Let's just say that when sending XML to third parties so that they can load them into their own systems, these two added elements often prove essential to a successful exchange of data.

Tricks and Traps

We have a few points to make here:

- You can extend the SQL query that produces XML using all the standard techniques that you have learned in this book. This includes a WHERE clause, GROUP BY elements, and so on.

- XML is a vast subject in its own right. Consequently, we are not able to explain how it is designed and how it works in this book.

21.15 Structuring XML Output

The marketing director has returned with another XML request. This time her agency needs the XML output presented in a specific way—some data needs to be presented as XML attributes and other elements need to be entities in a hierarchical structure. After a bit of work, you produce the following SQL:

```
SELECT          MD.ModelName AS "@Model"

                ,ST.Color

                ,ST.Cost AS "Costs/Purchase"

                    ,ST.PartsCost AS "Costs/Parts"

                    ,ST.RepairsCost AS "Costs/Repairs"

FROM            Data.Stock ST

INNER JOIN      Data.Model MD

                ON ST.ModelID = MD.ModelID

FOR XML PATH ('Stock')
```

Running this code produces the result that you can see in *Figure 21.30*—once you have clicked on the initial result in the query window.

```
XML_F52E2B61-18A...00805F49916B4.xml  ⇄ ✕ SQLQuery1.sql -...ADAM03\Adam (55))*
⊟<Stock Model="Testarossa">
    <Color>Red</Color>
⊟   <Costs>
        <Purchase>52000.0000</Purchase>
        <Parts>1500.0000</Parts>
        <Repairs>2175.0000</Repairs>
    </Costs>
  </Stock>
⊟<Stock Model="355">
    <Color>Blue</Color>
⊟   <Costs>
        <Purchase>176000.0000</Purchase>
        <Parts>2200.0000</Parts>
        <Repairs>5500.0000</Repairs>
    </Costs>
  </Stock>
⊟<Stock Model="911">
    <Color>British Racing Green</Color>
⊟   <Costs>
        <Purchase>15600.0000</Purchase>
        <Parts>0.0000</Parts>
        <Repairs>660.0000</Repairs>
    </Costs>
  </Stock>
⊟<Stock Model="924">
    <Color>British Racing Green</Color>
⊟   <Costs>
        <Purchase>9200.0000</Purchase>
        <Parts>750.0000</Parts>
        <Repairs>500.0000</Repairs>
    </Costs>
  </Stock>
```

Figure 21.30: *Structured XML output from a FOR XML query*

How It Works

XML allows you to define data as either attributes (like the model name in this example) or as elements (all the other data fields from the source query). Moreover, XML is very good at creating nested hierarchies of data. In this example, this means that all cost elements are grouped together as a subset of the data.

The XML query starts with the same SELECT query that you used in the previous example; however, this code is tweaked slightly to extend the XML structure.

As you saw in the previous section, XML defaults to displaying output as elements— that is, the data for each "field" is preceded by the element name inside < and >,

and it is followed by the same name inside < and > with a backslash added before the element name. In some cases, however, you may want to display data as XML attributes—that is, the name of the element appears inside another element (and the data appears in double quotes).

Displaying XML output as an attribute is as simple as adding an alias to the field that you want to transform into an attribute; however, the alias `must`

- Be enclosed in quotes
- Start with an @

The ability to create a nested hierarchy of XML output is also added when you are using field aliases. In this case, the alias must contain each required level of the output hierarchy separated by a forward slash.

Tricks and Traps

At this juncture, you need to know that

- We specifically chose not to include a ROOT element in this XML so that you can see the difference in the output.

- You can format the output as you would "normal" SQL and define decimals, the way date are presented, and so on.

- The aliases can be placed in either double or single quotes.

There is much, much more that we could add on the subject of XML output from SQL queries. However, this can rapidly become a specialist subject, so we prefer to start you on your way with a couple of examples and advise you to consult more focused resources if you need further details on this particular subject.

21.16 Outputting JSON

Now it is the sales director's turn. She needs to send data from the Prestige Cars' database to a web designer in something called JSON. Fortunately, SQL Server makes this really simple, as the following code snippet shows.

```
SELECT TOP 3   MD.ModelName
              ,ST.Color
              ,ST.Cost
              ,ST.PartsCost
              ,ST.RepairsCost
FROM          Data.Stock ST
```

```
INNER JOIN    Data.Model MD
              ON ST.ModelID = MD.ModelID
FOR JSON PATH, ROOT ('Stock')
```

Executing this code produces the result that you can see in *Figure 21.31*.

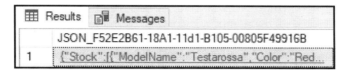

Figure 21.31: *JSON output from a FOR JSON query*

If you click on the output, you can see the result in a new query window. After a little formatting effort, it looks like the following code:

```
{
"Stock":
   [
      {
         "ModelName":"Testarossa",
         "Color":"Red",
         "Cost":52000.0000,
         "PartsCost":2200.0000,
         "RepairsCost":2175.0000
      }
,
      {
         "ModelName":"355",
         "Color":"Blue",
         "Cost":176000.0000,
         "PartsCost":2200.0000,
         "RepairsCost":5500.0000
      }
,
      {
         "ModelName":"911",
         "Color":"British Racing Green",
```

```
        "Cost":15600.0000,
        "PartsCost":0.0000,
        "RepairsCost":660.0000
      }
   ]
}
```

How It Works

Another structure that is frequently used to transfer data between heterogeneous systems is JSON. This stands for JavaScript Object Notation. Fortunately, SQL Server can generate JSON output extremely easily; all you have to do is add FOR JSON PATH to the initial SQL query.

In this example, the Stock and Model tables are joined so that you can select the model and color as well as various cost elements from the Stock table. Then you extend the query with FOR JSON PATH.

Generally, however, it is preferable also to add a ROOT element that then encloses the entire output. The complete line of SQL that converts a query into a JSON output query is

```
FOR JSON PATH, ROOT ('RootElement')
```

We realize that JSON is not intuitively comprehensible; however, it has become something of a lingua franca of the Internet age as far as sharing structured data between diverse systems is concerned. So, although a deep understanding of JSON structures may be overkill, understanding how to produce JSON datasets from SQL Server data is definitely not.

Tricks and Traps

We have a couple of points to make here:

- JSON is generally less easy to read by humans than XML.

- It is not necessary to reformat the JSON output. We have chosen to add some carriage returns and indents so that the structure of the data is a little easier to understand. In practice, the original JSON output from the SQL query can be used by any application that reads JSON without any manual intervention.

21.17 Defining JSON Output

Ten minutes after you produced the JSON data for the sales manager she sends you an email. The web designer wants the JSON data structured in a specific hierarchical way. After reading his definition of how the output should look you come up with the following SQL:

```
SELECT TOP 3    MD.ModelName
                ,ST.Color
                ,ST.Cost AS [Costs.Purchase]
                ,ST.PartsCost AS [Costs.Parts]
                ,ST.RepairsCost AS [Costs.Repairs]
FROM            Data.Stock ST
INNER JOIN      Data.Model MD
                ON ST.ModelID = MD.ModelID
FOR JSON PATH, ROOT ('Stock')
```

Once you have run the query, you can click on the output to get a closer look. We have formatted the result so that it looks like the JSON structure that you can see here:

```
{
    "Stock":
            [
             {
                "ModelName":"Testarossa",
                "Color":"Red",
                "Costs":
                        {
                            "Purchase":52000.0000,
                            "Parts":1500.0000,
                            "Repairs":2175.0000
                        }
             }
            ,{
                "ModelName":"355",
                "Color":"Blue",
```

```
        "Costs":
                {
                    "Purchase":176000.0000,
                    "Parts":2200.0000,
                    "Repairs":5500.0000
                }
        }
    ,{
        "ModelName":"911",
        "Color":"British Racing Green",
        "Costs":
                {
                    "Purchase":15600.0000,
                    "Parts":0.0000,
                    "Repairs":660.0000
                }
        }
    ]
}
```

How It Works

JSON is very good at structuring data. Specifically, it can contain many levels of nested hierarchies of data. In this example, the cost elements are contained at a sublevel in the final output. Once again, the Stock and Model tables are the basis for this query.

The extended JSON structure is attained by adding aliases to any source fields that need to be nested in the data hierarchy. More specifically, each level in the hierarchy is separated from other levels by a period, so defining an alias of "Costs.Purchase" creates a "Costs" sublevel containing a "Purchases" data element.

Tricks and Traps

There are a few points to make here on the subject of JSON formatting:

- When defining nested hierarchies of JSON data, you can enclose the alias in single quotes, double quotes, or square brackets.

- You can format the output as you would "normal" SQL and define decimals, the way dates are formatted, and so on, as you would for a standard SQL query.

We could add much, much more on the subject of JSON output from SQL queries, but since this requires an in-depth understanding of JSON, we instead advise you to consult more specialized resources if you need further details on this subject.

Conclusion

This chapter has taken you on a whirlwind tour of some of the SQL virtuoso techniques that you can use to hone your query output. From pivoting data via concatenated lists to adding complex subtotals in your reports or even replacing text in the final output, you have learned a useful variety of advanced ways to present data.

This chapter also concludes the book and your introduction to SQL Querying. I sincerely hope that you will put your learning to good use. Finally, we really hope that you have had fun learning SQL with SQL Server.

Core Knowledge Learned in This Chapter

The keywords and concepts that you have seen in this chapter are

Concept	Description
PIVOT	This operator allows you to create pivot tables.
GROUPING SETS	This operator lets you add multiple subtotals to aggregate queries.
STUFF()	This function is used to replace text at a specified position in a field.
STRING_AGG()	This function can be used to create commA.separated lists from the data in a column.
STRING_SPLIT()	This function creates multiple rows from commA.separated lists.
Recursion	A programming technique that iterates several times through, referring to itself.
Recursive CTE	A common table expression that is joined to itself to loop through a hierarchy or sequence.
FOR XML	This operator outputs the results of the query as XML.
FOR JSON	This operator outputs the results of the query as JSON.
PATH	Used with FOR XML or FOR JSON, this operator allows you to shape the output.
ROOT	Used with FOR XML or FOR JSON, this operator lets you specify a root element for the output.
HierarchyID	This data type is used to structure hierarchies.

APPENDIX A
Installing SQL Server

The only way to learn SQL is to practice using it. Unless you already have a SQL database that is available for you to use, you will need your own SQL Server instance. In this appendix, you will see how to set up your own personal SQL Server on your laptop or personal workstation. Then, in Appendixes B and C, you will see how to install SQL Server Management Studio to query SQL Server as well as the sample database that is used in the examples in this book.

Installing SQL Server

Microsoft has, fortunately, made it easy for anyone to learn SQL on a current version of its database software. Not only that, but it has made the latest version of the database freely available for development use. This version is currently not time-limited and will allow you to test all the code that is available in this book. It is called SQL Server Developer.

Microsoft currently describes SQL Server Developer (also called SQL Server 2019 development edition) as "a full-featured free edition, licensed for use as a development and test database in a non-production environment." What this seems to mean is that you can use it to learn SQL as long as you do not use it in a business—or indeed anywhere—to run or manage data.

> **Note: We will describe only how to install SQL Server Developer on the Windows platform here. If you want to set up SQL Server Developer on Linux, then please consult the Microsoft website.**

Here, then, is how to access, download, and install the database software:

1. Browse to the Microsoft SQL Server downloads page. It is currently at **https://www.microsoft.com/en-us/sql-server/sql-server-downloads**. It should look something like the one in *Figure A.1*.

Figure A.1: The Microsoft SQL Server downloads page

> **Note:** If the URL has changed since this book was published, then use your preferred search engine and look for SQL Server development edition.

1. Click the Download Now button under Developer Edition.
2. After a few seconds, the executable that links to the full download will appear at the bottom of the browser window, or a pop-up window will ask you if you want to run the download. This will depend on the browser you are using.

3. Click the executable link or the Run button (depending on your browser).

4. Confirm (if asked) that you want this app to make admin-level changes to your system. The installation type dialog will appear. It should look something like the one in *Figure A.2*.

Figure A.2: *The installation type dialog*

5. Click Basic. The license terms dialog will appear, looking like the one in *Figure A.3*.

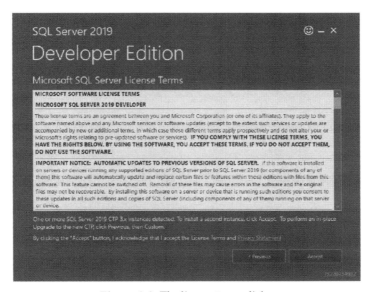

Figure A.3: *The license terms dialog*

6. Click Accept. The install location dialog will appear. It should look something like the one in *Figure A.4*.

Figure A.4: *The install location dialog*

7. Leave the install location as is and click Install. The download will begin, and the dialog shown in *Figure A.5* will appear while the download is carried out. Be warned that this can take a while, even with a fast Internet connection.

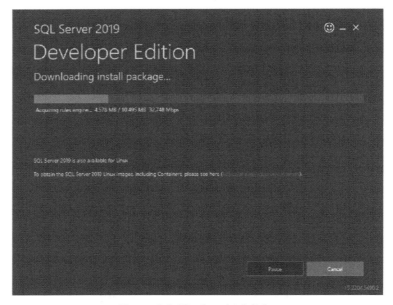

Figure A.5: *The download dialog*

8. The installation process will then extract the compressed files and begin the installation. You will see a dialog like the one in *Figure A.6*.

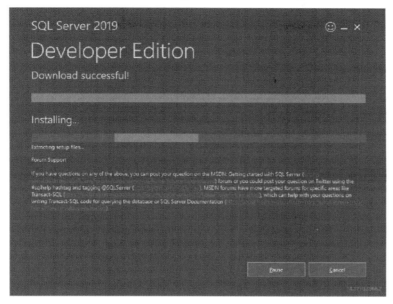

Figure A.6: *The installation dialog*

9. Once the installation is complete, you will see the successful completion dialog that is shown in *Figure A.7*.

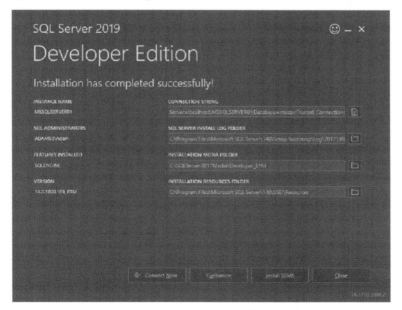

Figure A.7: *The successful completion dialog*

10. Click Close. A pop-up will ask if you really want to exit the SQL Server Installer. You can see this in *Figure A.8*.

Figure A.8: Exiting the SQL Server Installer

11. Click Yes.

Assuming that all ran smoothly, SQL Server 2019 is now installed on your computer. You can start using it to host databases.

Tricks and Traps

We have a couple of comments to make here.

- If there is already an older version of SQL Server installed on the destination computer, then a new instance (an independent version) of SQL Server 2019 will be installed as well. This will have no effect on the existing version of SQL Server.

- To install and run correctly, SQL Server 2019 requires a computer with at least the following:
  - o 6 GB of available disk space
  - o 1 GB of available memory
  - o A 2.0 GHz processor
  - o An 800 × 600 monitor

In practice, however, you will probably need considerably more memory and a much faster processor to run any viable database application.

Installing SQL Server Management Studio

Having a version of SQL Server that you can access is a good start, but you will nonetheless need an application that you can use to enter queries and see the results. In this appendix, you will see how to install SQL Server Management Studio, the application that we recommend using to enter and run queries when you are learning SQL with SQL Server.

Installing SQL Server Management Studio

As we explained in Chapter 1, one widely used tool for querying SQL Server is SQL Server Management Studio. Here is how you can download and install this particular piece of software, which Microsoft has, fortunately, made free to download and use:

1. Search for SQL Server Management Studio in your preferred search engine or click or use the following link: **https://docs.microsoft.com/en-us/sql/ssms/download-sql-server-management-studio-ssms**. You should see a dialog like the one shown in *Figure B.1*.

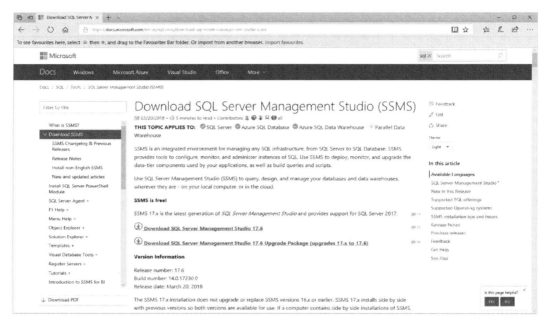

Figure B.1: *The SQL Server Management Studio download page*

2. Click Download SQL Server Management Studio 18.11 (or whatever the latest version currently is).

3. Run the download (this will depend on the browser you are using). You will see the installation dialog shown in *Figure B.2*.

Figure B.2: *The SQL Server Management Studio installation dialog*

4. Click Install. SSMS will be installed while the progress dialog is displayed, as in *Figure B.3*.

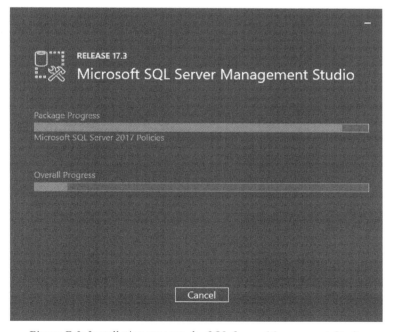

Figure B.3: *Installation progress for SQL Server Management Studio*

5. Once the installation has finished, the Setup Completed dialog will be displayed, as shown in *Figure B.4.*

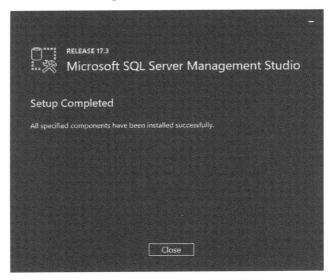

Figure B.4: The Setup Completed dialog

6. Click Close.

You can now launch SQL Server Management Studio and connect to the server you installed previously.

Tricks and Traps

We have one comment to make here.

- To launch SSMS, click the Start Menu button at the bottom left of the screen and scroll down the list of installed applications until you find Microsoft SQL Server Tools 2017. Expand this and you will see Microsoft SQL Server Management Studio, as shown in *Figure B.5.* Click on this to run SSMS.

Figure B.5: Running SQL Server Management Studio

APPENDIX C

Setting Up the Sample Database

To practice the SQL examples that you have seen (or will discover) in the course of this book, you will need to download and install the sample database that is the basis for learning SQL with the aid of this book.

This appendix will explain how to download the sample data, create the PrestigeCars database, and load the sample data into the PrestigeCars database so that you can practice your SQL.

Downloading the Sample Data

First you will need to download the sample data to a local directory.

1. In Windows Explorer, create a folder named **C:\SQLQueriesSampleData**.

2. Download the sample data file (**SQLQueriesSampleData.zip**) from the BPB website (**www.bpbonline.com**).

3. Extract the contents of the compressed file into the folder **C:\SQLQueriesSampleData**. The folder contents should look something like *Figure C.1*.

Name	Date modified	Type	Size
Chapter01.sql	16/11/2017 10:54	Microsoft SQL Server Query File	1 KB
Chapter02.sql	29/03/2018 13:55	Microsoft SQL Server Query File	2 KB
Chapter03.sql	29/03/2018 13:59	Microsoft SQL Server Query File	2 KB
Chapter04.sql	21/07/2018 12:54	Microsoft SQL Server Query File	3 KB
Chapter05.sql	21/07/2018 12:56	Microsoft SQL Server Query File	3 KB
Chapter06.sql	21/07/2018 12:57	Microsoft SQL Server Query File	3 KB
Chapter07.sql	22/07/2018 12:52	Microsoft SQL Server Query File	4 KB
Chapter08.sql	21/07/2018 13:05	Microsoft SQL Server Query File	7 KB
Chapter09.sql	21/07/2018 13:07	Microsoft SQL Server Query File	3 KB
Chapter10.sql	21/07/2018 13:09	Microsoft SQL Server Query File	2 KB
Chapter11.sql	21/07/2018 13:14	Microsoft SQL Server Query File	6 KB
Chapter12.sql	21/07/2018 13:18	Microsoft SQL Server Query File	9 KB
Chapter13.sql	21/07/2018 13:21	Microsoft SQL Server Query File	8 KB
Chapter14.sql	21/07/2018 13:24	Microsoft SQL Server Query File	7 KB
Chapter15.sql	21/07/2018 13:28	Microsoft SQL Server Query File	7 KB
Chapter16.sql	21/07/2018 13:31	Microsoft SQL Server Query File	3 KB
Chapter17.sql	21/07/2018 13:35	Microsoft SQL Server Query File	4 KB
Chapter18.sql	21/07/2018 13:37	Microsoft SQL Server Query File	6 KB
Chapter19.sql	21/07/2018 13:42	Microsoft SQL Server Query File	9 KB
Chapter20.sql	21/07/2018 14:17	Microsoft SQL Server Query File	10 KB
Chapter21.sql	21/07/2018 14:22	Microsoft SQL Server Query File	8 KB
SQLQueriesSampleData.sql	01/06/2018 08:49	Microsoft SQL Server Query File	1.703 KB

Figure C.1: The sample data folder contents

Creating the PrestigeCars Database

Now you will need to create a database into which you can load the sample data.

1. Run SQL Server Management Studio.

2. Right-click the Databases folder in SSMS and select New Database from the pop-up menu. You can see this in *Figure C.2*. The New Database dialog will appear.

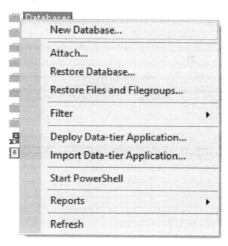

Figure C.2: Creating a new database.

3. Enter **PrestigeCars** as the database name. The New Database dialog will look something like the one in *Figure C.3*.

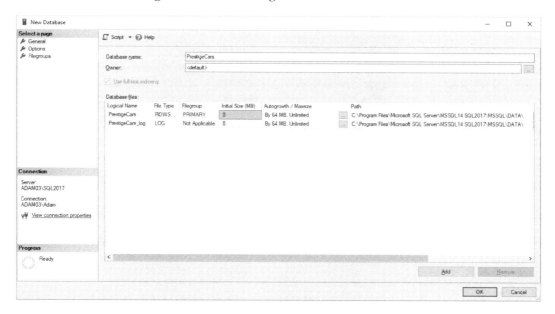

Figure C.3: Creating a new database

4. Click OK. The PrestigeCars database will be created.

Loading the Sample Data into the PrestigeCars Database

Finally, you need to load the sample data and all the database tables and views into the newly created PrestigeCars database.

1. In SQL Server Management Studio, click File⇨Open⇨File.

2. Browse to the file
   C:\ SQLQueriesSampleData\SQLQueriesSampleData.sql.

3. Click Open. The script will appear in a new query window.

4. Press **F5** to run the script and load the data.

You can now start querying the sample data contained in the PrestigeCars database.

Opening the Sample Queries

To save you having to type out all the sample queries in this book, hey are available in the download from the BPB Publications web site. If you have already downloaded the sample data as described in Section 1 of this Appendix, then you can jump directly to step 3.

1. In your web browser, navigate to
   www.bpbonline.com/sqlserver.

2. Download the sample data file (**SQLQueriesSampleData.zip**) from the BPB Publications website (**www.bpbonline.com**) and extract the contents into the folder **C:\SQLQueriesSampleData**.

3. Launch SQL Server Management Studio.

4. Click File⇨Open⇨File and navigate to
   C:\SQLQueriesSampleData.

5. Double-click the file containing the sample queries for the chapter that you are working on.

Index

Made in the USA
Coppell, TX
24 August 2023

20721208R00341